SOUTHERN BIOGRAPHY SERIES
Bertram Wyatt-Brown, Editor

Published with the assistance of the V. Ray Cardozier Fund,
an endowment created to support publication of scholarly books

# A Jackson Man

## AMOS KENDALL

### and the Rise of American Democracy

DONALD B. COLE

Louisiana State University Press

Baton Rouge

DESIGNER: Barbara Neely Bourgoyne
TYPEFACES: Adobe Caslon; Voluta Script Pro, display
TYPESETTER: Coghill Composition Co., Inc.
PRINTER AND BINDER: Thomson-Shore, Inc.

Library of Congress Cataloging-in-Publication Data

Cole, Donald B.
A Jackson man : Amos Kendall and the rise of American democracy /
Donald B. Cole.
p.   cm. — (Southern biography series)
Includes bibliographical references (p.   ) and index.
ISBN 0-8071-2930-5 (cloth : alk. paper)
1. Kendall, Amos, 1789–1869.   2. Politicians—Southern
States—Biography.   3. Journalists—Kentucky—Biography.   4. Cabinet
officers—United States—Biography.   5. United States—Politics and
government—1815–1861.   I. Title.   II. Series: Southern biography series.
E340.K33C65 2004
973.5'6'092—dc22
2003021390

The paper in this book meets the guidelines for permanence and durability
of the Committee on Production Guidelines for Book Longevity
of the Council on Library Resources. ⊗

To my friend
John J. McDonough

# CONTENTS

# PREFACE

At first glance Amos Kendall seems out of place in a southern biography series. After all, he grew up in Massachusetts, graduated from Dartmouth College, and lived for half of his life in Washington, D.C. But Kendall spent the first fifteen years of his career in Kentucky, years that transformed him from an elitist Yankee law student to a democratic political editor well versed in southern and western ways. When he became postmaster general, his refusal to allow the circulation of abolitionist pamphlets in Charleston, South Carolina, supported the interests of southern slaveowners. Kendall was a special person—one of the very few prominent antebellum politicians who successfully combined northern origins and southern experience. Andrew Jackson's secretary of state Edward Livingston and James K. Polk's secretary of the Treasury Robert J. Walker were others. Kendall's career reminds us that there was no single southern type.

Like every historian I am indebted to many people. Any assessment of Kendall as presidential adviser and postmaster general must start with Richard B. Latner's *The Presidency of Andrew Jackson: White House Politics, 1829–1837* and Richard R. John's *Spreading the News: The American Postal System from Franklin to Morse.* Although my interpretation of Kendall differs from both Latner's and John's, I learned a great deal not only from the books but directly from the authors as well. Dick Latner read and commented on the first draft of the manuscript; Richard John edited three different drafts and called my attention to a number of sources that I might otherwise have missed. William G. Shade, who read the first draft, enlightened and entertained me with his good-humored commentary. In addition my work benefited greatly from dissertations by Lynn L. Marshall and Terry L. Shoptaugh on Kendall, and by David Hochfelder on the telegraph. Terry lent me microfilms of Kendall's correspondence and journalism, and David read my chapters on the telegraph. Daniel Feller prodded me into placing Kendall in a broader setting than I had first intended. Bertram Wyatt-Brown made valuable suggestions for cutting the text.

Many others went out of their way to help me: Michael J. Olsen, archivist at Gallaudet University; Trace Kirkwood and James Holmberg at the Filson Historical Society; Mary Wolfskill at the Library of Congress; Sylvia Frank Rodrigue and George Roupe at Louisiana State University Press; manuscript editor Susan Tarcov; and George F. Skoch, who drew a fine map of Kendall's travels. Whenever I was in doubt, John J. McDonough, now retired from the Library of Congress, was at the other end of a telephone line. This book is dedicated to him.

I am grateful also to libraries for permission to quote from manuscripts in their collections: the Connecticut Historical Society; the Dartmouth College Library; the Duke University Rare Book, Manuscript, and Special Collections Library; the Filson Historical Society; the Gallaudet University Archives; the Maine Historical Society; the Massachusetts Historical Society; the Memphis/Shelby County Public Library and Information Center; the Missouri Historical Society; the New Hampshire Historical Society; the New-York Historical Society; the New Jersey Historical Society; the Princeton University Library; the University of Virginia Library; and the Library of Virginia.

Here in Exeter, Jacquelyn Thomas and the staff at the Phillips Exeter Academy Library were skillful, gracious, and supportive. My neighbor Dr. James C. Tucker patiently explained the various ailments that Kendall endured. And Tootie put in long hours working on the index. She and the family were always nearby to keep the book in perspective.

# ABBREVIATIONS

| | |
|---|---|
| *ASP:NA* | *American State Papers: Naval Affairs* |
| *Autobiography* | Amos Kendall, *Autobiography of Amos Kendall*, ed. William Stickney (1872; reprint, New York: Peter Smith, 1949) |
| BUS | Bank of the United States |
| *Compilation* | *A Compilation of the Messages and Papers of the Presidents, 1789–1897*, comp. James D. Richardson, 10 vols. (Washington, D.C.: Government Printing Office, 1897–99) |
| *DAB* | Allen Johnson and Dumas Malone, eds., *Dictionary of American Biography*, 20 vols. (New York: Scribner's, 1929) |
| Jackson Supplement | Supplement to the Andrew Jackson Papers (Wilmington, Del.: Scholarly Resources, Microfilm, 1986) |
| *JER* | *Journal of the Early Republic* |
| Kendall to John | Amos Kendall to John Kendall, Amos Kendall Papers, MHS |
| LC | Library of Congress |
| MHS | Massachusetts Historical Society |
| PMGLB | Postmaster General Letterbooks, RG 28, National Archives |
| *Register* | *Register of the Kentucky State Historical Society* |
| *Register of Debates* | *Register of Debates in Congress* |
| RG | Record Group, National Archives |
| *Statistical History* | *The Statistical History of the United States from the Colonial Times to the Present* (Stamford, Conn.: Fairfield, 1947) |

*A Jackson Man*

# INTRODUCTION

On her visit to the United States in the mid-1830s, the English writer Harriet Martineau met many of the most famous Americans of the day. No one, however, enthralled her more than a mysterious, undistinguished Democrat who had aroused fear and hatred in his opponents and had captured the imagination of Americans of all persuasions. Amos Kendall, she wrote, was

> supposed to be the moving spring of [Andrew Jackson's] administration; the thinker, planner, doer; but it is all in the dark. Documents are issued of an excellence which prevents their being attributed to persons who take the responsibility for them. . . . [W]ork is done of goblin extent and with goblin speed, which makes men look about them with a superstitious wonder; and the invisible Amos Kendall has credit of it all. . . . Every mysterious paragraph in opposition newspapers relates to Kendall. . . . [H]e is undoubtedly a great genius.[1]

Martineau had heard so much about Kendall's reputation for never being seen in public that as soon as she arrived in Washington she was on the lookout for him. Suddenly one evening, she recalled, "intimations reached me from all quarters, amidst nods and winks, 'Kendall is here:' 'That is he.'" At first she was taken aback by his strange, sickly appearance, but she soon decided that it worked to his advantage by keeping "the superstitious" in "dread of him." She surmised that he did not "desire the superstition to melt away; for there is no calculating how much influence was given to Jackson's administration by the universal belief that there was a concealed eye and hand behind the machinery of government." Martineau could not take her eyes off Kendall, who "was leaning on a chair, with head bent down, and eye glancing up at a member of Congress," but suddenly "he was gone."[2]

1. Harriet Martineau, *Retrospect of Western Travel,* 3 vols. (London, 1838), 1:236, 257–58.
2. Ibid., 258–59.

The Austrian-born writer Francis J. Grund was equally fascinated. He described Kendall sitting at his desk, brusquely interviewing job seekers without looking up from his writing. When Grund was introduced, Kendall made only "a slight motion forward" and "immediately sank back again into his chair." Instead of being offended by such discourtesy, Grund became one of Kendall's admirers. He respected his "extraordinary powers of mind, [his] indefatigable habits of industry, [his] calm, passionless [manner] and [his] unerring judgment." Kendall was proving, Grund was told, that "the various principles of democracy may be united into a system."[3]

It was Kendall's contributions to this system that attracted Martineau and Grund. As their French counterpart, Alexis de Tocqueville, expressed it, they had traveled to America seeking "the image of democracy . . . with its inclinations, its character, its prejudices, and its passions." Democracy had begun to catch hold in the United States in the 1790s, but how quickly and how fully it had developed depends on how it is defined. The traditional interpretation stresses forms of government and relates the rise of democracy to the creation of mass political parties in the 1830s. A recent school of thought sees its rise much earlier in the informal behavior of people of all types who created a participatory democracy through the use of social organisms such as salons, parades, festivals, and newspapers. Kendall, who edited newspapers and helped build a national political party, is a good source for both interpretations.[4]

The travelers realized that they were witnessing more than simply a change in government. The onset of democracy was intermixed with the rise of a commercial, capitalist economy stimulated by an expansion of banking, the construction of roads and canals, and the introduction of steamboats and railroads. Markets were growing; the young nation was on the move. Between 1790 and 1860 it would change from a federation of thirteen states and 4 mil-

3. Francis J. Grund, *Aristocracy in America: From the Sketch-Book of a German Nobleman* (1839; reprint, New York, 1959), 298–99.

4. Alexis de Tocqueville, *Democracy in America*, ed. Phillips Bradley, 2 vols. (1945; reprint, New York, 1980), 1:14. For the older view see Joel H. Silbey, "'To One or Another of These Parties Every Man Belongs': The American Political Experience from Andrew Jackson to the Civil War," in *Contesting Democracy: Substance and Structure in American Political History, 1775–2000*, ed. Byron E. Shafer and Anthony J. Badger (Lawrence, 2001), 65–92. For the newer view see David Waldstreicher, "The Nationalization and Racialization of American Politics: Before, beneath, and between Parties, 1790–1840," ibid., 37–63; and *In the Midst of Perpetual Fetes: The Making of American Nationalism, 1776–1820* (Chapel Hill, 1997). Andrew R. L. Cayton has questioned the influence and power of the earlier form of democracy. "We Are All Nationalists, We Are All Localists," *JER* 18 (1998): 521–28.

lion people tied to the Atlantic coast to a union (soon to be broken) of thirty-three states and 32 million people extending across the continent.

Hand in hand with the new government and economy went new institutions such as political parties and corporations and new liberal, individualistic values at odds with the virtuous republican ideals of the American Revolution. Making it all possible were remarkable advances in communication fostered by the spread of literacy and popular science, the expansion of newspapers and the post office, and the invention of the telegraph.

With all the new freedoms and choices, the period has been glorified as the age of the common man, but there was also a dark side. The capitalist economy produced a series of banking panics and recessions. There was a widening of the divisions between racial, ethnic, gender, and economic groups. Slaveowners grew defensive, planters and plain republicans pushed Indians aside, early arrivals united against immigrants, men sought to keep women in the home, and the gap grew between rich and poor.[5]

The changes were so far-reaching, so modernizing that we often turn to the antebellum years to learn more about ourselves. Since World War II no other period has been studied so exhaustively. Like Tocqueville we have been particularly curious about the nature of our early democracy and its relationship to the economic, social, and cultural changes of the era.[6]

Kendall contributed to and adapted to these trends. Though at first far from democratic, he made many contributions to the rise of democracy. His newspaper writing increased popular interest in politics. He joined in organizing first a political faction, then two different state parties, and finally the national Democratic party, all of which encouraged voters to participate in the

5. The political and social history of this period has been well covered. Among others see Robert H. Wiebe, *The Opening of American Society from the Adoption of the Constitution to the Eve of Disunion* (New York, 1984); Harry L. Watson, *Liberty and Power: The Politics of Jacksonian America* (New York, 1990); Charles Sellers, *The Market Revolution: Jacksonian America, 1815–1846* (New York, 1991).

6. Interest in antebellum America was sparked by Arthur M. Schlesinger's *The Age of Jackson* (Boston, 1945). For other interpretations of the era see Richard Hofstadter, "Andrew Jackson and the Rise of Liberal Capitalism," in *The American Political Tradition and the Men Who Made It* (New York, 1948), 44–66; Lee Benson, *The Concept of Jacksonian Democracy: New York as a Test Case* (Princeton, 1984); Sellers, *Market Revolution*; John Ashworth, *Slavery, Capitalism, and Politics in the Antebellum Republic*, vol. 1, *Commerce and Compromise, 1820–1850* (Cambridge, Eng., 1995); Robert H. Wiebe, *Self-Rule: A Cultural History of American Democracy* (Chicago, 1995); James L. Huston, *Securing the Fruits of Labor: The American Concept of Wealth Distribution* (Baton Rouge, 1998).

evolving system. During it all he was forced to adapt to the changes going on around him. Born on one of those small Massachusetts farms that stood somewhere between subsistence agriculture and market capitalism, he left home near the end of the War of 1812 to seek his fortune in Kentucky. There he became a jack-of-all-trades, a tutor, a lawyer, a postmaster, a newspaperman, finally a politician. In his later years he became postmaster general and business agent for Samuel F. B. Morse's telegraph. In almost all of these occupations he was swept up in the revolution in communications. He was the classic American self-made man.[7]

He also became the classic Jacksonian—the humble farm boy turned businessman who rallied behind Old Hickory—like Isaac Hill, Martin Van Buren, William L. Marcy, and Thomas Hart Benton. After carrying Kentucky for Jackson in 1828, he came to Washington, where he became the president's political adviser, patronage chief, and speechwriter, the author of his veto of the bill to recharter the Bank of the United States. He was a political operative; Bernard De Voto called him "a wirepuller on the highest levels"—"The Man to See" in the Jackson years. In many ways he was an earlier day Joe Tumulty or Tommy Corcoran.[8]

Until now there has been no biography of Kendall—perhaps because he was not a major figure and perhaps because an unsatisfactory autobiography and the absence of a large body of papers made the task seem difficult. The *Autobiography,* which was published shortly after his death, is actually a biography by his son-in-law, interspersed with Kendall's journal, letters, and editorials. It is much slanted in Kendall's favor and uneven in its coverage. One reviewer complained with good reason that it contained "comparatively little" about "the really important periods of his life"—meaning his years in politics. It does, however, reveal much about Kendall's personality. To compensate for the shortage of Kendall papers there are hundreds of valuable letters to and from Kendall in the papers of Andrew Jackson, Martin Van Buren, Francis P. Blair, Samuel F. B. Morse, Francis O. J. Smith (the telegraph man), and Kendall's son John Kendall. An indispensable source is the journalism of Kendall, his friends, and especially his enemies.[9]

7. Joyce Oldham Appleby has already analyzed the lives of hundreds of Kendall's contemporaries in *Inheriting the Revolution: The First Generation of Americans* (Cambridge, Mass., 2000).

8. Bernard De Voto, "The Easy Chair," *Harpers* 190 (1945): 501.

9. *Autobiography; North American Review* 116 (1873): 168. Kendall's papers were reportedly destroyed in a warehouse fire. John J. McDonough, *Index to the Andrew Jackson Papers* (Washington, D.C., 1967), xxi. There are two excellent doctoral dissertations. Lynn L. Marshall, "The Early

Before starting this study, I must offer a brief working definition of democracy. I understand it as a political culture based on ideals that have never been fully achieved. It has its roots in an egalitarian society in which the mass of the people enjoy what Gordon Wood has called "a rough equality of condition." They participate in a political system that enables them to shape public opinion and elect a government. The system provides organizations and procedures to promote the process. When officials take office, they carry out the will of the people. Unlike republicanism, which places limits on the power of the government and the people in order to protect liberty, democracy assumes that the majority can and should rule.[10]

In Kendall's day democracy was constantly evolving and many questions were yet unanswered. Who, for example, would be the "people" to vote and serve in the government? Would the government follow the wishes of the people? How would the government relate to the economy, democracy to capitalism?

Kendall's story offers an opportunity to look for answers.

---

Career of Amos Kendall: The Making of a Jacksonian" (Ph.D. diss., University of California, Berkeley, 1962); and Terry L. Shoptaugh, "Amos Kendall: A Political Biography" (Ph.D. diss., University of New Hampshire, 1984).

10. For definitions of democracy see Wiebe, *Self-Rule*, 1–11; Gordon S. Wood, *The Radicalism of the American Revolution* (New York, 1992), 231–32, 234 ("rough"), 243, 257–58; William G. Shade, *Democratizing the Old Dominion: Virginia and the Second Party System, 1824–1861* (Charlottesville, 1996), xiii–xv and passim; and Waldstreicher, "Nationalization and Racialization," 37–39.

PART ONE

# New England

# I

## DUNSTABLE

News of the fighting at Lexington and Concord reached Dunstable, twenty miles to the north, late in the evening of that fateful day. The townspeople were ready to act. Almost thirty of them, including nineteen-year-old Zebedee Kendall, had signed a pledge to "engage with each other in defence of our country, Priviledges and Libertys," and the town had voted "to have menite men . . . in readiness to march at the first notice." They had been drilling every week. Within a few hours militia captain Ebenezer Bancroft and fifty men were making their way southeast through Middlesex County to Cambridge.[1]

Two months later at Bunker Hill, Bancroft was severely wounded, and one of his soldiers lost an arm. During the siege of Boston the Dunstable militiamen took part in capturing Dorchester Heights, while back home their families were sheltering patriots fleeing from the city. The spirit of freedom was high; in June 1776 the town resolved that it would "risk life and fortune in ye cause" of independence. As the war spread outside of Massachusetts, the militia company, with Zebedee Kendall and a half dozen of his relatives in the ranks, fought at Ticonderoga, Philadelphia, and Saratoga.[2]

The unusual number of Kendalls in the militia company attests to their importance in the community. Dunstable was a Massachusetts town of six hundred people on the Merrimack River just south of the New Hampshire border. It had been founded in 1673, and for the next fifty years had served as a frontier garrison in the colonial wars. The coming of peace in the 1720s brought in permanent settlers of English stock, among them Zebedee's grandfather and grandmother, two great-uncles, and his father, John, then a baby.

---

1. Elias Nason, *A History of the Town of Dunstable, Massachusetts* (Boston, 1877), 106–13, 116, quotations, 112; Frederick Lewis Weis, *Early Generations of the Kendall Family of Massachusetts, Especially the Life of Lieutenant Samuel Kendall, Gentleman, 1682–1764, of Woburn, Lancaster, and Athol* (Lancaster, Mass., 1839), 166.

2. Nason, *Dunstable*, 113–29, quotation, 119.

The Kendalls bought land and started farming, the great-uncles married, and the family multiplied. In 1747 John eloped with Hannah Whitman, already five months pregnant, and within eight years they had a family of five children, the youngest of whom was Zebedee. By the time of the Revolution almost fifty Kendall children had been born in the town.[3]

As one of the town's core families the Kendalls performed vital civic duties and perpetuated community traditions. Only one or two families could rival them in number of members paying taxes. Everyone knew the Kendalls, for Zebedee's great-uncle Ebenezer ran a tavern that was used for elections and town meetings. He and Zebedee's father served on the committees that built a new meetinghouse. Zebedee's grandfather and his great-uncle Abraham were both elected selectmen. During the Revolution Zebedee's second cousin Asa chaired the committee of correspondence and held meetings of the minutemen at his home.[4]

The strong response of Dunstable and the Kendalls to the cause of freedom was typical of the reaction of dozens of Massachusetts country towns. The men who went off to fight were for the most part small farmers, whose primary concern was feeding their families, not making a profit. Typical farmers in Dunstable and throughout the state supported their families and a few animals—perhaps two or three cows, two pigs, a horse, and a pair of oxen—on twenty acres of improved land, half of it in hay and the rest in corn, rye, and pasture. Some of the farms were so small that the farmers had to exchange some surplus commodity, such as the labor of a son or daughter, for someone else's surplus grain.[5]

This homogeneous, small-town, farming society was rooted in the traditions of righteousness, duty, and hard work taught by the established Congregational church. The society in turn fostered a form of classical republicanism that believed in independence, civic virtue, simplicity, local power, and equal

3. Nason, *Dunstable*, 8–55, 77, 282–83; Weis, *Early Generations of the Kendall Family*, 166–67; Oliver Kendall, *Memorial of Josiah Kendall* (n.p., 1884), 1, 9–13, 31; *Vital Records of Dunstable, Massachusetts, to the End of the Year 1849* (Salem, 1913), 49–53, 150.

4. They ranked second in number of taxpayers in 1744 and tied for first in 1771. Nason, *Dunstable*, 75, 76, 79, 84, 86, 113, 117, 121; Bettye Hobbs Pruitt, ed., *The Massachusetts Tax Valuation List of 1771* (Boston, 1978), 204–7.

5. Bettye Hobbs Pruitt, "Self-Sufficiency and the Agricultural Economy of Eighteenth-Century Massachusetts," *William and Mary Quarterly* 41 (1982): 335. The median Dunstable farm had five acres of corn and rye, another five of pasture, and ten acres of hay. Pruitt, *Massachusetts Tax Valuation List*, 204–7.

rights for adult white males. Family and community were placed ahead of the individual. The farmers scorned the corruption, luxury, and exploitation that they associated with the commercial world of cities and the central rule of monarchs. Guarding these traditions and beliefs were core families such as the Kendalls.

But even small towns were close to markets and had economic classes and early forms of capitalism. In Dunstable and its five surrounding towns 8 percent of the taxpayers were lending money at interest. The total of over £7,000 on loan exceeded the annual rental value of all the real estate in those towns. In addition all of the towns but one exported grain. And property ownership varied greatly. The annual tax assessment (rental value) of most real estate in Dunstable was between £2 and £7, but five taxpayers had real estate valued between £17 and £28. The median of 20 acres of improved land was misleading, for two farmers owned more than 90 acres each, while many owned less than 10. Only an exclusive group of twenty farmers had more than a pair of oxen, while the large majority had none. Most notable was the dominance of a few wealthy families. In Dunstable the brothers Eleazer, John, and James Tyng owned 253 acres of improved land, three slaves, real estate valued at £68, and merchandise worth £200. When Eleazer died in 1782, he left his daughter Sarah an estate worth over £1,000.[6]

As the inequality suggests, this was not a democratic society. The town was dominated by the members of the church, who made up less than half of the adult population. Within this select group the older, more well-to-do men held the power. These elders and their wives sat in elevated pews in front of the minister, those paying the highest taxes occupying the best seats. Children and servants, including a score of black slaves, sat in the balcony. This religious hierarchy was matched by similar rankings in the militia and the town offices. Old militia officers never lost the deferential title of captain or lieutenant. The town historian, writing in the 1870s, refers to "classes" in eighteenth-century Dunstable.[7]

In 1780 Zebedee Kendall, now twenty-four, married Molly Dakin, twenty, of Mason, New Hampshire. The couple moved in with Zebedee's mother and father on Kendall Hill, close to the New Hampshire line, and soon built their own farmhouse close by. During the next decade Zebedee

6. Pruitt, *Massachusetts Tax Valuation List,* 190–95, 200–215, 246–51, 284–89; Pruitt, "Self-Sufficiency," 333–64; Nason, *Dunstable,* 151.

7. Nason, *Dunstable,* 93, 96–97, 99, 103–5, 111–12, 136 (quotation), 153.

served as selectman, overseer of the poor, and member of the church committee. In 1789 he was named deacon of the church, a position he held for the
next fifty years. In this capacity he taught in the Sabbath school and presided
over the sale of the thirty-two pews when the meetinghouse was rebuilt. All
the while he continued to take an active part in the musters of the militia
company. The leader of the third generation of Kendalls, he was a zealous
guardian of the republican tradition.[8]

After the war the townspeople remained true to the tradition. Determined to resist centralized power, they voted to adopt the Articles of Confederation but refused to ratify the Massachusetts constitution in 1780 because it
gave too much authority to the governor and too much freedom to the press
and Roman Catholics. Shays's Rebellion tested the town's loyalty to the state
government, for many of the Dunstable farmers were suffering the same burden of high taxes and heavy debts that led to the uprising. Even so, the town
supported the government and sent its share of militiamen to put down the
revolt. At the state convention to consider the United States Constitution, the
delegate from Dunstable voted for ratification. As political parties began to
emerge in the 1790s, Dunstable—like most of the other towns in Middlesex
County—voted Republican.[9]

Within the town a religious controversy had been brewing. Since 1755
Dunstable had been divided into two parishes, each with its own minister and
meetinghouse, one in the western part of town, the home of the Kendalls, and
the other to the east near the Merrimack River, where the Tyngs lived. By
1789 the arrangement had become so expensive that the parishioners agreed to
consolidate in one parish but were fighting bitterly over where to place the
meetinghouse. At this point widow Sarah Tyng Winslow, who had inherited
so much wealth from her father, offered to give the income from her estate to
endow the minister and support a central grammar school. She added the pro-
viso, however, that the parishioners must agree to use the eastern meetinghouse, which would have to be rebuilt, and put the grammar school next to it.
The offer was a financial godsend for the town, but the Kendalls and the others from the west stubbornly refused, protesting that they would have to walk
or ride too far to get to church or school. The eastern parish then broke away

8. *Vital Records of Dunstable*, 151; Weis, *Early Generations of the Kendall Family*, 166; Nason, *Dunstable*, 148–70.

9. Nason, *Dunstable*, 130–35, 146–49; Jonathan Eliot, ed., *Debates in the Several State Conventions on the Adoption of the Federal Constitution*, 5 vols. (Philadelphia, 1836), 2:179.

and eventually became the separate town of Tyngsborough, with all of the Tyng money.[10]

The Kendalls and their friends in Dunstable were left in a disastrous situation. Their numbers had been reduced to four hundred, they had very little money, and they faced the immediate problem of their meetinghouse. Over the next five years they spent more than they could afford in dragging the building several miles to the west and rebuilding it in the new center of town. Then they had to build their own school. There was also the problem of isolation, for Dunstable was now cut off from the Merrimack River, which flowed south through Tyngsborough. When the Middlesex Canal was completed in 1803, connecting the Merrimack with Boston, trade between central New Hampshire and Boston passed through Tyngsborough, not Dunstable.[11]

By 1840 Tyngsborough had developed into a thriving commercial town, mining granite and manufacturing barrels and shoes. It had profited greatly from the coming of the railroad and the rise of the mill towns Lowell, Massachusetts, and Manchester, New Hampshire, on the Merrimack. Its population had doubled. Dunstable, on the other hand, remained a poor farming community located on the rocky, hilly land away from the river; its population had risen only 50 percent. Perhaps the parishioners of Dunstable had anticipated the hardships that lay ahead, for in planning their meetinghouse they stipulated, somewhat defensively, that "the breastwork in the gallery" should not be "inferior" to the one in Tyngsborough.[12]

On August 16, 1789, two months after the parishes were separated, Amos Kendall was born, the son of Molly and Zebedee. The days leading up to the event must have been filled with anxiety, not only because of the church crisis but also because Amos would be Molly's sixth child in nine years. But August was a good time to have a baby. Molly's first five children had been born in the cold of fall and winter; this one came in the best part of the year. Now that the oppressive humidity of July was gone, the days were comfortable, the skies clear, and locusts hummed in the pleasant heat of the afternoon. Nestled on the western slope of Kendall Hill, the farm was protected by a pine grove to the north and by oak trees along the ridge. Looking across broad meadows to the south and west, the Kendalls could enjoy sunshine all day and see

10. Nason, *Dunstable,* 89–90, 143–46, 150–53, 161.

11. Ibid., 154–55; Christopher Roberts, *The Middlesex Canal, 1793–1860* (Cambridge, Mass., 1938).

12. John Hayward, *The New England Gazetteer* (Boston, 1839); Nason, *Dunstable,* 155.

Salmon Brook winding its way toward the Merrimack. With harvest time drawing near, corn was ripe in the fields, and apples were ready to pick in the orchards.[13]

Zebedee Kendall and his father were farming an average-sized farm with twenty-two acres of improved land. The meadowland along the brook provided hay for the horses, cows, and oxen, the plains above were used to pasture sheep, while eight acres next to the hill were planted alternately in corn and rye. The family had cleared part of the hillside for a potato field, leaving the rest for foraging. The Kendalls grew much of their own food and used wool from their sheep and flax from their garden to make their own clothing. They had a small cash income, some of which came from a patch of tobacco. With more livestock than they could pasture in summer and sometimes more grain than they needed, they rented a field for the animals twenty-five miles away in New Hampshire and paid for it either with grain or by dipping into their cash.[14]

Although Amos Kendall later had the reputation of having grown up poor, the truth is that the Kendalls were a middling, landowning family, above average in their community. They could not have been poor and still have held so many positions of trust. In addition they ranked in the first and second quartiles in property values. In 1771 Zebedee's father owned real estate worth well above the town median and produced one hundred bushels of grain, double his neighbors' production. And the Kendalls could borrow. Amos later mentioned that his father, "though not rich, could, by his credit, always command money." Even so, not one Kendall had gone to college or made the jump into the professional or merchant class. The family had neither the cash income, the large landholdings, nor the political and economic connections needed to push one of its members ahead in the restricted economy of the late eighteenth century.[15]

At the time of Amos's birth the farmers of New England were in the midst of a severe depression marked by farm foreclosures and a crisis in inheritance. Farms had usually been divided among sons; daughters were expected

13. *Vital Records of Dunstable*, 49–53; *Autobiography*, 1–2.

14. *Autobiography*, 1–2; Pruitt, *Massachusetts Tax Valuation List*, 204–7.

15. John Quincy Adams once called Kendall a "child of . . . poverty." John Quincy Adams, *Memoirs of John Quincy Adams*, ed. Charles Francis Adams, 12 vols. (Philadelphia, 1875–77), 8:28. In 1757 Zebedee's grandfather and one of his great-uncles paid the sixth and eighth highest taxes in the town. Zebedee occasionally made loans. Pruitt, *Massachusetts Tax Valuation List*, 204–7; *Autobiography*, 54, 68, 86.

to marry and live on their husbands' property. Now there was not enough land for the sons. Zebedee had been more fortunate than most because his only brother had either died or moved away, and his three sisters had all found husbands; but the situation was far less promising for his six sons and one daughter. By 1804, when Amos was fifteen, some of the pressure had been removed because the daughter and the two oldest sons had married and left. But the four remaining sons (of whom Amos was the second oldest) were still too many to be supported by the farm.[16]

With so many siblings and cousins to play with and so many older Kendalls to look up to, Amos should have had a happy, secure childhood, but his recollections were not very warm. His strongest memories were of having to get out of bed on cold mornings to tend his animal traps and of being scolded for taking the eyes from live fish to use as bait. He also remembered not being able to stand the sight of blood when hogs were slaughtered or to kill baby mice in the fields. He was shy, sensitive, and so sober and thoughtful that he was called "the Deacon."[17]

Why he became so somber needs explaining. Perhaps it was because of tension in the family over the cloudy future. Perhaps it was because of his father, who was a serious man. Perhaps it was the constant exposure to death and grief. After Amos was born, his mother bore six more children, and four of them died before the age of six. A baby sister died when Amos was five, another sister and a brother within two days when he was nine, and finally a baby brother when he was fifteen. Perhaps he lacked confidence in his siblings. He was terribly distressed, for example, when some of the boys in the town lured one of his older brothers into the woods one night to search for treasure and frightened him badly by hiding in the darkness and making terrifying noises. These and similar episodes led Amos to suspect that his brothers and sister were not as clever and sophisticated as the other children in town.[18]

Another reason may have been his health and physique. Thin and pale with a squeaky voice and spindly legs, he was often sick with colds and headaches and was much too weak to excel in outdoor, country life. Once when he and his brother George were foxhunting, they found themselves knee-deep in

16. Winifred Barr Rothenberg, *From Market-Places to a Market Economy: The Transformation of Rural Massachusetts, 1750–1850* (Chicago, 1992), 108–9; *Vital Records of Dunstable,* 49–53, 149–51, 220; Weis, *Early Generations of the Kendall Family,* 167.

17. *Autobiography,* 5–9.

18. *Vital Records of Dunstable,* 49–53; *Autobiography,* 5–6.

snow a mile and a half from home. After struggling to get back, Amos's legs gave out with still a half mile to go, and he had to lie huddled in the snow while George went to get a horse.[19]

As he grew older, the demands of farmwork became a burden. At the age of eleven he started doing chores for his grandparents in the morning and evening and spent the rest of the day working in the fields. At fifteen when his older siblings were gone and his father was laid up with arthritis, he and George had to take on much of the responsibility for the entire farm. Because of his frail physique he soon found the work "unusually severe." In later years he often looked back romantically and talked of giving up journalism and politics to return to farming, but such sentiments were little more than nostalgia.[20]

Amos's happiest memories centered on schoolwork. Obviously the brightest child in the family, he quickly mastered the arithmetic tables, bested his brothers and sisters in spelling bees, read the entire Bible, and devoured Jedidiah Morse's *American Geography*. While the other children played at noon hour and in the evenings, Amos spent the time reading books from the town's new social library. He also experimented with rudimentary mechanical devices and was intrigued with the idea of perpetual motion. Aware that his son was bookish, Zebedee encouraged him by giving him prizes and once by hiring a tutor, but neither Amos nor any of the Kendall children attended school regularly.[21]

Amos greatly admired his father. As in other Congregational families Zebedee ruled sternly and righteously and considered it his duty to control the lives of his children. He insisted on "grace before and thanks after" every meal and "morning and evening prayers" every day of the week. On Sundays the Kendalls read a chapter in the Bible and sang a hymn before leaving for two church services. At no time was there any card playing, dancing, drinking, or even playing the fiddle. His father was a kind and humane man. When Amos told him about using fish eyes for bait, Zebedee pointed out how wrong it was to treat animals so cruelly. He was the perfect example of the strict, republican family man of duty and civic virtue. He left a permanent mark on his son, who half a century later remembered him as a man of "ardent temperament."[22]

19. *Autobiography*, 10–11.

20. Ibid., 14 (quotation); *Kendall's Expositor* (Washington, D.C.), 17 Feb. 1842; Kendall to John, 24 Dec. 1848.

21. *Autobiography*, 4–5, 7, 322–23.

22. Ibid., 2–3, 8; Kendall to John, 10 Oct. 1852.

Once Zebedee recovered his health, he had to decide what to do with a puny fifteen-year-old son who was unusually precocious and not cut out for farming. He came to the conclusion that he must send him to college, a difficult task for a father with so little ready cash. The decision to send the smartest and least robust son to college while keeping the others on the farm was not uncommon. A few years earlier and sixty miles to the north, Ebenezer Webster had made the same decision, sending Daniel to Phillips Exeter Academy and Dartmouth.

As a first step Zebedee made an agreement with Joshua Heywood, the parish minister, to board Amos during the winter and instruct him in arithmetic and grammar. In return Amos would cut wood, care for the animals, and do other chores. It seemed a promising arrangement; Amos would prepare for college and might someday become a minister himself. But the plan failed, for Heywood, a hulking, dark, fierce-looking man, overworked Amos, bullied the young orphan girl who was doing the housework, and gave little instruction. Amos stuck it out all winter, but on returning home in the spring he prevailed on his father not to send him back. Instead of turning Amos toward the ministry, the winter with Heywood started his gradual alienation from the church.[23]

In the fall of 1805 Zebedee sent Amos to the academy in New Ipswich, New Hampshire, where he could board with his older brother Samuel, who had settled there. His father paid $8.20 for tuition and books, while Amos earned his board and room by working morning and evening on Samuel's farm. Academies had multiplied in New England, because teachers at the local grammar schools were too busy to provide the fundamentals of arithmetic and the classics required by colleges. New Ipswich had already prepared many students for Dartmouth College. Away from home for the first time, Amos was miserable. The diffidence that had plagued him throughout his boyhood only worsened as the other students made fun of his manners and appearance. He was terrified when called on to make his first declamation and delivered a memorized piece in a monotone with his eyes fixed on the wall across the room. The cruel preceptor "ridiculed him unmercifully," as Amos recalled, "comparing him to an immovable hydrant pouring forth his steady stream of water." After eleven weeks he returned home mortified and resentful.[24]

23. *Autobiography*, 11–12; Nason, *Dunstable*, 167.

24. Charles Henry Chandler, *The History of New Ipswich, New Hampshire, 1835–1914* (Fitchburg, Mass., 1914), 137–41; Leon Burr Richardson, *History of Dartmouth College*, 2 vols. (Hanover, 1932), 1:246; *Argus of Western America* (Frankfort, Ky.), 22 Oct. 1819; *Autobiography*, 12–13.

Far from defeated, however, he spent the winter practicing declamation in front of a mirror. When he returned to New Ipswich in the spring, he amazed everyone by delivering his first speech with "self possession and appropriate action." Before long he was performing so well in all subjects that he was even tutoring some of those who had laughed at him in the fall. As an old man he still remembered his triumph, but he never got over his fear of public speaking.[25]

In the fall of 1806 Zebedee informed Amos that he had to help pay for his own education and found him teaching positions for the winter. With the money he earned, Amos enrolled for the spring and summer at the academy in Groton, a town close to Dunstable. He did well scholastically but found that too much studying, like too much farmwork, "impaired his health, never very robust." Still dependent on his family, he had to return home for two weeks in order to "recruit his strength." This anxiety about his physical condition remained with him for the rest of his life.[26]

When Kendall completed his studies at the end of the summer of 1807, he had spent forty-seven weeks and $85 (half from his father) preparing for college. He was then examined and admitted to Dartmouth to start in the fall. It might have been more convenient for Zebedee to send his son to Harvard, which was much closer than Dartmouth, but that was out of the question. The Kendalls were unprepared socially and financially to send their son to a college that catered to upper-class young men, largely from the vicinity of Boston, many of them with liberal religious notions. Amos would have felt insecure at Harvard, where the students considered Dartmouth a "freshwater college" and doubted that a Dartmouth man could ever be "a fine gentleman." And Harvard was much more expensive. A thrifty student could survive at Dartmouth for considerably less than $150 a year, while it cost more than twice that much at Harvard.

The Kendalls could not afford even the $80 or $90 needed for the fall and winter terms at Dartmouth. So Amos—like scores of young men at the time—was allowed to postpone his entrance while he studied on his own and earned $13 and board and room teaching in the town across the state line in New Hampshire, also called Dunstable. The food was "wholesome, but coarse, consisting almost entirely of rye-bread, salt beef and pork, with potatoes and cabbages." The house was cold and drafty. There he sat in the evening "turn-

---

25. *Autobiography*, 13–14.
26. Ibid., 14–15.

ing first one side and then the other to a fire . . . with no sound around him but the wintry wind." The only luxury was going to bed, where he found some warmth in "an excellent feather-bed."[27]

Amos taught as many as sixty pupils of all ages for six hours a day, every day but Sunday. He taught eight subjects—writing, reading, spelling, arithmetic, English grammar, geography, and a special class for two boys in Greek and Latin. It was not easy to maintain order. He managed to get through the winter but had to come to the rescue of an unfortunate friend in another school who got into trouble by whipping a pupil. When Amos learned that the students planned to ride his friend out of the schoolyard on a rail, he exposed the plot. The boy's father then sued, but arbitrators, including Zebedee Kendall, who never failed to step in for Amos, ruled for the teacher. Despite the hard life, Amos carried away an idealized view of the New England free schools. The teachers, he recalled, kept "exemplary order," yet were "seldom tyrannical, and scarcely ever use[d] the rod." Teaching in such schools, he believed, "improved the young teacher quite as much as the taught."[28]

One of the benefits that he chose not to mention was the chance to be away from his father's control. He began to play cards and discovered that "dancing had now become a general amusement at private parties." One of these parties turned into an adventure. On a cold winter day he joined a group of young men and women on a sleigh ride that was to include a ball at a tavern in Chelmsford, Massachusetts, a dozen miles away. When the twenty-two sleighs—each with a couple—started out, the weather was bright and sunny, but by the time they reached their destination a heavy snowstorm had begun. The storm became so intense that they had to stay at the tavern all night. As they fought their way back through the heavy drifts the next morning, they stopped at several farmhouses to warm themselves. They noticed the men clearing the roads being treated to hot rum flip and quite likely sampled some themselves.[29]

By the spring of 1808 Amos could finally afford to enroll at Dartmouth. His character and values were now well developed. Born with intelligence and inner drive, he had absorbed the puritanical and republican ideals of his family

27. Ibid., 15–16; Richardson, *History of Dartmouth College*, 1:242–43. For the slighting references to Dartmouth by Oliver Wendell Holmes and John Quincy Adams see *Nation* 15 (1872): 124; and Adams, *The Diary of John Quincy Adams*, ed. David Grayson Allen et al., 2 vols. (Cambridge, Mass., 1981), 2:335.

28. *Autobiography*, 18; *Argus*, 22 Oct. 1819; Kendall to John, 13 Oct. 1851.

29. *Autobiography*, 16–18.

and community, especially those of his father. A difficult challenge lay ahead. The first Kendall to go to college, he would be taking a big step toward breaking free from the restraints imposed by the hierarchical culture of rural New England. Was he strong enough to succeed? Throughout his boyhood he had displayed a troubling insecurity. A shy, gloomy boy, he had had little faith in his siblings or his health, seemed dependent on his father, and had unfortunate experiences when he went away to school. But he had also shown perseverance and was beginning to display some independence. Even more important, the traditional society was showing signs of breaking up. In a new, more open society, young Kendall might be just the sort of person who could take advantage of the new opportunities. How he would respond to democracy was not at all clear. The first test would be at Dartmouth.

# 2

## NEW WORLDS

On a dark, chill morning in March 1808 Kendall rode to Amherst, New Hampshire, and took the stagecoach for Hanover. As he headed north over the hills, he went through towns that would later back Andrew Jackson as loyally as he would. He passed close to the homes of future political allies Isaac Hill, who was apprenticed to a printer, and Levi Woodbury, who was a junior at Dartmouth. The snow covering the roads was packed into ridges and hollows that caused the coach, equipped with runners, to rise and fall like a boat, making Kendall so motion sick that he ate nothing during the entire trip. Late at night on the second day the coach hit a stump and overturned, leaving Kendall to ride the final three miles on horseback. He did not reach Hanover until two o'clock in the morning.[1]

Dartmouth was one of dozens of new colleges spawned by the new society. In the years after 1770 the number had grown from nine to more than thirty, providing opportunities for thousands of young Americans. Many of the early Jackson men got their start at these colleges: Kendall and Woodbury at Dartmouth, William L. Marcy at Brown, Silas Wright at Middlebury, Franklin Pierce at Bowdoin, Roger B. Taney and James Buchanan at Dickinson, and Francis P. Blair at Transylvania.

Life in this young college offered Kendall so many new experiences that he later recalled it as a "new world." Hanover was a trading center overlooking the Connecticut River, four times as large as Dunstable. The center of town and college life was a spacious common, with a Congregational church at one end and four imposing Dartmouth buildings at the other. Daniel Webster would later call Dartmouth "a small college," but it was in fact the same size as Harvard, while Hanover was just as large as Cambridge.[2]

1. It was his first trip on a stagecoach. *Autobiography,* 18–20.
2. For "new world" see Kendall to Caleb Butler, 13 May 1835, Amos Kendall Papers, LC. For Webster's remark see George Ticknor Curtis, *Life of Daniel Webster,* 2 vols. (New York, 1870), 1:170. Hanover had a population of 2,000, and the enrollment at Dartmouth was about 170.

Kendall had an easy time breaking in because the first year at Dartmouth was not very demanding. The freshmen spent two-thirds of their time on the classics and the remainder on a smattering of mathematics, grammar, philosophy, and other subjects. The classes were routine affairs, with students reciting and presenting papers. What Kendall dreaded was the prospect of reading in front of a tutor and the entire freshman class. When finally called upon to speak, he stood with his back and elbows pressed tight against a wall to keep his hands from shaking. He performed so well that the tutor and the students could not believe that he had never given a college paper.[3]

Kendall found the informal education at Dartmouth far more stimulating than the formal curriculum. Almost all the students belonged to one of two large societies, the United Fraternity and the Social Friends, which sponsored debates and maintained libraries of some two thousand books apiece, as large as the college library. Kendall, who had exhausted the meager resources of the Dunstable library, could now choose from six thousand books—novels, poetry, plays, and tales of travel, as well as the classics and works on divinity, law, history, and philosophy. He could read current writers such as Scott, Weems, and Malthus, as well as those of an older generation, Edwards, Rousseau, Gibbon, and Johnson. Kendall later told his son that "the societies were of more use to me than all the teachings of Professors and Tutors."[4]

But it was from his classmates that Kendall learned most. Even though all seventy-one came from New England just as he did, their backgrounds were generally much different from his. They were more cosmopolitan, came from larger towns, and more than half were from comfortable, nonfarming families. A number of their fathers were doctors, lawyers, or clergymen, two were sheriffs, one a congressman, and one a judge. There could not have been many Republicans, for two-thirds came from Federalist towns, and Dartmouth was known as a Federalist college.[5]

3. Scholar George Ticknor, class of 1807, once remarked that he had "learnt very little" at Dartmouth. Richardson, *History of Dartmouth College*, 1:130, 213–14, 226, 242–56, 261–63 (quotation); *Autobiography*, 20.

4. Richardson, *History of Dartmouth College*, 251, 268–72; *Catalogue of Books in the United Fraternity's Library at Dartmouth College, June 1824* (Concord, 1824); *Autobiography*, 30; Kendall to John, 13 June 1850.

5. The median age was nineteen. George T. Chapman, *Sketches of the Alumni of Dartmouth College* (Cambridge, 1867), 150–59; *Dartmouth Graduates and Former Students* (n.p., n.d.), 161–63; Dartmouth College, Class of 1811, *Minutes of Their Meeting in 1849; Also Brief Biographical Notices of the Members* (Concord, 1850). Town population figures were taken from gazetteers at the New Hampshire Historical Society.

Kendall was a member of the Social Friends, but the men who influenced him the most were thirteen classmates who had formed a small, semisecret society called the Gymnasion Adelphon. The club, which he joined soon after his arrival, held weekly meetings, at which the members presented compositions or gave declamations. The character of these new friends gives a good indication of Kendall's values. He remembered them as "the best part of the class, both in morals and knowledge." Older, more sophisticated, and more scholarly than the others, they ranked at the top of their class and shared a moral idealism that was later reflected in their choice of professions. Instead of becoming lawyers like most of the class, five became clergymen, three were teachers, one a doctor, and one a poet-scholar. Bolder than their classmates, more than half of them sought careers outside of New England. Perhaps they were too bold; five of them were dead before they reached forty-five.[6]

The individuals whom Kendall most respected were club members Daniel Poor and Joseph Perry and a tutor, Francis Brown. Poor, who came from Danvers, Massachusetts, spent most of his life in Ceylon and southern India as a Congregational missionary. Perry taught school in New York City before serving in the national government. Brown, only a few years older than Kendall, became pastor of a Congregational church in Maine and then returned to Dartmouth as president at the time of the Dartmouth College Supreme Court case. He did much to save the college from being turned into a state university and died from overwork a few months after the decision. Kendall saw in these men the idealism of his father and also a scholarliness and worldliness that Zebedee lacked.[7]

Kendall's high moral standards often got him into trouble with his other classmates. One night his roommate and a few friends brought some stolen chickens back to the room, woke him up, and invited him to join them in a party. When Kendall called them thieves and refused to get out of bed, they tore off his bedclothes. On another occasion, after the class had completed its study of Homer, he attended a ceremony at which the students threw the pages of their textbooks into a basin of burning rum. As the ceremony grew

6. *Autobiography*, 26, 33, 61, 66 (quotation); Kendall to John, 13 June 1850; Kendall to Wright, 22 Nov. 1817, Nathaniel Wright Papers, LC. Half of the ten best students in the class and six of the sixteen members elected to Phi Beta Kappa were from the Gymnasion. *Catalogue of the Fraternity of Phi Beta Kappa, Alpha of New-Hampshire. Dartmouth College. 1832* (Hanover, 1832).

7. William A. Robinson, "Francis Brown," Frederick T. Person, "Daniel Poor," *DAB*, 3:114–15, 15:68–69; Kendall to John, 5 Sept. 1849; Kendall to Brown, 6 Nov. 1815, Dartmouth College Library.

noisier and the students drunker, Kendall became uncomfortable and left the room. Even when his strength of character won respect, it did not win friends. Late in the freshman year he impressed his classmates by talking two hotheads out of fighting a duel with pistols but then lost his classmates' approval by refusing to join a student protest when the two were expelled.[8]

Kendall started his sophomore year teaching school again and did not return to Dartmouth until March 1809. He found the students looking forward to sophomore quarter day when the tutors would read the names of the ranking students in the class. A tradition had grown that the winners would treat their classmates. Kendall hoped to be on the list, but he was morally opposed to the customary heavy drinking and hated the thought of spending money treating others. On the eve of quarter day, he circulated a resolution to do away with treating but got only thirteen signatures, almost all from the Gymnasion.

The next day tutor Brown and his colleague Samuel Ayer gave six of the seven awards to members of the Gymnasion (Kendall ranked sixth) and also, to everyone's surprise, announced that there would be no treating. Anyone who treated or allowed drinking in his room would be expelled. The students, of course, blamed the change on Kendall and his group. When he and members of the club went to Perry's room to celebrate, unhappy students forced their way into the room, slammed a decanter of rum on the table, and began drinking.

The faculty first held Perry responsible for the drinking in his room but then accepted the testimony of Kendall and his friends that two other students had brought in the rum. The two were promptly expelled. During the next few weeks angry students broke down Perry's door with a battering ram and came close to hitting Kendall with large timbers dropped from the third floor of the main college building, College Hall. They taunted Kendall and made fun of his pale complexion by calling him a ghost. In May most students, including Levi Woodbury, boycotted a special recitation put on by the ranking sophomore scholars and tried to drown out the proceedings by shouting, singing, and firing an old cannon. Kendall never forgave Woodbury for this.

Farcical as it was, the treating affair might have driven Kendall out of college had it not been for his friends in the Gymnasion. These men, he wrote later, "formed a phalanx which . . . the sons of dissipation were [not] able to break or terrify." Kendall remained unpopular but learned some valuable polit-

8. *Autobiography*, 20–25, 66.

ical lessons. He found that it was not wise to try to force his moral values on others and that he must learn to accommodate the majority. There would be no more crusades.[9]

Kendall had other educational experiences when he joined his parents in September for a trip to visit his sister Molly and his brother Zebedee junior on the Vermont frontier. For his father it was the chance for a traditional patriarch to check up on his children; for Amos it was an introduction to another new world. In passing through Woodstock, Vermont, one evening they attended a meeting of a new denomination called Christians, later the Disciples of Christ, which was a product of the Great Revival sweeping the frontier. Kendall was amazed by the emotional behavior at the meeting. With his confidence in his own denomination wavering, he listened closely to the "zealous conversation, singing and praying" and was surprised by the "active part" played by women.[10]

Even more memorable was his visit with his brother and sister east of Burlington. The young pioneers and their spouses had purchased land on credit, built rough shacks, and started farming and raising large families. They had not done well. Kendall's parents were distressed by their "poverty and destitution," but Kendall reacted more dispassionately. He later remarked that he had seen "how people live who settle on poor land." What bothered him most was not their miserable existence but his "conviction that they could never make the payments for their land, and were making improvements upon it for the benefit of others." His hard-hearted analysis proved to be correct; within five years both families had given up.[11]

In the spring of 1810, his junior year, Kendall took a bold step to improve his popularity. Up to that time he had never taken part in student pranks, but on the evening of June 19 he joined half of the student body in rounding up farmers' cattle and locking them in the basement of College Hall. When the tutors arrived to restore order, Kendall and a few others forced them to retire under a hail of stones. The next morning, his reputation already improved, he made more friends by drafting a clever memorial defending the students who had been caught. When the faculty let the students off scot-free, he became a hero.[12]

9. My account of the treating affair is based on ibid., 31–37, 66 (quotation).
10. Ibid., 40–41.
11. Ibid., 41–42.
12. Ibid., 46–50, 67.

The Fourth of July gave him another opportunity. Thomas Jefferson's Embargo Act had been so unpopular in New Hampshire that the Federalists had won the state election in 1809, but a year later the Republicans, led by Isaac Hill, now editor of the *New-Hampshire Patriot*, had regained control of the state. But not of Dartmouth, which remained Federalist to the core. Kendall's writing ability and the political sympathies that he had brought from Dunstable made him a natural leader of the Dartmouth Republicans. On being asked to recite a poem at the Fourth of July celebration, he indignantly refused, saying that the organizers were plotting to turn it into a Federalist affair. He and the Republicans then made plans for their own celebration and held their ground when the Federalists tried to stop them.

Kendall had improved as a politician. By casting suspicion on the motives of the Federalists and by devising a counterattack, he had attracted the support of 30 Dartmouth men, not bad in a Federalist college of 170. He had also become less zealous. At the Republican celebration on the Fourth he criticized the orations as "too Frenchified." A moderate, not a radical Republican, he could not bring himself to support Napoleonic France.[13]

His redemption was complete in his senior year. At the end of the fall his classmates voted him first in the class, and the Social Friends chose him to give their annual oration. He had already been elected to Phi Beta Kappa. At graduation time he ranked first in his class, followed by his friends Perry and Poor. But he continued to make enemies. After he and Poor were elected to an elite literary group, jealous members of the Social Friends tried to get the society to keep them from joining. Kendall and Poor defeated the plan by threatening to resign from the Friends. Kendall said privately that the society could not afford to let them resign because they were "the flower of the organization," the ones who "infused talent into its performances."[14]

One such performance was the tragedy "Palafox, or The Siege of Saragossa," which he wrote for commencement. Although the play was not a serious tragedy, it displayed his idealism and his hatred of Napoleon. Kendall was a busy man at commencement. He not only directed "Palafox" and played one of the parts but also joined in a poetic dialogue, participated in the exercises of the literary society, and gave the salutatory. Everything went smoothly even though a few of his enemies tried to unnerve him by blowing horns and ring-

---

13. My account of the Fourth of July is based on *ibid.*, 50–53.

14. Ibid., 53, 56–57, 59–63 (quotation); Dartmouth College, "Order of Exercises," 28 Nov. 1810, Dartmouth College Library.

ing the church bell during the literary exercises. After commencement he was so exhausted that he took to his bed for two days.[15]

As soon as Kendall reached home, he sat down and wrote a review of his college life. It is revealing how little he wrote about the community and family values that he had brought to college or the high ideals of his friends in the Gymnasion. Instead he dwelt on his search for individual popularity and success. The treating episode, he wrote, had destroyed his popularity, but his achievements and awards turned the tide. Life at Dartmouth had made him remarkably cynical and individualistic. "Man's opinion of right," he said, "is generally founded upon his interest," and the best way to get ahead was through "decision and firmness."[16]

Though not certain that he was yet a "man of decision," Kendall was pleased with himself. Only the eighth person in the history of Dunstable to have graduated from college, he had become something of an elitist. He liked the attention he had received in his senior year and enjoyed "seeing [his former] enemies at [his] feet." His admirers, he said, were impressed by his "versatility of mind" and "vivacity of imagination," which enabled him to produce "glowing pieces of composition." Kendall was describing the vindictiveness and writing style that would someday make him both hated and famous. The civic values that he had absorbed in Dunstable and had admired in his Gymnasion friends would not disappear, but they would often be tested by his determination to get ahead.[17]

He had already had such a test. A few weeks before graduation, he had learned that his old school, Groton Academy, was looking for a preceptor. This was the sort of position, offering the chance to do good in the community, that his friends in the Gymnasion were seeking; in fact one of them, Samuel Woodbury, was applying for it. Amidst his frantic preparations for commencement, Kendall somehow found time for a quick trip to Groton to look into the situation and get the advice and backing of his father's acquaintance William M. Richardson, a prominent attorney and postmaster in the town.

Richardson wasted no time on idealism. He told Kendall bluntly that teaching, even "as a temporary expedient, was to throw away a part of one's life." He advised him to become a lawyer and offered to provide him with legal

15. *Autobiography*, 59, 63–70.
16. Ibid., 66–67.
17. Ibid.; Nason, *Dunstable*, 216–17.

instruction and board and room. Kendall need only do legal chores, help in the post office, and sign a note to be paid later. He now had to choose between serving the community or advancing himself and making money through the law. The offer was too good to turn down. Not only would he be getting a good start on a career, but Richardson would be a valuable connection. On September 4, three days after reaching home, he moved to Groton.[18]

Although only a few miles from home, Groton was another new world for Kendall, for the town had much more to offer than Dunstable. His mentor was as scholarly as the members of the Gymnasion. A Harvard graduate and a learned student of the law, Richardson had a large practice and later in the fall would win a special election to Congress. Another attraction was the presence of two good friends, Samuel Woodbury, who had taken the preceptor's position, and Caleb Butler, who had been preceptor when Kendall was at Groton and was now studying law under Richardson.[19]

The Groton years, however, did not start well. While waiting for Richardson's current apprentice to leave, Kendall had to rent a room. His money soon ran out, and he was forced to spend the winter back home, "seeing very little company," cutting wood, and reading Blackstone, Coke, and Bacon. His "common lesson," he wrote glumly, "is eighty pages . . . too much, I am sensible, but I have scarcely anything else to do." He was happiest reading philosophy and daydreaming—making *"air-castles,"* he called it—of becoming a writer. He submitted a copy of "Palafox" to a theater company in Boston and entered two poems in a prize competition of the *Philadelphia Port Folio,* in each case unsuccessfully.[20]

After the dreary winter Kendall moved in with the Richardson family. During the state political campaign of 1812 he remained a Republican but resisted the call of politics. He turned down an opportunity to become a Republican editor, because he shared the common view that editors were nothing but disreputable, lower-class printers. Still tied to republican ideals of nonpartisanship and civic virtue, he wrote haughtily that he would not sacrifice his "conscience and . . . moral honesty to the unhallowed zeal of any party."[21]

18. *Autobiography,* 68–69 (quotation), 71, 78, 85–86.

19. Kendall to Caleb Butler, 19 May 1835, Kendall Papers, LC; Caleb Butler, *History of the Town of Groton* (Boston, 1848), 466–67; Charles Sumner Lobingier, "William Merchant Richardson," *DAB,* 15:579–80; *Autobiography,* 69, 71. Richardson was later chief justice of the New Hampshire Superior Court.

20. *Autobiography,* 69–70 (quotation), 78, 81–82.

21. Ibid., 71 (quotation), 75–76.

His moderate Republicanism carried over into foreign policy. He supported the declaration of war against Great Britain but continued to hate the idea of siding with the dictator Napoleon. He called Federalist talk of leaving the Union "madness" but refused to accuse Federalist state senator Harrison Gray Otis of conspiring with British spies. Otis's senate speech defending himself, he said, was "superior in manner to any [I] ever heard." This middle-of-the-road position was modeled on the views of Republicans such as Richardson and state senator Levi Lincoln.[22]

Kendall had no tolerance, however, for the "deluded" Federalist clergymen who were "hurling anathemas" at the Republicans. He denounced the Congregational minister David Chaplin for calling those who voted for war "devils" and for telling the young women of Groton to keep away from Republican "profligates." Such statements reinforced his growing doubts about the Congregational church, which was losing some of its strength in Massachusetts. Kendall had remained outwardly loyal to the church and had rarely missed an evening prayer service when he was at Dartmouth, but the events in Groton brought his loss of faith to the surface. "A portion of the congregation," he wrote, "first disbelieve, then hate, and at length desert their religious instructor."[23]

During a short visit in Boston with a college friend, Kendall shopped around for a new church by attending five different services. His comments showed that he had retained some of his conservative Protestant prejudices. He called the Roman Catholic ceremonies "ridiculous," the music "harsh," and the wall paintings designed for "ignorant" parishioners. Horace Holley's Unitarian Church service was no better. Kendall wrote scornfully that Unitarianism "might as well be called a forum; for it bears nothing of Christianity." He was thrilled, however, by Edward Dodge Griffin at the Park Street Congregational Church. His enthusiasm for the ruddy, white-haired revivalist suggests that Kendall was looking for an emotional evangelical message.[24]

Kendall's interlude in Groton gave him the chance to confront his physical limitations and his shyness. He failed miserably at being a militiaman like his father. The musters left him "completely exhausted," he became sick at the sight of a bleeding soldier, and after an accidental explosion, he fainted while using a needle to pick grains of gunpowder out of his hand. Before long he

---

22. Ibid., 71–73 ("madness"), 76 ("superior").
23. Ibid., 12, 65–66, 72–73 (quotation).
24. Ibid., 77–78.

had secured a surgeon's certificate excusing him from further musters. Meanwhile his health became a serious liability. After being vaccinated against smallpox in 1811 he developed such violent headaches that he had to return to Dunstable to be nursed back to health by his mother. In 1813 he had a severe attack of lung fever and lay in bed for three weeks, suffering so severely from headaches that he could not stand the noise of ringing bells. His many illnesses and his inability to stand the sight of blood ruled out the possibility of ever becoming a physician.[25]

He had better luck with his shyness, especially in dealing with women. While he was at Dartmouth, he had secretly taken dancing lessons, but he had rarely ventured into the social life of the town and was distressingly ill at ease when he did. But soon after he and Woodbury arrived in Groton, they were introduced to the three daughters of the Lawrence family, Susan, Mary, and Eliza. They were the sisters of William, Amos, and Abbott Lawrence, who were already establishing themselves as merchants in Boston. Kendall fell in love with the beautiful Eliza, who was only sixteen, but she quickly let him know that she was too young to become involved in a romance. He then turned his attention to the older but plainer Mary, and before long an engagement seemed to be in the offing.[26]

But it was not to be. Late in the fall of 1813, Richardson abruptly announced that he was planning to move to Portsmouth, New Hampshire, and would not be able to take his apprentice with him. Kendall was offered the chance to stay on with Richardson's successor, but thinking that this might be the time to go out on his own, he turned the offer down. His days as an apprentice were over. After six years in the new worlds of Dartmouth and Groton he was still a puritanical, civic-minded, not very democratic republican, but doubts were creeping in.[27]

25. Ibid., 69, 73–74 (quotation), 79–84.

26. Ibid., 40, 86–90; Robert Means Lawrence, *The Descendants of Major Samuel Lawrence of Groton, Massachusetts* (Cambridge, Mass., 1904), 6–7.

27. *Autobiography*, 85. Within a few months Richardson was named U.S. attorney for New Hampshire.

PART TWO

*Kentucky*

# 3

## DOWN THE OHIO

Kendall weighed several possibilities. The safest was to stay near Dunstable and Groton where he would be close to his parents and Mary Lawrence; more daring was to move to Boston where Mary's brothers were already doing well; or, most risky of all, he could leave New England. The last seemed unlikely because, except when he was in college, he had never ventured more than thirty miles from Dunstable, and for the last two years he had been studying law with an acquaintance of his father only five miles from home. And there was little family precedent; few if any of the Kendalls had moved out of New England.[1]

But instead of playing it safe Kendall decided to go. He later explained that "the depression of business" and the lack of "any rich or influential family connections" in New England had forced him into it. He was sure that he could do much better in the South or the West, "where there was a wider and clearer field for individual exertion." The explanation seems plausible. New Englanders had been moving out ever since the Revolution, the region was suffering from a wartime depression, and he had lost his only connection. But was the situation really bleak enough to force him to leave? Not everyone in New England was suffering. Some shrewd Yankees were making money in manufacturing, while others were profiting from privateering or from trading with the British troops in Canada. In fact the war made it difficult, even dangerous, to move west. There was no mass exodus. Hardly any of his classmates were leaving New England. There must have been other reasons for going.[2]

The reasons were personal. First, he was ready to go. He was no longer the shy, insecure boy who had taken the stagecoach for Hanover. Increasingly

1. *Autobiography*, 86.
2. Ibid., 85–86; Donald R. Hickey, *The War of 1812* (Urbana, 1989), 227, 230–31, 375; Amos Kendall to Wright, 22 Nov. 1817, Nathaniel Wright Papers, LC; Chapman, *Sketches*, 150–59.

independent, he was so intent on pursuing his own self-interest that he was willing to override the wishes of Mary Lawrence and his all-powerful father and take the risks of going west. There was also peer pressure. The classmates that he most admired were already well into their careers. Five members of the Gymnasion were close to being ordained, including Daniel Poor, who was making plans to go to India. Two others were about to start law practice, and another had become a doctor. Kendall, who kept track of such matters, must have felt that he had fallen behind. Furthermore, he could afford to go. His father agreed to advance him $200, and Richardson let him put off paying the $392 that he owed for board and tuition. Richardson also encouraged him to come to Washington, where he would introduce him to the right people. Kendall got ready to go.[3]

It was nothing new for Kendall's mother and father to say good-bye to their children, but Amos's departure was more painful than the other departures. The ones who had already left had stayed in New England and continued to farm; Amos was moving far away and had hardly any plans. There was a special irony because just as their son was about to leave, two of their older children, Zebedee junior and Molly, returned penniless from Vermont. Molly, whose husband had run away leaving her pregnant, had loaded her five children into a wagon and begun the two-hundred-mile trip home. Just forty miles short of her goal, she started labor and had to be taken in by strangers. At the final family dinner Zebedee spoke through tears, saying that they were unlikely to meet again in this world. He told Amos pointedly to be honest in his profession, and, "above all, to seek for salvation through a Saviour." Amos carried these words with him throughout his life.[4]

On Saturday, February 19, 1814, Kendall took the stage to Boston. The city was alive with talk of how badly the war was going. British ships were patrolling Long Island Sound and Chesapeake Bay. Only in the West, where American forces had gained control over most of Lake Erie, had there been any sustained success. Victories over Napoleon in Europe had now cleared the way for the British to stage a three-pronged attack on the United States by way of Lake Champlain, Chesapeake Bay, and New Orleans. The war was

3. There is also the possibility that Mary may not have tried very hard to hold him back. She first promised to become engaged and wait for him to get established but changed her mind after visiting her brothers in Boston. *Autobiography,* 85–89, 110. For Kendall's interest in his classmates see Kendall to Wright, 22 Nov. 1817, Wright Papers; Chapman, *Sketches,* 150–59.

4. *Autobiography,* 41, 86, 91 (quotation).

frustrating for Americans who wanted to migrate west. Plans for a national road and steamboat travel on the Ohio River were tempting them, but the war held them back.[5]

During the weekend Kendall must have had a few pangs of envy when he encountered several young men who were even further into their careers than his classmates. On visiting Mary Lawrence, who was in the city, he must have seen her brothers Amos and Abbott, who had just formed the mercantile firm of A. & A. Lawrence. On Sunday he attended the Brattle Street Unitarian Church to hear Edward Everett, not yet twenty, who had just been installed as minister. Perhaps with a touch of bravado, Kendall dismissed Everett as "a youth of great promise."[6]

About nine o'clock Monday morning Kendall climbed aboard the stagecoach for New York. Seated up high next to the driver he had a good view of the road, which angled south and west toward Connecticut. After traveling for forty hours, with only a four-hour stop for rest, the stagecoach pulled into New Haven near midnight. Unable to book passage on the packet to New York, he continued on by stagecoach for two more days, arriving in New York late Thursday afternoon, February 24. As he roamed the city during the evening, he found New Yorkers almost as worried as Bostonians about the war. Alarmed by the British ships lying off Sandy Hook, they were raising troops and making plans to defend the city.[7]

The following day Kendall took one of the new steam ferries across the Hudson River to New Jersey, where he boarded another stagecoach. By the time he reached Philadelphia, he had been on the road riding (and sometimes walking) for two exhausting days, with only a short overnight stop at Brunswick. Since rapid water transportation to Baltimore would not be available for another fifteen years, Kendall again had to settle for the stagecoach. The bumpy ride, dreary scenery, and long hours were taking their toll; the passengers became "sour," and Kendall had difficulty keeping his temper. Finally on Tuesday evening, March 1, he arrived in Washington.

Aside from the hour on the steam ferry, Kendall's journey had not introduced him to any of the new forms of transportation. For that reason and because of the miserable roads, the trip from Boston had taken more than nine days, no better than the speed of travel fifty or even a hundred years earlier.

5. Ibid., 91–92; Hickey, *War of 1812,* 151–83.

6. *Autobiography,* 92.

7. Ibid., 92–93.

He did, however, encounter new types of people—two young women from the West Indies, three "speculating merchants," a ship pilot, a horse racer, and three medical students from the South. He was delighted with the southerners' "agreeable manners," but he soon learned about southern honor when one of the students misunderstood something that he said and almost challenged him to a duel. The prudish Kendall was disgusted with the general conversation. The horse racer bragged about his "profligacies," while the students talked openly about their love affairs "with as little ceremony as a Northern man would tell a story."[8]

Tired and out of sorts, Kendall was in a somber mood when he stepped down from the stagecoach. The first sight to greet him was the Capitol building, presenting a "very gloomy appearance" as it loomed up in the dusk. In 1814 the Capitol was a modest building with two wings and no dome, but it seemed massive to Kendall. After losing his way several times, he finally found Richardson's boardinghouse and was warmly received by his mentor.[9]

As Kendall went about the city in the morning, he noted that the Capitol looked "much better by day than by night." He may have been cheered by a painting at an art exhibit on the way to Capitol Hill. The painting had caused much comment because it displayed a woman with "no other dress than a braid of pearls." Kendall called it something he would "never forget." At Dolley Madison's reception in the evening, he was just as cocksure as he had been describing Edward Everett. Even though three hundred "great men" and "many fine ladies" were present, he felt "no awe," and was "not much instructed." Showing no loyalty to a Republican president, he questioned whether James Madison had the ability "to manage the affairs of the nation."[10]

The next morning the president pro tempore of the Senate, Joseph B. Varnum of Massachusetts, whose home was near Dunstable, introduced Kendall to senators from Louisiana, Kentucky, and Ohio. He was told that the West had too many lawyers but needed family tutors. While waiting for something to turn up, he explored the city and attended the Sunday church service in the Capitol. The unsettled state of his political and religious views can be seen in his reaction to the Republican Baptist chaplain. Despite his own Republicanism, he disapproved of the preacher's "invectives" against the Federal-

8. Ibid., 93–95.

9. Ibid., 95.

10. Constance M. Green, *Washington: Village and Capital, 1800–1878* (Princeton, 1962), 21 ("no other"); *Autobiography*, 95.

ists. Kendall also appeared elitist and less than committed to social equality when he described the sermon as "ridiculous rant," good enough for soldiers but not for an "enlightened audience."[11]

On Monday Kendall received the welcome news that Senator Jesse Bledsoe of Kentucky wanted to hire him to tutor his children. He would start in April when Bledsoe returned from Washington and moved his family into Lexington. Deciding that he was not likely to get a better offer, he accepted, and on Wednesday, March 9, barely a week after his arrival, he was on the stagecoach for Pittsburgh. One of the other passengers was General Lewis Cass, just back from the Battle of the Thames and on his way to Michigan as the new territorial governor. He would later serve with Kendall in the Jackson and Van Buren cabinets. Kendall should have felt comfortable with Cass— they both came from old New England stock—but the general annoyed him with his surprising contempt for Yankees and their religion.[12]

Midday on Thursday the stagecoach reached Hagerstown, Maryland, headed north into Pennsylvania, and started along the road to Pittsburgh. After only a few hours the carriage broke down, and the passengers had to walk six miles to a wagon drivers' tavern. The exertion proved too much for Kendall, who became "excessively sick" and had to remain behind. Stranded in the Allegheny Mountains, he unhappily whiled away the time, writing a letter and conversing with the tavern keeper's daughters. Tedium turned to alarm on Sunday when three hundred militiamen arrived with no officers to control them. Still no democrat, Kendall complained that they were "without order . . . mean, dirty, ugly, and in every respect contemptible." If he ever got "safely through" the mountains, he would never again "be caught" in such a place.[13]

A much-relieved Kendall resumed his journey Monday morning, but he had not seen the last of the militia. Before the day was over, the stagecoach passed a bedraggled group of soldiers who had deserted because of inadequate food. His new riding companions were "a coarse but very intelligent" Irishman and F. G. Flügel, an "amiable, polite, and merry" young German headed for Cincinnati. Kendall got on so well with Flügel that he agreed to travel with him to Cincinnati before going on to Lexington. After three more days ca-

11. *Autobiography,* 96–97.
12. Ibid., 97.
13. Ibid., 97–98.

reening over wretched roads the stagecoach pulled into Greensburgh, half a day from Pittsburgh.[14]

Kendall was so motion sick from the long ride that he decided to complete the trip on horseback. When he reached Turtle Creek and had his first glimpse of Pittsburgh, his reaction was twofold. He was attracted by the romantic beauty of the "meandering" creek but was much more deeply moved by the sight of the city, so "enveloped in smoke and dust" that he called it "a very blacksmith's shop." After a week in the wilderness he was delighted to see signs of industrial activity and blurted out, "Here is my country."[15]

Pittsburgh was in the midst of a war boom, which had boosted its population to eight thousand. Already a center for outfitting ships, it had provided most of the equipment for the American fleet on Lake Erie. Kendall did not remain a stranger in the city for long. Armed with a letter of introduction, he called on bank president, later senator, William Wilkins and was treated with "marked kindness." He also introduced himself to the French-born editor of the *Western Gleaner*, who agreed to publish several of his poems.[16]

Because there were no stagecoach lines west of Pittsburgh, Kendall and Flügel intended to travel to Cincinnati on the Ohio River. "La Belle Riviere," as the French had called it, ran majestically south and west along the northern borders of Virginia and Kentucky until it emptied into the Mississippi. Often icebound in winter and clogged with sandbars in summer, it provided reliable transportation only in the spring and fall. The river was now free of ice, but high waves, swift currents, and sudden floods made it extremely treacherous. Kendall and Flügel could have bought passage on a sleek keelboat or on a large, broad flatboat, but they chose instead to buy a small skiff, row it down to Cincinnati, and then sell it. In this way they would save money but would constantly be in danger of drowning. The decision shows that even though he was weak physically, Kendall did not lack courage.[17]

After buying the skiff, they prepared to go, but at the last minute they met Major William T. Barry and his wife, Catherine, who owned a flatboat and were on their way to their home in Lexington. Barry was a thin, emaciated-

14. Ibid., 98–99.

15. Ibid., 99. For the interpretation of Kendall's reaction to Pittsburgh I am indebted to Marshall, "Early Career," 49.

16. *Autobiography*, 100.

17. Richard C. Wade, *The Urban Frontier: The Rise of Western Cities, 1790–1820* (Cambridge, Mass., 1959), 43; Hickey, *War of 1812*, 375; *Autobiography*, 100–101; Leland D. Baldwin, *The Keelboat Age on Western Waters* (Pittsburgh, 1941), 44–67, 140.

looking man weighing barely a hundred pounds, who, like Cass, had just returned from the Battle of the Thames. He and Kendall would work together in Kentucky and Washington for many years. Since Barry needed a skiff for side trips, he asked Kendall and Flügel to ride on the flatboat and tie their boat alongside. Before the end of the day, March 25, they were all off for Maysville, Kentucky.[18]

Encouraged by what he had seen in Pittsburgh, Kendall kept looking for more examples of civilization taming the wilderness. North of Steubenville, Ohio, he was rewarded when he and Flügel saw a coal mine dug into the bank of the river. Rowing ashore, they talked with two young entrepreneurs who bought coal from the mine and sold it four hundred miles downriver in Cincinnati. Kendall was excited to learn that the men had made almost enough profit on their first trip to pay for their boat. Two nights later he saw campfires and heard violins and the barking of dogs. These sights and sounds made the evening, he wrote, "singularly romantic," but as at Pittsburgh the real reason he was pleased was that they were the sights and sounds of civilization. Earlier civilizations did not count. On seeing one of the large Indian mounds in the region, he could not believe that such wonders had been built by "uncivilized Indians."[19]

After traveling night and day, they reached Maysville on the evening of April 2. The next day the Barrys departed for Lexington, following the same route as the one projected for the Maysville Road during the Jackson administration. Kendall thought well of Barry, who had charged him nothing for the boat ride and had treated him "like a gentleman," yet he saw the weaknesses in Barry's character that would lead to his downfall as postmaster general. Barry, he wrote, was "a very good man, but not a great man."[20]

Kendall's first impression of Kentucky was unfavorable. Always fastidious, he thought that Maysville suffered from "dirt and negligence." He and Flügel also found the skiff much less safe and comfortable than the flatboat. No sooner were they on the river than a heavy rainstorm forced them to go ashore and spend an uncomfortable night sleeping in a bed with sheets no softer than "coarse bagging." Seeking safety on the river the next day, they got permission to tie up alongside a keelboat and continued that way until on April 5 they reached Cincinnati.[21]

18. *Autobiography*, 101.
19. Ibid., 101–4; Marshall, "Early Career," 55.
20. *Autobiography*, 104–5.
21. Ibid., 105–6.

Here was Kendall's kind of civilization. With a population of six thousand Cincinnati had grown as rapidly as Pittsburgh and, according to one publicist, already had the "busy markets, the substantial public buildings, the . . . industrious inhabitants" of a great city. Kendall was most impressed by the large brewery and a "stupendous" six-story building on the riverbank. After trying for two days to sell the skiff, they finally gave it to a poor Spanish family. Then bidding his friend good-bye, Kendall crossed the river to the Kentucky side, left his trunk to be shipped, and started the last leg of his journey.[22]

The road to Lexington ran south for eighty-five miles. With no money to pay for a horse, he would have to travel on foot, a daunting prospect for someone with weak legs. The road would take him through a hilly, wooded, largely unpopulated region, inhabited, he feared, by wild animals. Starting in mid-afternoon, he walked sixteen miles, the last seven in the dark, before coming across a frontier cabin, where he spent a sleepless night on the floor. When he asked his host the next morning if the forest was dangerous, the man said no but added casually that it was full of wolves.[23]

Prudently stopping before dark the next day, Kendall spent a pleasant evening chatting with two men who were also on their way to Lexington. When one of them said that there were excellent opportunities for lawyers north of Cincinnati, Kendall, who was unsure of what lay ahead, almost turned around and headed back to Ohio. But he plodded on. After another day of walking, he was so stiff that he had to rest for a day and passed the time reading Nicholas Biddle's recently published history of the Lewis and Clark expedition. Early the next morning he met a farmer riding a horse and leading a second. Accepting the man's offer, he mounted the horse and accompanied the farmer to Georgetown, only fifteen miles from Lexington.[24]

Kentucky had not yet lived up to Kendall's expectations. The people he saw on his long walk lived on small farms in "miserable log habitations." He was disappointed that he had seen "very few slaves" and no plantations. On the morning of April 12, however, as he walked the final leg of his journey, Kentucky began to look more attractive. Now he was passing through "a fine country covered with beautiful plantations." The land was neither "hilly nor

22. Ibid., 106–7; Carlyle Buley, *The Old Northwest: Pioneer Period, 1815–1840,* 2 vols. (Bloomington, 1950), 1:21–22 (quotation).

23. *Autobiography,* 107.

24. Ibid., 107–9.

level, but gently waving, with an exuberance of verdure, many orchards in bloom, and many gardens laid out with taste."[25]

On this journey from Dunstable to Lexington Kendall had spent almost two months covering some 1,400 miles and passing through ten of the eighteen states in the Union. He had seen the War of 1812 from the vantage point of militiamen, officers, members of Congress, and critics of the war. He had taken the measure of Abbott and Amos Lawrence, Edward Everett, James and Dolley Madison, Joseph B. Varnum, Lewis Cass, William Wilkins, and William T. Barry, and received help from at least three. He had encountered immigrants from the West Indies, Ireland, Germany, France, and Spain. He had compared the mores of Yankees and southerners. His journey offers a glimpse of the republic melding into a democracy.[26]

Kendall too was changing. Although still a moralist with republican attitudes, accustomed to the certainties of Massachusetts farm life, he was beginning to adjust to an increasingly uncertain, liberal, capitalist, democratic world. So far he was more comfortable with capitalism than with democracy. He had started on his journey not knowing where it would take him or what he wanted to do. He still was not sure. As the trip unfolded, he had been forced to make quick decisions, such as accepting Bledsoe's offer and joining up with the Barrys. He had shown the ability to adapt, change plans, and make useful connections that could help him succeed on the American frontier.

25. Ibid. (quotations); Kendall to F. G. Flügel, 14 May 1814, Amos Kendall Miscellaneous Papers, Filson Historical Society, Louisville, Ky.

26. On the thirty days of actual travel, he moved at a pace of about 46 miles a day: from Dunstable to Washington, 515 miles, nine and a half days; Washington to Pittsburgh, 260 miles, six days; Pittsburgh to Maysville, 450 miles, eight and a half days; Maysville to Cincinnati, 63 miles, two days; Cincinnati to Lexington, 85 miles, four days.

# 4

## A YANKEE IN KENTUCKY

Kendall was now in the heart of Bluegrass Kentucky. The Bluegrass region occupies the northern hump of the state and was named for the color of the grass in springtime. The best part of the region is the gently rolling plain around Lexington in Fayette County, where fertile soil, a mild climate, and frequent rains produce bumper crops of corn, wheat, rye, tobacco, and hemp and offer rich forage for horses and sheep. The northern Bluegrass, through which Kendall had passed, is less attractive because of its inferior soil and its uneven hills and valleys.[1]

In 1814 Lexington was a thriving city of six thousand, with stone-paved streets and hundreds of brick houses. Already a center for manufacturing, it boasted ropewalks, textile mills, and bagging factories, as well as whiskey distilleries and ironworks. Wages and prices were high. Journeymen could earn enough in one day to eat for a week, while town lots were selling for the outlandish price of $500 a foot. Already a city of sophistication, Lexington supported a library of four thousand volumes, five or six times as many as in the Cincinnati library. Parents had a choice of three academies for their children. There were also three newspapers, an athenaeum, a theater, and a literary journal. The most notable institution was Transylvania University, which offered a traditional classical curriculum, similar to the one at Dartmouth. With its wealth and cultural trappings, Lexington had earned the reputation of being the Athens of the West.[2]

The plantations that Kendall had admired on approaching the city gave

1. Darrell H. Davis, *The Geography of the Bluegrass Region of Kentucky* (Frankfort, 1927).

2. Wade, *Urban Frontier*, 18–19, 49–51, 82, 169; Thomas P. Abernethy, *Three Virginia Frontiers* (Baton Rouge, 1940), 65; Bernard Mayo, "Lexington: Frontier Metropolis," in *Historiography and Urbanization: Essays in Honor of Stull Holt*, ed. Eric F. Goldman (Baltimore, 1941), 27, 30–31, 35; William Leavy, "Memoirs of Lexington and Vicinity," *Register* 41 (1943): 44–57, 119, 128–29, 143, 130–37, 258, 317–21, 332, 345–46.

the countryside a southern look. The widow of John Breckinridge, Thomas Jefferson's attorney general, lived in style at Cabell's Dale, named for her family. Henry Clay, who had migrated from Virginia, had built Ashland. The grandest estate was the five-hundred-acre Chaumiere des Prairies, where Colonel David Meade and his wife entertained lavishly. Some of the planters had as many as fifty slaves, but the median was about fifteen. Three-quarters of all heads of families in Lexington owned slaves, and a third of the population was black—an abrupt change for a Yankee like Kendall.[3]

He also began to notice new religious denominations and styles. Instead of Congregationalists, the Presbyterians were dominant in Lexington, especially among the upper classes, while the Methodists and Baptists were more common in the countryside. The Great Revival had started in southern Kentucky in 1800. The most famous revival of all took place a year later at Cane Ridge, north of Lexington, where thousands of Kentuckians attended emotional camp meetings that lasted for several days. These revivals greatly increased the size of the Baptist and Methodist denominations. Even though ready to change his religion, Kendall was scornful of the preachers at his first two Methodist services, one of whom was "bawling," the other "noisy," with "much flower, and some bombast."[4]

Kendall's career in Lexington began inauspiciously. After his grueling walk from Cincinnati, his left knee was so sore that he had to spend several days resting in his room at Postlethwaite's Inn. His trunk was slow in arriving, and he began to fear that it had been lost. To make matters worse, none of the people on whom he had counted did anything to help him. Jesse Bledsoe reneged on his offer of a job, apparently because he had decided not to move into Lexington, and then snubbed him when they passed in a tavern. The Barrys treated him politely but failed to introduce him to anyone. Lonely and lame in an unfamiliar world, he wrote that he had "suffered more mortification" than ever before in his life.[5]

Early in May his prospects finally brightened. When Henry Clay left for Europe in February to negotiate peace, his wife, Lucretia, returned to Ashland, where she had her hands full running the plantation and caring for seven

3. Wade, *Urban Frontier,* 124; Bernard Mayo, *Henry Clay: Spokesman of the New West* (Boston, 1937), 62–63, 89–93, 192–94; Leavy, "Memoirs of Lexington," 250–53.

4. Wade, *Urban Frontier,* 132–34; William E. Connelley and E. Merton Coulter, eds., *History of Kentucky,* 5 vols. (Chicago, 1922), 1:539; *Autobiography,* 105, 109.

5. *Autobiography,* 112–15 (quotation); Kendall to F. G. Flügel, 14 May 1814, Kendall Papers, Filson Historical Society.

children. Badly in need of a tutor, she offered Kendall $300, three times what Bledsoe would have paid, plus board and room, to tutor her five oldest children for a year. Kendall was delighted to accept. The turn of events came just in time, for he had only $17.75 left from the $216 with which he had left Dunstable. That same day, May 5, his trunk arrived.[6]

Working for Lucretia Clay was more than a financial bonanza. Only a short time before, Kendall had been living in a modest wooden house on a small Massachusetts farm; now he had moved into an enormous brick mansion on one of the great Kentucky plantations. His father owned at the most a dozen cows and two horses and tilled eight acres of crops; Henry Clay's fifteen slaves and more than a dozen free workers cared for a hundred head of cattle and one hundred horses and farmed three hundred acres. Zebedee could barely raise $300 for Amos's education; Clay spent $10,000 for Ashland and more than $1,000 to buy a one-fifth share of a racehorse.[7]

The change also had implications for Kendall's future. Clay would soon resume his career as Speaker of the House of Representatives, and people were already talking about him for president. He could easily become the powerful connection that Kendall desired. Some northerners might have found it compromising to work for a slaveholder, but Kendall, who was disappointed in not seeing slaves when he first arrived in Kentucky, had no such qualms. If getting ahead in Lexington meant accepting slavery, all the better.

Kendall's tutoring job was not an easy one. The two oldest children, Theodore, eleven, and Thomas, ten, showed no interest in studying and often flew into violent tantrums. At the start of one session Kendall had to drag Thomas kicking into the room. Twice he had to intervene when one of the boys threatened to kill a house slave. But Kendall's strength of character and his experience with unruly students were too much for the boys. They gradually learned to control their tempers and showed marked improvement in their studies.[8]

As a member of the Clay household, Kendall had an entrée into the Lexington social whirl. A poor dancer and a bashful conversationalist, he had a difficult time breaking in and often spent an entire evening "a silent spectator." He had not given up on Mary Lawrence, but he was perfectly willing to fall

---

6. *Autobiography*, 113–15.

7. Pruitt, *Massachusetts Tax Valuation List*, 204–7; *Autobiography*, 1–2; Robert V. Remini, *Henry Clay: Statesman for the Union* (New York, 1991), 73–74, 204–5.

8. *Autobiography*, 115–18, 122–24, 141–42; Remini, *Henry Clay*, 31 n. 45, 200–203; Henry Clay to Kendall, 30 Dec. 1815, *The Papers of Henry Clay*, ed. James F. Hopkins, Mary W. M. Hargreaves, Robert Seager II, and Melba Porter Hay, 11 vols. (Lexington, 1959–92), 2:116.

in love in Kentucky. On meeting one attractive woman, he wrote unhappily that he saw no hope of winning her, "plain, poor, and a Yankee as I am." Later he fell in love with Eliza Price, the belle of Lexington, but, realizing that he had no chance, berated himself for being such a "fool."[9]

Kendall was fortunate in having as his sponsor the thirty-three-year-old, "dark-eyed, dark-haired" Lucretia Clay, who took it on herself to give some polish to this shy, awkward Yankee. She made sure he was invited to the right parties, teased him about women, taught him how to make proper bows, and asked him gently why he always appeared so ashamed when he entered a room. Most important, she challenged his rigid, puritanical, often self-righteous opinions. When he bragged too much about New England, she called it "disgusting." Her attentions worked. Before long Kendall was dancing better and behaving more confidently with the fashionable young women. Lacking southern credentials, he relied on his poetry and his intellect to impress them. His poems were well received, and he enhanced his reputation as a Yankee intellectual by keeping up with contemporary works, such as Byron's romantic poem *The Corsair*, the short story *Zaida* by August von Kotzebue, as well as Maria Edgeworth's novel *Patronage* about life in Ireland.[10]

These parties were the sort of affairs at which some women were beginning to exercise political and economic influence. But Lucretia Clay appears not to have been one of them. Her Washington friend Margaret Bayard Smith, a prominent hostess, once remarked that Lucretia had "no taste for fashionable company." This may be an overstatement, but it does not seem likely that Kendall's sponsor provided the political or business connection that he hoped to get from the Clay household.[11]

Hoping to find such a connection, Kendall overcame his distaste for the militia and began to attend musters. He quickly found that militiamen in Kentucky were no better than those in Pennsylvania. Only two-thirds of the men showed up for musters, and many of those lacked muskets, bayonets, or uniforms. They were, he wrote, "an ill-armed, undisciplined rabble." The way they "threaten[ed] and ridicule[d] their officers [demonstrated] their sense of equality and their total want of subordination." In September it appeared that

9. *Autobiography*, 120 ("fool"), 133, 141, 171 ("plain"); Kendall to Flügel, 14 May, 4 July 1814 ("silent"), 10 Mar., 16 Aug. 1815, Kendall Papers, Filson Historical Society; Mayo, *Henry Clay*, 215.

10. Mayo, *Henry Clay*, 90–92 ("dark-eyed"); *Autobiography*, 117–18, 120–28 ("disgusting"), 141–45; Kendall to Flügel, 4 July 1814, 10 Mar. 1815, Kendall Papers, Filson Historical Society.

11. Margaret Bayard Smith, *The First Forty Years of Washington Society*, ed. Gaillard Hunt (1906; reprint, New York, 1965), 86–87; Remini, *Henry Clay*, 30–31.

he might have to join these men when the government called on Kentucky for militiamen to defend New Orleans. "Earnestly wish[ing] himself clear" of the whole affair, he resigned himself to going and was "considerably relieved" when he was not called.[12]

Kendall's scorn for the militiamen's "sense of equality" shows that he was still no democrat, but his experiences at musters did make him less snobbish and introduced him to democratic politics. On one occasion he ate watermelon and drank whiskey with some rough new friends until he was "stupid as a dunce." Since militia companies were basic units in Kentucky politics, they offered the soldiers a chance to participate in elections. At his very first muster he found that drinking and politics went together as the men formed a hollow square to hear a political stump speech and then "marched to the whiskey table." The speech impressed him more than he had expected. "A good orator [might] mislead the people," he wrote, but he also offered "much useful information." The militia was "a sort of primary assembly where future subjects of legislation [were] discussed."[13]

Despite his efforts to adapt, Kendall did not feel accepted and developed a rather low opinion of Kentucky. The people were "too chivalric—a mixture of generosity and barbarity" and too "absorbed with selfishness and money." At one party he stated dogmatically that there was "very little literary taste in Lexington." The only way to become "popular" was to "drink whiskey and talk loud, with the fullest confidence." He was not far off the mark, for many of the most popular figures in Kentucky at the time—including Henry Clay, Jesse Bledsoe, and William T. Barry—drank heavily and owed much of their success to their oratory. Lucretia Clay, predictably, was not amused. She said sternly that he was "too much prejudiced" in favor of New England and knew "very little" about Kentucky.[14]

Far from sure that Kentucky was right for him, he carefully maintained his ties with New England. During the summer he corresponded with his classmate Ether Shepley about politics and with at least four members of the Gymnasion. Much of the news from the North came from the "swarms of New-Englanders" who were "flocking" into Kentucky. Kendall was soon part of a circle of young Yankees, mostly well-educated law students, several of

12. *Autobiography*, 118–24, 128, 131.

13. Ibid., 119, 123, 126.

14. Kendall to Flügel, 4 July 1814 ("chivalric"), 10 Mar. 1815 ("selfishness"), Kendall Papers, Filson Historical Society; *Autobiography*, 122, 126 ("literary taste").

whom, like himself, had taken temporary jobs as tutors. Their futures were as indeterminate as his.[15]

At the end of the summer he still had no idea what he would do when his year with the Clays was up. He was considering law, teaching, business, and after listening to a few more speeches, Kentucky politics. His sights were unrealistically high. He refused to consider one teaching job even though it paid $750 a year, and concluded that teaching was "inconsistent with his ambition." His "aircastles" were now grander and more materialistic than his old dreams of becoming a playwright. "This day," he wrote, "I have been one hour a liberal-minded merchant . . . the next an elegant lawyer . . . basking in the sunshine of popularity, getting rich, and then thundering with Ciceronian eloquence in the Senate of the United States."[16]

He was easily swayed. On receiving a letter from William M. Richardson in October advising him to stick with the law, he decided to apply for a license. Since he would be examined by the court of appeals at the state capitol in Frankfort, he needed someone to introduce him to the members. William T. Barry agreed to do so, but on the appointed day he failed to show up, and Kendall had to ride the twenty miles to Frankfort by himself. Knowing that it was important to have a patron, he tried to get the well-known lawyer Robert Wickliffe to speak for him, but he was too busy. During the examination, which went on all evening and the next morning, he made so many errors that he began to think that he would fail. Just in the nick of time Barry and Wickliffe arrived and chatted privately with the justices, who soon announced that Kendall had passed. After this lesson in the importance of connections, Kendall was ready to practice law.[17]

He began to reconsider, however, when Lucretia Clay's brother John Hart asked him to manage $5,000 that he planned to invest in a grocery business. Kendall spent several days discussing the matter with his Yankee friends. First he leaned toward accepting because of "the prospect of riches," but then he remembered Richardson's advice. As he anguished over the decision, he made the telling remark: "Would to God that Mr. Clay was at home! for I should probably be decided by his opinion." In the end he did not have to choose, for Hart abruptly withdrew the offer.[18]

15. *Autobiography*, 120–24, 132 (quotation); Kendall to Simmons, 9 Jan. 1816, George A. Simmons Papers, Chicago Historical Society.

16. *Autobiography*, 124–25.

17. Ibid., 125, 128–31.

18. Ibid., 131–32.

At this point the War of 1812 intervened. Kendall was overly pessimistic about the way it was going. When he learned that New England Federalists had called an antiwar convention, he was so distressed that he impulsively made up his mind to return home and run for the Massachusetts legislature. The senseless plan, which he quickly abandoned, suggests just how uncertain he was about his future in Kentucky. By the end of the year he was filled with "doubt, fear, and dismay" and again yearned wistfully for Henry Clay. On learning that the peace talks were keeping the peace negotiators at Ghent, he complained that he would never reap "the advantages [he] had hoped from an acquaintance with Mr. Clay." Kendall's gloom, however, vanished quickly with the news of Andrew Jackson's victory at New Orleans. Anticipating Clay's American System, he expected all sections to "draw closer" and predicted that the United States would grow much stronger "under the fostering influences" of a "liberal" government.[19]

Kendall hoped to share in the prosperity because he was involved in one of the many land schemes being hatched after the war. When a company planning to buy land in the Indiana Territory offered him a job, he helped draw up a petition to Congress and volunteered to go to Indiana and inspect the site. But, as in other situations, his initial enthusiasm began to wane. He became annoyed when one of the stockholders, manufacturer James Prentiss of Lexington, tried to whittle down his pay. Furthermore the company had not yet raised enough money, and Congress was not expected to act on the petition for another year. On hearing unfounded rumors that Indians were attacking settlers in southern Indiana, Kendall quit the company.[20]

With his year at the Clays' nearing an end, he fell back on becoming a lawyer and thought again of combining law and politics. He joined the Tammany Society, the leading political club in the city, and agreed to write a Fourth of July oration for a local politician. But he was not at all sure that a poor Yankee could build a successful law practice in elegant Lexington. After scouting out the prospects in several neighboring counties, he went to Georgetown, the town where he had spent his final night before reaching Lexington. Although only fifteen miles to the north, Georgetown was strikingly different from Lexington. It served as the county seat of Scott County, which was outside of the heart of the Bluegrass and was far less developed than Fayette County. About the same size as Dunstable, Georgetown was a rural backwater

19. Ibid., 118, 125, 127, 133–39 (quotations).
20. Ibid., 135–38.

with none of Lexington's wealth and culture. No one there was likely to look down on him. The town had only one lawyer, and he was thinking of leaving. On the basis of this evidence, Kendall decided to start his law career in Georgetown.[21]

On May 10, only a week and a half after starting his search, Kendall turned the Clay children over to a new tutor and rode off to Georgetown. Once there, he made friends slowly, not from diffidence this time but because of his old feeling of superiority. After traveling in the best circles in Lexington, he looked down on the country folk in Georgetown. The town's leading tradesman, Major Herndon, was not a "man of the world," and the Baptist preacher had no education at all. Still expecting too much from his connections, he was disappointed when Herndon failed to introduce him to more than a handful of people. Worst of all, he could find very little legal business, and the other lawyer in town showed no inclination to leave.[22]

As the weather turned cold and rainy, he felt lonely and depressed. Needing someone to confide in, he thought of visiting his cheerful friend Flügel, who had moved to Vevay in the Indiana Territory. Kendall now dreamed of traveling to "a new country," where he could form "new societies and institutions," but was afraid that this constant "desire for change" would make him always "poor [and] unhappy." He had it wrong. In the old economy the search for change often led to poverty, as in the case of his brother and sister, but in the unfolding new economy it could be a path to success. In a few days the weather cleared. He fought off his despondency and decided to stay.[23]

One of the first events to alter his mood was a militia muster. "The time passed merrily," he wrote, as he listened to political speeches and came home with new friends "in high spirits," stopping at "almost every tavern" along the way. Several of the friends invited him to prepare a paper for a club meeting to be held the following week. Innocently expecting a literary gathering like those in Lexington, he was disappointed to find that most of the papers were "purely political, and of the most violent kind." But after reading his own paper and listening to the others, he was delighted to find that he could "out-write, if not out-speak," everyone there. The meeting was not a literary affair

21. Ibid., 134, 141–44; Davis, *Geography of the Bluegrass Region*, 8–27; Connelley and Coulter, *History of Kentucky*, 1:488; F. Garvin Davenport, *Ante-Bellum Kentucky: A Social History, 1800–1820* (Oxford, Ohio, 1943), 31.

22. *Autobiography*, 145.

23. Ibid.

but a regular session of the Scott County Republican party, held at Great Crossings, the home of the party leader, Congressman Richard M. Johnson.[24]

Colonel Johnson, a burly man with light reddish hair, had served in Congress since 1807. In the Battle of the Thames he won great fame by leading a cavalry charge and supposedly killing the Indian chief Tecumseh. Johnson and his five brothers sold supplies to the army and speculated in land. They were frequently in debt. He had never been accepted socially by the Lexington gentry, largely because he was living with a mulatto woman. The congressman was immediately interested in Kendall because he needed an editor for his party newspaper, the *Georgetown Minerva*.[25]

Five days after the club meeting Johnson arranged to have Kendall invited to the office of the publisher of the *Minerva*, Colonel Henderson. With little ado they offered him the chance to buy the printing business and become editor of the newspaper. He could pay for the business, they said, from future profits. Only two years earlier Kendall had considered newspaper editing beneath him, and Thomas Theobald, the proprietor of the tavern where he was staying, warned that Johnson was trying to get him under obligation and make him his political tool. He advised Kendall to "wash [his] hands" of the proposal. But Kendall needed a job and was confident he could remain independent of any political party. He told Henderson that he could not afford to buy the business but would consider editing the newspaper. First, however, he had to go to Lexington to attend the circuit court.[26]

Almost as soon as he reached Lexington, he came down with "bilious fever" (possibly a form of hepatitis), suffering such "excrutiating pain" that he believed himself "on the brink of the grave." Lucretia Clay, who was still waiting for her husband to return home, heard of Kendall's plight and sent her carriage to bring him to Ashland. For two weeks he could not even sit up in bed, and when he finally began to recover, he had very little appetite. When he left for Georgetown on July 15, he was so grateful that he could not express his emotions in words. His feeling of gratitude greatly affected his later relationship with Henry Clay.[27]

24. Ibid., 146–47.

25. Leland W. Meyer, *The Life and Times of Colonel Richard M. Johnson of Kentucky* (New York, 1932); *Autobiography*, 147.

26. *Autobiography*, 147–48.

27. Ibid., 148–49 (quotations); Kendall to Flügel, 16 Aug. 1815, Kendall Papers, Filson Historical Society. In evaluating this and Kendall's many other illnesses, I have relied upon Dr. James C. Tucker of Exeter, New Hampshire.

As Kendall resumed his search for a career, he was forced into business dealings in which change was sudden, rules were uncertain, and the participants were often naïve or unscrupulous. His long illness had been costly because it forced him to miss the court sessions at Lexington and Georgetown. Desperate for some kind of a job, he put aside his reservations and said that he would edit the *Minerva* and buy a half share of the business. At the same time the town postmaster offered to sell him the postmastership. Postmasters were officially appointed by the postmaster general, but the sale of offices was not uncommon. All it required was a friendly congressman to make the arrangements. When Johnson promised to help, Kendall agreed to become postmaster even though he worried that buying the office might seem unethical. On August 13 he wrote defensively in his journal that he felt "conscious of no moral wrong" and saw "the prospect of some profit." His father's moral scruples were wearing off.

Now needing money more than ever, Kendall arranged to assist the local schoolmaster in return for board and room. Then early in September he learned that the Indiana Land Company was offering higher pay and decided to rejoin and take part in laying out the new settlement. Expecting to leave soon, he abandoned his law practice and asked Henderson, the postmaster, and the schoolmaster to release him from their agreements. Kendall's constant shifting of plans is breathtaking. Over one summer he had made arrangements to practice law, buy a newspaper, teach school, run a post office, and was now ready to throw them all up for a land company.

Ten days later his plans changed again. When he studied the company's new constitution, his old misgivings returned, and he backed out of the project. After consulting Johnson and the postmaster, he completed arrangements to buy the postmastership and half of the *Minerva*. He was confident that running the two businesses together would give him an advantage over rival editors because the post office would provide ready access to the news. By October 2 he had closed both deals, agreeing to pay $180 each of the next four years for the post office and $200 for five years for the newspaper—$1,720 in debt tacked on to the $600 he already owed Richardson and his father. For a young Yankee only a few years removed from a tiny farm, this debt of $2,320 (more than $30,000 in today's money) was a heavy burden.[28]

---

28. *Autobiography,* 150–61. In estimating the present-day value of sums of money I have turned to John J. McCusker, *How Much Is That in Real Money? A Historical Price Index for Use as a Deflator of Money Value in the Economy of the United States* (Worcester, Mass., 1992).

Kendall's law practice was not completely dead. Eager to get some expo-sure, he had signed on as an unpaid co-lawyer to defend a man charged with murder. The trial, which took place October 5–7, gave him the chance to find out whether he could "make a speech." Although he was nervous and forgot about a third of what he had planned to say, he did reasonably well. Several persons said that he had made them cry; one even called him the greatest ora-tor ever to speak in Georgetown. He was so pleased with the praise and the verdict of manslaughter rather than murder that he decided to stick with his law practice in spite of all his other commitments.[29]

The next day Kendall brought out the first issue of the *Minerva*. He had grand ideas. With his franking privilege as postmaster he expected to get news by letter from agents all over the United States. Since the letters would reach Kentucky twice as quickly as newspapers, he would have the news long before his competitors. His most ambitious project was a religious journal. To gather information and solicit subscriptions he planned to get the names of clergy-men from hundreds of postmasters. He sent a letter to his old tutor Francis Brown, who had just taken over as president of Dartmouth, asking him for lists of theologians and religious publications as well as a "course of reading" not only on religion but also on literature and science. There is no evidence that Brown, already tied up with the Dartmouth College case, ever replied to this presumptuous letter. The journal never got off the ground.[30]

For a few weeks Kendall's newspaper business went smoothly, but sud-denly he discovered that Henderson had not been honest with him. Hender-son owed Johnson's brother-in-law Robert J. Ward $2,000 and had put up his half of the business as security. He had also transferred $800 of Kendall's promissory notes to secure a debt to Johnson's brother James. Kendall had bought half of a newspaper from a man who did not have title to it. He was now in debt to the Johnsons and under their control.

Angry and frightened, he thrashed about for a solution. On January 16, 1816, he shut down the newspaper and made plans to go on the road to collect some $2,000 in unpaid subscription fees. In a sharp letter to Richard M. John-son he intimated that he had been deceived and said that he would not own property controlled by someone who might "influence [his] opinions." He

29. *Autobiography*, 158–59.
30. Kendall to Francis Brown, 6 Nov. 1815, Amos Kendall Papers, Dartmouth College Library; *Autobiography*, 159–60; Kendall to Flügel, 11 Oct., 2 Dec. 1815, Kendall Papers, Filson Historical Society.

wrote defiantly in his journal that if the Johnsons planned to control him, they would not find him as "smooth to their hands" as they expected.

But Kendall soon realized that he could ill afford to antagonize Colonel Johnson, who, aside from Henry Clay, was his only possible connection in Kentucky. After receiving a reply from Johnson promising to straighten everything out, Kendall quickly sent back a conciliatory letter and then left on his collection trip. Soon after he returned, James Johnson took the *Minerva* off his hands and canceled his debt. Kendall would remain as editor of a new newspaper, the *Georgetown Patriot,* with himself and two journeyman printers listed as publishers. The Johnsons, however, would own everything. Kendall, who was already keeping his post office arrangement secret, now agreed to cover up this sham as well. He rationalized that if he found that he could not be "independent," he would "quit."[31]

Meanwhile, Kendall was encouraged by the progress of a lawsuit concerning a tract of eight hundred acres near Georgetown that had been surveyed and entered on the county books by a Virginian named Bullock. An absentee landlord, Bullock had received no formal grant and had made no improvements. In his absence a speculator had claimed the property, received a grant, and then sold the land in small lots to eight or nine settlers. In December 1815 Bullock's sons had hired Kendall to evict the families. Since the situation was similar to the one his brother and sister had faced in Vermont, Kendall should have been sympathetic toward the settlers, but he also had to consider his fee. If he ousted the settlers, he would receive two hundred acres, by far the largest fee in his career. Self-interest prevailed. Before the case reached court, he arranged a settlement in which the settlers could either rebuy their land at five-sixths of its value or vacate and receive a small sum for improvements. It was not a generous settlement because in either case they would have to go to court to get back their original payments. The settlers vacated, and Kendall got his fee.[32]

After two years in Kentucky Kendall could look back on more than his share of failures. Despite the backing of Lucretia Clay and the popularity of

31. *Autobiography,* 158–70.

32. Ibid., 163, 168–70, 180. Historians such as Charles Sellers and John Ashworth who portray Kendall as an agrarian have overlooked this case. Sellers, *Market Revolution,* 304–5, 312–13, 318, 324–25; Ashworth, *"Agrarians" and "Aristocrats": Party Political Ideology in the United States, 1837–1846* (Cambridge, Eng., 1983), 15, 23, 24, 25, 31, 227. Kendall wrote later that he had been uneasy about the ruling in the land case, but his uneasiness did not prevent him from siding with absentee landlords. *Autobiography,* 180.

his poetry, he was never accepted in Lexington. His experience in the militia was predictably unhappy. His business ventures—the grocery, the land company, and the *Minerva*—went nowhere and caused him enormous anxiety. Aside from the Bullock case he made almost nothing as a lawyer. The post office brought in very little, and he could not live on his editor's salary, which was only $150 a year. He had nibbled at the edges of politics but still considered it beneath him.

The failures were neither surprising nor unusual. Although he had a college education, two years of legal training, and many interests, he was not really skilled in anything, not even the law. Years later when he was involved in telegraph patent cases, he wryly admitted that he was not as good a lawyer as many of his adversaries. He was a Yankee jack-of-all-trades, in some ways a literary Eli Whitney, who as a young man also traveled from New England to take a tutoring job in the South. America was filled with jacks-of-all-trades who lacked the proper training for the new specialized occupations that were springing up.[33]

But the many failures did not mean that he would continue to fail. He was unusually intelligent, determined, and adaptable. He knew how to write, and he still had big dreams. Two rough years in Kentucky had rubbed off some of his elitism and republicanism and introduced him to slavery, evangelicalism, land speculation, journalism, and more important, democracy, partisan politics, and frontier capitalism. He was not yet committed to any of them, but perhaps he could take advantage of his talents and his experiences to find the right career.[34]

33. Kendall to Samuel F. B. Morse, 6 Dec. 1849, Samuel F. B. Morse Papers, LC.

34. Donald B. Cole, "A Yankee in Kentucky: The Early Years of Amos Kendall, 1789–1828," *Proceedings of the Massachusetts Historical Society* 109 (1997): 24–36.

# 5

## POLITICAL EDITOR

During his first few months editing the *Georgetown Patriot* Kendall held onto his republican ideals of civic virtue and nonpartisanship. He called party politics "contemptible" and condemned any editor who would "libel . . . the character of a respectable citizen . . . for the good of a party." He promised that "no personal abuse" would ever "flow from his pen." His job, he wrote, was to "promote learning, refine manners," and "watch over the morals of the community." Pointing to flaws in Kentucky social behavior, he attacked "the spirit of gambling and drunkenness" and pleaded with voters not to drink on election day.[1]

Kendall also maintained the liberal nationalism with which he had greeted the end of the war. He confessed great satisfaction at seeing "wave after wave" of migrants "carrying civilization and refinement" westward and increasing American wealth and power. They must not be "restrained," he wrote, until they reached "the western ocean." He praised Congress for "extending the internal communication of the country by roads and canals, and . . . protecting manufactures by a tariff of duties." He also wrote two articles supporting the new Bank of the United States (BUS) as essential for the national government. His only reservation was the fear that the BUS placed too much power in "the hands of a few individuals."[2]

But politics would be hard to avoid. The state and congressional elections would be held the first week in August, and the people were up in arms about the Compensation Act. On March 7, 1816, a House committee chaired by Richard M. Johnson had recommended that the pay of members of Congress, then $6 a day, be changed to an annual salary of $1,500, or approximately $12 a day. With the help of Henry Clay, who was back from Europe and once

1. *Georgetown Patriot,* 20, 27 Apr., 4, 11, 26 May, 3 Aug. 1816.
2. Ibid., 20, 27 Apr., 11, 18 May 1816.

again Speaker of the House, the bill passed quickly and was signed into law. There was a massive outcry. All across the country resolutions were passed attacking the measure as "high-handed," "reprehensible," and extravagant. Johnson commented that the bill "excited more discontent than the alien or sedition laws." Later, on the Fourth of July, celebrations were filled with speeches and toasts denouncing the new law. Critics were particularly angry at the unrepublican pretentiousness of replacing a daily wage with a salary and the statement by one congressman that at $6 a day congressmen could not live like "gentlemen."[3]

The uproar was an example of the growth of popular participation in politics that had been going on since the era of the Revolution. Even though the first political party system had not proven durable and a truly democratic system of government was not yet in place, Americans found other ways to make their opinions known. The same sort of parades and celebrations that had stirred up opposition to British rule were later used to comment on the ratification of the Constitution and to challenge or defend Federalist rule in the 1790s. Political participation reached a high point in 1798 when lower-class Republican printers used their newspapers to attack the Alien and Sedition Acts.[4]

The involvement of Johnson and Clay made the Compensation Act a particularly sensitive subject in Kentucky. As soon as they returned home and started running for reelection, they had to attend militia musters and other democratic gatherings to answer angry questions and defend the act. Kendall was in a "delicate" position. He wanted to remain free to speak his mind but could ill afford to alienate either Clay or Johnson by opposing their position. After waiting for two years he had finally received an invitation in May to visit Clay at Ashland. The Speaker was even more "agreeable" than he had hoped, and within half an hour they were chatting in a "familiar" way. The conversation, however, was about the coming election, not about Kendall's career. Kendall also talked with Johnson's brother James but could not get a firm agreement on editorial policy.[5]

For a while Kendall managed to remain independent. He even refused to

---

3. C. Edward Skeen, "*Vox Populi, Vox Dei:* The Compensation Act of 1816 and the Rise of Popular Politics," *JER* 16 (1986): 253–74 (quotations, 259–60).

4. Waldstreicher, *In the Midst of Perpetual Fetes;* and Simon P. Newman, *Parades and Politics in the Street: Festive Culture in the Early American Republic* (Philadelphia, 1997).

5. *Autobiography,* 171–72 (quotations); Remini, *Henry Clay,* 146; *Patriot,* 3 Aug. 1816.

publish an article submitted by the Johnsons and mildly criticized the Compensation Act. But when asked to give a poem on the Fourth of July, he turned partisan. Instead of attacking the Compensation Act as so many were doing, he delivered a patriotic ode in which he praised Johnson for his heroism at the Battle of the Thames. Later he defended the Compensation Act by saying that members of Congress should be paid well enough to live like gentlemen and should not have to shine their own shoes or live in cheap boardinghouses. On being told that congressmen should be willing to live as plainly as soldiers, he answered that few gentlemen would want to live on such simple fare. He also appeared condescending by ridiculing the misspellings, grammatical errors, and less than cultivated writing style of opponents of the act. His haughty behavior aroused so much hostility that he was threatened and had to go about armed with a knife.[6]

These unnerving events pushed Kendall down the road toward democracy. Realizing that he had taken the wrong side of a popular issue, he looked for a question on which he could agree with the majority. Since he knew that Federalism had been hated during the war, he started using the term to attack his adversaries. In most cases it did not apply because there was no longer a Federalist party in Kentucky, but it did apply to John Pope, a former Federalist U.S. senator who was running against Clay. Pope had been nominated by a militia company, but Kendall contended that only sixteen men had attended the meeting and that thirty-nine others had drawn up counterresolutions. When an opposition editor used the word of the captain of the company to refute the charge, Kendall took advantage of the opening. Federalists, he said, may "believe a captain in preference to his entire company," but "simple republicans . . . pay more regard to the voice of *thirty-nine* than one."[7]

Democratic arguments like this struck such responsive chords that Kendall began to understand how democratic politics worked. The people were not immediately affected by the Compensation Act, but the act had aroused their resentment. "The sensation which has been excited" by the political campaign, he wrote in the *Patriot,* would remind the candidates of their "dependence on the people" and "the necessity of . . . consulting their opinions."[8]

6. *Autobiography,* 172, 175–78; Marshall, "Early Career," 146–49; Robert P. Hay, "Amos Kendall's Ode to Freedom," *Register* 68 (1970): 239–51. Jeffrey L. Pasley correctly calls Kendall "a measured opponent of the Compensation Act" but does not explore his embarrassing efforts to defend it. Pasley, *"The Tyranny of Printers": Newspaper Politics in the Early American Republic* (Charlottesville, 2001), 32.

7. *Patriot,* 17, 24 Aug. (quotation), 7 Sept. 1816.

8. Ibid., 10 Aug. 1816, quoted in Marshall, "Early Career," 154.

Johnson and Clay won reelection, faring much better than most of their congressional colleagues, less than 30 percent of whom were reelected. Of the fourteen western congressmen voting for the compensation bill, they were the only ones to retain their seats. Kendall deserved more credit for Johnson's success than for Clay's. Much of Johnson's majority came from his personal popularity in Scott County, but in the rest of the congressional district to the north and west, where he was not so well known, he needed the help of the *Patriot.* It was in this district, not in Clay's, which included the heart of the Bluegrass, that Kendall would stake his future.[9]

He had suddenly found a career in the burgeoning field of political journalism. Responding to the new economy, the number of newspapers in the United States had risen from less than a hundred in 1790 to almost four hundred in 1810; by 1830 it would exceed eight hundred. Scores of young men— including Thomas Ritchie in Virginia, Isaac Hill in New Hampshire, and Charles Hammond in Ohio—were launching successful careers in this new field. They would become leaders of the revolutions in journalism and democratic politics that followed the War of 1812.[10]

Kendall quickly joined both revolutions. It may seem odd that someone whose opinions had been so republican and elitist should suddenly become a partisan democrat, but as his own shifts of career suggest, sudden change was becoming the norm. Furthermore it was hard not to be democratic in Kentucky, where all adult white males were eligible to vote and where members of the lower house had to be reelected every year. Kendall's experiences in the militia and political clubs had made politics seem attractive. And journalism offered a promising career. As his attitudes changed, his reputation began to grow. Politicians appreciated his energy, his shrewdness, and his imaginative writing style, while businessmen were impressed by the financial understanding he had displayed in his articles on the BUS.

One of those most interested was William Gerard, half owner of the *Argus of Western America* in Frankfort and a director of the Bank of Kentucky. With the BUS making plans to establish branches in Lexington and Louisville, Gerard needed an editor who could influence state banking legislation.

---

9. Normally 50 percent were reelected. Johnson carried Scott County 1,052 to 430, the rest of the district 2,588 to 2,357. Skeen, *"Vox Populi,"* 266; *Patriot,* 24 Aug. 1824.

10. For statistics see Allan R. Pred, *Urban Growth and the Circulation of Information: The United States System of Cities, 1790–1840* (Cambridge, Mass., 1973), 21. For the expansion of the political press during and after the War of 1812 see Pasley, *"Tyranny of Printers,"* 348–99.

He also needed political help because he had antagonized Johnson by opposing his reelection. In September Gerard asked Kendall if he would be interested in buying a half interest in the *Argus*.[11]

After his painful dealings with Henderson, Kendall should have rejected the offer out of hand. Accepting it would put him deeper in debt and would force him to give up his law practice and postmastership and break his agreement with the Johnsons. But his success in the election had whetted his appetite, and he was tempted by the chance to make money editing a large newspaper in the state capital. Moreover, he was losing money as a lawyer and postmaster and was making only $150 a year as editor. The Johnsons, who were just as self-interested, were willing to let him go because they expected him to bring the *Argus* over to Colonel Johnson's side. Gerard removed the last obstacle by arranging a loan from the Bank of Kentucky. By mid-October Kendall had bought half of the *Argus* for $2,000 and had moved to Frankfort.[12]

He was now living in a town of 1,400 people that had grown up in the steep, narrow valley of the Kentucky River. It was located in Franklin County, another of the counties north and west of Lexington that were far less prosperous and patrician than the counties in the heart of the Bluegrass. When Kendall arrived, the town was in an uproar because newly elected Republican governor George Madison had died unexpectedly, leaving Lieutenant Governor Gabriel Slaughter to take over his duties.[13]

Even though Slaughter was also a Republican, Kendall was alarmed because the new governor had aligned himself with the remaining Federalists by appointing John Pope secretary of state. Expecting no patronage from Slaughter's Federalist-leaning faction, Kendall and Gerard decided to start a faction of their own. In the first issue of the *Argus* they showed their partisanship by attacking Slaughter and starting a campaign to block Pope's confirmation. The quarrel between Gerard and Johnson was patched up, and Kendall won the backing of Clay's Lexington newspaper, the *Kentucky Reporter*. Kendall's faction was so popular in the lower house that he and Gerard were elected printers for the legislature, but since the faction lacked strength in the senate, Pope was confirmed.[14]

11. *Patriot*, 7 Sept. 1816; *Autobiography*, 179–81, 184. The Kentucky constitution of 1799 was one of the first to adopt white manhood suffrage. John E. Kleber, ed., *The Kentucky Encyclopedia* (Lexington, 1992), 225.

12. *Autobiography*, 179–83.

13. Ibid., 182–83.

14. *Argus*, 1 Nov. 1816; *Patriot*, 2, 9, 16, 23, 30 Nov. 1816; *Autobiography*, 183–86.

As the 1817 campaign got under way, Kendall changed his tack. Pointing out that Slaughter had not been elected governor by the people, he insisted that instead of letting him finish out Madison's four-year term, the state should hold a new election. The people, he said, had the right to choose. The New Election faction carried the August election by a wide margin. William T. Barry, Jesse Bledsoe, and prominent lawyer George M. Bibb of Frankfort, who had joined the movement, were elected to the state lower house. After the election the victors celebrated at the home of Eliza Price and carried Bibb and Kendall about the room on their shoulders. It was ironic that the belle of Lexington, who had turned up her nose at Kendall, should host the affair. The victory, however, meant little, for a new election bill was rejected in the senate. Kendall's faction won again in 1818, but by this time even he seemed to have lost interest in the subject. Slaughter remained governor until he retired in 1820.[15]

During the elections Kendall had shown a sense of humor and considerable skill in political give and take. When old Federalist Humphrey Marshall wrote articles entitled "Plain Truth," calling him a fool, Kendall replied with "Plainer Truth" signed by "A Fool," making it clear that the real fool was Marshall. When the humorless Federalist editor George W. Hunt scolded him for using "violent language," Kendall replied lightheartedly that perhaps he was guilty of "vanity" but surely not "violence."[16]

Not all the exchanges were humorous. In the 1817 campaign Kendall criticized John N. Farnham of the Federalist *Frankfort Commentator* so harshly that Farnham challenged him to a fistfight. The scrawny Kendall was not eager to fight, but he knew that in the culture of Kentucky he would have to defend his honor. He reluctantly accepted the challenge and would have been badly hurt if Gerard and his journeyman printers had not come to his rescue. A few weeks later editor Moses Bledsoe of the *Commentator* knocked him down several times. James Johnson warned Kendall that the assault would be repeated and gave him a small pistol. Riding back to Frankfort soon afterward, he encountered Bledsoe on a lonely section of the road. As Kendall told the story, he brandished his pistol, and Bledsoe fled. Kendall may have embellished the incident, but it did much for his political reputation.[17]

In May 1817 Kendall took full command of the *Argus* when Gerard sold

15. *Autobiography,* 185–90, 198; *Argus,* 14 Feb., 2 May 1817, 30 Apr. 1819.

16. *Autobiography,* 184–85, 188–89.

17. Ibid., 190–96; *Argus,* 25 Sept. 1818.

his half share to Gervas E. Russell and J. B. Russell, who chose to be silent partners. Financial stability seemed assured by a circulation of 1,500, the largest in the state, and the printing contract with the legislature. Kendall made the *Argus* a lively, informative, four-page weekly. In one issue, for example, he wandered engagingly from the publication of Cooper's *The Pioneers* (3,500 copies sold the first six hours) to the death of Bonaparte's mother (the exact sums of money left to each heir) to Byron's "Vision of Judgment" (a piece of "blasphemous libel"). He continued to support the BUS and federal internal improvements and still called for a vigorous policy of territorial expansion. He was confident that his fellow countrymen, seeking to become rich, would transform "the dark woods" of Indian warfare to "bright fields" of grain. His liberal, capitalist vision for the spread of civilization was similar to that of Henry Clay, but it had not led to a political connection with the Speaker.[18]

One reason that Kendall lost interest in a new election in 1818 was that he had fallen in love. Any remaining ties with Mary Lawrence had been severed in August 1815 when she sent word that she would never move to Kentucky. After hearing the news Kendall wrote F. G. Flügel to say that he was seeking a wife. "She need not be a beauty," he wrote, but since he was "a poor man," she "must . . . be willing to supervise [housework] and even labor herself." On learning that Flügel was married and had an unmarried sister-in-law staying at his house, Kendall decided to visit.[19]

In June 1816, before the compensation election campaign heated up, he set out for Flügel's home in Vevay, Indiana, halfway down the Ohio River from Cincinnati to Louisville. The Ohio Valley was booming, for Indiana had just been admitted to the Union. A few months later seven-year-old Abraham Lincoln crossed the river with his family on their way to Little Pigeon Creek, Indiana. When Kendall reached Vevay, he was disappointed in Flügel's sister-in-law, but he was impressed by the Swiss winegrowers, who were "growing rich" selling wine for $1.50 a gallon. Wherever he went, Kendall was on the lookout for ways to make money.[20]

18. *Argus*, 17 Oct., 7, 21 Nov. 1817, 15 Jan. 1819, 26 Apr. 1821, 28 Mar. 1822, 26 Feb. 1823 ("blasphemous"), 30 Jan. 1824; Tom K. Barton, "Henry Clay, Amos Kendall, and Gentlemen's Education: State-Supported Higher Education as a Political Issue in Kentucky, 1815–1825," *Rocky Mountain Social Science Journal* 3 (1966): 50–51; *Argus*, 18 Apr. 1827, cited in Edwin N. Hopson, notes for unfinished Ph.D. diss. on Amos Kendall, Filson Historical Society; ibid., 1 Nov. 1816, quoted in Marshall, "Early Career," 164 ("dark woods").

19. Kendall to F. G. Flügel, 16 Aug. 1815, Kendall Papers, Filson Historical Society.

20. *Autobiography*, 173–74.

In the spring of 1818 he finally found the right woman. Mary B. Woolfolk was one of seven children of William and Nancy Woolfolk, who lived in the countryside near Louisville. Kendall, who liked to stress his modest origins and those of his wife, called William Woolfolk a "plain, honest farmer," but on an unguarded occasion he referred to him more accurately as "a planter." Woolfolk owned at least a dozen slaves and ran a plantation of over six hundred acres. He also operated a mill, speculated in land, and held other pieces of property, including more than 1,200 Virginia land warrants. Though not as wealthy as Henry Clay, he had a larger plantation and almost as many slaves.[21]

Mary, who was in her late twenties, was a practical, down-to-earth woman with simple tastes, perfect, he thought, for someone "doomed" to "temporary and perhaps lasting poverty." Kendall loved her for her "goodness of heart." In his proposal he showed unusual sensitivity toward women. Not only did he speak to Mary's mother as well as her father, but he also showed awareness of the risks women took in marriage. Many women, he told Mary, came to "prefer the once dreaded state of 'single blessedness' to the miseries of a husband cruel, capricious, and improvident." He would never be such a husband, he said with moral conviction, because he did not have "a single vice."[22]

The Woolfolks granted permission but with a special condition. Mary had "an unfortunate brother and sister . . . not capable of taking care of themselves." Her father had arranged in his will that after he and his wife died, Mary would care for them and receive eight slaves for their support. Kendall accepted the condition because he was in love with Mary, but humanitarianism may also have been involved. There is a good chance that the children were deaf-mutes, and in his editorials Kendall had shown great concern for such unfortunates. Furthermore, the large number of slaves must have been an attractive inducement. Eight slaves—depending upon their ages and capabilities—were worth perhaps $500 each, or a total of $4,000, more than enough to pay off his entire debt. Kendall deeply felt "the want of property" and told Mary that he would "do anything which was not mean, dishonour-

21. Ibid., 237; *Argus*, 22 Oct. 1823 ("plain"); Kendall to Flügel, 4 Apr. 1839, Kendall Papers, Filson Historical Society ("planter"); "Will of William Woolfolk, 8 Aug. 1822," *Filson Club Historical Quarterly* 6 (1932): 192; United States Census Schedules, 1810, Jefferson County, Ky., RG 29, reel 7, p. 26; *American State Papers: Public Lands*, 6:398.

22. Kendall to Mary Woolfolk, 8, 12 July 1818, Kendall to Mary Woolfolk Kendall, 7 Mar. 1819, in *Autobiography*, 238–42.

able, or wicked, to become rich." The two were married at the Woolfolk plantation on October 1, 1818.[23]

Kendall was an affectionate husband. When Mary was away, he counted the hours until she returned and often felt the urge to write her a love letter. There were moments of friction—Amos was fussy, and Mary sometimes lost her patience—but all things considered, the two were happily married. After several years in a small, inexpensive house, they rented a larger one two blocks from the capitol building, where they had a pleasant yard with a cherry tree. They owned four slaves—undoubtedly from the Woolfolks—and kept a cow. Children came regularly—Mary Anne in 1820, then a boy who died, followed by Adela in 1822, and William Zebedee in 1823.[24]

When Kendall married, he had just turned twenty-nine. He was not yet old, but he seemed so because his hair was gray and would soon be white. His gaunt, narrow face, sallow skin, and thin, frail body also conveyed the appearance of age. At five feet nine and a half inches, he was a bit above average height, but since he bent over when he walked, he looked much shorter. In an age that took great stock in phrenology, Kendall's large head and high forehead attracted attention. Most striking of all were the large gray-blue eyes and prominent hooked nose set above a small firm mouth and oval jaw. His sharp eyes gave some indication of his fierce ambition, while the tightly pursed lips suggested his moralism and intolerance.[25]

Kendall was a fastidious, self-righteous man, constantly worried about his health. When Mary went away for a few days, he was upset at having his routine disturbed. "The coffee is not made on time," he sulked, "the dinner is cooked badly, the cow is not milked, the house is not kept clean." One fall he had an unpleasant experience when he fell into the water while fording a river. He was so cold, he wrote Mary, that he looked desperately for some place to sit before a fire. But when he finally reached a tavern, he thought it was too filthy and could not bring himself to stop. The next day he complained that his back hurt and that he "felt a little of the rheumatism lurking in [his] legs."

---

23. Mary Woolfolk to Kendall, n.d., Kendall to Mary Woolfolk, 12 July, 9 Sept. 1818, in *Autobiography*, 237, 239–40; *Patriot*, 19 Oct. 1816; *Argus*, 3, 23 Sept., 19 Nov. 1823; G. Glenn Clift, comp., "Kentucky Marriages and Obituaries—1787–1860," *Register* 36 (1938): 174.

24. They also had boarders—perhaps a maid and apprentice printers. Kendall to Mary Woolfolk Kendall, 7 Mar. 1819, 9 Sept. 1820, 11 May 1822, in *Autobiography*, 241–44; United States Census Schedules, 1820, Franklin County, Ky., RG 29, reel 22, p. 66; Weis, *Early Generations of the Kendall Family*; Kendall to Flügel, 4 Apr. 1839, Kendall Papers, Filson Historical Society.

25. U.S. Passport Application no. 27051, 23 June 1866, National Archives, RG 59.

Sometimes his self-righteousness got him into trouble. In the summer of 1822 he caught a young boy taking cherries from his tree and was so incensed that he gave him a whipping. A few days later the boy's father knocked Kendall to the ground and kicked him. Kendall told his side of the story in the *Argus,* the father sued, and Kendall countersued. The foolish affair was not settled until Kendall paid one cent in damages.[26]

Kendall was unusually introspective. More than anything else he feared being considered a coward or looking foolish to women. After his fights with Farnham and Bledsoe he admitted to himself that he had lacked "daring" but was proud that he had not shown "cowardice." Although he dreaded "the necessity of killing" a man, he convinced himself that if necessary he would have the nerve to "shoot down [an] adversary in the streets." In describing one of his unsuccessful courtships, he conceded that he lacked the "impudence" needed to "take [women] by storm."[27]

He was especially introspective about religion. Although he had drifted away from strict Calvinism, he remained deeply religious. Much in awe of his father, he believed that religion had given Zebedee the "energy of character" that kept him from committing wrong. He only wished that he had such character. In 1821, while praying alone, he underwent what he called "the process of conversion." As he recalled it, "a sensation of wonderful serenity" came over him, and he became "perfectly but quietly happy." The conversion, however, did not last, and from then on he was determined not to join any church. He was afraid that if he did, he would be a "disturber of the peace" of that institution. Convinced that most church members were hypocrites, he considered himself unfit to live up to the high moral standards of any denomination.[28]

Yet he continued to think and write about Christianity. In 1823 he endorsed the new Bible Society in Frankfort. He also wrote several "Sunday reflections" trying to prove the existence of a "Supreme Being." There must be a God, he insisted, because otherwise it would be impossible to explain the harmony of the sun, moon, and stars. Kendall saw a connection between the grand design of the universe and the system of perpetual motion that had "haunted his mind" since childhood. He did not cut himself off from orga-

26. Kendall to Mary Woolfolk Kendall, 7 Mar. 1819, 9 Sept. 1820, in *Autobiography,* 241–43; Marshall, "Early Career," 285–86.

27. *Autobiography,* 196–97 ("daring"); Kendall to Wright, 22 Nov. 1817, Nathaniel Wright Papers, LC ("impudence").

28. Kendall to John, 10 Oct. 1852 ("energy"); Kendall to the Rev. G. W. Samson, 25 Dec. 1861, in *Autobiography,* 655–56 ("conversion").

nized religion and soon got over his supercilious attitude toward Methodists and Baptists. Mary Kendall, a devout Methodist, often invited her preacher to the house. Kendall himself knew many prominent Baptists, including the Johnsons and the eloquent Baptist preacher Jacob Creath. He also renewed his interest in the Disciples of Christ, whom he had first encountered in Vermont.[29]

Kendall found an outlet for his religious concerns in Freemasonry. He had become active in the Masons soon after arriving in Lexington and had many Masonic friends, including Clay, Bibb, and Barry. In June 1823 he delivered a Masonic address in which he tried to answer his own religious questions. He began by stressing the need for a Christian model. Jesus Christ could not fill the need, for no one could match him; but John the Baptist, who had "all our passions," was "entirely within reach." Kendall may have been thinking of his own earthly model, his father, who seemed beyond his reach. The task for Masons, he said, was to restore God's moral world, which had been destroyed by human passions. He warned his fellow Masons against a trinity of vice: idleness, which was "the devil's Threstle-Board," intemperance, which "breaks down every barrier," and profanity, which was so "*heaven-daring.*"[30]

Kendall had become an important figure in the community. In addition to his newspaper editing and his religious work, he drew up a town ordinance regulating the treatment of slaves, served on a committee investigating the condition of cellars and ponds, was appointed to a commission rebuilding the county jail, and was a member of the county board of education. On one occasion he performed five and a half days of work with a horse and cart on a county road. Like his forebears in Dunstable, he had become one of the guardians of virtue in Frankfort.[31]

Only two years after calling party politics "contemptible," Kendall had become one of the better-known political editors in the state. By accepting challenges and carrying a pistol he had proven himself in Kentucky politics. His sudden rise was another example of the abrupt twists and turns of his career and demonstrates the unusual openness and indeterminacy of life in the early

29. In 1831 he was still experimenting with perpetual motion. *Autobiography,* 259–65, 323–25.

30. Louis Collins, *History of Kentucky,* 2 vols. (Covington, 1882), 1:28, 29, 525–26; Amos Kendall, *An Address on the Principles of Masonry* (Frankfort, 1823).

31. Nettie Henry Glenn, *Early Frankfort, 1786–1861* (n.p., n.d.), 84, 93–94, 96; L. F. Johnson, *The History of Franklin County, Ky.* (Frankfort, 1912), 72; *Argus,* 7 Feb. 1822; Baxter Ford Melton Jr., "Amos Kendall in Kentucky, 1814–1829: The Journalistic Beginnings of the 'Master Mind' of Andrew Jackson's Kitchen Cabinet" (Ph.D. diss., Southern Illinois University, 1978), 153.

republic. But after so many failures, he tended to exaggerate his successes. He took too much credit for the victory in 1817, saying that a pamphlet of his had changed the whole "current" of the election. He presumptuously used the pseudonym "Democrat" and claimed that his faction spoke for the voters. In a letter to a friend he boasted that even though "the political atmosphere [was] filled with storms," and "the bolts occasionally scath[ed]" him, they could not "hurl [him] from the cloud."[32]

He was getting a little ahead of himself. Even though he had shown a remarkable aptitude for democratic politics and had embraced democracy, he did not represent the voters and was not yet the leader of a real party. His influence was limited because he remained at odds with the governor and had not won the support of the voters on any significant issue. In these early political battles he had dealt with congressional pay and the question of a new election, neither of which affected people's lives. Even he admitted—much later—that the people were not deeply concerned about holding a new election. He would not be a real political leader until he had faced a vital economic issue.

32. *Autobiography,* 189 ("current"); Kendall to Wright, 22 Nov. 1817, Wright Papers ("political").

# 6

## THE RELIEF WAR

In the spring of 1818 Kentucky and the West reveled in postwar prosperity. Bad harvests in Europe and the reopening of foreign markets had driven up farm exports, while improvements in transportation made it easier to get produce to market. A great increase in the number of state-chartered banks and the resumption of the westward movement encouraged land speculation and led to a threefold increase in the sale of public land. As a result farm prices in the Ohio Valley, already inflated, rose another 30 percent over the values of 1815. Paper money was in good supply. Fifteen years later the economist William M. Gouge commented that "the first months of the year 1818 were the golden age of the western country. Silver could hardly have been more plentiful in Jerusalem in the days of Solomon, than paper money was in Ohio, Kentucky, and the adjoining regions."[1]

Gouge, who hated paper money, was being sardonic. In his mind there had been far too much paper circulating in the West. Kentucky was a case in point. Theoretically, the only bank in the state in 1815 was the Bank of Kentucky with its central office in Lexington and branches in other towns. The state owned half of the stock, appointed half of the directors, and required the bank to back its notes with a safe level of specie. But in addition private individuals and institutions were issuing their own notes. The amount of paper money was further increased in 1817 when the BUS opened branches in Lexington and Louisville. To cap it all, the legislature chartered forty-six new banks, each authorized to issue $25,000 in banknotes with no specie restrictions. Kentucky now had a lending institution for every 6,700 free inhabitants.[2]

1. *Statistical History*, 121, 239; William M. Gouge, *A Short History of Paper Money and Banking in the United States* (1833; reprint, New York, 1968), 129.

2. Sandra F. VanBurkleo, "'The Paws of Banks': The Origins and Significance of Kentucky's Decision to Tax Federal Bankers, 1818–1820," *JER* 9 (1989): 462.

The new economy could bring bad times as well as good. American manufacturing was already suffering from a postwar flood of foreign imports. Then at the height of the farm boom in 1818 good harvests in Europe and new trade restrictions abruptly reduced the demand for American foodstuffs. As the flow of trade turned against the United States, its banking system came under extreme pressure. Toward the end of the summer the BUS, which had stimulated the boom with generous loans, now began to contract.

The BUS was not entirely responsible for what followed; western investors who borrowed unwisely and bid up prices also had themselves to blame. But the result of the contraction, especially in Kentucky and the West, was disastrous. During their first year in operation the two Kentucky branches of the BUS had steadily accumulated the notes of the other Kentucky banks. When the branches started demanding specie for the notes and started calling in loans, the effect was felt all over the state. The Bank of Kentucky was forced to redeem so many notes and call in so many of its own loans that by November the amount of its notes in circulation had been cut in half. When the newly chartered independent banks also had to call in their loans, unhappy debtors began to refer to them as the "forty thieves." A sudden reduction in world prices made the situation worse. By 1820 wholesale prices in Cincinnati had dropped 30 percent, and the price of wheat had been cut 60 percent. The financial contraction came to be called the Panic of 1819.[3]

A severe depression hit Kentucky. Property values were cut in half, farmers faced foreclosure, and businessmen were on the verge of bankruptcy. Among the most hard hit were the Johnson brothers, who owed $30,000 to the BUS and lost money when the new bank at Georgetown suspended specie payments. Lexington did not escape. Its landlocked location was already keeping it from taking full advantage of steam transportation, and it suffered a heavy blow when the Lexington Manufacturing Company went out of business.[4]

The postwar boom and bust forced Americans to look anxiously at the growth of capitalism. Ever since the days of the Revolution Americans had believed in the idea that every man had the right to the fruits of his labor.

3. Ralph C. H. Catterall, *The Second Bank of the United States* (Chicago, 1902), 31, 51–52; *Autobiography*, 199–204; VanBurkleo, "'Paws of Banks,'" 462; *Statistical History*, 121, 124.
4. *Argus*, 13 Feb., 26 Mar. 1818; Marshall, "Early Career," 201–2; Leavy, "Memoirs of Lexington," 128.

David Ricardo later turned this doctrine into the labor theory of value (that the worth of any object was the labor put into it), and it became the basis for anticapitalist movements. It had no such radical connotation in America, where the availability of endless land supposedly made government restraints on capitalism unnecessary.

The panic, however, reinforced the fears of some that capitalism led to corruption and disaster. Others, more adaptable, were confident that in the long run it would prove beneficial. The third and largest group reacted tentatively and inconsistently. Although not opposed to capitalism, they resented the privileges that capitalists were receiving from government—the speculative profits from fluctuations in the value of public lands and government banknotes, the benefits from protective tariffs, and the special rights granted to large corporations. In the West they were quick to blame the panic on one of these corporations—the BUS.

Kendall represented the third group. Facing vital economic issues for the first time, he reconsidered his views frequently over the next few years. He believed that workers had the right to the fruits of their labor, but was no reformer. His first reaction to the panic was to turn against the BUS, calling it a monopoly and accusing it of destroying the independent banks. To some extent he was expressing the fear, mentioned earlier in the *Georgetown Patriot,* that the government had given the BUS too much power. He also had a political motive: the majority in Kentucky was against the BUS.[5]

His change of heart ended the good feeling between the *Argus* and the *Kentucky Reporter,* which continued to follow the lead of Henry Clay and support the BUS. In early October 1818, the day after he was married, Kendall delivered a broadside against the BUS, calling its directors "brokers, stock-jobbers and shavers." When the *Reporter* struck back, he started a five-part attack on the BUS. "The honest yeomanry of the country," he wrote, was "arrayed" against a "monster" that cared for nothing but money. A small investor himself, he expressed the resentment against the BUS felt by many disappointed investors in the West. The quarrel between the *Reporter* in Lexington and the *Argus* in Frankfort was the start of a struggle between the well-established heart of the Bluegrass near Lexington and the less highly devel-

5. Huston, *Securing the Fruits of Labor,* 1–13, 25–26. I have followed Huston in using the term "his" labor to conform with usage at the time. Ibid., 8 n. 5. For Kendall and the fruits of labor see Kendall, *Address on the Principles of Masonry.*

oped second tier of Bluegrass counties to the north and west in the vicinity of Frankfort and Georgetown.[6]

Kendall resumed his attack in the spring with a series of articles rebutting John Marshall's defense of the BUS in *McCulloch v. Maryland.* He argued that the BUS violated the doctrines of states' rights and strict construction of the Constitution and said that the founding fathers had never dreamed of giving Congress the power to establish such a corporation. With his states' rights, anti-BUS position Kendall had now moved away from the nationalism of his early days in Kentucky. The main reason was the panic, but he also may have been influenced by the old states' rights arguments of Virginians such as Spencer Roane, John Taylor, and Thomas Ritchie, who had not been swayed by the nationalist republicanism of Clay and John Quincy Adams. Alarmed by Marshall's nationalist interpretation of the Constitution, these Old Republicans defended the agrarian way of life and the supremacy of state governments. This resurgence of traditional republicanism would bring a number of Republicans, both northern and southern, into a new party, the party of Andrew Jackson.[7]

The first official response to the panic in Kentucky came from a reactionary group of legislators aptly called the Disorganists, who blamed the panic on greedy bankers and demanded the abolition of every bank in the state. This absurd proposal was turned down, but the Disorganists managed to pass a bill placing an annual tax of $60,000 on each of the two branches of the BUS. It was later ruled unconstitutional by the federal circuit court.[8]

County meetings held in the spring of 1819 were more realistic. The main contest was between Reliefers, who wanted to use the power of the state government to relieve debtors, and Anti-Reliefers, who defended creditors. A majority of the meetings, including a well-publicized gathering at Frankfort, proposed relief measures postponing the payment of debts and allowing banks

6. *Argus,* 24 July, 2 Oct. ("brokers"), 13 ("yeomanry"), 20, 27 Nov., 4, 18 Dec. ("monster") 1818. It is customary to speak of the inner and outer Bluegrass. I have subdivided some of the inner Bluegrass into the heart near Lexington (Fayette, Clark, Woodford, Jessamine, and Bourbon Counties) and the second tier (Franklin, Mercer, Scott, and Harrison Counties). Davis, *Geography of the Bluegrass Region.*

7. *Argus,* 8, 15 Jan., 2 Apr., 7, 14, 21, 28 May, 4, 11, 18, 25 June, 2, 9, 23 July 1819; *Autobiography,* 207–22.

8. *Journal of the Senate of the Commonwealth of Kentucky,* 1818 sess., 198–99; *Journal of the House of Representatives of the Commonwealth of Kentucky,* 1818 sess., 166; VanBurkleo, "'Paws of Banks,'" 168, 463–74.

to suspend specie payments and issue more paper money. Once again Frankfort and the second tier of counties were at odds with Lexington and the heart of the Bluegrass. Three of the meetings that called for relief were held in the second tier; only one in the heart of the Bluegrass, which was more in sympathy with creditors than debtors.[9]

Kendall took no consistent position. At one time he sounded like a Disorganist, saying that the people had "bitter hostility" against all banks and that it might be a good idea to "abolish the whole system" of private banking. He professed no sympathy for debtors. Those who had "contracted debts" beyond their "ability to pay" would have to take "the consequence." No good Republican would try to "relieve hair-brained adventurers and visionary speculators from the effects of their rashness and folly." After the Frankfort meeting he was willing to let banks suspend specie payments and issue new banknotes but insisted that they resume specie payments as soon as possible and refused to consider the postponement of debts.[10]

His position changed again in June when President James Monroe and Andrew Jackson visited Frankfort. On the eve of the visit Kendall swung back a little toward nationalism by saying that Kentucky needed higher tariff duties to protect agriculture and manufacturing. He also used the opportunity to underscore his democratic sentiments. No one, he said, should "prostrate himself in the dust or kiss the President's toe." Every "freeman" should say to himself: "*I am as good as the President. Why should I worship my own servant?*" Monroe's visit gave Kendall his first opportunity to see Jackson, but he showed very little interest in the general.[11]

The relief movement gained momentum in the fall of 1819. By this time Kentuckians owed banks at least $10 million, almost $3 million of it to the BUS. Robert Wickliffe of Lexington and other BUS lawyers had started a major drive in the circuit court to collect these debts and by November had won judgments in twenty-six cases. With property being "sacrificed . . . for less than half its value," a "deeper gloom" hung over the state than had "ever [been] witnessed" before. The legislature responded with a stay act delaying payment of debts for two years unless creditors accepted the notes of the Bank of Kentucky. Since the law protected the bank as much as the debtors, many

9. *Argus,* 14, 21 May 1819; Murray N. Rothbard, "The Frankfort Resolutions and the Panic of 1819," *Register* 61 (1963): 214–19.

10. *Argus,* 1 Jan. ("bitter," "contracted"), 21 May, 11 June, 10 Sept. 1819 ("abolish").

11. Ibid., 18 (quotation), 25 June, 2 July 1819.

Reliefers were dissatisfied and began to call for a new state bank that would significantly increase the amount of money in circulation. Kendall neither supported nor opposed the stay bill.[12]

The debate over relief showed how artificial the New Election campaigns had been. At the Frankfort meeting George M. Bibb, a New Election man, had joined forces with Federalist John Pope in support of relief measures. During the legislative session Kendall often found himself agreeing with Governor Slaughter. Both opposed the BUS and the independent banks and accepted the stay bill with reluctance. With Slaughter's administration coming to an end, the New Election faction, already split by the fight between Frankfort and Lexington, no longer had a common foe to hold it together.[13]

The election of 1820 provided an opportunity for a referendum on relief. The gubernatorial candidates—Generals John Adair and Joseph Desha, Colonel Anthony Butler, and U.S senator William Logan—were quite similar. Each was a Republican, all but Butler had been in Congress, and all but Logan had served in the War of 1812. The best known was "the Old Warrior" General Adair, who had fought at New Orleans, the least known Colonel Butler, a land speculator, who had family ties with the New Election faction. The idea of a referendum died quickly when all candidates came out for relief. Kendall's views on the candidates were colored by politics, not ideology. He was neutral toward Logan and Desha but dead set against Adair, who had cooperated with Governor Slaughter in opposing the election of Richard M. Johnson to the U.S. Senate. Since Butler had New Election connections, the faction came out in his favor.[14]

During the campaign Kendall enlisted the editorial help of Francis P. Blair, the clerk of the Franklin County circuit court. Blair had grown up in Frankfort and had graduated from Transylvania the same year as Kendall from Dartmouth. Even more gaunt than Barry or Kendall, he was a sickly consumptive weighing less than one hundred pounds, who fully expected to die

12. Frank F. Mathias, "The Relief and Court Struggle: Half-way House to Populism," *Register* 71 (1973): 156; VanBurkleo, " 'Paws of Banks,' " 476–84; *Niles' Weekly Register* (Baltimore) 16 (1819): 255 ("sacrificed"); Samuel Reznek, "The Depression of 1812–22: A Social History," *American Historical Review* 39 (1933): 31 ("gloom"); *Autobiography*, 227; *Argus*, 28 June 1821.

13. *Argus*, 14 May 1819, 2 Feb. 1820, 28 June 1821; G. Glenn Clift, *Governors of Kentucky* (Cynthiana, Ky., 1942), 19–23.

14. Frank F. Mathias and Jasper B. Shannon, "Gubernatorial Politics in Kentucky, 1820–1851," *Register* 88 (1990): 247; *Argus*, 27 Apr., 22 June 1820; Marshall, "Early Career," 228–29; Shoptaugh, "Amos Kendall," 83; *Frankfort Commentator*, 10 Aug. 1820.

before he reached forty. Some considered Blair ugly because of his prominent teeth and unusually large head, but he was a man of great charm and had many friends. Married with four children, he owned two slaves, lived on a 130-acre farm, and had enormous debts of almost $40,000. Like Kendall he had inherited republican principles but had adopted liberal democratic views.[15]

Since the candidates did not differ on relief, the election was fought over personalities, not issues. Kendall and Blair worked aggressively to tear down Adair, who was in the lead, with personal attacks. They called the general a Federalist, a "military adventurer," and other familiar epithets, some of which backfired. During the three-day election Kendall and his friends met every evening in his office and received reports on the voting. When on the second night it became apparent that Butler had no chance, they made a final effort to stop Adair by instructing Butler supporters to vote for Logan. This, however, failed. Adair won by five hundred votes over Logan, each with about twenty thousand votes; Desha and Butler trailed far behind. The panic crisis brought 74 percent of the eligible voters to the polls, the highest in Kentucky to that time, considerably greater, for example, than the 63 percent turnout in 1812.[16]

Kendall's campaigning had helped bring out the voters, but in the end he had suffered a personal defeat. He had picked a fight with the strongest candidate and had backed the weakest, a man so unprincipled that he later embarrassed President Jackson with his corrupt behavior as minister to Mexico. Butler came in last and even failed to carry Franklin County. Worse still, Kendall's behavior cost him any chance of having influence in the new administration. He and Adair never spoke for the next three years; his only tie with the administration was with the new lieutenant governor, William T. Barry. Kendall's opponents enjoyed his discomfiture. He and his "minions," they wrote, had met in his *"regal* chamber" to plot and *"regulate the affairs of the state,"* but even though they sent out "heralds on flying horses" at the last minute, they could not save the day.[17]

15. Elbert B. Smith, *Francis Preston Blair* (New York, 1980), 3–13, 229.

16. *Argus,* 22 June (quotation), 6, 20, 27 July, 17, 31 Aug. 1820; *Commentator,* 10 Aug. 1820. Charles Sellers oversimplifies the election when he argues that Adair won "on a platform of radical relief." Adair, like the others, supported relief, but he ran as a military hero and won for that reason. He carried only two of the twelve counties most in favor of relief. Sellers, *Market Revolution,* 170; *Argus,* 31 Aug. 1820; Mathias and Shannon, "Gubernatorial Politics," 247; Lynn L. Marshall, "The Genesis of Grass-Roots Democracy in Kentucky," *Mid-America* 47 (1965): 276.

17. Joe Gibson, "A. Butler: What a Scamp!" *Journal of the West* 11 (1972): 235–47; Washington *Globe,* 12 June 1837; *Commentator,* 10, 17 Aug. 1820.

Despite the personal nature of the campaign, it was by default a victory for debtor relief. When the legislature convened in October 1820—almost two months early because of the panic—the Relief party was in the majority. After lengthy debate they passed—and Adair signed—two important measures. The first established the Bank of the Commonwealth and authorized it to issue $3 million in notes backed not by specie but by the good name and public lands of the state. Debtors could borrow up to $1,000 from the bank. The second, the Replevin (or Stay) Act, revised the legislation passed earlier in the year. Debts could still be postponed for two years, unless creditors accepted notes of the Bank of Kentucky or the Bank of the Commonwealth, in which case the delay would be only one year or three months, respectively.[18]

Now Kendall had to take a stand. Earlier in the year he had published an article on the labor theory of value. Although he did not give up his belief that the fruits of labor belonged to the laborer, he did oppose Ricardo's thesis that the value of any object was entirely the labor put into it. "The universal source of value," Kendall declared, was "the desire of mankind to possess" any given item. Gold and silver were in demand because they "contained more value in the same bulk" than other commodities. Governments had not given them this quality, and government paper money had "no value in itself." This con-fused position—support for the theory of the fruits of labor, but opposition to legislative paper money designed to help the worker—kept him on the fence.[19]

But when the bills were passed, he found it politically expedient to go along with the Reliefers. Many of his friends, including Bibb, Blair, and Barry, were in the Relief party; Relief men controlled the legislature; and the *Argus* printing contract was up for renewal. So Kendall remained silent and was soon reelected printer and, oddly enough, a director of the new bank. When he hesitated for a month before accepting the post, his lack of conviction was so obvious that he was attacked as a "weathercock" by one of his rival editors.[20]

Even after he became a director, Kendall was lukewarm about the relief measures. He said that the Replevin Act should never be used to "exempt"

18. The relief program was not as radical as it might have been. The legislators defeated several attempts to abolish the Lexington-based Bank of Kentucky. House, *Journal,* 1820, 11–13, 195, 358; Senate, *Journal,* 1820, 120, 237, 261; *Argus,* 28 June 1821; Mathias, "Relief and Court Struggle," 158–60; Shoptaugh, "Amos Kendall," 86.

19. *Autobiography,* 229–36; Marshall, "Early Career," 241–43.

20. House, *Journal,* 1820, 291; Shoptaugh, "Amos Kendall," 87–88; *Argus,* 1 Feb. (quotation), 30 Aug., 6 Sept. 1821.

property from sale. The new bank was an "experiment" and an "evasion" of the constitutional clause prohibiting states from issuing bills of credit. He hoped it would become a specie-paying bank. He was alarmed by the rapid decline in the value of the Commonwealth notes, which by the middle of 1821 were worth only seventy cents in gold. His concern put him in the strange position of siding with Lexington merchants, who suffered losses when they used the notes to satisfy their East Coast creditors. The declining value of the notes increased the friction between Lexington, the home of the Kentucky Bank, and Frankfort, the headquarters of the Commonwealth Bank. The Kentucky directors not only continued to pursue overdue debts—almost $900,000 from Franklin County alone—but also refused to help prop up the value of the Commonwealth notes.[21]

The Kentucky Bank and the Anti-Relief party gained an ally in 1821 when Henry Clay retired from Congress and returned to Lexington. Clay was a former director of the bank and had just taken a job with the BUS that pitted him against the debtors that the Relief party was trying to help. He had been given the responsibility of recovering overdue loans in Kentucky and Ohio. In this capacity he introduced lawsuits involving hundreds of thousands of dollars and won an important suit against the Johnsons. Although he avoided taking a public stand, it was apparent that he backed the Anti-Relief position.[22]

The Relief War reached its high point late in 1821 when the legislature passed a stay law forbidding the forced sale of any property for less than three-quarters of its value unless the creditor accepted notes of one of the two state banks. But a reaction was setting in. Although the relief program had saved thousands of debtors from sacrificing valuable property, it had a damaging effect on the overall economy. The decline in the value of the notes of the two banks had forced the citizens to pay a high price for goods imported from outside the state. When the Commonwealth dollar dropped to forty cents in the fall of 1822, the state started withdrawing notes in order to restore the value of the others. After $2 million in notes had been burned, the value of the remaining notes began to rise. At the same time improved economic conditions

21. *Argus,* 18 May 1820 ("exempt"), 1 ("experiment"), 15 Feb., 1 Mar., 12 Apr. ("evasion"), 9 Aug. 1821, 28 Mar., 2 May 1822; Marshall, "Early Career," 246–48; Murray N. Rothbard, *The Panic of 1819: Reactions and Policies* (New York, 1962), 103–5; Mathias, "Relief and Court Struggle," 160–61.

22. Harry R. Stevens, "Henry Clay, the Bank, and the West in 1824," *American Historical Review* 60 (1955): 843–44; Remini, *Henry Clay,* 176–77, 197–98, 207–8.

in the United States and Europe bolstered the state economy. With less need for relief, the legislature ended stay laws on all future contracts.[23]

The Relief War was over, but the political conflict continued. On May 13, 1822, Judge James Clark of the Bourbon County circuit court ruled that the Replevin Act of 1820 violated the contract clauses in the state and federal Constitutions. Even though the act had become an anachronism, the decision stirred partisan passions. Reliefers opposed the decision, Anti-Reliefers supported it, and the terms of the struggle were broadened. Instead of defending debtors against creditors, Reliefers contended that they were defending the rights of the voters exercised in the legislature against the power of vested interests expressed in the courts. Anti-Reliefers replied that they were defending the Constitution. The bitterness was increased by the two U.S. Supreme Court cases of *Green v. Biddle,* in which the court overturned a Kentucky law against absentee landlords. Reliefers were more than ever convinced that the courts, state and federal, were thwarting the will of the people. As the replevin case went to the state court of appeals, the Relief War was becoming the Court War.[24]

Once the Relief War was redefined as a battle over popular rights, Kendall no longer had any difficulty committing himself to the Relief party, which he considered to be the democratic side. If judges overturned legislative acts, he said, the legislature had the right to remove them. When Anti-Reliefer Robert Wickliffe, who was running for the legislature, retorted that the state and federal Constitutions—not the state legislature—had supreme authority, Kendall called him an "ultra federalist."[25]

Kendall was less ambivalent about education than he was about money and debts. During the Relief War he turned out a series of republican, increasingly democratic editorials proposing a state system of free common schools. With such a system, he said, "intelligence, virtue and good principles [would]

23. Rothbard, *Panic of 1819,* 54, 106–8; Dale Royalty, "Banking and the Commonwealth Ideal in Kentucky, 1806–1822," *Register* 77 (1979): 99–107; House, *Journal,* 1822, regular sess., 10–16; *Argus,* 9, 16 Jan. 1823; Mathias, "Relief and Court Struggle," 162; *Niles' Register* 23 (1822–23): 245–46, 321, 355, 387.

24. Mathias, "Relief and Court Struggle," 166–67; Arndt M. Stickles, *The Critical Court Struggle in Kentucky* (Bloomington, 1929), 30–31; *Argus,* 27 June, 4, 11 July 1822; House, *Journal,* 1822, special sess., 67–73; Sandra F. VanBurkleo, "Green v. Biddle," in Kleber, *Kentucky Encyclopedia,* 390.

25. *Argus,* 27 June, 4, 11 July, 12, 26 Sept. 1822, 9 July, 17 Sept., 1 Oct. (quotation), 26 Nov. 1823. Wickliffe was elected.

be the only passport to office." No republic could "be well governed unless all or a majority of the people [were] capable of governing." Using terms that would later find favor with the Jackson movement, he pointed out that "farmers and mechanics" could not afford to support their children at Transylvania University. The state should make up for this by *"dispens[ing] the blessings of at least a common education to every citizen."* The state passed a bill modeled on this plan, and Kendall wrote a report based on a study of American school systems, but lack of financing kept the plan from being carried out.[26]

Meanwhile Kendall's dream of having a political connection with Henry Clay was beginning to come true. In 1819 the Speaker helped the *Argus* get a printing contract with the State Department, and Kendall supported Clay when he delivered a speech in the House attacking Jackson for invading Spanish Florida. Early the next year, Clay gave Kendall advance notice of his plans to retire from Congress, while Kendall, at Clay's urging, asked Kentucky slaveholders to support the Missouri Compromise.[27]

Later in the year the relationship became stronger. Clay wrote to Kendall, suggesting that Secretary of State John Quincy Adams had not won enough land from Spain in the Adams-Onis Treaty. He obviously wanted Kendall's help against Adams in the next presidential campaign. Kendall responded with several editorials protesting against the provision in the Peace of Ghent that gave the British rights on the Mississippi and insisting that the next president should come from the West. The Washington *National Intelligencer,* which was backing Adams, tried to dismiss the upstart *Argus* with sarcasm, but Kendall, who liked the attention, fired back with editorials praising Clay and denouncing the system of "dynasties" that would make Adams president.[28]

Clay was also getting help from Massachusetts congressman Jonathan Russell, who had served with Clay and Adams at the Ghent conference. In the spring of 1822 Russell made public a copy of a letter purporting to show that Adams had been willing to give the British navigation rights on the Mis-

26. *Autobiography,* 255–57; *Argus,* 8 ("be well"), 15 ("intelligence"), 22, 29 Oct., 12, 19 Nov. 1819, 25 Jan., 13, 20 Sept., 4 Oct., 13 ("farmers," "raise"), 20 Dec. 1821, 3 Jan., 21 Mar. 1822; Barton, "Henry Clay," 50–52.

27. Clay knew about the contract well before it was made public. Kendall criticized Jackson in the Florida affair even though his friend Richard M. Johnson defended the general. Clay to Josiah Meigs, 11 Jan. 1819, Clay to Kendall, 8 Jan. 1820, Clay, *Papers,* 2:633n, 752–53; *Argus,* 19 Feb., 19 Mar., 2 Apr. 1819, 2, 9 Mar. 1820.

28. Clay to Kendall, 16 Apr. 1820, Clay, *Papers,* 2:822–24; *Argus,* 15, 22, 29 Nov. 1821, 24, 31 Jan. (quotation), 28 Feb., 28 Mar. 1822.

sissippi in exchange for American fishing rights off the shores of Canada. In June Clay hired Kendall to continue the fight with a series of anonymous articles for an Ohio newspaper. Within a few weeks Kendall had drawn up four "Letters to the People of Ohio," attacking Adams for giving up the Mississippi to Britain and Texas to Spain. Some of the material appeared in an editorial in the *Argus* accusing Adams of selling out the West. Adams was so irritated by the letters that he published a pamphlet defending himself against these and related charges.[29]

Using the pamphlet as an excuse for answering back, Kendall revised the four letters into a personal attack on Adams, which appeared in the *Argus* in the spring of 1823. One of his most telling points was that before the War of 1812 Adams had minimized the seriousness of the British and Indian threat in the upper Mississippi Valley. Left unchecked, British agents had "poisoned the minds of these children of the forest," thus causing "murders" all over the Northwest. Kendall's assumption that Indians could be so easily influenced was part of the prevailing white image of the Indians as childlike. It would become a major part of the Jackson program.[30]

By 1823 Kendall had developed a good working relationship with Clay. He felt free to give advice and had not hesitated to set conditions for his Ohio letters. He promised to do all he could for Clay, saying that his services would only partly compensate for the "kindness" of Lucretia Clay when he was "moneyless, friendless, and powerless." Clay followed his advice and promised to "communicate freely" with him about his presidential campaign. But despite all this, Kendall never gained Clay's confidence, and the two were never close socially. In addition their opposing views on the Relief War stood in the way of a close relationship.[31]

As Kendall's public life began to take on broader dimensions, his private life was suddenly disrupted. Late in the fall of 1822—while he was attacking Adams and publishing his report on education—his father-in-law, William Woolfolk, died, leaving Mary a considerable amount of property. Finally with

29. Remini, *Henry Clay*, 215–17; Kendall to Clay, 20 June 1822, Clay, *Papers*, 3:236–38; *Argus*, 18 July 1822; William Tanner to Kendall, 1 July 1828, in ibid., 16 July 1828; Adams, *Memoirs*, 6:49; John Quincy Adams, *The Duplicate Letters, the Fisheries and the Mississippi: Documents Relating to Transactions at the Negotiation of Ghent* (Washington, 1822), 232–43.

30. Clay, *Papers*, 3:237n; *Argus*, 31 Oct., 7, 14, 21 Nov. 1822, 6 Feb., 19 Mar.–28 May, 2 Aug. 1823; Amos Kendall, *Letters to John Quincy Adams, Relative to the Fisheries and the Mississippi* (Lexington, 1823), passim (quotations 17, 23).

31. Kendall to Clay, 20 June 1822, Clay to Kendall, 23 June 1822, Clay, *Papers*, 3:236–40.

some capital to invest, Kendall used the inheritance as security to buy an abandoned gristmill five miles east of Frankfort and started converting it into a paper mill. He looked forward "with fond and eager hopes to the time when he would be able to retire" from the "political turmoil" and live in wealth at his mill.[32]

On October 3, 1823, his dreams were suddenly shattered when Mary complained of a headache and a high fever. After an illness of only ten days she died, leaving him a widower with three children, ages three, one, and a few months. In the extravagant language of the times Kendall's obituary described Mary's "near perfection," her devotion to her children, and her hopes for eternal life. It also offered a few hints about his own personality. His social and political defensiveness came through when he mentioned Mary's willingness to "live humbly," her indifference to "the superior dress [and] furniture" of her neighbors, and her hostility toward anyone who had "spoken evil" of him. His uncertainty about his religious future can be inferred from his remark that Mary died certain that "the gates of heaven would be opened to her."[33]

Mary's death had serious financial consequences for Kendall. In accordance with William Woolfolk's will, much of the property that Mary had inherited reverted to the Woolfolk family when she died, stripping Kendall of most of his security for the mill. He would somehow have to get another loan or give up his plans. Shortly after Mary's death he was dealt a second setback when the legislature voted to transfer half of the state printing from the *Argus* to the rival *Frankfort Commentator*.[34]

Like so many Americans Kendall had had a difficult time responding to the Panic of 1819. The panic shocked him, made him reassess his assumptions, but did not change his fundamental approach to American life. He was still a moderate adapting to capitalism and democracy. To describe him as a radical relief man as some have done makes no sense. Kendall never supported the sweeping changes in society that are usually attributed to the term "radical." After the ups and downs of his early years in Kentucky the shift from boom to bust was not an entirely new experience. So he continued on as before, re-

32. Mary and Amos did not take the "unfortunate" children. They stayed with Mary's mother. "Will of William Woolfolk." The mill was located on fifty acres at Mount Pleasant, a small settlement on Elkhorn Creek. Ebenezer Hiram Stedman, *Bluegrass Craftsman, Being the Reminiscences of Ebenezer Hiram Stedman*, ed. Frances L. S. Dugan and Jacqueline P. Bull (Lexington, 1959), xi–xii, 148–54, 219; *Argus*, 22 Oct. 1823 (quotation).

33. *Autobiography*, 265–68.

34. House, *Journal*, 1823, 277; Kendall to Clay, 19 Feb. 1825, Clay, *Papers*, 4:78.

acting quickly, almost impulsively, with little concern for consistency. Sometimes he spoke out sharply against banks and paper money, but when the
replevin and bank bills were passed he accepted them. Beneath his inconsistency, however, was a fundamental shift from his old pro-BUS liberal nationalism to an anti-BUS states' rights position. Although he did not realize it,
the Panic of 1819 had turned Kendall toward the Jackson party.[35]

35. Charles Sellers, for example, surely goes too far in describing Kendall in the Relief War as
one of the "portendors of Jacksonian radicalism." Sellers, *Market Revolution,* 304.

# 7

## THE COURT WAR

Kendall had little time to grieve. A few days before Mary died, the court of appeals declared the Replevin Act unconstitutional, and a few weeks later the legislature convened. Having lost in court, the Reliefers sought to remove the three justices, but they were unable to get the necessary two-thirds majority. The best they could do was to push through a resolution denouncing the court decision and defeat the Anti-Relief protest that followed.[1]

The resolution and protest were the first volleys in the election of 1824. As its candidate for governor the Relief party chose General Joseph Desha, the farmer from the outer Bluegrass who had placed third in the election of 1820. A tall man with "small deep-sunken" eyes, he had fought in the Indian War of 1794 as well as the War of 1812. The Anti-Relief party nominated Christopher Tompkins, a well-known lawyer from central Kentucky, who had been elected to the legislature when he was only twenty-five. He had no military record. Later in the year a third candidate, William Russell, entered the race.[2]

Although a true party system had yet to develop, the leadership of the two parties revealed deep differences. Those in command of the Relief party were invariably lifetime Republicans, half had served in the War of 1812, almost all lived near Frankfort in the second tier of counties north and west of Lexington, and only one could be considered a member of the wealthy elite. On the other hand about half of the Anti-Relief leaders had been Federalists, none had been in the war, half lived in the heart of the Bluegrass near Lexing-

1. The Reliefers lost the election for speaker and could not prevent the repeal of the Replevin Act, which had run its course. *Argus,* 15 Oct. 1823, 7 Jan. 1824; House, *Journal,* 1823, 295–97; Senate, *Journal,* 1823, 214–20; Stickles, *Critical Court Struggle,* 39; *Niles' Register* 25 (1823–24): 275.

2. Desha was committed to relief and had carried five of the leading relief counties in 1820. Earl Gregg Swem, ed., *Letters on the Condition of Kentucky in 1825* (New York, 1916), 15–16; Mathias and Shannon, "Gubernatorial Politics," 249.

ton, and half were men of wealth. In short the Relief leadership was closer to the small-farm, small-business, militaristic tradition in the Kentucky hinterland than was that of the Anti-Relief party, which related better to the plantation, commercial world of Lexington.[3]

Kendall ran the Relief campaign, which meant that he orchestrated the party message, edited the party newspaper, communicated with other editors and politicians, helped select and advise candidates, organized party dinners and parades, got people to vote, and kept track of the voting during the three-day election. It was the first time he had been given such overall control of a real party. His immediate task was to shape a message. Realizing that the public was tired of complex economic issues, he went in search of a simple democratic theme that would appeal to the majority.

The inspiration for the theme came from two dinners. At the first, on January 17, 1824, about fifty members of the Anti-Relief party gathered at Washington Tavern in Lexington to honor the wealthy lawyer, planter, and legislator Robert Wickliffe. Two of the most striking toasts were one giving thanks to the Kentucky judiciary and another asking the Lord to "have mercy upon [the] transgressions" of the Relief party. A week later about 150 Relief men came to the same tavern to honor retiring lieutenant governor William T. Barry. This time the toasts called the judges "the essence of aristocracy" and the people the "source of all rightful power."[4]

Another Relief toast caught Kendall's attention. The people of Kentucky, it went, knew how badly "the Holy Allies of Europe" and "the Aristocrats and Monarchists of America" had treated the majority of the people on the two continents. The toast referred to the so-called Holy Alliance of European powers, which was resisting liberal uprisings on the continent. Kendall was intrigued. Only a few weeks earlier he had praised President Monroe for his

3. This comparison was based on a study of ten leaders in each party. The ten Relief leaders were Adair, Barry, Bibb, Blair, Desha, Kendall, Johnson, Attorney General Solomon P. Sharp, lieutenant governor nominee Robert McAfee, and soon to be elected U.S. senator John Rowan. The Anti-Relief leaders were Clay, Pope, Tompkins, Wickliffe, Humphrey Marshall, state representative Robert J. Breckinridge, Judge James Clark, Frankfort lawyer John J. Crittenden, Congressman Ben Hardin, and House Speaker George Robertson. Of the Reliefers only Rowan was from the elite and only Barry from the heart of the Bluegrass. The only Anti-Reliefer from the second tier was Crittenden.

4. *Argus,* 4 Feb. 1824; Billie J. Hardin, "Amos Kendall and the 1824 Relief Controversy," *Register* 64 (1966): 200–201.

doctrine warning the Alliance not to interfere in the Americas. He had found his theme: the rights of the common people were being threatened by a dangerous, aristocratic conspiracy. He would link it to the Holy Alliance.[5]

In the next few weeks Kendall wrote a series of editorials, which he called "Wictorian Dinner: An 'Expose' of the minority 'System' of Kentucky; Or The curtain drawn from the Holy Alliance of America." The word "Wictorian" was apparently taken from the name of the chief villain, Robert Wickliffe. The first chapter was the best. After describing how "the priests, monks, friars, bigots and nobles" of Europe had prevented "government of the people," he warned that a similar Holy Alliance—the BUS, the Supreme Court, and the Kentucky court of appeals—was doing the same in Kentucky. Their wealthy representatives had sat at the Wictorian dinner plotting to undermine democracy in the state. He went on to give inflated estimates of just how rich they were. Wickliffe was supposedly worth half a million dollars; officers of the Lexington branch of the BUS represented a million; and another group of bankers was put at two million. The three succeeding chapters were in the same vein. Much of this of course was hokum—what connection did the Holy Alliance have with Kentucky?—but the essays attracted attention because they were aimed at the ordinary voter, made fun of rich people, and tapped into a powerful American feeling of resentment against wealth and power.[6]

The message of a second series, written by Francis P. Blair, was similar to that of the first, but not the style. Kendall delighted in long essays, elaborate metaphors, involved, complex sentences, and witty phrases. Blair wrote short essays, with short sentences and blunt opinions. Using terms from the revolutionary era, he called the Anti-Reliefers the Court party and the Reliefers the Country party. This was a false analogy because the Reliefers, who had been in power for four years, were the Court or central party. But Kendall's readers understood Blair's point: The Anti-Relief party "love[d] great men," while the Relief party considered the people "the source of all power."[7]

The final two series, undoubtedly by Kendall, continued the theme of court and country. The essays traced the origins of the relief struggle back to the battle between the Court party and the Country party in England, and

5. *Argus*, 17 Dec. 1823.

6. Ibid., 11, 18, 25 Feb., 3 Mar. 1824; Hardin, "Amos Kendall and the 1824 Relief Controversy," 201–2.

7. *Argus*, 30 Jan., 25 Feb., 3, 10, 17, 24 Mar. 1824.

followed it through the struggle between monarchists and antimonarchists in the colonies and between Federalists and Republicans in the republic. Since both of the Kentucky parties consisted almost entirely of Republicans and neither supported monarchism, these analogies were as specious as Blair's.[8]

But the theme was strong. Like most politicians at the time, Kendall and Blair were identifying the Relief party with republican concepts. Their party, they said, was fighting to preserve purity and liberty against corrupt, Anti-Relief conspirators. The principal enemies, the BUS and the "rich and well born" aristocrats, were relying on the courts to crush farmers and debtors. Kendall added the patriotic argument that the BUS was under the influence of foreign stockholders. Again the arguments defy logic. Kendall himself had been no friend of debtors during most of the panic, and the Anti-Relief party also believed that it was protecting the people. As for the Holy Alliance, no one was more opposed to it than Anti-Relief man Henry Clay. As Kendall was writing the "Wictorian Dinner," Clay was in Congress attacking the Alliance for threatening Greek independence.[9]

Kendall used republican words because he felt comfortable with them, but he was also becoming the master of a new democratic language. Like other democratic writers he replaced the old deferential, formal style with one using nicknames, slogans, humorous and lighthearted attacks, intimate glimpses of friends and foes, peppered from time to time with familiar biblical and Shakespearean references. Citing the net worth of his opponents was a good example. This combination of old and new language became the standard political style of antebellum America.[10]

The message got through, and the readers responded favorably. They accused the Anti-Relief party of "intrigue, cunning and deception" and thanked Kendall for his "bold stand" in defense of "the rights . . . of the people." It is entirely possible, as an opposition editor alleged, that Kendall wrote some of

8. Ibid., 17 Mar.–28 July 1824. The four series appeared in twenty-seven installments containing some 115,000 words.

9. Amos Kendall [Patrick Henry], *The Wictorian Dinner* (Frankfort, 1824), iv; Remini, *Henry Clay*, 222.

10. In this section I have drawn on Major L. Wilson, "The 'Country' Versus the 'Court': A Republican Consensus and Party Debate in the Bank War," *JER* 15 (1995): 619–47, especially 644–47; and Andrew W. Robertson, *The Language of Democracy: Political Rhetoric in the United States and Britain, 1790–1900* (Ithaca, 1995), 68–81.

these letters himself, but he denied it and had them reprinted in other Relief party newspapers. Further evidence of Kendall's success can be inferred from the irate response of the Anti-Relief men, who dubbed him "Poor Amos the Yankee, . . . the lying editor," and on one occasion waylaid him and beat him with a cane.[11]

Final proof came in the election. Again Kendall contributed to getting out a large vote, though the turnout (69 percent) was lower than the 74 percent in 1820, when the panic brought so many Kentuckians to the polls. Desha won almost 60 percent of the vote, far greater than Adair's plurality of 33 percent in 1820. Public anger over the court decisions played a part in the result, as did the reduction in the number of candidates from four to three. But the size of the victory was mainly because of Kendall's democratic message.[12]

The results of the presidential election were less clear-cut. Of the four candidates in 1824 only Henry Clay and Andrew Jackson were running in Kentucky. The absence of a valid party system in the state can be seen in the inability of the Relief party to agree on whom to support. Kendall and his friends Barry, Blair, and Johnson remained committed to Clay, while others—Desha, Bibb, and Attorney General Solomon P. Sharp—were Jacksonians. Forerunners of a party system can be seen, however, in the county and district meetings held by both the Clay and Jackson parties.[13]

Although Clay carried the state easily with a 73 percent majority, Jackson had pockets of strength in Kentucky that later developed into Democratic strongholds. The strongest were two counties in the outer Bluegrass: Jefferson County, which included Louisville, and Campbell County, across the Ohio River from Cincinnati. Jackson would have done even better if he had had Kendall's support. Kendall, however, stood by Clay, describing him as "the

---

11. *Argus*, 3, 31 Mar., 12, 19 ("intrigue") May, 2, 9, 16, 23 June, 7 July, 25 Aug. 1824; *Danville Advertiser*, quoted in Arndt M. Stickles, *Eminent Early Kentuckians* (Frankfort, n.d.) ("Poor").

12. Mathias and Shannon, "Gubernatorial Politics," 249–50. Desha's identification with the Relief movement contributed to his victory. There was a strong correlation between Desha's best counties and the strongest Relief counties. Marshall, "Genesis of Grass-Roots Democracy," 275–76.

13. *Argus*, 21 Nov. 1822, 30 Apr., 4, 11 June 1823, 24 Apr., 28 July, 4, 11 Aug., 6, 20, 27 Oct. 1824; Johnson to John J. Crittenden, 7 Mar. 1824, Richard M. Johnson, "The Letters of Colonel Richard M. Johnson of Kentucky," ed. James A. Padgett, *Register* 39 (1941): 187; Richard P. McCormick, *The Second American Party System: Party Formation in the Jacksonian Era* (Chapel Hill, 1966), 214–15.

Grecian Pericles, without his propensity to war" as opposed to Jackson the military man. He also protected Clay by maintaining the myth that he was not committed to either side in the Relief War. As a result Clay won 94 percent of the vote in Franklin County.[14]

The 1824 elections had a powerful effect on Kentucky politics. Adapting the term "Court party" that Kendall and Blair had introduced, the Reliefers demanded that the new administration "drive" the "old court" judges from office and set up a "new court." Before long the party names New Court and Old Court had replaced Relief and Anti-Relief. Desha took office convinced that he had a popular mandate to get rid of the old court of appeals. At the same time the emergence of the Jackson and Clay organizations in the presidential election added a national dimension to state politics and speeded up the realignment of parties.[15]

Kendall was finally on good terms with a governor. Desha said that he liked Kendall because he "appeared disposed to be very friendly, and was of my own politics." Afraid that "grammatical errors" might creep into his message to the legislature, he asked Kendall to go over it and correct any mistakes. Kendall agreed at once, saying that they "must swim or sink together." He now had a relationship much more equal than the one with Clay and one that prepared him for his future work as adviser and speechwriter for Jackson.[16]

The team of Desha and Kendall was another step toward a party system. Though less famous and less of an icon than Adair, Desha was a better party leader. In fact he was so partisan and stubborn that he never became very popular. As one observer noted, his enemies said "many harsh things of him" and even his friends said "but little for him." After a year of Desha's "obstinacy & perversity," Old Court state representative John J. Crittenden swore that he could not "live under [such] domination." Kendall soon found how stubborn the new governor could be. After thanking him for his editing, Desha promptly restored much of the original wording. As a result, the message

14. Jasper B. Shannon and Ruth McQuown, *Presidential Politics in Kentucky, 1824–1848* (Lexington, 1950), 1–3; *Argus*, 18 Feb., 5 May 1824. Kendall's attack on Jackson as a military man is a good example of the "anti-image" M. J. Heale describes in *The Presidential Quest: Candidates and Images in American Political Culture, 1787–1852* (London, 1982), 188–212.

15. *Argus*, 8, 22 Sept., 3 Nov. 1824; Stickles, *Critical Court Struggle*, 49.

16. *Argus*, 8 Sept. 1824; Desha to Kendall, 6 May 1831, "Correspondence between Governor Joseph Desha and Amos Kendall—1831–1835," ed. James A. Padgett, *Register* 38 (1940): 9–10.

lacked Kendall's distinctive rhetoric and, surprisingly, said nothing about the court of appeals.[17]

The legislative session got off to a terrifying start. Early in the morning of November 4 a fire broke out in the capitol building, burning it to the ground. Forced to move to a nearby church, the legislature was slow dealing with the question of the court of appeals. The New Court party finally got a vote on removing the justices but again failed to muster a two-thirds majority. The party then offered a bill reorganizing the court—a procedure that got rid of the justices and required only a majority vote. The bill passed and was taken up by the house on December 21. An angry debate ensued. What had started as an effort to discipline justices had become—in the minds of the Old Court party—a devious, radical attempt to overturn the constitution. After three days of wrangling, the bill finally passed early in the morning of December 24. Old Kentuckians later recalled it as Christmas Eve.[18]

Kendall was exuberant. In addition to reorganizing the appeals court, his party had recovered the speakership of the house and had returned all of the printing to the *Argus*. His friends Barry and Blair were named chief justice and clerk of the new court. Kendall warned the old justices that if they resisted, the governor would call out the militia and scatter them. When they refused to give up their records, Blair climbed into the court office through a back window and stole the books.[19]

The New Court hubris was short-lived. Soon after the New Year 1825 the Old Court leaders took a leaf from Kendall's book and appealed to the people. Calling the Reorganization Act unconstitutional, they promised to protect the people by defending the constitution and held protest meetings in at least sixteen Bluegrass counties, many of which had supported Desha. The justices of the old appeals court refused to step down and made plans to hold their regu-

17. Swem, *Letters,* 14–15; Crittenden to Clay, 26 Dec. 1825, Clay, *Papers,* 4:948; "Correspondence between Governor Joseph Desha and Amos Kendall," 9; Desha, "Governor's Message," 1 Nov. 1824, in *Argus,* 3 Nov. 1824.

18. There was another way to remove the judges—amending the constitution—but that would also have taken a two-thirds vote. *Argus,* 3, 10 Nov. 1824; John Harvie to Clay, 4 Nov. 1824, Clay, *Papers,* 3:878–80; House, *Journal,* 1824, 437–38, 440–41, 454; Senate, *Journal,* 1824, 241; Stickles, *Critical Court Struggle,* 47–51; Swem, *Letters,* 7, 20–29.

19. Stickles, *Critical Court Struggle,* 57–62; *Argus,* 5 Jan. 1825; Smith, *Francis Preston Blair,* 20–21.

lar session in the fall. Adopting the watchword "victory or death," the Old Court party vowed to give "no quarter" in the next election.[20]

The party received unexpected help from the ugly case of Governor Desha's son Isaac, who had been arrested the previous fall on charges of robbery and murder. After the trial was moved to a court close to the governor's home, Isaac was found guilty, only to have the judge order a new trial. Old Court men promptly accused him of repaying the governor for past favors and predicted that if the young man was ever convicted, his father would pardon him. The judge was burned in effigy, and the case became a heavy liability for the New Court party.[21]

A more complex problem for Kendall was his relationship with Henry Clay. In the 1824 presidential election Jackson had won a plurality in the electoral vote but lacked the necessary majority. The election went to the U.S. House of Representatives, which had to choose from the three leading candidates—Jackson, John Quincy Adams, and William H. Crawford. Each state delegation would have one vote. Clay had been eliminated, but since he had carried Kentucky, Missouri, and Ohio, he was in a position to influence the delegations from those states and thus decide the election. Because popular sentiment in Kentucky strongly favored Jackson over Adams and Crawford, the state legislature passed a resolution calling on Clay and the other Kentucky congressmen to cast the state's vote for Old Hickory. Kendall pressed Clay to announce that he was for Jackson.[22]

Clay, however, ignored the advice. On January 8, 1825, he wrote Blair saying that he intended to vote for Adams, not because he preferred him but because he was the better "choice of evils." He asked Blair and his friends to encourage their congressmen to do the same. When told about the request, Kendall faced a difficult decision. He wanted to maintain his connection with Clay, but if he did, he risked alienating many of his friends who were moving to Jackson. Choosing to stick with Clay, Kendall wrote to his congressman, David White, urging him to vote for Adams.[23]

20. Swem, *Letters*, 29; Stickles, *Critical Court Struggle*, 59, 66; *Argus*, 23 Feb. 1825; George Robertson to Crittenden, 25 May 1825, John J. Crittenden Papers, LC (quotation); Kendall to Clay, 19 Feb. 1825, Clay, *Papers*, 4:78–79.

21. Jeanette H. McCarthy, "The Strange Case of Isaac Desha," *Register* 60 (1962): 293–303; Blair to Clay, 11 Feb. 1825, Clay, *Papers*, 4:64–67; *Argus*, 19 Jan., 9 Feb., 5 Oct. 1825; Stickles, *Critical Court Struggle*, 73.

22. Kendall to Clay, 22 Dec. 1824, Clay, *Papers*, 3:901–2.

23. Clay to Blair, 8 Jan. 1825, Blair to Clay, 24 Jan. 1825, ibid., 4:9–10, 41.

Meanwhile on January 9 Clay promised Adams that he would back him for president. A month later the House elected Adams, with the Kentucky delegation (including White) and the delegations from the other two Clay states voting in Adams's favor. Directly afterward Adams named Clay secretary of state. The series of events caused a tremendous uproar. Jacksonians denounced Clay for making a "corrupt bargain" with Adams. In Kentucky hundreds turned against him for disobeying the resolutions of the legislature, and more New Court politicians, including Johnson and Barry, went over to Jackson.[24]

Kendall and Blair remained loyal to Clay but were obviously discomfited. They told Clay that "the general impression [was] unfavorable" toward him and warned that Jackson was likely to win the next election. The motive behind Kendall's loyalty was financial. He wanted to protect his printing contract with Clay's State Department and hoped that Clay would give him a loan so that he could build his paper mill. There was also the chance that Clay would offer him a job in the State Department. Clay had reasons to cooperate. A loan would keep Kendall on his side in the next presidential election; a job in Washington would help the Old Court by getting Kendall out of the state.[25]

Kendall kept after Clay unabashedly. In February he warned Clay that the only reason he had not deserted him was his debt to Lucretia Clay. He described the loss of the Woolfolk money and asked Clay to be on the lookout for "any opportunity" that might be to his "advantage." In March he told Clay that he was finding it hard to "defend" him. Repeating the story of his hard luck, he said that he needed $2,000–$3,000 in order to "abandon all local party politics and spend the rest of [his] life on [his] farm."[26]

Responding to the pressure, Clay offered Kendall a position in the State Department at $1,000 a year, which Kendall considered inadequate. When they met in June, Clay loaned him $1,500 and repeated his offer of a job. There was no agreement on the latter, but during the state election campaign that summer Clay passed the word that Kendall was about to move to Washington. He was so convincing that Old Court leader George Robertson told his followers that "they would not have [Kendall] to contend with much longer."

24. Remini, *Henry Clay*, 252–67.

25. Ibid., 259; Kendall to Clay, 21 Jan., 19 (quotation), 20 Feb. 1825, Clay, *Papers*, 4:35, 77–79; Albert D. Kirwan, *John J. Crittenden: The Struggle for the Union* (Lexington, 1962), 71; *Argus*, 4 Feb., 23 Mar. 1825.

26. Kendall to Clay, 19 Feb. ("any"), 23 Mar. ("defend," "abandon") 1825, 11 Oct. 1826, Clay, *Papers*, 4:77–79, 134–36, 5:776.

Clay may have been stretching the truth for political purposes, but on the other hand Kendall may have left him with the false impression that he would accept the job. He actually had no intention of going to Washington, for he had borrowed $2,000 from his brother-in-law Thomas S. Page and planned to use the combined $3,500 to build the mill. Worried about the rumor, which suggested that he had been bought off, Kendall burned Clay's letters and later accused him of "interfer[ing]" in the election. Yet their relationship remained intact.[27]

The 1825 election was a great victory for the Old Court leaders. Their dramatic appeal and their protest meetings had convinced the public that Desha's party had acted arbitrarily in dismantling the court of appeals. Now they could claim that the Old Court was the party of the people. Desha's popularity declined when the state was unable to find a jury to try his son. Barry was heckled badly in Lexington, while Kendall was pilloried as a "broker in slander." Barely half a year after its Christmas Eve debacle, the Old Court party won back the house and held half the seats in the senate.[28]

As the public waited for the legislature to deal with the court issue, nothing was certain, and violence seemed possible. Two appeals courts were in session, and no one knew which would prevail. Despite its loss in August, the New Court party still controlled the executive, shared power in the senate, and even had an outside chance of electing one of its members—former attorney general Solomon P. Sharp—speaker of the house. Sharp, however, was being accused of having seduced a woman named Ann Cook and having fathered her stillborn child. Old Court editor Patrick Darby was spreading the seduction story in such lurid detail that a fight between him and Sharp seemed imminent. Public outrage grew when Isaac Desha was found guilty for the second time and once again the judge ordered a new trial. After threats were made against the two Deshas, the governor hired a bodyguard and was seen carrying "a huge pair of horse pistols" into church.[29]

27. Kendall to Clay, 28 Apr., 4 Oct. (quotations) 1825, ibid., 4:305–6, 718–20; *Argus*, 28 May 1828; Marshall, "Early Career," 340–41, 351–53; Remini, *Henry Clay*, 277–78.

28. *Danville Advertiser*, 18 Aug. 1825 (quotation), *Argus*, 11 May 1825, both from Hopson, notes for unfinished Ph.D. diss.; Stickles, *Critical Court Struggle*, 71, 81–83; Thomas Bodley to Clay, 23 Aug. 1825, Clay to Kendall, 18 Oct. 1825, Clay, *Papers*, 4:588, 746–48.

29. Connelley and Coulter, *History of Kentucky*, 2:637; *Argus*, 29 June, 13 July, 5, 19 Oct. (quotation), 30 Nov. 1825, 11 Jan., 22 Feb. 1826; J. W. Cooke, "'Pride and Depravity': A Preliminary Reexamination of the Beauchamp-Sharp Affair," *Border States* 6 (1987): 1–12; *Niles' Register* 29 (1825–26): 97–98; *Danville Advertiser*, 16 Sept. 1825, from Hopson, notes for unfinished Ph.D. diss.

At two in the morning on November 7, opening day of the legislature, the possibility of violence became reality. Sharp answered a knock at the door and was stabbed to death by an unknown assailant. In the legislature that day the news of the murder overshadowed everything else. Although most related it to Sharp's alleged seduction of Ann Cook, now Ann Beauchamp, many suspected that it had been planned by Sharp's Old Court enemies—most likely Patrick Darby. With Sharp dead, George Robertson of the Old Court party was quickly elected speaker.[30]

The grisly murder provided a grim setting for Desha's message to an already hostile legislature. The message, written by Kendall, was intensely partisan. Just as in the 1824 campaign, the governor seized the high ground by using republican language to accuse the Old Court of a conspiracy. The people, he said, were in a state of "agitation" because of threats to "the purity of their republican institutions." By foreclosing on loans, the BUS had turned farmers into "tenants" and had gained control of their vote—a "systematic attack" upon the legislature that was "nothing short of despotism." The governor refused to abandon the Reorganization Act and warned that if the old judges continued to resist, he would not "shrink" from enforcing it. The provocative words raised the hackles of Old Court men.[31]

They refused to be cowed. On November 14 they pushed a bill through the house repealing the Reorganization Act and two days later passed a series of sarcastic, tartly worded resolutions answering the governor's message. What were the "particular causes" of the "agitation"? What "real estate" had the BUS "seized," and could he name "their tenantry"? What proof did he have that the BUS "controlled" these tenants? Did he intend to call out the militia?[32]

Kendall replied evasively. He was disappointed that the resolutions showed so little respect for the governor. The causes of the "agitation" were so "obvious" that anyone not seeing them must "be ready to surrender our republican representative government." Though refusing to give names, he insisted that the BUS controlled its tenants because it had the power to "drive [them] from their homes." The war of words ended in a stalemate. The house tabled the governor's reply and cleared the BUS of any wrongdoing, but the

---

After being pardoned by his father in 1827, Isaac Desha went to New Orleans, where he killed another man, confessed both crimes, and died of fever. McCarthy, "Strange Case," 302.

30. Theodore W. Clay to Henry Clay, 11 Nov. 1825, Clay, *Papers,* 4:816–18; Fred M. Johnson, "New Light on Beauchamp's Confession?" *Border States* 12 (1993): 13.

31. Desha, "Governor's Message," 7 Nov. 1825, in House, *Journal,* 1825, 7–22.

32. House, *Journal,* 1825, 56–58, 88–91; *Niles' Register* 29 (1825–26): 228–29.

bill repealing the Reorganization Act failed in the senate. When the legislature adjourned on December 21, John J. Crittenden feared that "anarchy" was approaching.[33]

Amidst the turmoil Kendall was making plans to take a new wife. During the fall he had hired an unemployed papermaker named Alexander Kyle and was soon attracted to his daughter Jane, who was only seventeen, less than half Kendall's age. This time the courtship was far less romantic than it had been with Mary, for then he was seeking love, now he was looking for someone to care for his three children. Jane too may have had practical motives, for Amos could offer her many more comforts than she had at home. But there must also have been love and physical attraction because they had a long marriage and many children. They were married on January 5, 1826.[34]

There was no time for a honeymoon because Kendall was deeply immersed in the Sharp murder case. Suspicion had turned to Ann Beauchamp's husband, Jeroboam, whom she had married several years after having the stillborn child. There was a good possibility that she had goaded her husband, who was rather unstable, into murdering Sharp to avenge the seduction. He was arrested on November 12, 1825. Kendall thought that Beauchamp had committed the murder, not just for revenge but also because he was an ardent Old Court man and had been provoked by Patrick Darby. Already antagonistic toward Darby, Kendall threw himself into a vicious, personal war with the man, mocking his "sweet face" and calling him a "cats-paw" who consorted with prostitutes.[35]

Kendall's unrestrained, passionate efforts to show that Darby had collaborated in the murder—a charge that he could not document—reveal a man under a great deal of pressure. He was newly married, his party had been badly beaten, and the legislature had taken away his entire state printing contract. His mill was finally producing paper, but he was afraid that low water would

33. "Correspondence between Governor Joseph Desha and Amos Kendall," 8–10; Desha, *Governor's Message in Reply to the Resolutions Adopted in the House of Representatives on the Motion of Mr. Breckinridge* [14 Dec. 1825] (Frankfort, 1825), 1–17; *Niles' Register* 29 (1825–26): 292; Clay, *Papers*, 4:916n; Stickles, *Critical Court Struggle*, 84–91; Crittenden to Clay, 26 Dec. 1825, Clay, *Papers*, 4:948.

34. Kendall to Clay, 25 Dec. 1825, Clay, *Papers* 4:942–43; "Kentucky Marriages and Obituaries, 1787–1860," *Register* 36 (1938): 255.

35. Cooke, "'Pride and Depravity,'" 1–9; Johnson, "New Light?" 13–14; *Argus*, 9, 16, 23, 30 Nov. 1825. 11 ("sweet"), 25 Jan., 1, 8, 15, 22 Feb., 22, 29 Mar. 1826.

force him to close down later in the year. With so much going wrong, he became bitter and suspicious, accusing postmasters of holding up his mail and railing at merchants and lawyers who were suing him for small debts. He even claimed that the Old Court wanted to murder him.[36]

The outcome of the Beauchamp trial did not make Kendall feel any better. Beauchamp was found guilty and hanged on July 7. While awaiting execution, he wrote two confessions, the first implicating Darby but the second exonerating him. Darby promptly used the second confession to sue Kendall for libel. Kendall protested that he had never directly accused Darby of murder, but he had to admit that his suspicions had taken a "wrong direction." A long trial seemed in the offing.[37]

The Sharp murder case dominated the 1826 election. When it was finally over, the New Court had suffered another bad defeat, losing both houses. It was the worst campaign Kendall had run. By focusing attention on the Sharp murder and failing to prove his case, he lost any opportunity to debate the merits of the Reorganization Act. Whether the New Court could have won anyway is questionable. Already convinced that the Reorganization Act was unconstitutional, the public resented Desha's administration for blocking its repeal. Prosperity, furthermore, had returned to Kentucky, and the public wanted an end to the bickering.[38]

Kendall now felt more pressed than ever. He summed up his situation in a letter to Clay, asking him to renew the $1,500 loan. "The ill feeling generated by our political warfare," he complained, "has induced most of my political enemies to bring suits against me." Weary of political editing, he intended to sell his newspaper, pay off his debts, and get out of politics.[39]

Clay extended the loan, but the pressures continued, and Kendall soon succumbed. On September 6 the *Argus* tersely announced that he was suffering from a "severe indisposition"—later identified as "the flux" or violent diarrhea—that was keeping him from writing. But Kendall was sicker than that. Joseph Desha, who visited him several times, realized how "very low" he had

36. William B. Blackburn to Clay, 9 Dec. 1825, Clay, *Papers,* 4:888–89; *Argus,* 11 Jan., 1 Feb., 1, 29 Mar. 1826; Desha to Kendall, 6 May 1831, "Correspondence between Governor Joseph Desha and Amos Kendall," 11; Marshall, "Early Career," 371.

37. Cooke, "'Pride and Depravity,'" 9–10; *Argus,* 24, 31 May, 23 June, 12 July (quotation), 2 Aug. 1826.

38. Stickles, *Critical Court Struggle,* 103; *Niles' Register* 30 (1826): 5.

39. Kendall to Clay, 8 July 1826, Clay, *Papers,* 5:534–35.

sunk and for a while was afraid that his friend might die. Almost a month passed before he began to recover.[40]

During the first part of the Court War Kendall finally began to exert the "strong influence" in politics that he had boasted of so prematurely. He had built a political party, the New Court, with a mixture of republican and democratic ideas—liberty, egalitarianism, majority rule, states' rights, and opposition to corruption and privilege. In an age in which politics had become public entertainment, he knew how to appeal directly to the voters with imaginative stories and sharp personal attacks. But after his victory in the election of 1824 and the passing of the reorganization bill, his successes came to an end. Troubling questions arose: Was he a Clay man or a New Court man? Would he continue his political career or retire to his mill? Was he stable enough and committed enough to succeed in democratic politics?

40. *Argus,* 6 Sept. 1826; Kendall to Clay, 11 Oct. 1826, Clay, *Papers,* 5:776; Desha to Kendall, 6 May 1831, "Correspondence between Governor Joseph Desha and Amos Kendall," 13–14.

# 8

## JACKSON

Late in September Desha was happy to find that Kendall had "mended" enough to "walk about the house." For some time the governor and Richard M. Johnson had been trying to bring him into the Jackson camp. On being asked in August whether he would support Jackson or Adams in 1828, Kendall had snapped back that he intended to remain neutral. Still critical of Jackson, he said that he "disliked" the general's "violent . . . tyrannical disposition," his lack of "capacity," and his "moral character, particularly the way he obtained his wife."[1]

But the Jackson men thought they could bring him around. When Washington publisher Duff Green, an early Jackson supporter, visited Kentucky in September, several Jacksonians assured him that Kendall could be induced to join the party. Johnson said flatly that Kendall would come out for Old Hickory as soon as he could raise $1,500 to pay off his debt to Clay. Green did not talk with the sick Kendall, but he told Johnson that he was willing to advance the money.[2]

When Desha arrived to talk politics, Kendall was of several minds. He had never cared much for Jackson, and he valued his relationship with Adams's secretary of state Henry Clay. But he had also gone on record as a westerner opposed to Adams, and the chance to pay off his loan was appealing. Ideologically, he had started as a nationalist Republican in line with Adams and Clay but after 1819 had adopted the states' rights, strict constructionist views of many of the Jackson men.

In the end political pressure was decisive. Kendall was well aware that the

1. Desha to Kendall, 6 May 1831, "Correspondence between Governor Joseph Desha and Amos Kendall," 12–14.

2. Duff Green, *Facts and Suggestions, Biographical, Historical, Financial, and Political. Addressed to the People of the United States* (New York, 1866), 29; *Globe*, 8 Oct. 1834.

New Court party was losing its fight with the Old Court and needed the infusion of strength that the Jackson movement was bringing. He also knew that almost all of his New Court friends, now even Francis P. Blair, had gone over to Jackson. Desha increased the pressure. The Jacksonians, he said, already had newspapers in Louisville and Lexington and were determined to have "a thoroughgoing Jackson paper" in Frankfort. Either Kendall could come out for Jackson in the next two days or the Jacksonians would set up their own newspaper. Knowing that Frankfort was not big enough for another press, Kendall hesitated for only "a few moments" and then gave in. He told Desha that he suddenly felt "strong enough to write" and would "compose a column" supporting Jackson.[3]

On October 4 Kendall announced that he was backing Jackson because he considered the general's beliefs more Jeffersonian than the "consolidating principles" of Adams. Even now he refused to cut loose from Clay. He said that he owed much to the Clays and reminded his readers that while he had opposed Adams for president in 1824, he had backed Clay. To avoid any misunderstanding he wrote Clay, assuring him that he would never cast "any imputation" on his "integrity or honor." With this qualified endorsement of Jackson, Kendall became the last prominent public figure in Kentucky to go over to Old Hickory. The move was more out of weakness than strength.[4]

The local Jacksonians were delighted. Desha was confident that "however mincing" Kendall might be at first, he would soon "warm to the cause" and "do the subject justice." Johnson told Jackson cheerfully, "Kendall deserves great credit for his independence. He is equal to Duane at his best." This was strong praise, for William Duane had won Jackson's admiration when he was indicted under the Sedition Act for his Jeffersonian writings. The Adams men reacted differently. According to publisher William W. Worsley of Louisville, Kendall cared only for money and would "write for that man, or that party, which pays him best."[5]

Both sides overstated the case. Kendall was hardly being independent, and his decision was as much political as financial. In the short run the shift cost him money because it put his federal printing contract, worth $300 a year,

3. "Correspondence between Governor Joseph Desha and Amos Kendall," 14.

4. *Argus,* 4 Oct., 1 Nov. 1826; Kendall to Clay, 11 Oct. 1826, Clay, *Papers,* 5:776.

5. "Correspondence between Governor Joseph Desha and Amos Kendall," 15; Johnson to Jackson, 27 Oct. 1826, *Correspondence of Andrew Jackson,* ed. John Spencer Bassett and John Franklin Jameson, 7 vols. (1926–35; reprint, New York, 1969), 3:212; Worsley to Clay, 11 Dec. 1826, Clay, *Papers,* 5:989–92.

at risk. Henry Clay was already in the midst of a wholesale shakeup of newspaper patronage. By the end of the year he had removed contracts from thirty-three of the eighty-odd newspapers authorized to print the federal laws and had given them to friendly presses. On December 22 he canceled the *Argus* contract.[6]

Once the printing was removed, Kendall broke with Clay. The secretary, he announced defiantly, had cut the "family tie" and "turned [him] out," leaving him free to change his course. He would not let himself "be crushed by the wheels of [Clay's] ambition." It is worth noting that Clay did not reply. The end of the relationship, after all, meant far less to him than it did to Kendall. Clay had lost a useful but in his mind not especially important functionary; Kendall had lost a connection that he had cultivated for a dozen years.[7]

The break between the two men coincided with the end of the Court War. In the December session of the legislature a bill repealing the Reorganization Act was passed over Desha's veto. The session was humiliating for Kendall, who was subjected to frequent ridicule. Old Court legislators made a habit of mocking him as "Amos," uttering the name, as Kendall reported, with "a suitable grin, a significant gesture . . . followed by an eloquent pause."[8]

While Kendall was jumping on the Jackson bandwagon, a state two-party system was emerging. Richard P. McCormick has attributed the new system to the personal rivalry between Clay and Jackson, but it seems more likely that it was a direct continuation of the Old Court–New Court conflict. Both Kendall and Clay observed that New Court men were going over to Jackson and Old Court men to Adams. Clay's brother-in-law James Brown made the reasonable comment that New Court men had turned to the presidential contest to regain the power they had lost in the court fight. There was striking continuity among the party leaders of 1824. All nine of the surviving Relief leaders had become Jacksonians, and nine of the ten Anti-Reliefers, Adams men. The

6. *Argus,* 15 Nov. 1826, 10, 24 Jan. 1827; Culver H. Smith, *The Press, Politics, and Patronage: The American Government's Use of Newspapers, 1789–1875* (Athens, Ga., 1977), 256–57.

7. *Argus,* 10, 24 Jan., 7 Mar. 1827. Clay's supporters later attacked Kendall for ingratitude. In 1838 Harriet Martineau gave a garbled version of how the Clays rescued Kendall when he had the fever and then hired him as a tutor. The ungrateful Kendall later deserted to Jackson. Of course it was Lucretia Clay alone who hired Kendall and saved him from the fever—after he had worked at Ashland. Martineau, *Retrospect of Western Travel,* 1:259–60.

8. Stickles, *Critical Court Struggle,* 102–4; House, *Journal,* 1826, 173; Senate, *Journal,* 1826, 160; *Argus,* 13 Dec. 1826.

only exception was Anti-Reliefer John Pope, who had moved into the Jackson party.[9]

The Jackson men were already a step ahead of their opponents. In Jefferson County, one of the few carried by Jackson in 1824, Major Allan Campbell had formed a party with a central committee in Louisville and subcommittees in the wards and the militia companies. In November 1826 he put on a successful Jackson dinner at which New Court men and even a few from the Old Court got "tipsy" together. Porter Clay warned his brother that once the Jackson "Demegogus" got the people "arroused, you might as well attempt to control the currant of the Mississippi."[10]

Abandoning any thought he may have had of giving up politics, Kendall soon replaced Campbell as the most talked about Jackson man in Kentucky. Worsley wrote Clay to warn him that Kendall would be coming to Campbell's next Jackson dinner. Adams congressman Francis Johnson, who was running for reelection in southern Kentucky, complained that his opponent, Joel Yancey, was riding about the district reading selections from "Amos" to the people. Johnson was afraid that the "Frankfort junto" of Kendall and Blair would replace Yancey with a stronger candidate once Yancey had stirred the people up. Kendall complained so much about losing the printing that the Adams party suspected correctly that he was using the "*Amos* affair" to win the sympathy of the public.[11]

Kendall's maneuvers were worth reporting because the Kentucky election of 1827 was considered a preview of the coming presidential election. With Adams assured of sweeping New England and Jackson expected to carry Pennsylvania and the South, Kentucky was one of three important swing states, Ohio and New York the others. The election had added significance because Kentucky would be choosing congressmen as well as state officials. Clay promised that the Kentucky Adams party would gain seats in Congress.[12]

9. McCormick, *Second American Party System*, 209–10; *Argus*, 28 Feb. 1827; John J. Marshall to Clay, 5 Jan. 1827, Clay to James Brown, 27 Mar. 1827, Brown to Clay, 12 June 1827, Clay, *Papers*, 6:16–17, 361, 666. For the continuity thesis see Everett W. Kindig, "Western Opposition to Jackson's 'Democracy': The Ohio Valley as a Case Study, 1827–1836" (Ph.D. diss., Stanford University, 1974), 149–59. For the analysis of party leaders in 1824 see chapter 7, pp. 81–82.

10. Campbell to Jackson, 4 Feb. 1827, Andrew Jackson Papers, LC; McCormick, *Second American Party System*, 216; Worsley to Clay, 3 Nov. 1826, Porter Clay to Clay, 22 Feb. 1827, Clay, *Papers*, 5:861, 6:223.

11. Worsley to Clay, 3 Nov. 1826, Thomas Metcalfe to Clay, 31 Mar. 1827, Francis Johnson to Clay, 8 Apr. 1827, Clay, *Papers*, 5:861, 6:381, 413.

12. Clay to John W. Taylor, 4 Apr. 1827, Clay, *Papers*, 6:395; *Argus*, 3 Oct. 1827. The Kentucky congressional elections had been shifted from the even-numbered to the odd-numbered years and the next election moved from 1826 to 1827.

During the election Kendall spent far more time writing partisan articles than he did discussing issues. When the Adams newspapers called Old Hickory a gambler, Kendall retorted that Jackson had gambled only as a youth, while Adams had gambled at billiards in the President's House. He denounced an article in the *Frankfort Commentator* describing Jackson's marriage to Rachel as adulterous even though he had once made similar comments himself. He also defended Jackson against the charge that he had illegally executed six militiamen. Then taking the offensive, he repeated the story that Adams had once procured a woman for the czar of Russia.[13]

This sort of partisan writing encouraged Kendall's enemies to call him a hack journalist. John Quincy Adams described him as an "author to be let," and Virginia congressman Henry A. Wise later referred to him as "a pen for the political malice of Mr. Clay's party." If so, Kendall was not alone. The election of 1828 brought to the fore on both sides dozens of aggressive newspapermen, whose slashing, no-holds-barred style has often aroused contempt. Among the most effective Jacksonians were Isaac Hill of the *New-Hampshire Patriot,* who introduced the story of the czar, and Duff Green of the *United States Telegraph,* who spread the charge that Clay had bargained with Adams. They were matched by Adams men Charles Hammond of the *Cincinnati Gazette,* who started the adultery charge, and John Binns of the *Philadelphia Democratic Gazette,* who circulated thousands of handbills depicting the coffins of the militiamen.[14]

These men were much more than hacks. In the years following the Constitutional Convention the political press became a central institution in the American political system and its editors key political figures. They spoke for their party, established the party line, defended the party candidates, and attacked their opponents—the sort of duties Kendall was performing in Kentucky. They must be judged in the context of the moralistic, religious, and changing age in which they were living. With their intuitive understanding of the popular mind, they were able to shape election debates by making and responding to moral charges that the public took seriously. Often ruthless but not unprincipled, they used the press to build parties and in so doing spread democracy.[15]

Of all the partisan attacks in the Kentucky campaign, the bargain charge was the most important. The charge was broadened in March 1827 when Clay

13. *Argus,* 8, 15, 29 Nov. 1826, 2, 28 Feb., 7, 14 Mar., 18 Apr., 8 Aug. 1827.

14. Adams, *Memoirs,* 8:28; Henry A. Wise, *Seven Decades of the Union* (Philadelphia, 1871), 117.

15. For a perceptive reconsideration of the partisan press see Pasley, *"Tyranny of Printers,"* 1–23.

was accused of having bargained with Jackson as well as Adams. According to the story, Clay had offered to support Jackson in 1825 if the latter promised not to keep Adams as secretary of state. Jackson endorsed the charge and said that he had rejected the offer. As soon as Clay reached Lexington in late May, he published an "indignant denial," and two weeks later he repeated it at a dinner for a thousand of his followers.[16]

But the election hinged more on party rallies and Jackson's military reputation than on anything else. In late July William T. Barry stirred up a crowd of three thousand with a bold speech praising Jackson as a war hero. On the eve of the election, which was held August 6–8, several thousand Jackson men almost caused a riot when they paraded through Lexington wearing hickory leaves on their hats. The momentum carried the Jacksonians to victory. They pulled even in the house, improved their position in the senate, and increased the number of their congressmen from four to seven in a delegation of twelve. On hearing the news, Charles Hammond told Clay sarcastically that the result was not "as favorable as [Clay had] anticipated."[17]

Buoyed by his first victory in three years, Kendall turned to national politics. Just after the Kentucky election Congressman James Buchanan of Pennsylvania, who had brought the offer from Clay to Jackson, embarrassed Old Hickory by admitting that Clay had never made such an offer. Seeing an opportunity to get into the controversy and divert attention from Buchanan's gaffe, Kendall announced on August 22 that he and others knew beforehand about the bargain between Adams and Clay. He was basing his statement on what Blair had told him in 1825 after receiving Clay's letter saying that he intended to vote for Adams. Kendall was manipulating the facts. He had not read the letter himself, and the letter said nothing specific about Clay's becoming secretary of state. He also hid the fact that if there had been a bargain, he was part of it because he had urged his congressman to vote for Adams rather than Jackson.[18]

On the same day Kendall sent his first letter to Jackson. The timing was exquisite. Jackson was disturbed by Buchanan's admission and was ready for any revelation about Clay. In addition he was excited about the Kentucky elec-

16. Remini, *Henry Clay,* 317–18; Clay, "Address," 29 June 1827, "Speech at Lexington," 12 July 1827, Clay, *Papers,* 6:728–30, 763–77.

17. *Argus,* 25 July, 15, 22 Aug., 5 Sept. 1827; Thomas Smith to Clay, 1 Aug. 1827, Hammond to Clay, 10 Aug. 1827, Clay, *Papers,* 6:839–41, 876–77. Congressional Quarterly, *Guide to United States Elections,* 3d ed. (Washington, D.C., 1994), 948.

18. *Argus,* 1, 22 Aug. 1827; Remini, *Henry Clay,* 319; Clay to Blair, 8 Jan. 1825, Clay, *Papers,* 4:9–11.

tion, which showed, he said, that the "free men" of Kentucky had refused to "yield to the mandates of *a dictator*." Although he did not know Kendall personally, he knew enough about him to say once that he was "*an able writer*." Kendall wrote brashly that he had published the editorial in order to "sustain" Jackson because he was "embarrassed" by the way in which the general's advisers, including Duff Green, had handled the Buchanan affair. He sent a second letter five days later reassuring Old Hickory that the Buchanan fiasco had raised more doubts about the Adams men than about the Jacksonians. Kendall was not only trying to ingratiate himself with Jackson but also hoped to convince the general that the bargain charge was still a good weapon, and he wanted to involve the Kentucky party in the national campaign.[19]

Once Kendall had reopened the bargain charge, he was harshly attacked by Adams editors, who said that he had "put himself up to the highest bidder, and was knocked down to Jackson." He retaliated by starting a series of letters to Clay that would appear in the *Argus* over the next year. In the first letter, on September 26, he repeated what he had told Jackson—that he had learned from a "confidential friend" that Clay would be made secretary of state. In the second, two weeks later, he put the blame on Clay for reviving the subject. Kendall would use his letters to drag out the bargain charge through the entire campaign.[20]

During these months of partisan charges, Kendall had been engaged in reorganizing the state party. On August 20, two days before he wrote to Old Hickory, a central committee of twenty Jackson men, including Kendall and Blair, sat down to prepare for the 1828 gubernatorial and presidential elections. Because presidential electors would now be chosen on a statewide basis instead of by districts, the Jacksonians had to pull their loosely connected militia, county, and district units into a tightly knit statewide structure. Under Kendall's guidance, a centralized party began to take shape. A central committee, already dubbed the "Frankfort Junto," would control county committees through special "trusty agents." Within the counties local subcommittees would choose delegates for county conventions, which in turn would select delegates for a state nominating convention. The Jacksonians would use this democratic organization to choose candidates and get out the voters.[21]

19. Jackson to William Moore, 4 Jan. 1827, Jackson to John McLean, 21 Aug. 1827, Kendall to Jackson, 22, 27 Aug. 1827, *The Papers of Andrew Jackson*, ed. Harold D. Moser et al., 6 vols. to date (Knoxville, 1994–), 6:251, 379–84.

20. *Argus*, 19 ("put"), 26 Sept. ("confidential"), 10 Oct. 1827.

21. Ibid., 5 Sept. 1827; McCormick, *Second Party System*, 216–18; Kendall to Blair, 9 Jan. 1829, Blair-Lee Papers, Manuscripts Division, Department of Rare Books and Special Collections, Princeton University Library ("trusty").

They went into action in September. On the tenth, seven hundred Jackson men attended a barbecue at Cedar Cove near Frankfort, where they marched, gave toasts, and passed resolutions. Then on the twenty-sixth, the same day as the first letter to Clay, Kendall made a dramatic announcement in the *Argus*. Warning conspiratorially that the Adams party was "secretly organiz[ing]," he called on the Jacksonians to take "public measures to counteract" this plot. He asked all friends of Jackson to form county committees and prepare for a state convention on January 8, 1828, the anniversary of the Battle of New Orleans.[22]

The revitalized party had much in common with Jackson organizations in New Hampshire and New York. At the top, the Frankfort Junto was comparable to Isaac Hill's Concord Regency in New Hampshire and Martin Van Buren's Albany Regency in New York. Each was controlled by a small group of leaders, drawn generally from lawyers, editors, small bankers and businessmen, men socially below the aristocracy of the state. The three parties all adhered to Jeffersonian principles and operated through party patronage, a party press, and an intricate system of committees.

Most important, the leaders of the three groups shared a common faith in the value of political parties. Casting aside the eighteenth-century notion that parties were designed only to serve the interests of their leaders, they portrayed them as valuable institutions that would protect the nation from dangerous men, reduce sectionalism, and spread democracy. Van Buren and the Albany Regency have received most of the credit for these ideas, but many editors in a number of organizations shared the belief. Although fiercely devoted to the Jackson party, Hill thought it was better for a voter to support his opponents rather than remain impartial. He "view[ed] the idea of an impartial paper as preposterous." Kendall's description of a centuries-long struggle between the party of the aristocracy and the party of the common people was almost identical with Van Buren's view of parties in *The Origin and Course of Political Parties in the United States*.[23]

Kendall, Hill, and Van Buren were themselves much alike. They had been brought up in poor-to-middling, farming families on the edges of Massachu-

22. *Argus*, 12, 19, 26 Sept. 1827; McCormick, *Second American Party System*, 216–18.

23. There were also strong Jackson parties in Virginia and Tennessee. Donald B. Cole, *Martin Van Buren and the American Political System* (Princeton, 1984), 96–98; Richard Hofstadter, *The Idea of a Party System: The Rise of Legitimate Opposition in the United States, 1780–1840* (Berkeley, 1969), 242–71; Pasley, *"Tyranny of Printers,"* 21–22, 354 (quotation); Martin Van Buren, *Inquiry into the Origin and Course of Political Parties in the United States* (1867; reprint, New York, 1967).

setts, Kendall and Hill on the New Hampshire border, Van Buren just across the border in New York. They were little men, highly intelligent, crafty, insecure about their place in society, eager to make money, and above all inordinately ambitious. But their personalities differed. Hill, who was crippled as a child and whose father was insane, grew up harsh and vindictive; while Van Buren, whose good-natured father ran a tavern, was amiable and gracious. Kendall, a deacon's son, was never as bitter as Hill, or as charming as Van Buren. Hill would become a senator and governor, Van Buren was already a senator and would some day be president, but Kendall never aspired to such positions.

Kendall's interest in bringing Kentucky into the national Jackson movement can be seen in his effort to get William T. Barry to run for governor. He considered Barry, who lived in Lexington, the best person to heal a growing rift between the Frankfort wing of the party, led by Kendall, Blair, Johnson, Desha, and Lieutenant Governor Robert McAfee, and the Louisville wing, headed by John Pope, editor Shadrach Penn, Senator John Rowan, and Congressman Charles A. Wickliffe. McAfee and Pope both wanted to run, but Kendall thought they would destroy party unity, especially Pope, who had been causing him trouble for years.[24]

In a letter on September 17, Kendall told Barry that if he carried Kentucky, Jackson would win the presidential election, and Barry would have "saved his country." And if he lost, he could count on "the aid of [his] friends" and the "favorable feelings" of Jackson. Kendall was trying to convince Barry to run by appealing to his patriotism and by holding out the prospect of federal patronage, both of which depended on a link between the Kentucky and the national parties. He could not, however, get Barry to make an immediate decision.[25]

To strengthen the link Kendall decided to go to Washington and talk with the party leaders. The trip would also give him a chance to see about the loan that Green had promised. With debts now in excess of $7,000 and still growing, he was very much in need of cash. The only good financial news he had had recently was that Patrick Darby had dropped his libel suit.

During the first part of the journey, which took him to Cleveland, Buf-

24. Kendall to Barry, 17 Sept. 1827, Andrew J. Donelson Papers, LC. The hostility between the two groups can be seen in John Pope to Jackson, 19 Feb. 1829, and Worden Pope to Jackson, 31 May 1829, Jackson Papers.

25. Kendall to Barry, 17 Sept. 1827, Donelson Papers.

falo, Albany, and New York, he had a firsthand look at the stunning improvements in transportation—the carefully crowned macadam roads in Ohio, the
National Road, which had reached Zanesville, Ohio, the Erie Canal, and the
steamboats on the Hudson. The canal boats with their heated cabins, he
wrote, offered "the most comfortable way of travelling in the world." He
mused that the canal would give New York such economic power that it would
soon control western trade and become "dangerous, perhaps, to the Union."
He was thinking like a southerner.[26]

And like a slaveowner as well. After owning slaves for seven or eight
years, Kendall had become as paternalistic as a southern planter, describing
himself as a kind master who treated his "negroes" as though they were his
"children." Thus on his way through Ohio he was perturbed to meet a "bitter
enemy of all slaveholders," who insisted that no one owning slaves could be a
true Christian. Kendall hotly replied with one of the standard proslavery arguments of the day. Although he did not believe that anyone should be enslaved
permanently, he opposed emancipation until "negroes could, in some way, be
separated from whites." Kentucky would free its slaves, he said, if Ohio would
receive them. He doubted whether "those who are loud for emancipation
would like to have our freed slaves for their neighbors."[27]

Reaching New York on November 10, Kendall tried to see Van Buren
about his loan but had to be satisfied with leaving him a letter. He then headed
north for a visit in Dunstable. Thirty-eight years old, he had not been home
for almost fourteen years. His moving description of the final few hours of his
journey shows how wrenching an experience it had become. Although not an
emotional man, he started to cry when he saw his mother and father at the
window of the old farmhouse. His mother, who was sixty-eight, looked the
same, but his father, four years older, had failed badly, had lapses of memory,
and could barely get about, his eyes so dim that he did not recognize his son.[28]

26. *Argus*, 20, 27 June 1827, 12, 19 Mar. 1828; Melton, "Amos Kendall in Kentucky," 203–5;
Kendall to Clay, 8 July 1826, Robert Scott to Clay, 3 Sept. 1827, Clay, *Papers*, 5:535 n. 3, 6:993;
Robert Johnston to Jane Kendall, 18 Oct. 1827, Amos Kendall Papers, Dartmouth College Library;
"Letters from Amos Kendall," 14, 17 Oct., 16 Nov. 1827, in *Argus*, 24 Oct., 6 Dec. ("dangerous")
1827; Kendall to Jane Kendall, 25 Oct., 7 ("the most"), 15 Nov. 1827, in *Autobiography*, 270–74.

27. "Letter from Kendall," 17 Oct. 1827, in *Argus*, 24 Oct. 1827; Kendall to Clay, 8 July 1826,
Clay, *Papers*, 5:534.

28. Kendall to Jane Kendall, 15 Nov. 1827, in *Autobiography*, 272–74; Kendall to Van Buren, 10
Nov. 1827, Martin Van Buren Papers, LC; "Letter from Kendall," 16 Nov. 1827, in *Argus*, 6 Dec.
1827.

Three weeks later on December 3, Kendall took the stagecoach from Boston to Albany, visited two of his brothers, and continued, almost entirely by steamboat, to Washington. The speed of transportation was noticeable; between New York and Washington he spent only two days of actual travel compared to four and a half in 1814. When he arrived on December 14, he found the city much changed. Most striking for Kendall were the population, which had almost doubled, and the Capitol building, which now had an impressive rotunda.[29]

It was an auspicious time for the Jackson party. After winning elections in New Hampshire, Ohio, Indiana, and New York, as well as Kentucky, the party had taken over both houses of Congress. In the week before Kendall's arrival the Jacksonians had elected Andrew Stevenson of Virginia Speaker of the House and Duff Green printer for the Senate, and had won majorities on almost all the important congressional committees. With two Jackson senators and seven Jackson congressmen, Kentucky had one of the largest and most influential delegations in the Congress.[30]

Little wonder then that Kendall received a friendly greeting. He was invited to dinner by Stevenson and New Hampshire senator Levi Woodbury, whom he had not seen since their days at Dartmouth. Van Buren and Green were most gracious and quickly arranged a loan of $2,000. Green and Senator Thomas Hart Benton of Missouri may have talked about jobs, because he later had offers from both of them. He surely talked about the bargain charge. Clay was becoming so concerned about the attacks that he was preparing a major address defending himself. When it appeared on December 29, not long after Kendall left, the Jackson central committee in Washington was ready with an answer. Kendall's growing notoriety can be seen in the opposition charges that he was one of the authors. Even though he denied the rumor, it is hard to believe that he did not contribute in some way.[31]

When he arrived home—barely ten days before the party convention in January—the Jacksonians appeared to be losing ground. Despite their strong showing in August, they had been unable to elect their first choice for speaker

29. *Autobiography*, 89–90. See also Kendall to Jane Kendall, 15 Nov., 15 Dec. 1827, in *Autobiography*, 272–76; "Letter from Kendall," 18 Dec. 1827, in *Argus*, 2 Jan. 1828.

30. Robert V. Remini, *The Election of Andrew Jackson* (Philadelphia, 1963), 166–69; Perry M. Goldman and James S. Young, eds., *The United States Congressional Directories, 1789–1840* (New York, 1973), 197–204, 210.

31. Kendall to Jane Kendall, 15 Dec. 1827, 23 Jan. 1829, in *Autobiography*, 274–76, 281; Clay, "Address," 29 Dec. 1827, Clay, *Papers*, 6:1394–96; *Argus*, 30 Jan., 25 June 1828; *Globe*, 8 Oct. 1834.

of the house or to return the printing to the *Argus*. Barry had agreed to run for governor, but the rifts between Frankfort and Louisville and between New Court and Old Court men had not been resolved. In order to get Barry nominated at the convention, Kendall and his Frankfort friends had to accept Robert Breckinridge and John P. Oldham, both of Louisville, as chairman of the convention and lieutenant governor. When Oldham turned the nomination down, the party quickly agreed upon an Old Court man, John Breathitt, from southern Kentucky. Kendall, who now had the ticket he wanted, was himself elected to the state central committee and the committee to write the party address.[32]

He also shaped the campaign. As in the election of 1824 a symbolic Kendall theme—this time the bargain charge instead of the "Wictorian Dinner"—played a central role. Kendall's letters to Clay, Clay's address, and the Jackson response had brought the story national attention. Deciding that it was time to take a stand, Clay's friends in the Kentucky senate offered a resolution on January 18 declaring the charges "false and malicious" and made for "party purposes." The resolution was a blunder, for it led to a hearing and gave Kendall an opportunity to elaborate his version of the bargain charge.[33]

He startled the senate by revealing that Clay had secretly hired him to write the four "Letters to the People of Ohio" attacking Adams. He also accused Clay of trying to bribe him by offering him a job in Washington. Finally he brought in witnesses to support his claim that Clay had mentioned a bargain with Adams in his letter to Blair. The testimony was damaging for Clay because it portrayed him as two-faced, first conspiring against Adams and later making a bargain with him. Blair, who had the only copy of the crucial letter, refused to testify, saying that the contents were confidential, but his real reason was to avoid undercutting Kendall by releasing a letter that said nothing specific about a bargain. At the end of the hearing the Adams senators passed a resolution exonerating Clay of any wrongdoing, but the hearing had left the opposite impression.[34]

During the spring of 1828 the two sides continued to fight over the letter. Aware that it contained uncomplimentary remarks about Adams, Kendall

32. House, *Journal*, 1827, 4–11; *Argus*, 6, 26 Dec. 1827, 16 Jan. 1828; *Niles' Register* 33 (1827–28): 277, 316; Leonard P. Curry, "Election Year—Kentucky, 1828," *Register* 55 (1957): 197, 199–201.

33. Senate, *Journal*, 1827, 256–57; *Argus*, 23, 30 Jan. 1828.

34. Senate, *Journal*, 1827, 298–99, 302–9; *Argus*, 23, 30 Jan., 6, 13 Feb. 1828; Blair to Clay, 31 Dec., 22 Jan., 4 Feb. 1828, Charles S. Todd to Clay, 18 Feb. 1828, Clay, *Papers*, 6:1403–5, 7:54, 74–76, 104.

taunted Clay to display his famed "boldness" and "courage" by forcing Blair to release it. Under great pressure to prove his innocence, Clay decided to get a copy of the letter and show it to trusted backers, who would publish edited excerpts supporting his position. When word got out that Clay had asked Blair for a copy, it was Kendall's turn to be alarmed. Fearful that the letter would offer no proof of a bargain, he pleaded with Blair not to release a copy; but Blair, thinking that Clay would not dare publish it, had already sent him one. As soon as Clay received the copy, he dispatched duplicates to his campaign managers, including Kentucky party chairman John Harvie in Lexington. When Kendall asked permission to see the letter, Harvie reluctantly agreed but would not let him take notes.[35]

Unfortunately for Clay, Kendall had an excellent memory and was able to reconstruct the letter almost verbatim. By July 9 he was ready to discuss the letter and the bargain charge in another of his public letters to Clay. Assuming the role of underdog, he said he was but "a humble Editor," while Clay was "high in office and clothed with power." We have been told, he wrote, that Clay would publish the Blair letter; "we listen for the thunder; we look to see where the bolt will fall. It bursts—and what have we?" Nothing. He then announced that he had seen the letter and quoted the exact wording of several passages. In addition to describing Adams as the best "choice of evils," Clay had also disclosed his "strong personal objections" to both Jackson and Adams. Kendall could not produce any specific reference to a bargain, but he quoted remarks that seemed to allude to one. Clay had mentioned, for example, that a friend of Adams had promised that Clay's "future interests" would best be served by supporting Adams.[36]

The bargain charge showed once again how clever—and unscrupulous— Kendall could be. He had created the equivalent of a modern soap opera and damaged Clay's reputation with very few solid facts. There was probably no corrupt bargain between Adams and Clay. It was not surprising that Clay chose Adams, whose economic program was like his own, over Jackson, whom he distrusted and disliked. Nor is it surprising that Adams appointed Clay, who had experience in foreign affairs, secretary of state. But the public was less generous. Many held the republican belief that Clay and Adams had joined in

35. *Argus,* 6 Feb. 1828 (quotation); Kirwan, *John J. Crittenden,* 76–77; Clay to Blair, 8 Jan. 1825, Clay, *Papers,* 4:9–11; *Kentuckian* (Frankfort), 17 Apr., 8 May, 3 July 1828; Kendall to Blair, 26 June 1828, Blair-Lee Papers; Marshall, "Early Career," 411–15.

36. Kendall, "Letter V to Henry Clay," in *Argus,* 9 July 1828.

a conspiracy, while others held the democratic view that Clay had acted corruptly by ignoring the will of the people of Kentucky and voting for Adams. In the new culture of democracy, politicians were expected to follow the instructions of the voters.

The Jacksonians took full advantage of these sentiments. Through the party press they made the bargain charge a major part of their campaign. Thomas Hart Benton spread the story in the West, and just before the presidential election the *United States Telegraph* in Washington carried all the details. Pointing out that "the mass of the people" received "their information from the newspapers," Kendall boasted that his letters to Clay were being read everywhere. In an increasingly democratic age still concerned about preserving public virtue, the charge aroused great public interest. Realizing this, Clay took the charge seriously but, struggling to defend himself, succeeded only in keeping the story alive. In his later years he admitted that his decision to become secretary of state and his handling of the bargain charge had been among his greatest political mistakes.[37]

With only a few weeks to go before the state election, the Jacksonians were running a new-style campaign. Unlike earlier candidates, who rarely campaigned themselves, Barry had taken his message into many parts of the state—even to the southern counties along the Tennessee border. Preacher Jacob Creath was lining up Baptist votes. Lexington postmaster Joseph Ficklin, who owed his appointment to Barry and Johnson, was accused of holding up bags of Adams party handbills. Congressman Thomas P. Moore was using materials forwarded by Gulian Verplanck of the Albany Regency. Blair bragged that they had "almost every Jackson man ticketed & riveted to the polls."[38]

The intense campaigning led to a record turnout of over 74 percent,

37. Glyndon G. Van Deusen, *Life of Henry Clay* (Boston, 1937), 224–25; Edward Bates to Clay, 6 Oct. 1828, Clay, *Papers*, 7:485; *United States Telegraph*, 8, 9, 16 Oct. 1828; *Argus*, 9 July (quotation), 1 Oct. 1828. For the story of the bargain charge from Clay's point of view see Kirwan, *John J. Crittenden*, 70–81, and Remini, *Henry Clay*, 270–72, 321–22. Catherine Allgor supports the position that in the eyes of the public Clay had acted corruptly. She also argues, unconvincingly, that there was a bargain between the two men. Allgor, *Parlor Politics: In Which the Ladies of Washington Help Build a City and a Government* (Charlottesville, 2000), 185–86, 194.

38. Barry to Susan Taylor, 3 Dec. 1827, 11 Apr., 3 June 1828, William T. Barry Papers (typescripts), Filson Historical Society; *Argus*, 30 Apr. 1828; Benjamin W. Dudley to Clay, 17 Aug. 1827, Richard Hawes to Clay, 29 Jan. 1828, Clay, *Papers*, 6:917, 7:62–63; Moore to Verplanck, 29 May 1828, Gulian C. Verplanck Papers, New-York Historical Society, cited in Remini, *Election of Andrew Jackson*, 210; Blair to Desha, 30 Oct. 1828, Joseph Desha Papers, LC.

slightly higher than in the panic election of 1820. But it did not bring a Jacksonian victory. Barry's close identification with the New Court party proved too heavy a handicap. As one observer remarked, "hundreds, nay thousands of Genl. Jackson's Old Court friends could not be prevailed on to vote for Barry." Encouraged by Barry's difficulties, the Adams party increased its efforts. Clay returned to Kentucky in July and was seen at the Fayette courthouse each day of the election. The Jacksonians won control of both houses and elected Old Court John Breathitt lieutenant governor, but Barry lost by close to two thousand votes.[39]

For the first time in Kentucky the two-party system carried over intact into the presidential election. The Jacksonians continued to ignore issues and base their campaign on images, slogans, and negative attacks on the opposition. They played up Jackson's image as the "Hero of New Orleans" and the "incorruptible patriot." They drew upon old republican traditions and new democratic ideas by calling themselves both the "Republican" and the "democratic Jackson" party. Crying that the "fate of the Republic is to be decided," they called for "*Liberty or Monarchy*" and "Jackson and Reform." The meaning of the latter was unclear. Jackson was promising a republican reform program of retrenchment and rooting out corruption, but Kendall hoped to root out the Adams men and establish a system of party patronage. The Jacksonians never let up on Adams and Clay—especially Clay—constantly reminding the voters of the corrupt bargain.[40]

The efforts of both parties to mobilize the electorate brought out 68 percent of Kentucky voters, greater than the 56 percent nationally, far greater than the 25 percent Kentucky turnout in the presidential election of 1824, but less than the percentage in August. Jackson carried Kentucky by a wide margin, 39,394 to 31,460. His victory helped catapult him into the presidency, for just as expected, he swept the South and Adams New England, making Kentucky, Ohio, and New York crucial states. Jackson won all the electoral votes in the first two and a majority in New York.[41]

39. William B. Lewis to Van Buren, 8 Aug. 1828, Van Buren Papers; Curry, "Election Year," 201–4; Mathias and Shannon, "Gubernatorial Politics," 253–56.

40. *Argus*, 16 Jan. (quotation), 28 May (quotation), 6, 20 Aug., 17 Sept., 22, 29 Oct. (quotations) 1828; Robert P. Letcher to Clay, 27 Aug. 1828, Clay to Richard Pindell, 15 Oct. 1828, Clay, *Papers*, 7:441, 501; Johnson to Jackson, 22 Aug. 1828, Richard M. Johnson, "The Letters of Colonel Richard M. Johnson," *Register* 39 (1941): 272–73; Curry, "Election Year," 204–8.

41. Svend Petersen, *A Statistical History of the American Presidential Elections* (New York, 1963), 18–20; Shannon and McQuown, *Presidential Politics*, 4.

It has been said that Jackson did not do especially well in Kentucky. Adams was so unpopular in the South, so the argument goes, that Jackson carried every southern state, and only in Kentucky was the election at all close. The difference supposedly was a strong backlash caused by the attacks on Clay. Thus Kendall and the bargain charge were more liabilities than assets. This view, however, fails to take into consideration two points: Unlike the rest of the South, Kentucky had the beginnings of a two-party system, and the Jacksonians had just lost the governorship to their opponents. Kendall could not afford to run a soft campaign. Had it not been for the Jacksonians' democratic methods and party propaganda, Adams might have carried Kentucky. As it was, Kendall's party won a solid victory in Henry Clay's home state.[42]

The voting patterns give some early clues about Jacksonian Democracy. Jackson's strength—like Desha's in 1824—lay in underdeveloped, rapidly growing counties such as Kendall's second tier near Frankfort, counties that had been most in favor of relief. These early Jacksonians were striving, upwardly mobile people, who resented the privileges of the established aristocracy represented by the planters and merchants in the heart of the Bluegrass. They had responded enthusiastically to Kendall's "Wictorian Dinner" in 1824 and his bargain charge in 1828. Jackson and Kendall would appeal to them again with the BUS veto in 1832.[43]

Kendall had every intention of taking advantage of his success. He already had offers from Green to be assistant editor of the *United States Telegraph* and from Benton to set up a newspaper in St. Louis but rejected both because his eyes were on Jackson. On November 19 he wrote a letter of congratulations to the general. Perhaps sounding him out on party patronage, Kendall said that he looked forward to "a new era of reform" and commented that the election

42. Curry, "Election Year," 207–8.

43. In this paragraph I have drawn heavily from Marshall, "Genesis of Grass-Roots Democracy," especially 284–87. See also Shannon and McQuown, *Presidential Politics*, 4–6. Jackson won eight of the ten strongest relief counties and nine of the ten with the fastest rate of growth. One other pattern, to which Marshall alludes only in passing, is the role of personal influence. The influence of leaders such as Kendall and Blair in Franklin County, Johnson in Scott County, Pope in Washington County, Wickliffe in Fayette County, James Clark in Clark County, and Thomas P. Moore in Mercer County either reinforced or outweighed the influence of the socioeconomic characteristics in Marshall's analysis. The importance of personal influence in the Jackson party can also be seen in the split between Frankfort and Louisville. The two regions voted in roughly similar fashion during the Relief War but split because of personal rivalries.

showed that the people of Kentucky would not "sanction . . . a corrupt administration." Jackson sent back a friendly letter but said nothing about a job or
reform. Nonetheless, Old Hickory had Kendall in his plans. Early in December a messenger arrived from the president-elect offering Kendall an unspeci-
fied position in the new administration. He promptly accepted.[44]

Eager to be on hand when appointments were being made, Kendall made
plans to leave for Washington as soon as possible. His ostensible purpose
would be to carry the electoral returns to Congress. He said nothing about the
possibility of a job because he wanted to avoid raising the specter of another
corrupt bargain. He did, however, suggest that he planned to stay in Washington by starting the process of selling the mill and the *Argus.* Jane and the family
would remain behind until he was appointed and could afford to bring them
to Washington. The family was growing. After losing her first child, Jane had
given birth to a healthy daughter early in 1828 and was expecting another child
next summer. That would give them five children, all under ten.

Now committed to a career in Washington, Kendall was leaving a state
political party that was well organized at every level but lacked real political
power. An Adams man was governor, and even though the Jackson party held
majorities in both houses, a swing group of Old Court/John Pope Jacksonians
often voted with the Adams men. The party managed to return the printing
to the *Argus* but again could not elect its preferred candidate for speaker. In
addition the candidacy of Pope kept Kendall's wing from reelecting
Richard M. Johnson to the U.S. Senate. Only after a month of haggling did
the party compromise on George M. Bibb.[45]

Kendall left for Washington on December 21. In two years he had broken
with Clay, built a new-style political party, and carried Kentucky for Jackson.
Although the party was not truly democratic—it was open only to adult white
males and it preferred to obscure issues rather than deal with them—it took a
major step toward democracy by creating useful structures for getting people

44. Green to Richard M. Johnson, 10 Aug. 1828, Green to Kendall, 17 Sept. 1828, Duff Green
Papers, LC; Benton to Kendall, 24 Aug. 1828, *Massachusetts Historical Society Proceedings* 13 (1873–
75): 306–7; Kendall to Jackson, 19 Nov. 1828, Jackson to Kendall, 25 Nov. 1828, Jackson Papers;
*Autobiography,* 303.

45. *Argus,* 17, 24 Dec. 1828; House, *Journal,* 1828, 4–5; Senate, *Journal,* 1828, 117–19; Johnson to
John T. Johnson, 2 Jan. 1829, Richard M. Johnson, "The Letters of Colonel Richard M. Johnson,"
*Register* 39 (1941): 276–77; Leslie Combs to Clay, 31 Dec. 1828, Clay, *Papers,* 7:583–84; Blair to
Desha, 22 Dec. 1828, Desha Papers.

into politics. Kendall had developed a message and style in which he appealed directly to ordinary people like himself through republican imagery and democratic assaults on wealth and privilege. The bargain charge, which summed up much of that appeal, was a key weapon in defeating John Quincy Adams. Kendall was now taking his style of democracy to Washington.

PART THREE

*Washington*

# 9

## REFORM

On the morning of December 23 Kendall was in Cincinnati, waiting uneasily for his steamboat to start up the Ohio. The river was icing over so rapidly that the departure time had been postponed to three in the afternoon, and there was a good chance that the run would be canceled. Three o'clock finally arrived, and much to Kendall's relief, the steamboat got under way. By the time he reached Wheeling two days later the river was filled with ice, and steamboat travel was suspended. After spending Christmas night in a tavern, he left by stagecoach the next day and reached Washington on the evening of December 29.[1]

Kendall went directly to the boardinghouse of Obadiah B. Brown on E Street near the General Post Office and moved in with Richard M. Johnson, who was finishing out his term in the Senate and would be elected to the House in August. Brown was a Baptist minister who doubled as a clerk in the General Post Office. He was also a Jacksonian insider, whose parlor served as a meeting place for members of the party. Kendall described him as "a cheerful, jolly man, who loves good eating and drinking and delights in a joke." With five children, two grandchildren, and three boarders, Brown and his wife offered a lively, friendly home. Kendall enjoyed himself there immensely, chatting with politicians and postal clerks, learning about the Baptist church, and occasionally reading aloud some of his poetry.[2]

He was quickly reassured about his prospects. His congressional friends Johnson, Thomas P. Moore, and Charles A. Wickliffe were certain that that he would be appointed as a principal clerk or an auditor. The latter would pay $3,000 a year. He also had offers from several politicians who were already maneuvering to succeed Jackson and could use a writer. Postmaster General

---

1. Kendall to Jane Kendall, 26 Dec. 1828, 4 Jan. 1829, in *Autobiography*, 276–79.
2. Kendall to Jane Kendall, 4, 15 Jan. 1829, in ibid., 277–80.

John McLean, who had campaigned for Jackson while serving under Adams, promised a clerkship if he kept his job. A spokesman for Martin Van Buren, who was in Albany serving as governor of New York, offered to appoint him chief clerk if the Little Magician was named secretary of state. Vice President John C. Calhoun was prepared to make him an auditor.[3]

Duff Green and Senator John H. Eaton of Tennessee, the most influential Jackson men in the city, had their own plans for Kendall. Green promptly renewed his earlier offer of an editorship. Eaton, who mistrusted Green, urged Kendall to accept, so that he could keep an eye on the publisher. As an alternative Eaton asked Kendall to set up his own press and said he would see to it that he got a share of the congressional printing. Kendall refused to bite. If he accepted an offer from any one person, he reasoned, the rest would become his enemies. He had developed a particular distaste for Green, who, he said, considered himself "the ruler of the nation." The House and Senate soon elected Green printer, but Kendall was unconcerned because he had decided to work for no one but Andrew Jackson.[4]

After attending a few parties Kendall became convinced that Washington needed moral and social reform as much as political. In telling Jane about the dinners, he wavered back and forth from rural, wide-eyed excitement to Yankee frugality and puritanical disapproval. The "big bugs," he began, "invite you to dine with them at five o'clock. . . . and it is eight, nine, or ten, before the dinner is over." At the Jackson dinner on January 8 "the company did not all leave the table until eleven o'clock, and then many of them could scarcely leave it at all." He reassured Jane that only the "very rich" gave dinners; he would not waste their money on such affairs. As for the women, "They lace up too tight and expose their shoulders too much." All in all he believed that "if there is more extravagance, folly, and corruption anywhere in the world than in this city I do not wish to see that place. . . . There is great room for *reform* here." Kendall saw himself as a moral, country outsider in a wicked court city.[5]

He was not the only one, however, for other Jackson editors, looking for jobs, were frequent guests in Brown's parlor. One was the slender, young, reserved Gideon Welles, editor of the *Hartford Times*. Kendall also became ac-

---

3. Kendall to Jane Kendall, 4 Jan. 1829, in ibid., 277–79; Kendall to Blair, 3 Feb. 1829, Blair-Lee Papers.

4. Kendall to Jane Kendall, 4, 23 Jan., 10, 14 Feb. 1829, in *Autobiography*, 177–79, 280–85; Green to Johnson, 10 Aug. 1828, Green Papers; Kendall to Blair, 3 Feb. 1829, Blair-Lee Papers.

5. Kendall to Jane Kendall, 15 (quotations), 23 Jan., 10, 14 Feb. 1829, in *Autobiography*, 279–85.

quainted with Isaac Hill, whose aggressive editorials in the *New-Hampshire Patriot,* had won Jackson's admiration. Another new friend, the robust and amiable Mordecai M. Noah of the *New York Courier and Enquirer,* could tell stories almost as well as their host. These new friends deferred a bit to Kendall because he was the only one who had exchanged letters with Old Hickory.[6]

By early February the editors were getting edgy waiting for Jackson, whose arrival had been delayed because of the tragic death of his wife, Rachel. When he finally arrived on February 11 and settled in at Gadsby's new National Hotel, Kendall suggested that they pay a call. The next day a dozen of them went over to the hotel. As they were about to go in, jolly Mordecai Noah found himself at the head of the line. Looking back at grim, bent-over Isaac Hill, he supposedly said with a smile, "Hill, you are the ugliest of the clan, of a hungry aspect enough. I am fat and plump: you should lead us on, and as soon as the old president sees this picture of starvation, he will surrender at once."[7]

The story, though perhaps apocryphal, does justice to the event, for Jackson succumbed. He greeted each man individually and over the next few weeks had private talks with many of them. Most of them eventually got jobs, and during his administration Jackson appointed fifty-nine editors to office. His willingness to pay such attention to editors was remarkable, for previous presidents had held them in low regard. John Quincy Adams called the Jackson newspapers "the foulest presses," and his friend Senator Samuel Bell of New Hampshire referred to editors as "skunks." Jackson, who prized loyalty, responded warmly to the editors because he was grateful for the way they had defended him when Rachel was accused of adultery. They shared a common bond; they had all come to Washington as outsiders, determined to reform the government.[8]

These appointments support the argument that the Jacksonians represented a new sort of political movement relying on ordinary people, often of humble background, rather than the established leaders of society. Hill and Nathaniel Greene, editor of the *Boston Statesman,* escaped poverty by becoming newspaper apprentices before they were fifteen. Duff Green and Kendall

6. John Niven, *Gideon Welles: Lincoln's Secretary of the Navy* (New York, 1973), 58–64. For the editors' correspondence (or lack of it) with Jackson, see Harold D. Moser et al., eds., *Guide and Index to the Microfilm Editions of the Papers of Andrew Jackson* (Wilmington, Del., 1987).

7. "Letter from Amos Kendall," 11 Feb. 1829, in *Argus,* 25 Feb. 1829; Niven, *Gideon Welles,* 64; *Niles' Register* 48 (1835): 147 (quotation).

8. Adams, *Memoirs,* 8:215; *Washington National Journal,* 3, 8 Dec. 1829, 11 May 1830.

started life on marginal farms. Not all, of course, fit the stereotype. Both Gideon Welles and Mordecai Noah came from well-to-do families. But taken as a whole, the prominence of the editors contributed to the democratization of American politics.[9]

Kendall had looked forward to talking with Jackson as much as he had to meeting Clay. He knew that his views were similar to the general's—faith in states' rights and egalitarian democracy, a concern for what they called reform, and hatred for the BUS—but he needed to know more. So he was delighted two days later when he was the first editor invited in for a private conference. Their talk started well as Jackson promised him a position as either an auditor or a principal clerk. Kendall was soon unnerved, however, when the general mentioned that he intended to appoint John Pope, who was a friend, to the seat on the Supreme Court left vacant by the recent death of Thomas Todd of Kentucky. By suggesting Pope, who had alienated the majority wing of the state party, Jackson showed that he either knew little about Kentucky politics or, even worse, was uninterested in party patronage. Kendall, Johnson, and Moore had already decided on William T. Barry for the seat, and Kendall had written Pope a nasty letter, attacking him for his selfishness in the Senate election and telling him not to expect a federal position.[10]

Kendall blurted out that the delegation preferred Barry and after the conversation rushed off a letter to Francis P. Blair telling him to have letters supporting Barry sent to Jackson. At least four were mailed from Kentucky, and several others were submitted by members of Congress. Kendall's experience was almost identical with Van Buren's two months later when Jackson decided to appoint another friend, party maverick Samuel Swartwout, port collector for New York. Kendall fared better, but not because of the letters, most of which arrived too late. Jackson came down in favor of Barry because of the advice of Kendall and others in Washington and because he appreciated Barry's hard work in the Kentucky election.[11]

9. Niven, *Gideon Welles*, 64. For the concept of a new type of party see Lynn L. Marshall, "The Strange Stillbirth of the Whig Party," *American Historical Review* 72 (1967): 425–44; for the contrary view see Sidney H. Aronson, *Status and Kinship in the Higher Civil Service: Standards of Selection in the Administrations of John Adams, Thomas Jefferson, and Andrew Jackson* (Cambridge, Mass., 1964). For the editors and the democratization of politics see Pasley, *"Tyranny of Printers,"* 18–21.

10. Kendall to Jane Kendall, 14 Feb. 1829, in *Autobiography*, 283–85; Kendall to Blair, 9 Jan., 14 Feb. 1829, Kendall to Pope, 11 Jan. 1829, Blair-Lee Papers.

11. Pope to Jackson, 19 Feb. 1829, Richard M. Johnson et al. to Jackson, 18 Feb. 1829, R. B. McAfee et al. to Jackson, 20 Feb. 1829, Robert L. McHatton et al. to Jackson, 20 Feb. 1829, Joseph

Shortly before his inauguration Jackson called Kendall in again and expanded on his political views. In explaining reform he stopped short of party patronage but did say that he would remove anyone who had interfered with the election or had been appointed for political reasons or against the will of the people. He also outlined a "middle and just course" on the tariff and the distribution of surplus funds to the states for internal improvements. Kendall was much encouraged, for Jackson's grounds for removal seemed to open the door for patronage, and his moderate states' rights program was compatible with his own.

As Kendall recalled the meeting, Jackson had been very flattering. He said that Kendall was qualified to be a department head and added dramatically that if the "storm waxed violent against his measures," he would not hesitate to put him in a different position, which Kendall took to mean as editor of a new party newspaper. Even discounting the source, the conversation suggests that he had risen rather rapidly in Jackson's estimation. Old Hickory liked Kendall, felt comfortable with him, and wanted someone around who was well educated and wrote well. He also had been won over by Kendall's political successes. In the summer of 1828 Duff Green told a Kentucky friend that Kendall was one of the two or three Kentuckians with the best "claim upon Gen'l Jackson" for a position. The November results strengthened this claim. Jackson, who hated Clay, must have been impressed by Kendall's ability to popularize the bargain charge and carry Clay's home state.[12]

He certainly had the election in mind in selecting his cabinet. After choosing his two strongest campaign managers, Eaton and Van Buren, for war and state, he rewarded his base of power in the South by naming inconspicuous Senators John Branch of North Carolina and John M. Berrien of Georgia for secretary of the navy and attorney general. To satisfy Pennsylvania he made Congressman Samuel D. Ingham secretary of the Treasury. He was thinking of reappointing John McLean of Ohio postmaster general, but the two could not reach an understanding. McLean had developed the doctrine that postmasters held office as a public trust and would not be removed unless it was

---

Desha to Jackson, 23 Feb. 1829, James Taylor to Jackson, 23 Feb. 1829, Joseph Ficklin to Jackson, 25 Feb. 1829, Jackson Papers.

12. Richard B. Latner makes a strong argument for the influence of Kendall and other westerners in the Jackson administration. Latner, *The Presidency of Andrew Jackson: White House Politics, 1829–1837* (Athens, Ga., 1979), 4, 17–22. Kendall to Blair, 7 Mar. 1829, Blair-Lee Papers. Kendall to Jane Kendall, 25 Feb. 1829, in *Autobiography,* 285–86; Green to Presley Edwards, 9 July 1828, Green Papers.

proved that they had violated that trust. When it was suggested that he would have to remove some of them more arbitrarily, he demurred. The problem was solved by making Barry postmaster general and giving the seat on the Supreme Court to McLean. The shift proved to be invaluable for the political power of the Kentucky Jacksonians.[13]

The new cabinet members were less distinguished than the incumbents. While almost everyone in Adams's cabinet enjoyed a national reputation, only Van Buren had comparable renown in Jackson's. Though not as lowly as the editors, the cabinet appointees were rather ordinary people—so ordinary that Jackson and Kendall tried to make a virtue of it. Jackson remarked that his new administrators were capable "men of business." Kendall added that "the *great men*" might "find much fault" with the cabinet, but he expected it to be "useful" instead of "splendid." The selections showed, he said, that common people could attain "the highest offices" in the land.[14]

On the morning of inauguration day Kendall joined the "dense current" of citizens walking up Pennsylvania Avenue toward Capitol Hill. From the west front of the Capitol he looked back and spied "the hero" striding up the avenue, protected by a cadre of veterans of the Revolution. Kendall then went around to the east front where a crowd of 15,000–20,000 people filled the space below the steps. Exactly at noon Jackson appeared dressed in a plain black suit and delivered his inaugural, covering much of the ground that he had gone over with Kendall. On the question of reform he promised to "extinguish . . . the national debt" through "strict and faithful economy" and pledged to "counteract those causes" that had put "power in unfaithful or incompetent hands." Although this seemed to justify removals, it was still not the forthright endorsement of party patronage Kendall wanted.[15]

The demand for patronage was intense. For the first time in twenty-eight years the party in power was being replaced, and there were thousands in town seeking jobs. Margaret Bayard Smith, who had lived in Washington throughout the twenty-eight years, said that her friends in the administration feared a "general proscription." Just how far the Jacksonians went in establishing party

13. Richard R. John, *Spreading the News: The American Postal System from Franklin to Morse* (Cambridge, Mass., 1995), 79–81, 214–16. "Letter from Kendall," 20, 25 Feb., 11 Mar. 1829, in *Argus*, 4, 11 Mar., 1 Apr. 1829; Kendall to Blair, 7 Mar. 1829, Blair-Lee Papers.

14. Kendall to Blair, 7 Mar. 1829, Blair-Lee Papers; "Letter from Kendall," 25 Feb. 1829, in *Argus*, 11 Mar. 1829.

15. "Letter from Kendall," 5 Mar. 1829, in *Argus*, 18 Mar. 1829; Jackson, "First Inaugural Address," *Compilation*, 2:436–38.

patronage has been the subject of much discussion. Ever since the election Duff Green had been promising that Jackson would "reward his friends and punish his enemies." After all, said Green in the *United States Telegraph,* Old Hickory had been selected by "the people" as "the agent of reform." Jackson, however, insisted that he intended only to weed out corrupt and incompetent officials. Contemporaries and nineteenth-century civil service reformers accused the Jacksonians of starting a spoils system, and recent historians have renewed the charge. On the other hand several studies have shown the percentage of removals somewhat lower than expected. Kendall's story offers another chance to review the subject.[16]

The Kentucky Jacksonians had no qualms about a spoils system. Soon after the inaugural Kendall wrote Blair, asking him to prepare the public for "a revolution in the U.S. offices." When one of his constituents apologized for seeking a position, he replied that everyone else was doing the same. He later told Blair that every Jackson man in Kentucky wanted a job. The Kentuckians believed that they had an inside track because Jackson needed a strong party in Kentucky to keep Clay from staging a comeback.[17]

Kendall had already sent Blair a blueprint for rebuilding the party. To keep everyone informed Blair was to send copies of the *Argus* to each company of militia. With so many Kentuckians expecting jobs in Washington, the party needed "new men" at home; if successful they would have "irresistable claims" on Jackson. He told Blair to choose county agents and a central committee and also a good man for federal marshal because in 1830 the marshal would have the power to appoint federal census takers for each county. He authorized Blair to promise prospective county agents that they would get these jobs, "thus proving that fidelity to the cause should not go without its rewards." Kendall listed five candidates for marshal and asked Blair to find out how

16. Thomas P. Moore to James B. Gardiner, 14 Feb. 1829, Kendall Papers, Dartmouth College Library; Smith, *First Forty Years of Washington Society,* 299; *Telegraph,* 3 (quotations), 8, 18, 24 Nov. 1828; Jackson to Susan Decatur, 2 Apr. 1829, Jackson, fragment, 1831, Jackson, *Correspondence,* 4:22, 6:504; James Parton, *Life of Andrew Jackson,* 3 vols. (New York, 1860), 3:206–27. Richard R. John argues that the Jacksonians established a spoils system in *Spreading the News,* 206–56, and "Affairs of Office: The Executive Departments, the Election of 1828, and the Making of the Democratic Party," in *The Democratic Experiment: New Directions in American Political History,* ed. Julian Zelizer, Meg Jacobs, and William Novak (Princeton, 2003). Erik M. Eriksson shows a low overall rate of removal in "The Federal Civil Service under President Jackson," *Mississippi Valley Historical Review* 13 (1927): 526–29.

17. *Autobiography,* 307–8; Kendall to Blair, 30 Apr., 2 July 1829, Blair-Lee Papers.

much each could be counted on to "promot[e] the views and interests of our party."[18]

For the next two years Blair and Kendall worked in tandem. Kendall sent information from "headquarters" in Washington and paid part of the expense of handbills and extras. One of Blair's chief responsibilities was to make the important post offices "safe" for the party. If he could "collect the evidence of abuse" and recommend good replacements, Kendall would see to it that Adams men were removed. Kendall kept Blair informed when the administration made a futile attempt to take over the boards of the BUS branches in Lexington and Louisville. He was an irrepressible cheerleader. "Be up and doing," he would say, "organize, organize" and "a fig for the fainted [*sic*] hearted men who are ready to surrender."[19]

They succeeded. Kendall and his Kentucky friends won a host of early appointments and secured printing contracts for the *Argus* and other newspapers. At least a dozen important Adams postmasters were turned out, Thomas P. Moore was named minister to Colombia, and two young party men were appointed to foreign missions. In some of the appointments, however, Kendall had to accommodate the wishes of the Pope/Louisville wing of the party. Two postmasterships and the position of federal attorney went to Pope's friends, and when Kendall tried to remove the Frankfort postmaster, an Adams man, Pope's wife saved him by writing to Jackson. Kendall even had to accept the appointment of Pope himself as governor of the Arkansas Territory.[20]

Despite the compromises, Kendall was immensely pleased and was soon as cocky and arrogant as he had been after the passing of the Reorganization Act. He was far from impressed with the people he met in Washington, few of whom were "men of strict honesty" or "exalted talents." If Blair did his job, Kendall would see that he was "promoted," and someday Blair might rise as high as Kendall had. He totaled up what the administration had done for "Old Kaintuck." Barry would receive $6,000 a year; Moore $1,800; Pope $3,000; and Kendall expected $3,000. Kendall was particularly elated by the possibilities of patronage in the post offices. From now on, he told Blair, postmasters in Kentucky would hold their positions as "tenants at [Barry's] will." You can

18. Kendall to Blair, 9 Jan. 1829, Blair-Lee Papers.

19. Ibid., 9 Jan. ("safe")), 10 Mar. ("Be up"), 12 Apr., 22 Nov. 1829; Robert V. Remini, *Andrew Jackson and the Bank War* (New York, 1967), 49–55.

20. Kendall to Blair, 9 Jan., 14 Feb., 7, 10, 14 Mar., 12 Apr. 1829. Nine of the postmasters removed were among the most highly paid. John, *Spreading the News*, 224–25.

imagine, he wrote gleefully, how those "poor devils" who abused Barry last year must now feel.[21]

Jackson had held back the appointments of Kendall and other controversial figures to avoid the hostility that would have arisen had he sent them immediately to the Senate, then in special session. Soon after the session adjourned on March 17, he appointed Kendall, Hill, and his Tennessee friend William B. Lewis, who was living in the President's House, to the Treasury Department, and two months later he added New York banker Thomas L. Smith. The appointments attracted great attention because of the size and prestige of the Treasury. The largest of the five federal departments in Washington, it employed over half of all departmental personnel in the city. Three-quarters of these treasury clerks worked under eight prominent accounting officers: a register, two comptrollers, and five auditors. In 1829 this hierarchy had become almost a permanent civil service. The register and first auditor had served since George Washington's time, and five of the others at least a dozen years.[22]

Jackson had replaced half of this respected staff with four undistinguished, inexperienced party men, two of whom were printers and three of whom had been involved in political controversy. Hill, who became second comptroller, had published lurid stories about Adams. Lewis, second auditor, had participated in an unsavory salt lick deal with the Chickasaw Indians, and Kendall, fourth auditor, had orchestrated the bargain charge. Only Smith, register, had escaped notoriety.[23]

These removals and the many that followed convinced the opposition and traditional Jacksonians such as Thomas Ritchie of Virginia that a proscription was under way. According to one of Clay's friends, the appointments showed that Jackson was determined "to honour vice, to reward friends, and to punish

21. Kendall to Blair, 3 Feb. ("men"), 7 ("promoted"), 10 ("old") Mar. 1829, Blair-Lee Papers.

22. The Treasury Department had 169 employees; the next largest, the General Post Office, had 44. Kendall to Jane Kendall, 22 Mar. 1829, in *Autobiography*, 287; Leonard D. White, *The Jacksonians: A Study in Administrative History, 1829–1861* (New York, 1954), 163; *Globe*, 10 May 1832; William F. Sherman, comp., "Inventory of the Records of the Accounting Officers of the Department of the Treasury," National Archives, RG 217, Inventory No. 14, 1987, 250–54.

23. Removed in 1829 were Register Joseph Nourse, Second Comptroller Richard Cutts, Second Auditor William Lee, and Fourth Auditor Tobias Watkins. In 1836 Jackson removed First Comptroller Joseph Anderson and First Auditor Richard Harrison. When Jackson left office, only Third Auditor Peter Hagner and Fifth Auditor Stephen Pleasanton remained. *Globe*, 10 May 1832; Sherman, "Inventory," 250–54.

enemies." The Jacksonians, however, maintained that they were simply carrying out Jackson's promises of reforming the government. A year and a half later Duff Green, who had led the drive for spoils, announced defensively that the administration had removed only 10 percent of all government officials, but the figure is misleading. The Jacksonians removed a much higher percentage of the important, higher-paid officials. During his eight years in office Jackson removed 45 percent of the 610 officials appointed directly by the president. A comparison of the rosters of the five government departments in Washington in 1829 and 1831 shows the same pattern. Of all 297 officials, most of whom held good jobs, 19 percent had been removed, and for the 33 top-level officials the removal rate was 58 percent.[24]

Furthermore, the rate was high in the more visible parts of the government and in offices where spoilsmen were in direct control. Thirty-six percent of the land registers and receivers were removed within the first six months, and removals in the diplomatic and consular fields reached 25 percent by the end of Jackson's administration. Second Comptroller Hill and Secretary of State Van Buren removed, respectively, 22 percent and 40 percent of the officers under their command.[25]

The story of the Post Office further confirms the pattern. The Post Office was the largest agency in the United States government; by 1831 three-fourths of all federal civilian employees were postal officers. When Barry took over, he announced that he would remove only those guilty of improper behavior, but Green and Kendall soon convinced him to change his mind. By late spring he had dismissed Washington postmaster Thomas Munroe and several key Kentucky postmasters. He told his daughter that he could not be expected to retain "personal or political enemies."[26]

24. Green was referring only to those dismissed from office. The total number leaving office for any reason—including death or retirement—was considerably higher. Philip R. Fendall to Clay, 24 Mar. 1829, Clay, *Papers*, 8:16. Green's figure has been confirmed by later studies. Eriksson, "Federal Civil Service," 526–29. For presidential removals see Carl R. Fish, "Removal of Officials by the Presidents of the United States," *Annual Report of the American Historical Association for the Year 1899*, 2 vols. (Washington, 1900), 1:84. For the departments see *Globe*, 10 May 1832.

25. *Globe*, 10 May 1832; Malcolm J. Rohrbough, *The Land Office Business: The Settlement and Administration of American Public Lands, 1789–1837* (New York, 1968), 276; John M. Belohlavek, *"Let the Eagle Soar!" The Foreign Policy of Andrew Jackson* (Lincoln, Neb., 1985), 274; John Niven, *Martin Van Buren and the Romantic Age in American Politics* (New York, 1983), 238; Eriksson, "Federal Civil Service," 533.

26. *Statistical History*, 710; *Niles' Register*, 38 (1830): 105; Barry to Susan Taylor, 16 May, 11 June 1829, "Letters of William T. Barry," *William and Mary College Quarterly* 13 (1904–5): 239–42; Kendall to Blair, 30 Apr. 1829, Blair-Lee Papers; Richard R. John, "Managing the Mails" (Ph.D. diss., Harvard University, 1989), 284–85 n. 63.

One of the Kentucky postmasters removed was James W. Hawkins of Frankfort, the postmaster who had been saved by John Pope's wife. Kendall finally got him ousted in May by making trumped-up charges that Hawkins had mismanaged government funds. If Kendall had had his way, the position would have gone to Lewis Sanders, who was negotiating to buy his share of the *Argus,* but it went instead to Richard M. Johnson's brother Benjamin. In either case it was a clear example of party spoils. Once Hawkins was gone, Kendall put pressure on Barry to remove the two assistant postmasters general, Abraham Bradley and his brother Phineas, whose careers rivaled those of the veterans in the Treasury Department. Barry resisted until late in the summer when Abraham Bradley provoked a quarrel by denouncing Hawkins's removal. Kendall then charged Bradley with conspiracy and forced Barry to dismiss both brothers. It was, however, a Pyrrhic victory because Abraham raised doubts about Barry's competence by publishing a letter documenting his "total unfitness" for the office.[27]

Barry had now settled into a pattern of ousting high-ranking officers while retaining most lesser figures. By 1831 he had removed the top three officials in the General Post Office but only two of the forty clerks. His policy for postmasters was the same. In his first year he removed 29 percent of the highest-paid postmasters and only 5 percent of the rest. Most of these well-paid officials were in the New England and Middle Atlantic states, where the Jacksonians were working to build up their party.[28]

Some years later Thomas Hart Benton used the 5 percent figure to argue that the extent of the spoils system had been exaggerated, but James Parton retorted that the Jacksonians removed almost all of the postmasters from the offices "worth having." He placed the responsibility on party spoilsmen. Parton was correct. Without Jackson's blessing his administration had established a system of party patronage with emphasis on prominent, high-ranking officers and on specific offices where men like Hill and Van Buren were in control.[29]

27. Kendall to Blair, 12, 30 Apr., 2 July 1829, Blair-Lee Papers; Kendall to Blair, 12 May, 21 June, 3 July 1829, Blair Family Papers, LC; *Argus,* 24 June, 26 Aug., 21 Oct. 1829; *Niles' Register* 37 (1829): 76, 90–91, 98–99, 119; Washington *National Intelligencer,* 30 Sept. 1829; John, *Spreading the News,* 222.

28. *Globe,* 10 May 1832; John, *Spreading the News,* 223–25. The percentage of removals of all postmasters was high in Hill's New Hampshire (24 percent) and Van Buren's New York (10 percent). *Niles' Register* 38 (1830): 105.

29. Thomas Hart Benton, *Thirty Years' View,* 2 vols. (New York, 1854), 1:159–62; Parton, *Life of Andrew Jackson,* 3:210.

Early Monday morning, March 23, Kendall walked up E Street and Pennsylvania Avenue to the brick Treasury Building near the President's House, and started in as fourth auditor. He had announced in the *Argus* that he would carry out the president's program of reform, which stressed saving money and rooting out corruption. He would have ample opportunity because his duties were to review all navy accounts, which made up a quarter of federal expenditures. When he found that the office subscribed to more than two dozen newspapers, he immediately canceled the subscriptions. During the first week he discovered that he was being asked to receive, frank, and forward a steady stream of letters. Since postage was customarily paid by the recipient, the procedure saved the addressee money at the expense of the government. At the end of the week he announced abruptly that he would "inflexibly obey" the law requiring that such mail should be returned to the sender's post office.[30]

The opposition reacted with rather bad grace. The editor of the *Baltimore Patriot* sneered at Kendall's "inflated" writing style, blaming it on his "vanity," which had doubtless been brought on by his "temporary elevation" to high office. Adams senator Josiah S. Johnston of Louisiana later commented that Jackson's "professions of economy" had "dwindled down" to "paltry savings in News Papers." The self-righteous Kendall called the editor of the *Patriot* "insolent" and said he did not plan to use government funds to reward editors.[31]

Kendall also took a stern look at the way the navy accounts were being handled. On his first day he ended a policy of paying midshipmen $1.50 per diem for time spent in New York taking examinations. The second day he stopped one of his clerks from moonlighting as agent for citizens with claims against the navy. He no longer allowed claims of $7 a cord for firewood, the New York City rate, in places where the price was lower. Sometimes overly zealous, he got into trouble when he falsely accused one of his clerks of stealing from a pension fund.[32]

He had strong support from his superiors. Treasury secretary Samuel D. Ingham extended Kendall's policy of canceling newspaper subscriptions to the

30. *Autobiography*, 308–12; *Niles' Register* 37 (1829): 125. Kendall was not very busy at first. His letterbooks show that he wrote an average of only fifteen letters a day the first few months. Fourth Auditor, Miscellaneous Letters, National Archives, RG 217, vol. 28, 102 ff.

31. *Niles' Register* 37 (1829): 125; Josiah Johnston to Clay, 8 July 1829, Clay, *Papers*, 8:73; *Autobiography*, 313.

32. *Autobiography*, 310–16.

entire department, and navy secretary John Branch said that he was deter-mined to "reform his department." He and Kendall enlisted the support of a veteran official who promised to give them evidence of corruption. After two weeks Andrew Jackson called Kendall in and urged him to review accounts with "the utmost strictness." Kendall, who had just had his first dinner with the president, did not hesitate to give him "a variety of suggestions." The invi-tation to the dinner had been arranged by Van Buren, who described Kendall as someone destined to become "influential." At the dinner, which was also attended by Lewis and Van Buren's New York friend James A. Hamilton, Kendall found the Little Magician "very attentive."[33]

Kendall needed the president's support when he began cutting claims of marine officers by as much as 25 percent. In a scathing report on May 28 he attacked the officers' perquisites in great detail. The commandant of the corps was authorized to receive about $1,500 a year in pay and extras, but thanks to special allowances he collected twice as much. Kendall blamed the system on loose "*constructions*" of the Constitution, which gave legislative powers to members of the executive, who had "no direct responsibility to the people." He also pointed out that marine officers received greater compensation for duty on shore than at sea. Now was the time, he said, to "mend" the system and "infuse into the government a principle, a tone, and an energy, which shall last at least for a generation."[34]

There was an immediate uproar. Lieutenant Colonel William Anderson, the fourth-ranking officer in the corps, took his case to Senator Littleton Tazewell of Virginia, a member of the Senate Naval Affairs Committee. Taze-well was an aristocratic, strict-construction, old-school republican. He and his Virginia colleague, John Tyler, were Jacksonians but were not sure of Jackson's republicanism. Without reading the report Tazewell accused Kendall of using an antirepublican broad construction of the Constitution to increase the power of the executive—the opposite of Kendall's position.[35]

Kendall was so bothered by the rebuke that he sent Tazewell a copy of his report, pointing out that he had strictly opposed the doctrine of broad con-struction, "*especially*" anything that gave legislative power to the executive. The

33. Ibid., 313–14, 316; James A. Hamilton, *Reminiscences of James A. Hamilton* (New York, 1869), 130.

34. Kendall to Blair, 24 May 1829, Blair-Lee Papers; Kendall to the Secretary of the Navy, 28 May 1829, *ASP:NA*, 3:581–88. At the end of 1829, only 10 of 50 marine officers were on sea duty. Ibid., 270–71, 431–33.

35. *ASP:NA*, 3:431–32.

senator backed off, saying that he approved of Kendall's stance. On reading Tazewell's reply, Jackson told Kendall that he was pleased to have "our course . . . approved by such [an] enlightened friend." It was reassuring for Kendall to have Jackson refer to his stand as "our course" and comforting for both men to be recognized as strict-construction republicans.[36]

With this encouragement Kendall continued to search for ways to eliminate disorder, waste, and dishonesty. He started an overhaul of the navy book-keeping system by ordering naval officers at the various yards to send in regular accounts of all expenditures. He brought order to the pension fund and changed the way the navy drafted funds from the Treasury. After revising his study of marine pay he sent it to Congress along with a much more definitive study—a "tremendous document," he told Blair—of the pay and allowances of all officers in the navy.[37]

Real reform, however, required the cooperation of Congress. The House and the Senate had tried to control expenses by itemizing appropriations, but the navy had found ways around the regulations—as Kendall well knew—by providing extra allowances and by transferring funds from one category to another. To solve the second problem he proposed replacing "specific appropriations" with "specific accountability." The secretary could use the money as he pleased but would have to make an accounting at the end of the year. Congress did not accept the proposal, but it was later included in the reorganization of the Post Office.[38]

After two months of republican retrenchment, Kendall finally turned to party patronage. Using the excuse that the Adams men, who held twelve of the sixteen positions in his office, were showing "indolence," he decided that they had to be "reformed." On June 1, he told Jane, he "turned out six clerks"; it was "the most painful thing" he had ever done. Kendall's removal of almost 40 percent of his staff was comparable to the removals by Hill and Van Buren.

36. Kendall to Tazewell, 24 June 1829, Amos Kendall Letter (#9210-D), Albert and Shirley Small Special Collections Library, University of Virginia Library; Jackson to Kendall, 2 July 1829, Jackson Supplement.

37. Kendall, "Statement Relative to the Pay and Emoluments of the Officers of the Marine Corps," 25 May 1830, *ASP:NA*, 3:581–88; Branch, "Statement of the Pay, Emoluments, and Allowances of Every Officer, and Agent of the Naval Service, including the Marine Corps," 28 May 1830, in ibid., 685–752; Kendall, Letters of Instructions, 30 Mar. 1829, 14 Aug. 1829, Fourth Auditor, Miscellaneous Letters, vol. 28; James D. Daniels, "Amos Kendall: Cabinet-Politician" (Ph.D. diss., University of North Carolina, 1968), 87; Kendall to Blair, 18 Mar. 1830, Blair-Lee Papers.

38. White, *Jacksonians*, 131–35.

His new staff of eleven Jackson men and five from the opposition included two Kentucky friends. He had hoped, he told Jane apologetically, that he could "find something" for her father, Alexander Kyle, but he would never "do for a clerk" and was too old to be a messenger.[39]

To make sure that the new staff understood the moral side of Jacksonian reform, Kendall issued a circular on office behavior—one of the first federal codes of ethics. He started with an eloquent paragraph nicely balanced between the ideals and realities of the new democratic politics. Everyone, he wrote, "should consider himself hired by his fellow-citizens" but must realize that he holds his office "at the will of the Auditor and the Secretary of the Treasury." Kendall hoped that "the painful business of making removals [was] at an end," but the clerks should understand that their jobs depended on their "industry and fidelity."[40]

Adhering to the moral standards that he had learned from his father, he warned clerks to "guard against the slightest violation of principle." Taking "a few quills or a little paper" from the office was just as wrong as stealing money from the treasury. He would not tolerate "gambling [or] intemperance." Above all there was to be no "foolish aping of men of wealth." Persons making such a "vain show" were the kind who would "swindle" the "farmers, mechanics, and merchants" who paid the clerks' salaries. To keep the office clear of corrupt influences, the clerks were not to accept gifts, entertain visitors, or converse with "loungers." He had previously announced publicly that "the interest of the country demands that this office shall be filled with *men of business*, and not with *babbling politicians*." Later, as Kendall became more identified with administration politics, the opposition would throw these statements back at him.[41]

Kendall's most conspicuous contribution to reform was uncovering the peculations of his predecessor, Tobias Watkins. By mid-April Kendall had unraveled a tangled skein of events showing that Watkins had misappropriated more than $3,000. Delighted by the revelations, Jackson told an old friend that he was preparing to arrest "*a rat*" that had been caught "marauding on the Treasury." The arrest took place on May 1.[42]

39. Kendall to Blair, 21 June 1829, Blair-Lee Papers; Kendall to Jane Kendall, 1, 8 June 1829, in *Autobiography*, 292–93; *Globe*, 10 May 1832.

40. *Autobiography*, 317.

41. Ibid., 318–20; *Niles' Register* 36 (1829): 125.

42. *Autobiography*, 290, 314–15; Kendall to Blair, 21, 30 Apr. 1829, Blair-Lee Papers; *ASP:NA*, 3:735; Jackson to John C. McLemore, Apr. 1829, Jackson, *Correspondence*, 4:19–21; *Niles' Register*, 37 (1829): 235, 275–80, 360.

The case had great political importance because it supported Jacksonian allegations about corruption in the Adams administration. Unlike the other treasury officials, Watkins had been a partisan figure. He had helped Clay answer the bargain charge; and if Adams had won the election, Watkins would probably have replaced McLean as postmaster general. Both sides reacted in partisan fashion. Kendall instructed Blair to redouble his charges of "abuse and corruption" and tell the public that "reform" was taking place. Blair ran the story in the *Argus* and reminded his readers that Watkins had written for Henry Clay. The Adams editors tried to make the best of a bad situation. Several painted Watkins as a martyr, and another dismissed the charges because they had been made by the "reckless" and "vindictive" Kendall.[43]

Watkins was brought to trial on June 2. Two months later he was convicted of "improperly" obtaining $3,050, fined that amount, and sentenced to nine months in jail. When his sentence expired, he was held in jail for inability to pay his fine, which Jackson refused to remit. A year and a half after the trial John Quincy Adams visited Watkins in his "solitary cell" and commented that Jackson's "rancor" was still "insatiate." Watkins was not released until March 1833.[44]

Kendall and Jackson lived up to their promises of rooting out corruption and saving money. Within a year the administration uncovered defaults totaling $457,000, predominantly in the Treasury and Navy Departments. Kendall took the lead in cutting expenses. By the end of the first year he estimated that he had saved $800,000 in the Navy Department, or two-thirds of the total savings of the government. And in 1832 he announced that the department had saved an average of $500,000 a year for three years. The estimates were too modest. In Jackson's first three years he spent $4,000,000 less than Adams in his last three, and half of the savings came from the navy. This frugality won the praise of Old Republican former congressman Nathaniel

43. *Niles' Register* 37 (1829): 359; Mary W. M. Hargreaves, *The Presidency of John Quincy Adams* (Lawrence, Kan., 1985), 56, 270; Clay to John Sloane, 20 May 1827, Samuel L. Southard to Clay, 23 July 1829, Clay, *Papers*, 6:572–74, 8:80; Kendall to Blair, 21 Apr. 1829, Blair-Lee Papers; *Argus*, 13 May 1829; *National Journal*, 4 May 1829, in Daniels, "Amos Kendall," 83–84; Adams, *Memoirs*, 8:290.

44. *Niles' Register* 37 (1829): 235–40, 275–80, 309–11, 341–44, 358–60, 373, 389, 421; *ASP:NA*, 3:735–36; Francis T. Brooke to Clay, 11 July 1829, Clay to Samuel L. Southard, 9 Aug. 1829, Clay, *Papers*, 8:76, 84; Robert V. Remini, *Andrew Jackson and the Course of American Freedom, 1822–1832* (New York, 1981), 189; Adams, *Memoirs*, 8:290; *Congressional Globe*, 25th Cong., 3d sess., app., 389.

Macon of North Carolina but severe criticism from the *National Intelligencer,* which accused Kendall of damaging the morale of the navy.[45]

During their first year in office Jacksonians had made it clear that their promise of reform included retrenchment and ridding the government of corruption. They were less forthcoming about whether it included a system of patronage. Even though they had obviously started such a system, they dared not admit it because the idea was far too unpopular. Whatever it was called, their policy of removals has received and deserves much criticism. The system was often venal and inefficient. It weakened the ideal of public trust and seriously hampered the work of the government. The damage it caused in such places as the Land Office, the Post Office, and the federal armory at Harpers Ferry has been well documented. At the same time, however, it must be said that party patronage was an essential part of an emerging political party system and thus an important contribution to American democracy. Party editors with insufficient sources of income, like Isaac Hill, Francis P. Blair, and Nathaniel Greene, depended on contracts and federal positions in order to keep going. One historian has called such patronage "a primitive, necessary form of public campaign financing." Democracy is not always neat and orderly, and it is sometimes corrupt.[46]

45. Kendall to Blair, 21 Apr., 24 May, 2 July 1829, 25 Apr. 1830, Blair-Lee Papers; *Autobiography,* 298–99; "Central Hickory Club Address," 9 Oct. 1832, in *Globe,* 13 Oct. 1832; Macon to Van Buren, 9 Aug. 1830, Van Buren Papers; *Intelligencer,* 11 Sept. 1830; *Globe,* 18 Dec. 1830. Adams's expenditures 1826–28: total, $49,600,000; Navy, $12,400,000. Jackson 1829–31: total, $45,600,000; Navy, $10,400,000. *Statistical History,* 719.

46. For skepticism about Jacksonian reform but a positive attitude toward Kendall see Edward Pessen, *Jacksonian America: Society, Personality, and Politics,* rev. ed. (Homewood, Ill., 1978), 313–17. For corruption in the Jacksonian patronage system see Rohrbough, *Land Office Business,* 271–94; John, *Spreading the News,* 206–56; Merritt Roe Smith, *Harpers Ferry Armory and the New Technology: The Challenge of Change* (Ithaca, 1977), 252–304. The quotation is from Pasley, *"Tyranny of Printers,"* 399.

# IO

## PARTY BATTLES

At the end of July 1829 the Watkins case was in the hands of the judge, and the president was planning to take a vacation. For months Kendall had been promising Jane, who was about to have a baby, that he would soon be home to take his family to Washington. On July 29 he started for Kentucky, but instead of rushing back, he took a leisurely trip down the Valley of Virginia to White Sulphur Springs. Here he spent a week enjoying the waters in the company of wealthy southern planters—a self-indulgence that seems inconsistent with his character. The best that can be said is that he was worn out and felt the need of a rest.[1]

By the time Kendall finally reached Frankfort, he found that Jane had given birth to a boy, named Andrew, who lived only a few months. Kentucky was still a closely divided state; the Jackson party had won ten of the twelve congressional races in the August election but had lost its majorities in both houses of the legislature. Kendall's return sparked some partisan fighting. The Adams press called his charges against Clay, Hawkins, and Watkins trumped up; the Jackson men praised him for "crush[ing]" corruption and ridding his office of "*aristocratic privileges.*" In thanking his friends Kendall attributed his success to his early experiences on the farm, which had taught him how unfair it was for farmers to save a little money and then have to give it to the government. These Jacksonian statements, opposing corruption, privilege, and high taxes, and defending democracy, farm life, and frugality, reflected the blend of republicanism and democracy that the Jacksonians were establishing in Washington.[2]

1. Kendall to Jane Kendall, 1 May, 7–8 Aug. 1829, in *Autobiography*, 291, 294–95.
2. Hill to Susan Hill, 4 Sept. 1829, Isaac Hill Papers, New Hampshire Historical Society; Clay to Josiah S. Johnston, 26 Aug. 1829, Clay, *Papers*, 8:89–90; *Argus*, 24 June, 1 July, 12, 26 Aug., 23 Sept. 1829; *Autobiography*, 321–22 (quotation).

During the next month Kendall struggled to put his business affairs in order. He was unable to get Lewis Sanders to buy his half share of the *Argus*, but one of his former partners, Gervas E. Russell, stepped forward and took it off his hands. Selling the mill property proved more difficult, and when he and the family left for Washington early in October it was still unsold.[3]

Kendall had rented a house in a "charming" part of Georgetown, where expenses would be $200 a year cheaper than in the city. Jane's only complaint was the smoky wood stove, which he solved by having a coal grate installed. Kendall hoped to hold the family's expenses to $1,500 a year and use the other half of his $3,000 salary to pay off his debts. It was a reasonable plan—many government clerks were getting by on much less—but it would require some discipline. He warned Jane that they could not live as elegantly as "the *very first*" society in Washington. She could not expect to attend "the great parties" or spend any more for clothing than in Kentucky. Instead of owning a horse and carriage, they would rent a hack for seventy-five cents an hour. He reassured her, however, that she would enjoy living in Georgetown because their neighbors would be "more plain and more agreeable" than in the city. Like Amos, Jane would start as an outsider.[4]

Although only forty, Kendall had aged so prematurely that his brother George had not recognized him when they met two years before. Pale, white haired, dressed warmly to ward off the cold even on hot days, he was a strange sight. John Barton Derby of Boston, who had come to Washington in June 1829 seeking a job, recalled him as "buttoned up to the throat in a white broadcloth great-coat,—a white linen handkerchief was bound close about his head, and his countenance was pale and cadaverous. I never remember recoiling from any human spectacle, with such an instinctive antipathy and disgust." When they shook hands, Derby "felt a thrill of cholera stealing" over his body. "What, Mr. Kendall," he exclaimed, "has the political enemy been using his physical power on your . . . head?" "No," Kendall answered, "I am suffering with the sick head-ache." Derby "breathed more freely after he was gone."[5]

<hr />

3. A. G. Meriwether had previously bought the Russell brothers' half share. Kendall, *Autobiography*, 258–59; Kendall to Blair, 3 Feb., 30 Apr. 1829, Blair-Lee Papers; *Argus*, 9, 23 Sept. 1829.

4. Kendall to Jane Kendall, 8 June 1829, in *Autobiography*, 293 (quotations); Kendall to Joseph Desha, 9 Apr. 1831, "Correspondence between Governor Joseph Desha and Amos Kendall," 8; Kendall to Blair, 29 Oct. 1830, Blair-Lee Papers; Kendall to W. W. Corcoran, 12 Oct. 1830, Conaroe Papers, Historical Society of Pennsylvania.

5. Kendall to Jane Kendall, 15 Dec. 1827, in *Autobiography*, 274; John Barton Derby, *Political Reminiscences* (Boston, 1835), 58–59.

Derby's image of Kendall—so like the one in the Anti-Relief newspapers—was unfair. He published it from memory in 1835 when he had become a Whig and had every reason to paint a sorry picture of a Democratic spoilsman. Others who knew Kendall better treated him more gently. U.S. Treasurer John Campbell of Virginia described him as a "little fellow" and "a very tender man." Campbell's brother David said that Kendall had "a very intelligent face," was "very modest," and seemed to be "a plain unassuming man, with a gray head." But Derby's image stuck.[6]

Kendall returned to work on October 12 and found Andrew Jackson deeply enmeshed in a political struggle with Washington society. Under the Virginia Dynasty the upper-class ladies of the city had played a significant role in governmental affairs. The gossip, banter, and exchange of ideas in the women's sphere of dinner parties and receptions gave Dolley Madison, Margaret Bayard Smith, and other prominent women an unusual degree of influence. This expansion of women's power was still another example of the unofficial spread of democracy in the early republic. As a whole, upper-class Washington society was far from democratic, and the ladies hated the intrusion of Jacksonian democracy.

Accustomed to setting the rules of society, these ladies had been highly critical of John H. Eaton and Margaret O'Neale Timberlake for having an affair while Margaret's husband, John Timberlake, was serving as purser on the U.S.S. *Constitution.* When Timberlake died aboard ship in 1828 and the Eatons married soon afterward, the society leaders refused to entertain them. The ostracism of the Eatons extended into the administration. Vice President John C. Calhoun, cabinet secretaries John Branch and Samuel D. Ingham, their wives, and widower John M. Berrien all joined in. To the president's intense embarrassment they were followed by his secretary Andrew J. Donelson and his hostess, Donelson's wife, Emily.

An infuriated Jackson, whose beloved Rachel had also been accused of adultery, defended the Eatons and was supported by Martin Van Buren, William T. Barry, and William B. Lewis. At one level the Eaton affair became a social struggle between outsiders and insiders. At another it pitted married couples against unattached men. Among the Eatons' backers were Jackson, Van Buren, and Lewis, all widowers, Isaac Hill, whose wife was home in New

6. John Campbell to David Campbell, 1 May 1829, David Campbell to Maria H. Campbell, 27 May 1829, Campbell Family Papers, Duke University Rare Book, Manuscript, and Special Collections Library.

Hampshire, and Richard M. Johnson, who was already defying society by living with a mulatto woman. At still a different level it became a political fight between the friends of Calhoun and those of Van Buren to determine which of the two men would succeed Jackson. But at the heart of the matter were two different views of democracy.[7]

As outsiders and Jackson loyalists with conventional views on the role of women, the Kendalls had no sympathy for Washington society and no reservations about accepting the Eatons. Jane liked Margaret Eaton and became one of her few female friends in the administration. Their friendship and Amos's good relationship with navy secretary Branch led the president to ask him to try bringing Branch and John Eaton together. It was an important assignment, for the president was thinking of removing Branch from the cabinet.[8]

But events were in motion that would make it impossible for Kendall to mediate. While he was away in Kentucky, holdover Adams men in his office had examined Timberlake's navy accounts and found them $14,000 in arrears. A few days after Kendall returned, he, Branch, and John Eaton received anonymous letters charging that remittances from Timberlake to John Eaton had caused the default. Accusations that Eaton and Timberlake had been conniving to defraud the government were also being circulated in pamphlets. The charges were damaging to an administration that supposedly was reforming Washington.[9]

On investigating, Kendall immediately became suspicious. The letters were in uniform handwriting and unusually vicious. One taunted Kendall for being "vigilant in discovering abuses among public oficers" but "vent[ing his] spleen [only] on worms." Another told Eaton, "Revenge is sweet, and I have you in my power, and I will roast you, and boil you, and bake you." He also discovered that letters from Eaton and pages from Timberlake's account book had been removed from the purser's papers. Finally, he was surprised to find no inventory of Timberlake's property at the time of his death.[10]

7. Allgor, *Parlor Politics*, 190–238; Kirsten E. Wood, "'One Woman So Dangerous to Public Morals': Gender and Power in the Eaton Affair," *JER* 17 (1997): 237–75. See also John F. Marszalek, *The Petticoat Affair: Manners, Mutiny, and Sex in Andrew Jackson's White House* (New York, 1997); Smith, *First Forty Years of Washington Society*, 252; Adams, *Memoirs*, 8:185.

8. Leon Phillips, *That Eaton Woman: The Defense of Peggy O'Neale Eaton* (New York, 1974), 66; Barry to Susan Taylor, 16 May, 25 June 1829, Barry, "Letters," 13:239–41, 242–43; Kendall to Blair, 22 Nov. 1829, Blair-Lee Papers.

9. Kendall to John Branch, 22 Feb. 1830, *ASP:NA*, 3:654–55.

10. *ASP:NA*, 3:654–55.

Eaton, furthermore, offered a plausible explanation for the remittances. Back in 1823 the Metropolis Bank had foreclosed on properties worth $12,000 owned by Margaret's father, William O'Neale. Eaton had come forward and bought back the property, promising to resell it and turn any profit over to the O'Neales. A year later Eaton loaned about $1,600 to Timberlake to clear his previous accounts so that he could become purser on the *Constitution*. The remittances in question were sent by Timberlake to repay the loan and help salvage O'Neale's property.

Kendall began to suspect that Eaton and Timberlake were the objects of a conspiracy. His suspicions turned to Lieutenant Robert Beverley Randolph of Virginia, who had become acting purser of the *Constitution* when Timberlake died and had taken over his accounts and property. The lieutenant was a descendant of the famous Randolph family and was on excellent terms with Senators Littleton Tazewell and John Tyler. He had been in the navy since 1810 and ranked among the top third in seniority of all naval officers. His accounts had been reviewed, found satisfactory, and closed by Tobias Watkins in the fall of 1828.[11]

The deeper Kendall got into the case, the more convinced he became that Randolph was guilty. When first questioned, the lieutenant said that Timberlake had left only a small sum of money and that it had all been used to repay his Mediterranean debts. Randolph also denied that there had ever been an inventory. But Commodore Daniel T. Patterson, who had been captain of the *Constitution,* said that the purser had left a great deal of money and that there was an inventory. Not wanting to handle such a "delicate" case alone, Kendall got permission from Jackson to have Patterson and Second Comptroller Isaac Hill join in the investigation.[12]

In challenging a prominent Virginian and bringing in Hill and Patterson, Kendall made the case even more political than it was already. After almost a year of the Jackson presidency a number of southern leaders such as Vice President Calhoun and Senators Tazewell and Tyler were losing confidence in the president because of his appointments policy and what they viewed as autocratic, antirepublican behavior. The Timberlake case increased their doubts. Defending Timberlake and Eaton (and thus Jackson) were two of the president's most loyal politicians, Kendall and Hill, and one of his most loyal mili-

---

11. Lyon G. Tyler, ed., *Encyclopedia of Virginia Biography* (New York, 1915), 2:351–52; *ASP:NA,* 3:402–34, 654–64; Kendall to Blair, 22 Nov. 1829, Blair-Lee Papers.

12. Kendall to Branch, 22 Feb. 1830, *ASP:NA,* 3:654–55.

tary men, Patterson, who had served with Old Hickory at New Orleans. On the other side were the two Virginia senators, one of whom, Tazewell, had already crossed swords with Kendall.

In an official examination on February 12, 1830, Randolph admitted that there had been $11,000 in Timberlake's accounts but continued to insist that he, Randolph, had accounted for it legitimately. When Kendall refused to give him access to Timberlake's papers, the lieutenant flew into a rage and threatened to complain to Tazewell and Tyler. The threat was not an idle one, for the Senate had not yet confirmed Kendall and Hill and only a week earlier had called for reports from them on the Timberlake case. On February 25 Kendall received another anonymous note in the same handwriting as before. Randolph, the note read, had complained to his "bosom friends" Tazewell and Tyler, who had "expressed the utmost indignation" at Kendall's refusal to make the papers available. To show that he could not be intimidated, Kendall wrote Tazewell a note saying that Randolph's threats had fallen "powerless." On March 3 he sent a report to the Senate outlining his suspicions about Randolph. "I will do nothing to shield Major Eaton," he wrote, but "I will not be deterred from doing justice to him . . . by the threats of . . . open enemies or masked assassins." He then turned the Timberlake case (now the Randolph affair) over to a navy court of inquiry.[13]

Early in the Timberlake case the president had asked Kendall to help him prepare his first annual message to Congress. Within a few weeks Kendall produced statements on Indian affairs, the BUS, and political reform, which went a long way toward defining the policies of the administration. Kendall's experiences in Kentucky had taught him that Indians were an inferior, childlike, warlike people blocking the movement of civilization westward. He had become involved in the Indiana Land Company because he thought that the Indian menace had been removed, but had then lost interest because of rumors of Indian raids. In his letters to John Quincy Adams in 1823 he had described the Indians as "children of the forest," whose minds were easily "poisoned" by the British. That same year he had said that the Indians' "minds must be turned from the wild pursuit of game to . . . the cultivation of the earth." He believed that educating the Indians was a waste of time.[14]

13. Tazewell to Jackson, 17 Feb. 1830, Kendall to Branch, 22 Feb. 1830, Kendall to Tazewell, 24 Feb. 1830, ibid., 3:591–92, 655–57, 669.
14. Kendall, *Letters to John Quincy Adams*, 17; *Argus*, 19 Mar. 1823.

This scornful attitude, typical of his time, was reflected in his draft. Efforts to "reclaim" the Indians from their "wandering life," he argued, had proven unsuccessful. "Surrounded by the whites with their arts of civilization," the "savage[s]" were "doom[ed]" to "weakness and decay" unless a policy of removal was adopted. The statement, which was consistent with Jackson's views, was used in the message and became the first step toward the passage of the Indian Removal Act six months later.[15]

Kendall's draft on rechartering the BUS was not quite as influential. The charter would not expire until 1836, but Jackson was so opposed to the BUS that he wanted to include the subject in his message. When he asked his advisers to suggest changes in the BUS, Kendall returned a draft with ideas from his days in Kentucky. The BUS, he said, was unconstitutional because Congress lacked the powers to set up a private corporation outside of the District of Columbia and exempt it from state taxes. The only proper bank would be one attached to the Treasury, located in the district, and with all the stock belonging to the government. Again his ideas mirrored Jackson's.[16]

Worried about what Jackson would say in the message, supporters of the BUS—Van Buren, Eaton, and Lewis—brought in James A. Hamilton of New York to help with the writing. Hamilton dismissed Kendall's draft, saying that it was written "in a loose, newspaper, slashing style," and drew up a less specific, less hostile statement. Since Jackson was not yet ready to attack the BUS openly, he went along with Hamilton's draft. In his message he questioned the constitutionality of the BUS and wondered if a national bank "founded upon the credit of the Government" might better serve the country.[17]

In order to get his own ideas before the public Kendall sent a letter to his editor friend Mordecai M. Noah, which appeared as an editorial in the *New York Courier and Enquirer*. The letter raised troublesome questions about the BUS: Was it necessary now that most of the federal debt had been retired? Might not state banks show that they were safe enough to receive the federal deposits now in the BUS? Did these banks need protection against the BUS? Would state legislatures tell their senators how to vote on the question of recharter? The editorial prepared the way for a future war on the BUS.[18]

---

15. "Drafts of First Annual Message," Jackson Papers; Jackson, "First Annual Message," *Compilation*, 2:456–59.

16. Kendall to Jackson, 20 Nov. 1829, Jackson Supplement.

17. Hamilton, *Reminiscences*, 150; Jackson, *Correspondence*, 4:97n; *Compilation*, 2:462.

18. *Niles' Register* 37 (1830): 378; Isaac C. Pray, *Memoirs of James Gordon Bennett and His Times* (New York, 1855), 111, 148.

Kendall's draft on political reform had the most immediate impact of the three. The constant talk about spoils, the rush of job seekers to Washington, and the large number of removals had led to an angry protest. Adams men and some of the southern Old Republicans in the Jackson party were likening the president to a corrupt eighteenth-century English king dispensing favors. Jackson, who had never countenanced a spoils system, was disturbed by the criticism and wanted to explain his position.

In his draft Kendall used republican ideas to justify a democratic reform. "Few men," he warned, can "long possess office and power without being more or less corrupted." By remaining in office they "pervert government from its legitimate ends and make it an engine for the support of the few at the expense of the many." Regular removals of such men would "promote that rotation in office which constitutes a leading article in the republican creed." These words, which Jackson used with only slight changes, became the Jacksonian rationale for political removals. Instead of a corrupt spoils system in which kings gave out jobs, Kendall described removals as a democratic system in which the jobs belonged to the people and were rotated among them.[19]

Soon after sending in the annual message, Jackson started forwarding 243 appointments, including 20 editors, to the Senate for confirmation. Coming on the heels of his call for rotation in office, the unprecedented number of appointments brought out more protests. Resolutions were presented in the Senate questioning the president's power to make removals without due cause. To reduce the criticism, Jackson sent in the less controversial appointments first, leaving editors like Kendall, Hill, and Noah for last. Hill, who knew he was a target, was so alarmed that he sent word back to New Hampshire that there would be no further removals in the state until he was confirmed.[20]

The nominations of Kendall and Hill were sent to the Senate on February 10, 1830, two days before Kendall began his examination of Randolph. After a month's delay, Kendall's nomination and his report on Timberlake were both sent to a select committee made up of three Jacksonians (Tazewell, George M. Bibb, and Hugh Lawson White of Tennessee) and two Adams men (Ezekiel Chambers of Maryland and Samuel Bell of New Hampshire). Kendall had

19. "Drafts of First Annual Message," Jackson Papers; Jackson, "First Annual Message," *Compilation,* 2:448–49; Wood, *Radicalism of the American Revolution,* 301–5.

20. Eriksson, "Federal Civil Service," 523; *Register of Debates,* 21st Cong., 1st sess., 457–70; *National Journal,* 3, 8 Dec. 1829, 11 May 1830; *Intelligencer,* 27 Sept. 1832; Hill to Henry Starks, 13 Jan. 1830, Hill Papers.

nothing to fear from Bibb and White but could expect no mercy from the other three. Tazewell was an open enemy, Chambers had accused Kendall of partiality in the Timberlake case, and Bell, the leader of the Adams party in New Hampshire, had nothing but contempt for editors.[21]

Kendall was worried about being confirmed because the Jacksonians had only nominal control of the Senate, and three of them—Tazewell, Tyler, and William Smith of South Carolina—were expected to vote against him. He also feared that other Jackson men, put off by his reputation as a spoilsman, might join them. And if there was a tie, he had little confidence in the vote of Vice President Calhoun. Unable to mingle comfortably with senators, he felt isolated and—as had happened before—became sick and depressed. His only solace came from Andrew Jackson, who promised him another job if he was rejected—some said as a third assistant postmaster general.[22]

Jackson was also worried. He had been unable to bring the Eaton affair to an end and dared not do anything drastic. He knew, for example, that if he dismissed John Branch, Branch's two fellow North Carolinians in the Senate would vote against Kendall and Hill. Jackson also faced a number of roadblocks in Congress. His hopes of starting a movement against the BUS dimmed when reports favorable to it were brought into both houses. His Indian policy was in doubt after Adams senator Theodore Frelinghuysen of New Jersey delivered a moving speech against removal of the tribes. And most dangerous of all, radicals in South Carolina were claiming the right to nullify federal laws and were planning to raise the issue on April 13 at the Jefferson birthday dinner.[23]

The day before the dinner the Senate dealt Jackson a severe setback by rejecting Isaac Hill by a vote of thirty-three to fifteen. Hill had attacked Adams so virulently during the campaign that only the most loyal Jackson men stood up for him. The defeat exposed weaknesses in the party, which could not deliver the votes of nine key southerners. The rift between Jackson and the more radical southerners widened at the dinner when the president delivered a toast rebuking Calhoun and the doctrine of nullification. Encouraged by the turn of events, critics of the spoils system offered resolutions in the Senate calling removals "a gross violation of our constitutional rights." Only with great difficulty could Jackson senators table them.[24]

21. *Senate Journal,* 21st Cong., 1st sess., 423; Kendall to Blair, 1 Mar. 1830, Blair-Lee Papers.

22. Adams, *Memoirs,* 8:179, 197. Kendall to Blair, 28 Jan., 1, 18 Mar., 25 Apr. 1830, Blair-Lee Papers.

23. Johnston to Clay, 14 Mar. 1830, Clay, *Papers,* 8:181–83; Adams, *Memoirs* 8:184.

24. *Senate Journal,* 447; *Register of Debates,* 21st Cong., 1st sess., 368, 385–96.

The nomination of Kendall had now become all-important. It was said that the men around Jackson would "give any office in their gift" to have him confirmed. Clay and Daniel Webster expected a close vote. If there was a tie, Clay's friend Josiah S. Johnston doubted that Calhoun would vote against Kendall, knowing that his action would split the Jackson party. They were all correct, for on May 10 the Senate voted twenty-four to twenty-four on the nomination, and Calhoun, not yet ready to confront Jackson, broke the tie in Kendall's favor. Kendall survived primarily because his Kentucky background made him much more palatable to the South than Hill. Only three southern Jacksonians voted against him—Tazewell, Tyler, and Smith. The Jackson party held together.[25]

But more party discord had already begun as Calhoun and Van Buren started maneuvering toward the next election. In December Duff Green began to drum up support for Calhoun in New England and tried to enlist Gideon Welles of Connecticut. "Shocked" by what he considered disloyalty to Jackson, the editor refused. At about the same time publisher James Watson Webb of the *New York Courier and Enquirer* suggested Van Buren as the next party candidate. By early spring, however, Van Buren had decided that the best way to stop Calhoun was to have the president run again. In short order the *Courier and Enquirer* and the *Albany Argus* recommended Jackson's renomination, and in a few weeks the New York and Pennsylvania legislatures renominated the president.[26]

Once Kendall had sided with Eaton in the Randolph affair, his relationship with Calhoun and Green deteriorated. He noted that Calhoun was treating him "coolly" and that Green spoke "harshly" of members of the administration not "friendly" with Calhoun. On March 1 he warned Blair that if there was a break in the cabinet, Green would attack Jackson, thereby forcing the president to set up a new party organ. Remembering Jackson's remark about someday needing him in a different position, Kendall predicted that he would become the editor.[27]

25. Johnston to Clay, 14 Mar., 30 Apr. (summary)(quotation), Clay to George Watterson, 8 May 1830, Clay, *Papers*, 8:181–83, 198, 203–4; Webster to Jeremiah Mason (summary), 8 May 1830, *The Papers of Daniel Webster: Correspondence*, ed. Charles M. Wiltse and Harold T. Moser, 7 vols. (Hanover, N.H., 1974–86), 3:405; *Senate Journal*, 457.

26. Welles to Hill, extract, 24 Apr. 1830, in Kendall to Welles, 10 Mar. 1831, Gideon Welles Papers, LC; Niven, *Gideon Welles*, 74–76; Webb to Van Buren, 19 Dec. 1829, Van Buren Papers; *Albany Argus*, 3 Apr. 1830.

27. Kendall to Blair, 28 Jan. ("coolly"), 1, 18 Mar., 25 Apr. 1830, Blair-Lee Papers; Kendall to Blair, fragment, c. Apr. 1830, Blair Family Papers ("harshly").

Thus somewhat by default he was drawn toward the Van Buren camp. On March 18 he told Blair that Calhoun was too impatient and urged Blair to come out in favor of Jackson's renomination. Amazed by the unobtrusive way in which Van Buren operated, he reported that the Little Magician "glide[d] along as smoothly as oil and as silently as a cat" and had "the entire confidence of the President." Kendall preferred Van Buren to Calhoun but treated him warily because he considered him a rival for the president's ear. A devoted Jackson man, Kendall never became a Van Buren man.[28]

The conflict between Van Buren and Calhoun became entangled in the rejection of Hill, who was one of Van Buren's strongest supporters. Aware that Jackson was angry about the rejection, Kendall devised a plan to have Hill elected senator from New Hampshire. The plan hinged on having incumbent Levi Woodbury announce that he would not be a candidate for reelection when the legislature voted for senator in June. Kendall approached friends in New Hampshire and put articles in the Baltimore and New York newspapers announcing Woodbury's intention not to run. Woodbury reluctantly agreed but then reneged in June, only to be badly beaten by Hill in the legislature. The return of Hill in place of Woodbury, who had been flirting with Calhoun, would be to Van Buren's advantage.[29]

Despite the acrimony Jackson's congressional program was faring well. By the time the session adjourned at the end of May, the Senate had confirmed all but 7 of his 243 nominations. Mordecai M. Noah was rejected the same day that Kendall was confirmed, but later the Jacksonians took advantage of key absences to push him through on reconsideration. The Indian removal bill passed on May 28, and in the last few days of the session the president successfully vetoed three internal improvement bills, including one for the Maysville Road in Kentucky. Jackson was also pleased by Kendall's report on the Randolph affair, which cleared Eaton of any misdoing and left little doubt that Randolph had mishandled Timberlake's accounts.[30]

But party problems remained. Jackson further antagonized the southern nullifiers by accusing Calhoun of having recommended that he be censured for his invasion of Florida in 1818. Calhoun, he wrote on May 30, had tried to

28. Kendall to Blair, 18 Mar., 25 Apr. 1830, Blair-Lee Papers.

29. Kendall to Blair, 25, 30 Apr., 24 June 1830, ibid.; Niven, *Gideon Welles*, 76–78; Donald B. Cole, *Jacksonian Democracy in New Hampshire, 1800–1851* (Cambridge, Mass., 1970), 92–95; Hill to John Langdon Elwyn, 13 Apr. 1830, Hill Papers; Woodbury to Benjamin Pierce, 15 May 1830, John Hubbard to Woodbury, 30 May 1830, Levi Woodbury Papers, LC.

30. Jackson to James A. Hamilton, 29 May 1830, Jackson, *Correspondence*, 4:139–40.

"destroy [his] reputation." There was also a northern party problem, for the Indian Removal Act and the Maysville Road veto had annoyed northern and western Jackson men. On June 1 Kendall warned Hill that many of these men had "gone home much dissatisfied." He expected Clay's friends to make "a mighty effort . . . to rouse the country." With his flair for finding conspiracies he suggested that "the Union itself" might be threatened if Clay's efforts were not "promptly met and counteracted." As a first step he asked Hill to have the Jackson majority in the New Hampshire legislature pass a resolution endorsing the president's policies. Hill, whose election to the Senate was about to be voted on in the legislature, passed Kendall's draft resolution along, and it carried, as Kendall recalled, with "narely a verbal alteration."[31]

Kendall had been thinking about "a new division of parties" for some time. Back in February he had warned Blair that Old Hickory would consider anyone who supported the BUS an enemy. Blair needed no lecturing, for he had recently written several angry editorials in the *Argus* against the BUS. In another letter to Blair on April 25 he predicted that the Jackson party would soon consist of "the democracy of the northern, middle, western and part of the southern states, who will go for reform in all the branches of the government, a gradual reduction of duties so as to bring down the revenue . . . [and] the lopping off all the *splendid appendages* to the government." The opposition would come mainly from "the furious anti-tariff men of the South and the furious tariff men of the north."[32]

With this moderate states' rights platform Kendall was staking out a position less reliant on the South and midway between the southern nullifiers and the northern nationalists. He was looking ahead to the emerging two-party system: one party, the Jackson Democrats, willing to compromise on the tariff and attacking the BUS; the other, the Whigs, based on an alliance of Clay and Calhoun. But first he, Van Buren, the president, and others of like mind would have to deal with the dangerous split in the administration.

---

31. Jackson to Calhoun, 3, 30 May 1830, ibid., 4:136, 140–44; Kendall to Hill, 1 June 1830, Hill Papers; Kendall to Blair, 10 July 1830, Blair Family Papers.

32. Kendall to Blair, 1 Mar., 25 Apr. 1830, Blair-Lee Papers.

# II

## THE KITCHEN CABINET

On his way back to the Hermitage in late June 1830 Andrew Jackson wrote an angry letter to William B. Lewis. It was time, he said, to replace Duff Green as party spokesman. The president was outraged by Green's failure to reply to the congressional reports defending the BUS. Calhoun controlled Green, he expostulated, just as a puppeteer pulled the strings on his dolls. Jackson's letter was the first step toward a crisis in the administration and ultimately the formation of the Democratic party.[1]

Lewis shared the letter with Kendall, and the two men began looking for an editor. Lewis, a Van Buren man, approached Claiborne W. Gooch, who was copublisher of the *Richmond Enquirer* and close to the Little Magician. Kendall, on the other hand, consulted William T. Barry, and the two men decided to write to Francis P. Blair. Knowing that Jackson was not ready to cut his ties with Green, Kendall made it clear in his letter that the new paper would have to coexist with the *United States Telegraph*, even though it would be the "*real* administration paper." Gooch was very much interested, but he made too many demands and soon fell out of the running. The matter then dragged on until October when the president returned from Tennessee and readily agreed that Blair was the man for the job.[2]

In spelling out the terms of the arrangement Kendall listed the same priorities that he had shared with Blair in earlier letters. The newspaper would have to support "a thorough reform in the government" and take a stand against the BUS. It must be "mildly opposed to the South Carolina nullifiers, in favor of a judicious tariff, . . . the payment of the national debt, . . . and . . .

1. Jackson to Lewis, 26, 28 June 1830, Jackson, *Correspondence*, 4:156–58.
2. Kendall to Blair, 10 July 1830, Blair Family Papers (quotation); Kendall to Blair, 22 Aug., 2–4, 14 Oct. 1830, Blair-Lee Papers; Blair to Kendall, 24 Dec. 1842, Van Buren Papers; Michael W. Singletary, "The New Editorial Voice for Andrew Jackson: Happenstance or Plan?" *Journalism Quarterly* 53 (1976): 672–78.

leaving the states to manage their own affairs." Blair must also agree to be pledged to Jackson alone, not to Van Buren or anyone else. This was a balanced states' rights program designed to hold the southern base while reaching out to other interests.[3]

To make sure that Blair took the job, Kendall made it as attractive as possible. Although Green would keep the congressional printing, Blair could count on executive patronage worth at least $4,000 a year and eventually $15,000. Dress for the family would be no more expensive than in Kentucky. Blair, an avid hunter and fisherman, could hunt deer in Virginia and catch "cats, perch, pike, rock, sturgeon . . . shad and herring" in the Potomac. This rosy picture helped win over Blair and his wife, Eliza, and as soon as Blair settled his debts, he accepted the job.[4]

To keep peace in the party Kendall tried to convince Green that Blair was coming as an ally, not as a rival. A second newspaper was needed, he explained, to help the party compete with the six opposition presses in the city. Green was not fooled. He called on Barry and Eaton, "threatened, protested and remonstrated," but finally said grudgingly that he would meet Blair "on friendly terms." For the time being he was no more interested in open warfare than Kendall and Jackson.[5]

The appointment of Blair was a coup for Kendall. His rivals Lewis and Van Buren would have much preferred the traditionally republican Virginian Gooch over the more democratic westerner Blair. Calhoun and Green of course would have preferred no one at all. Kendall had deftly added Blair to his growing list of party friends in Washington. He had sent Blair the names of these friends so that the new editor would know where to turn for help and patronage. The list included prominent figures such as Van Buren, Barry, Eaton, and Lewis, and lesser men—Treasurer John Campbell, Register Thomas L. Smith, Second Comptroller James B. Thornton (who had replaced Isaac Hill), and Land Commissioner Elijah Hayward. This was an emerging core of Jackson loyalists within the administration.[6]

3. Kendall to Blair, 2–4 Oct. 1830, Blair-Lee Papers.

4. Kendall to Blair, 22 Aug., 2, 29 (quotation) Oct., 1 Nov. 1830, ibid.; Smith, *Francis Preston Blair*, 9, 13, 33, 41–42; Kendall to Blair, 20 Nov. 1830, Blair Family Papers.

5. Kendall to Green, 7, 10 Nov. 1830, Blair-Lee Papers; Blair to Green, 13 Oct. 1830, in *Globe*, 30 Mar. 1831; Kendall to Blair, 20 Nov. 1830, Blair Family Papers (quotation).

6. Kendall to Blair, 22 Aug., 2 Oct. 1830, Blair-Lee Papers; *Globe*, 19 Mar. 1831; *Autobiography*, 373–74; Kendall to Hill, 26 Nov. 1830, Miscellaneous Manuscripts, Kendall, Amos, New-York Historical Society; Kendall to Blair, 20 Nov. 1830, Blair Family Papers.

After a perilous three-week carriage trip through the Kentucky and Virginia mountains, Blair reached Washington the last week in November. On the final day the carriage overturned, leaving him with a long gash on his head. For weeks Kendall had been telling Lewis and others to "wait till Blair comes," for then they would have someone who could talk back to Duff Green. When the new editor finally arrived, Lewis was disappointed to see a sickly man, all skin and bones, who spoke in a dirgelike voice. Noting the patch on his head, Lewis remarked unsympathetically, "Mr. Blair, we want stout hearts and sound heads here."[7]

The Old General, a better judge of character than Lewis, immediately took to "Blaar," as he called him, and insisted that he sit next to him at a state dinner that evening. The two men were much alike: both loved the outdoors, were handy with firearms, and hated the BUS. As soon as Blair bought a home and could keep cows, he began leaving pails of milk at the President's House. Jackson in return entertained the Blairs and twice took them along on a summer vacation. Jackson, who was six feet one and weighed 140 pounds, was now surrounded by three Kentuckians—Kendall, Blair, and Barry—as cadaverous as he. The four could not have weighed 500 pounds.[8]

The Blairs chose to live in Washington, but the Kendalls stayed put in Georgetown. The family continued to grow. Baby Andrew had died, but Jane had given birth to another daughter, and her parents, Alex and Eleanor Kyle, had arrived from Frankfort with her brother, her sister Eliza McLaughlin, and her sister's young son James. There were also four slaves, giving Kendall sixteen mouths to feed.[9]

Perhaps the new newspaper would help, for Kendall was to write articles, share other responsibilities, and receive part of the profits. He had asked Blair to bring along a back file of the *Argus,* which would save him "much thought" when he took up some of the old Kentucky issues. Since the party had no money to set up a press, he hired a job printer. Freed from the drudgery of publishing, Blair would be able to spend his time writing and "pushing [his]

7. Smith, *Francis Preston Blair,* 42–43; Parton, *Life of Andrew Jackson,* 3:337.

8. Parton, *Life of Andrew Jackson,* 3:337–38; Smith, *Francis Preston Blair,* 92.

9. Eliza had lost her husband either by death or by separation. Kendall to Blair, 2–4, 29 Oct. 1830, Blair-Lee Papers; United States Census Schedules, Scott County, Ky., RG 29, 1820, 121, 140, Georgetown, District of Columbia, 1830, 141; Kendall to Isaac Hill, 13 July 1830, Kendall Papers, Filson Historical Society; Kendall to Isaac Hill, 26 Nov. 1830, Miscellaneous Manuscripts, Kendall Papers, New-York Historical Society.

acquaintance with government officials and members of Congress." He would need only a clerk and a boy to fold and mail the newspapers. Kendall was happy to hire Alex Kyle and his son to perform these tasks.[10]

The first issue of the newspaper, which they called the *Globe*, appeared on December 7, barely a week after Blair's arrival. It was timed to coincide with the convening of Congress. Underlining their opposition to an activist central government, they placed on the masthead the motto: "*The world is governed too much.*" The purpose of government, they maintained, was to protect men from evil—often from government itself. Only by reelecting Jackson could Americans save themselves from the "splendid schemes" of foolish politicians.[11]

As Kendall had promised Blair, the paper replaced the *Telegraph* as the party organ. Using their ties with other editors, they quickly established a network of Jackson papers, exchanging editorials with presses such as the *New-Hampshire Patriot*, the *Richmond Enquirer*, the *Albany Argus*, and the *Argus of Western America*. They defended democracy and states' rights, rotation in office and economy in government, and increasingly attacked the BUS.[12]

For these first few months Blair and Kendall shared the writing. As in Kentucky, Kendall's pieces were more imaginative, learned, and humorous than the blunt, ferocious attacks written by Blair. Sometimes the content gives Kendall away, sometimes the metaphors, sometimes the sophisticated vocabulary. He was always partisan. An example of humor was a piece entitled "The Penates" and signed "Vox Populi, Vox Dei" admonishing editor Hezekiah Niles for worshiping the household gods Adams and Clay. Vox Populi quoted an imaginary French visitor who found Adams men "sullen, haughty," Clay men "cunning, impudent," but Jackson men "confiding, philanthropic." Two attacks on Calhoun, supposedly submitted by Kentuckians, were almost certainly written by Kendall—especially the one from "a gentleman of much political information in Franklin county." Less funny but more significant was a

10. Kendall to Blair, 2–4, 14 ("much") Oct. 1830, Blair-Lee Papers; Kendall to Blair, 20 Nov. 1830, Blair Family Papers ("pushing"); Kendall to A. Kyle, 19 Feb. 1831, Kendall Papers, Dartmouth College Library.

11. The *Globe* was a four-page semiweekly with politics, general news, excerpts from books and other newspapers, and sharp editorial comment, similar in many respects to the *Argus*. *Globe*, 7 Dec. 1830.

12. *Globe*, Dec. 1830–Mar. 1831.

series of two dozen commentaries by Kendall on Jackson's message to Congress.[13]

Although the *Globe* was a journalistic and political success, it was not making money. Blair was often slow paying the printer, and Kendall had to give up any claim on sharing in the profits. He began to write less often and left more of the responsibilities to Blair. Seriously in need of funds, the new editor traveled to Baltimore, Philadelphia, and New York in March 1831 and raised $6,000. With the new capital he set up his own printing shop and launched a daily edition. By July he had two thousand subscribers, about half as many as either the *Telegraph* or the *National Intelligencer*. Jackson pressed cabinet members to provide printing jobs, but even with this help Blair did not come close to attaining Kendall's goal of $15,000 a year of executive printing.[14]

The cold, snowy winter of 1830–31 was not a happy one for the president. The Eaton affair continued to plague him, and he and several of his closest friends were ill much of the time. Jackson suffered constant pain from two bullets in his arm and chest, and John H. Eaton was so sick with diphtheria that he came close to dying. Because of the sickness and the standoff with Washington society the president's dinner parties had "run down pretty low," with "scarce any ladies attend[ing] them."[15]

For a time Calhoun and Green tried to cooperate with Jackson. They hoped to get Jacksonian votes in the printer elections and saw no reason to antagonize the president until they knew whether he intended to run for a second term. But after the *Globe* announced that Jackson would run and both houses elected Green printer, Calhoun decided to act. On February 17 he published an "Address" in the *Telegraph* denying the charge that he had tried to have Jackson censured for his Florida invasion. He did admit, however, that he had believed Jackson guilty of "exceed[ing his] orders." He insisted that Van Buren and his friends had brought up the charge as part of a plot to destroy him.[16]

13. Ibid., Dec. 1830–Mar. 1831, especially 12, 15 Jan. and 12 Mar. 1831; Powrie V. Doctor, "Amos Kendall, Propagandist" (Ph.D. diss., University of Georgia, 1940), 48; Kendall to Jackson, 3 Dec. 1831, Blair-Lee Papers.

14. Blair to Kendall, 24 Dec. 1842, Van Buren Papers; *Globe*, 7, 11 May, 13 June, 1 July 1831; Parton, *Life of Andrew Jackson*, 3:338; Smith, *Francis Preston Blair*, 47.

15. Jackson to Mary Eastin, 1 Jan. 1831, Jackson Supplement; Everett to Charlotte B. Everett, 19 Jan., 17 Feb. (quotation) 1831, Edward Everett Papers, MHS.

16. Everett to Charlotte B. Everett, 8, 19 Jan. 1831, Everett Papers; "The Autobiography of Martin Van Buren," ed. John C. Fitzpatrick, *Annual Report of the American Historical Association*

Obviously well prepared for the address, the chain of Jackson newspapers answered back. The *Richmond Enquirer* cited Calhoun's "unrestrained ambition," while the *Globe* said that he had admitted to attacking Jackson. The *New York Evening Post* called him a liar. The *Albany Argus* defended Van Buren with material from the *New-Hampshire Patriot,* the *Hartford Times,* and the *Rhode Island Republican Herald.* Jonathan Harvey of New Hampshire cheerfully reported that "Duff [was] intensely disappointed" at the way the Jacksonians had responded.[17]

Kendall had been waiting for this chance ever since bringing Blair to Washington. He was well armed, because he had a copy of a letter from Gideon Welles to Isaac Hill in 1830 describing Green's efforts to get Welles to back Calhoun. The letter gave Kendall the chance to show that Green and Calhoun had been disloyal to Jackson, and he exploited it just as he had used Clay's letter in 1828. He kept the subject alive and his target on the defensive by releasing information bit by bit. He hoped to force Green to publish other documents, but if he refused, "the inferences," Kendall said, would hurt him more than "the truth." Remembering his difficulty with Clay's letter, he warned Welles never to claim more for any document than it actually contained.[18]

Kendall first used part of Welles's story to refute the idea that Van Buren had started the controversy. Green, he noted, had been plotting for Calhoun ever since Jackson became president. Finally on April 6 Kendall published an extract from Welles's letter to prove that Green had held "conversations" with newspaper editors in December 1829. Following his own advice not to claim more than he could prove, he did not say that Calhoun was planning to run in 1832. He simply quoted Green as saying that Calhoun's "claims could not be postponed another four years."[19]

---

*for the Year 1918,* 2 vols. (Washington, D.C., 1920), 2:376–81; *Globe,* 22 Jan. 1831; *Niles' Register* 39 (1831): 405, 437; *Telegraph,* 17 Feb. 1831.

17. *Richmond Enquirer,* 19, 24 Feb. 1831; *Globe,* 19 Feb., 2 Mar. 1831; *Albany Argus,* 7 Mar. 1831; Harvey to Welles, 6 Mar. 1831, Gideon Welles Papers, box 1, folder 4, Connecticut Historical Society.

18. Niven, *Gideon Welles,* 80–81; Welles to Van Buren, 27 Dec. 1830, Van Buren Papers; Kendall to Welles, 24 Jan., 21, 26 Feb., 2, 4, 8, 10, 19 Mar., 1, 7, 8, 15, 22 Apr. 1831 (quotations, 2, 8 Mar.), Gideon Welles Papers, LC; Welles to Kendall, c. 2 Feb. 1831, Welles Papers, Connecticut Historical Society.

19. *Globe,* 23, 26 Feb., 2, 9, 12, 19 Mar., 6 Apr. 1831; *Telegraph,* 26 Feb., 18 Mar. 1831; *Niles' Register* 40 (1831): 71–72; Kendall to Welles, 19 Mar., 1 Apr. 1831, Welles Papers, LC.

Kendall, Blair, and the other editors had blunted the attacks of Calhoun and Green but had not saved the administration. Van Buren realized that the struggle would never end as long as the cabinet was divided. Dismissing Calhounites Branch, Ingham, and Berrien would not help; the public would only blame the dismissals on Van Buren and the Eaton affair. But if Van Buren resigned first, then the three could be ousted, and the president could form a united cabinet. After Van Buren broached the idea to Jackson, the president discussed it with Lewis, Eaton, and Barry and endorsed the plan. On April 7, Eaton resigned, followed four days later by Van Buren. Jackson then forced Branch, Ingham, and Berrien to resign.[20]

After failing with plain "men of business" in his cabinet Jackson reverted to the old formula of appointing distinguished men from good families. He and Van Buren would continue this formula until 1841. Having feuded with southern nullifiers, he chose men with broader views—none from the Old South. Minister to Great Britain Louis McLane of Delaware was brought back to become secretary of the Treasury while Van Buren replaced him in London. Senator Edward Livingston of New York and now Louisiana became secretary of state, Roger B. Taney of Maryland attorney general, northerners Lewis Cass and Levi Woodbury secretaries of war and navy.

Jackson had lost his cabinet, and there was no certainty that he could save his party. The opposition, now being called National Republicans, felt that the administration was falling apart. Edward Everett, who had left the ministry and was now congressman from Massachusetts, predicted "a general breaking up of the [Jackson] party" that would threaten "the Union," while Clay said that the party was "on the verge of dissolution." Jackson was angry and depressed, as he fretted about the Eaton affair, which was still not settled.[21]

Kendall, who had seemed so confident in dueling with Green, was now a bit unsure. In breaking up the cabinet Jackson had consulted with Lewis and Barry but not with him. The president was also becoming very friendly with Blair. The new cabinet was not made up of the ordinary sort of people Kendall preferred; he was not at all sure how he would get along with the new secretary of the Treasury. Working too hard as usual, he was at one of those points

20. Van Buren, "Autobiography," 402–7; *Globe*, 20 Apr. 1831; Ingham to Berrien, 20 Apr. 1831; Royce McCrary, ed., "The Long Agony Is Nearly Over," *Pennsylvania Magazine of History and Biography* 100 (1976): 237; *Richmond Enquirer*, 14 May 1831; *Niles' Register* 40 (1831): 179.

21. *Niles' Register* 40 (1831): 128; Everett to Charlotte B. Everett, 22 Feb., 4, 10 Mar. 1831, Everett Papers; Clay to Francis T. Brooke, 1 May 1831, Clay, *Papers*, 8:342.

where he was close to exhaustion. Kendall's uneasiness can be seen in his defensive, ugly letter to Joseph Desha written just after Jackson had decided to break up the cabinet. Desha had demanded repayment of $500 that he had loaned Kendall in 1826. Kendall replied that he had not "expect[ed] ever to be asked for it." He pointed out that he had spent many weeks writing Desha's official messages and had never received any compensation. If necessary, he said menacingly, he was ready to publish "a true history of these transactions." He hoped Desha would "cease to press" him.[22]

At this low point in the administration Jackson and his partisans took up the task of revamping the party and laying the groundwork for the coming presidential election. Blair began to call for "The March of Reform" against "*the American Aristocracy*" on behalf of "the working man." Lewis was meeting state leaders and keeping Jackson informed about Duff Green. Van Buren left to mend fences in New York before going to England. And early in May Kendall set out on a trip to New England to build support for the new administration and counteract the efforts of Green, who was on a similar trip to Connecticut and Massachusetts. Kendall and Jane and four of their children reached Boston on May 11 and stopped at the home of Kendall's brother Samuel in Medford, five miles north of the city.[23]

For the next two days Kendall met with Boston politicians. Although the Jackson party in Massachusetts was one of the weakest in the country, its central committee exercised considerable power because it held all the federal offices in Boston. At the head of the party was Port Collector David Henshaw, a well-to-do banker and publisher sympathetic with Green and Calhoun. Cracks were beginning to appear in Henshaw's organization. When he tried to raise money from the federal officeholders, Port Surveyor John McNeil, a hero in the War of 1812, refused to let his department contribute.[24]

McNeil and Port Naval Officer Leonard Parker called on Kendall to complain about the friendly manner in which Green had been treated when he visited Boston a few days before. Henshaw had given him a dinner and had spent four days escorting him about the state. Wherever he went Green had

22. Kendall to Joseph Desha, 9 Apr. 1831, "Correspondence between Governor Joseph Desha and Amos Kendall," 7–9. There is no evidence that Kendall paid the debt.

23. *Globe*, 1, 21 June 1831; Kendall to Welles, 27 Apr. 1831, Welles Papers, LC; Kendall to Lewis, 17 May 1831, Lewis to Kendall, 25 May 1831, "Origin of the Democratic National Convention," *American Historical Magazine* 7 (1902): 267–72.

24. Arthur B. Darling, *Political Changes in Massachusetts, 1824–1848* (New Haven, 1925), 67–75, 78–84, 93, 173–81.

told his listeners that Calhoun "must be run for Vice President." Kendall promised the two talebearers that he would be back in Boston in a week or so and would give Henshaw "a piece of [his] mind."[25]

Accompanied by McNeil on horseback, Kendall and his family proceeded on to Dunstable. It was a pleasant ride for Kendall: summer was coming on, leaves were making their first soft appearance, and he was bringing his wife and children to meet his mother and father. He found his parents as he had left them, still living on Kendall Hill. Their time was running out, though not as fast as he had feared; Molly Kendall would live two more years, Zebedee eight. Later that day Eliphalet Case, editor of the Jackson newspaper the *Mercury* in the mill town of Lowell came over to tell Kendall of a "rising Jackson spirit" in the Massachusetts interior. The spirit was far better, he said, than the selfish attitude in Boston, where Henshaw's men were "*content with the possession of the offices*" and had failed to give the interior towns any guidance in "the affairs of party."[26]

On May 16 Kendall and McNeil rode up along the Merrimack River to Concord, New Hampshire, to visit Isaac Hill. New Hampshire was rapidly becoming the banner Jackson state in the Union, with Jackson men holding two out of every three seats in the legislature. Hill and his Concord Regency ran the state and influenced politics in Vermont and Maine as well through political connections and a network of newspapers.[27]

Kendall was concerned, for he had no idea whether Hill approved of the appointment of his rival, Levi Woodbury, to the cabinet. He felt better when Hill assured him that the appointment would do some "good" in New England and that he no longer had any "fear of [Woodbury's] going for Calhoun." Kendall then turned to the question of the vice presidency, which was threatening to widen the split in the party. Hill again reassured him by promising to "do anything which is proper to unite the party." He was a Van Buren man, but for the sake of harmony he was willing to accept a southerner such as the strict states' righter Judge Philip P. Barbour of Virginia.[28]

Before returning to Dunstable Kendall sent a report to Lewis, criticizing

25. Kendall to Lewis, 17 May 1831, "Origin of the Democratic National Convention."

26. Ibid.; Weis, *Early Generations of the Kendall Family*, 166–67.

27. Kendall to Lewis, 17 May 1831, "Origin of the Democratic National Convention"; Cole, *Jacksonian Democracy in New Hampshire*, 5, 78–81, 162–68.

28. Kendall to Lewis, 17 May 1831, "Origin of the Democratic National Convention."

Henshaw and discussing the vice presidency. In reviewing candidates for the office he revealed his coolness toward Van Buren by saying that "he ought not to be [run]." After dismissing several other northerners because they would not run well in the South, he concurred with Hill's suggestion of Barbour. This letter, like the one to Blair setting the party line for the *Globe*, shows that despite his interest in the northern wing of the party, Kendall had not forgotten the South.[29]

In his reply Lewis agreed with Kendall's criticism of Henshaw and suggested that the party rely more on McNeil and Parker. As for vice president, he dismissed not only the northern candidates but also Barbour, who, he feared, "would not be acceptable to Pennsylvania or New York." Lewis wanted to wait a year and then hold a nominating convention—a plan that served the interests of his favorite, Van Buren, who needed time to regain his popularity. He wondered if Hill could arrange to have the Jackson majority in the legislature make such a proposal. The New Hampshire Jacksonians obliged with a resolution calling for a convention in Baltimore in May 1832, and the plan was soon accepted by the party.[30]

Kendall lingered in Dunstable longer than he had expected. Soon after he got back from Concord, his seven-month-old daughter Elizabeth became dangerously ill and died within a few days. All the while Jane was suffering from a persistent foot infection—perhaps a bad case of poison ivy—incurred, Kendall believed, on one of their "rambles" in the fields. Her feet became so swollen and sore that she could not walk. Because of the funeral and Jane's infection their departure was put off until early June.[31]

Stopping in Boston on the way back, Kendall was gratified to learn that the Massachusetts party was falling in step with the Jackson administration. It showed new interest in the interior by scheduling its next state convention for Worcester, toward the middle of the state, rather than Boston. Later in the summer the organization cut its ties with Calhoun by setting up a new party newspaper. When Kendall arrived home on June 15, he must have felt better about his role in the party. Not only had he paved the way for a party convention, an important step toward a mass party, but he had also improved the

29. Ibid.

30. Lewis to Kendall, 25 May 1831, ibid.; *Globe*, 6 July 1831.

31. Kendall to Lewis, 17 May 1831, "Origin of the Democratic National Convention"; Kendall to Woodbury, 2 June 1831, Woodbury Papers (quotation).

administration's ties with Massachusetts and northern New England. Further-more, Van Buren would soon be in England, leaving Kendall more room to operate in Washington.[32]

Kendall arrived just in time for the final chapter of the Eaton affair. While he was away, Samuel D. Ingham, who was about to leave office, had sharply attacked Jackson and the Eatons. Eaton sent him a challenge, which Ingham rejected. Late in the afternoon of June 17 Eaton and a band of his cronies marched past the Treasury Building threatening Ingham and then followed him back to his house. When Ingham left town during the night a week later, Jackson wrote to Van Buren that it was a "Parthian flight," and Kendall told Hill that Ingham had become the "laughing-stock" of the nation. A short time later the Eatons also left Washington, ending the Eaton affair.[33]

Just who won the affair is hard to decide. Since Jackson had lost his cabi-net and the Eatons had left Washington, never to return for any length of time, the ladies of Washington could claim victory. But in the long run they had lost. The dreary parties in the winter of 1830–31 were a forerunner of what was to follow. Under the Jacksonians the dinners and receptions lost their im-portance and women lost their influence. The all-male Jacksonian version of democracy took over.[34]

The Eaton affair strengthened the power of Jackson's inner circle, which was well represented in the rowdy conclusion. Kendall, Lewis, Thomas L. Smith, and John Campbell were with Eaton that evening; Hill and Van Buren anxiously awaited the outcome; and Blair published Eaton's version of the event in the *Globe*. They all believed that Eaton had defended his honor and that Ingham (and by proxy Calhoun and Green) had lost theirs.[35]

There was a changing of the guard in Washington. Between March and June 1831, five key figures had departed: Van Buren of the Jackson men, and Calhoun, Branch, Ingham, and Berrien of the opposition. Two others—Eaton and Green—were on their way out. Even Jackson himself left in late June for

32. McCormick, *Second American Party System*, 46–47; Darling, *Political Changes*, 93–97, 181–91.

33. Kendall to Welles, 20 June 1831, Welles Papers, LC; Kendall to Hill, 15 July 1831, Hill Pa-pers; Jackson to Van Buren, 23 June 1831, Jackson, *Correspondence*, 4:301–2; *Niles' Register* 40 (1831): 331, 415; Adams, *Memoirs*, 8:371–73.

34. Allgor, *Parlor Politics*, 235–38.

35. Kendall denied any involvement in the fracas but admitted being in the neighborhood at the time. *Globe*, 19 July 1831. For the role of manhood in the episode see Wood, "'One Woman So Dangerous,'" 237–75, especially 268–70.

a seaside vacation. Until the new cabinet took over, party affairs were in the hands of Kendall, Lewis, Barry, Blair, and other partisans.[36]

The opposition had been alarmed for some time at the steady rise of these advisers. Green had accused *"Amos Kendall & Co.* of undermining the popularity of general Jackson" and had predicted that the "embrace of Amos Kendall, Martin Van Buren, [and] William B. Lewis [would] be the embrace of death of the *'republican party.'* " *Niles' Register* reminded its readers that Kendall had once tried to get a job from Henry Clay. John Branch coined a popular phrase by blaming "malign influences" for Jackson's decisions.[37]

A few of Jackson's friends urged him to get rid of Kendall and company. His longtime friend Alfred Balch warned that "there exists in Washington 'a power behind the throne greater than the throne itself.' " Kendall, he said, should "let you wholly alone," and Lewis should "see you" only on "ceremonious" occasions. Congressman Benjamin Chew Howard of Maryland urged the "retirement" of Kendall and Lewis. To all this Jackson, who still prized loyalty, replied that he had no intention of driving away "individuals who have been sincere in their friendship for me."[38]

Jackson's opponents were soon calling these individuals the "Kitchen Cabinet." Although the term did not appear in the press until March 1832, it began to show up in private correspondence the previous summer and fall. John S. Barbour of Virginia and Nicholas Biddle both used the expression, and Blair wrote rather defensively in August that "neither the *kitchen* nor *parlor* cabinets [could] move Jackson."[39]

The Kitchen Cabinet was never a formal organization and it had not sprung up overnight. Ever since Jackson took office he had relied upon a small group of advisers—first Green and the Tennessee clique of Eaton, Lewis, and Donelson; then the northerners and westerners, Van Buren, Kendall, Hill,

---

36. Woodbury and Livingston had already arrived but would need time to get involved. Jackson to Lewis, 26 June 1831, Jackson, *Correspondence*, 4:303.

37. *Niles' Register* 40 (1831): 72 ("Amos"), 165 ("embrace"), 191, 192, 253, 300–301, 350, 427; 41 (1831–32): 38–39 ("malign"); *Telegraph*, 12 April 1831; *Telegraph*, n.d., in *Globe*, 13 Apr. 1831; Richard B. Latner, "The Kitchen Cabinet and Andrew Jackson's Advisory System," *Journal of American History* 65 (1978): 371–74.

38. Alfred Balch to Jackson, 21 July 1831, Jackson to Richard G. Dunlap, 29 Aug. 1831, Jackson, *Correspondence* 4:314–16, 336; Jackson to Benjamin Chew Howard, 4 Aug. 1831, Jackson Papers.

39. Barbour to Blair, 11 Sept. 1831, Blair-Lee Papers; Biddle to Robert M. Gibbes, 13 Dec. 1831, Nicholas Biddle Papers, LC; Thomas H. Clay, "Two Years with Old Hickory," *Atlantic Monthly* 60 (1887): 197–98.

Barry, and Blair. Of the latter none could quite match Van Buren; Jackson admired his poise, legal skill, and political experience. The president lost confidence in Green and Donelson and was forced to give up Hill and Eaton. Van Buren was sent to England. That left Kendall, Lewis, Blair, Barry, and less-well-known figures such as Smith, Campbell, and Hayward in the Kitchen Cabinet.[40]

Contemporaries had no doubt who was the head of the group. A survey of comments about Jackson's advisers in 1831, mostly in the press, shows forty-eight references to Kendall, eighteen to Lewis, nine to Blair, eight to Barry, and a few scattered. There were also, of course, many references to Van Buren, but these dealt mainly with him as one of the two principals in the struggle for power, not as a member of the Kitchen Cabinet. And, of course, he would not be back in Washington for over a year. Relishing the attention, Kendall told Hill defiantly that his enemies wanted to get rid of him but would not succeed.[41]

Jackson's decisions to defend the Eatons and bring Blair to Washington had destroyed his cabinet and put his party in danger. But there were hopeful signs. The president and his closest advisers were organizing a new party, based on patronage, state organizations, a national convention, a chain of newspapers, and a Kitchen Cabinet. Jackson was firmly in command, but Kendall had his finger in almost every pie. It remained to be seen how he and the new party would fare with a new cabinet and with the most divisive issue of the day—the recharter of the BUS.

40. For the best discussion of the Kitchen Cabinet see Latner, "Kitchen Cabinet," 367–88. For the role of Lewis see Louis R. Harlan, "Public Career of William Berkeley Lewis," *Tennessee Historical Quarterly* 7 (1948): 118–31. See also Kendall to Blair, 20 Nov. 1830, Blair Family Papers.

41. The comments were made between February 9 and December 11, 1831, and were drawn from the *Register of Debates*, 21st Cong., 2d sess., the *Telegraph,* the *Globe,* the *Intelligencer, Niles' Register,* the *Richmond Enquirer,* the papers of Andrew Jackson, John C. Calhoun, Henry Clay, and Nicholas Biddle, and a few other sources. See also Kendall to Hill, 15 July 1831, Hill Papers.

Portrait of Amos Kendall by Daniel Huntington that hangs in
the president's office of Gallaudet University
*Courtesy Gallaudet University Archives*

William T. Barry, who carried Kendall down the Ohio River
and later left him a mess in the Post Office (1833)
*Courtesy Library of Congress*

Henry Clay in 1825, the year John Quincy Adams
named him secretary of state
*Courtesy Library of Congress*

*Globe* editor Francis P. Blair in later years
*Courtesy Library of Congress*

Portrait of Kendall's second wife, Jane Kyle Kendall,
by Daniel Huntington, which hangs next to
Kendall's at Gallaudet University
*Courtesy Gallaudet University Archives*

Martin Van Buren, Kendall's rival for
Jackson's ear (1835). From a portrait by Henry Inman.
*Courtesy Library of Congress*

John C. Calhoun, whose break with Jackson
shaped the Democratic party
*Courtesy Library of Congress*

Political cartoon of Andrew Jackson in 1833 attacking him for
his vetoes and supposedly regal behavior
*Courtesy Library of Congress*

Margaret (Peggy) Eaton, whose marriage to John H. Eaton destroyed
the first Jackson cabinet. Painting by Henry Inman.
*Courtesy Library of Congress*

Samuel F. B. Morse, who hired Kendall to be his agent and made
him a millionaire. Photograph by Mathew B. Brady.
*Courtesy Library of Congress*

Edward M. Gallaudet, superintendent of the Columbia Institution for the
Deaf and Dumb and the Blind, in 1864 at the age of twenty-seven.
Photograph by Alexander Gardner.
*Courtesy Gallaudet University Archives*

Kendall's mansion at Kendall Green, ca. 1860
*Courtesy Gallaudet University Archives*

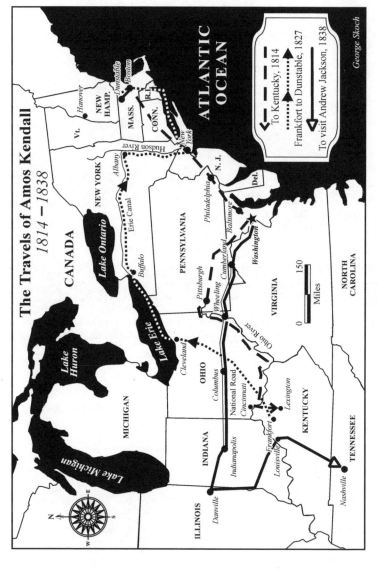

Travels of Amos Kendall, 1814–1838

# 12

## THE BANK VETO

The voters felt intensely about the BUS because it was so large and so powerful. There is nothing quite like it today. Its capital was double the annual expenses of the federal government, it held a quarter of all bank deposits, and
its banknotes made up 20 percent of money in circulation. Americans reacted
to the BUS in the same way that they had to the Panic of 1819. A rapidly
dwindling group who still resisted change looked on it as the epitome of all
that was wrong with the new age. Large numbers, who wholeheartedly accepted capitalism, considered the BUS essential to prosperity. They argued
that it provided loans, regulated state banks, and transferred federal funds. In
between there was a substantial group that accepted capitalism but opposed
the power and privileges of the BUS.

Feelings were never more intense than during Jackson's first term when
the BUS dramatically expanded its activity. Between 1830 and 1832 its notes
and loans increased 60 percent, its deposits 40 percent. At any time the BUS
could contract these loans and demand specie for the millions of dollars of
state banknotes in its possession. The prospect brought back memories of the
panic and made the BUS a central political issue. National Republicans, more
in tune with capitalism than were Jacksonians, largely supported it. Many
Jacksonians, particularly Kendall, Blair, and the president, saw it as an undemocratic monopoly. They thought it unfair that the BUS was exempt from state
taxation and had the use of the federal deposits without paying interest. But
enough Jackson men accepted the BUS to give it majority support in Congress.[1]

Jackson had raised the question of the BUS in his 1830 annual message by
suggesting that Congress replace it with "a branch of the Treasury department
. . . without power to make loans or purchase property." Kendall and Blair

---

1. *Statistical History*, 623.

followed in January and February 1831 with a series of articles, one of which revived the issue of BUS ownership of real estate in Kentucky. On February 2 Thomas Hart Benton offered a Senate resolution against renewing the BUS charter, which still had five years to go. He warned that the "monster . . . aggravate[d] the inequality of fortunes; to make the rich richer, and the poor poorer." The resolution failed by only three votes. By spring the *Globe* was attacking the "monied power" and calling the BUS unconstitutional. When an article against the BUS appeared in the *New-Hampshire Patriot* while Kendall was in New England, the opposition assumed that he had written it.[2]

Much would depend on the new cabinet. As a group the new secretaries believed in the power of the federal government and in most cases favored the BUS. Livingston and McLane supported it vigorously, while Cass and Woodbury saw the need for some sort of national bank. Only Taney opposed the BUS. The bank's president, Nicholas Biddle, recognized the new cabinet as "a fortunate change for the Bank" but realized that he would have trouble with Jackson's inner circle. In a showdown between the two cabinets he was afraid that "the kitchen would predominate over the Parlor."[3]

Now that he was at the head of the Kitchen Cabinet, Kendall felt that it was time to move closer to the center of power. At the end of June he and his family (but not the Kyles) rented a house near the State Department, where he would be only a short walk from the President's House and not far from his own office in the Treasury Building. He would also be near the office of the *Globe*, which had been shifted to the Octagon House on 18th Street. Kendall's move to the city was the start of changes in his lifestyle that would make it increasingly difficult for him to make ends meet.[4]

Kendall was uneasy about the new cabinet officers. He shared their opposition to nullification but not their approval of the BUS. Socially he was worlds apart from every one of them. In addition he was in the awkward position of serving under a new secretary of the Treasury who would have preferred having his own man as fourth auditor. Kendall came from the same part of New England as Cass and Woodbury, but he was suspicious of both—the former because of their conversation on the stagecoach from Washington and the lat-

2. Jackson, "Second Annual Message," 6 Dec. 1830, *Compilation*, 2:529; *Globe*, 8, 12, 19, 22, 26 Jan., 5 Feb., 27 Apr., 25 May, 1 June 1831; Benton, *Thirty Years' View*, 1:187.

3. Taney, "Roger B. Taney's 'Bank War Manuscript,'" ed. Carl B. Swisher, *Maryland Historical Magazine* 53 (1958): 121–28; Biddle to J. Hunter, 4 May 1831, Biddle to N. B. Gibbes, 13 Dec. 1831, Biddle Papers.

4. Lewis to Jackson, 1 July 1831, Jackson, *Correspondence*, 4:309; *Globe*, 18 May 1831.

ter because of the episode at Dartmouth and Woodbury's link with Calhoun. Woodbury soon annoyed him even more by badgering him for reports. Kendall replied brusquely that he had just "risen from a sickbed" and would hand in the reports as soon as he had the "time and health." With "a little reflection," the secretary would surely realize that his "admonitions" showed a presumption of "neglect on my part, neither just to me, nor the most agreeable to my feelings."[5]

Within the Kitchen Cabinet two significant changes were working to Kendall's advantage: Martin Van Buren was gone, and William B. Lewis was losing some of his power. Lewis had embarrassed Jackson by intervening in the election of a Pennsylvania congressman and had annoyed him by continuing to support the BUS. He was never as enthusiastic about the use of party patronage as Kendall would have liked. In December 1831, perhaps at Jackson's request, he moved out of the President's House. Although he still continued to advise the president, his influence was limited.[6]

Despite his increasingly strong position, Kendall remained circumspect in dealing with the president. When Blair offered him $800 a year to write regularly for the *Globe*, he wanted to accept but was worried about Jackson's reaction. The president had continued the Adams policy of prohibiting officials from editing or publishing political newspapers, but he had permitted several, such as Mordecai M. Noah, to write occasional articles. Kendall was so nervous about asking Jackson's permission that he put it off for two months.[7]

He finally wrote the president on December 3. If he had not "stepped forward," he started, there would never have been a *Globe*. His only pay had been the satisfaction of "defending [Jackson's] administration and character." He would gladly go on writing for nothing, but he was so poor that he had "to stint" his family "in the comforts of life." His health had become so "feeble" that "at no distant day" he might die and leave his loved ones to charity. All he wanted was permission to devote "some of those hours which others spend in luxurious dinners and rounds of parties" to writing for the *Globe*. Jackson

5. John A. Munroe, *Louis McLane: Federalist and Jacksonian* (New Brunswick, N.J., 1973), 331; Woodbury to Kendall, 10 Mar. 1832, Kendall to Woodbury, 10 Mar. 1832, Gustavus Vasa Fox Papers, New-York Historical Society.

6. Harlan, "Public Career of William Berkeley Lewis," 125–31; Parton, *Life of Andrew Jackson*, 3:224–25; Ann Maria Lewis to Andrew Jackson, 3 Dec. 1831, Jackson, *Correspondence*, 4:314n.

7. Blair to Kendall, 30 Sept. 1831, Kendall to Jackson, 3 Dec. 1830, Blair-Lee Papers. Jackson allowed Taney to continue his private law practice while he was attorney general. Taney, "Bank War Manuscript," 226.

had every right to reject this sentimental, self-pitying request, but he was just as sentimental as Kendall and promptly gave in.[8]

The most influential member of the regular cabinet was treasury secretary Louis McLane, who greatly impressed the president with his balanced economic program. McLane proposed lowering tariffs to please the South while maintaining protection for key manufactures. Even more important, he wanted to recharter the BUS with just enough reforms to satisfy antibank sentiment. He and Livingston had already approached Biddle and were trying to bring about a compromise. After listening to McLane, Jackson no longer seemed unalterably opposed to the BUS.[9]

The president was having a difficult time dealing with his new administration because he had not yet recovered from the sickness and depression that had gripped him during the cabinet debacle. In October he ran a high fever from an infection caused by the bullet in his arm. Jackson was concerned about the reemergence of Henry Clay, who had been elected to the Senate and nominated for president by the National Republican party. The selection of such a well-known advocate of the BUS was a boon to Biddle. Determined to have a harmonious administration, Jackson held regular meetings of the cabinet, avoided confrontation, and made little effort to hold McLane back.[10]

The questions of party control and rechartering the BUS came to a head late in the fall. In preparing his annual message, Jackson showed much more deference to McLane and Livingston than to Kendall and Taney. Disregarding a draft of an entire message by Kendall, the president allowed Livingston to write an introduction that sounded more National Republican than Jacksonian. At the end of the message Jackson passed over an antibank statement by Kendall in favor of a proposal by McLane to leave the future of the BUS up to Congress. The annual message was so unusually conciliatory that the *National Intelligencer* remarked on its "subdued tone."[11]

Even more startling was McLane's treasury report, which included plans for a protective tariff and a proposal to recharter the BUS. Antibank, states'

8. Kendall to Jackson, 3 Dec. 1831, Blair-Lee Papers.

9. Munroe, *Louis McLane*, 302–13; Jackson to Van Buren, 6 Dec. 1831, Jackson, *Correspondence*, 4:379.

10. *Globe*, 25 Oct. 1831; Louis McLane to Van Buren, 11 Aug. 1831, in Van Buren, "Autobiography," 579; James C. Curtis, "Andrew Jackson and His Cabinet: Some New Evidence," *Tennessee Historical Quarterly* 27 (1968): 157–64.

11. Taney, "Bank War Manuscript," 121–28; "Drafts of Third Annual Message," Jackson Papers; Jackson, "Third Annual Message," *Compilation*, 2:544–58; *Intelligencer*, 9 Dec. 1831.

rights Jacksonians believed that McLane was trying to gain control of the party. New York congressman Churchill C. Cambreleng compared the report to those of Alexander Hamilton, while John Randolph could not believe that Jackson would "waver" so on the BUS. Blair prepared a scorching attack on the report but toned it down when McLane threatened to resign. Even after it was rewritten, McLane was displeased because Blair called the report much "more favorable" to the BUS than were the views of the president.[12]

Hoping that he could win Jackson's support for a recharter bill, Biddle hesitated at pushing for a bill on his own. In mid-December, however, Clay convinced him to move at once so that the bill could be part of the 1832 presidential campaign. They reasoned that Jackson would hardly veto a recharter bill only a few months before the election. Early in January 1832 Biddle's memorial for recharter was brought to both houses of Congress, and within a month the Ways and Means Committee of the House had drawn up a bill. The prospects for passage seemed excellent.[13]

But the progress of the Bank bill and two other developments late in January served to reenergize Jackson's fighting spirit. Always quick to personalize politics, Old Hickory felt that Biddle and Clay were challenging him by bringing up the bill in an election year. He was also angry when Van Buren's nomination to be minister to Great Britain was defeated, with Vice President Calhoun casting the deciding vote. Calhoun boasted that his vote would "kill" Van Buren, "kill him dead," but he underestimated the strength of the Jackson party. The Jacksonians held scores of meetings and wrote hundreds of letters of protest, while the *Globe* published editorials from all parts of the Union defending Van Buren.[14]

The other development was a clumsy attempt by the McLane and Van Buren camps to get rid of Blair. There was some logic in the move, for Blair had annoyed both groups. He had not only fought with McLane over the treasury report but also antagonized the Van Buren people by stating that nei-

12. Munroe, *Louis McLane*, 310–16; Cambreleng to Jesse Hoyt, 29 Dec. 1831, in William L. McKenzie, *The Life and Times of Martin Van Buren* (Boston, 1846), 230; Randolph to Jackson, 19 Dec. 1831, Jackson, *Correspondence*, 4:386; *Globe*, 9, 17 Dec. 1831; McLane to Blair, 19 Dec. 1831, Blair-Lee Papers.

13. Clay to Biddle, 15 Dec. 1831, *The Correspondence of Nicholas Biddle Dealing with National Affairs, 1807–1844*, ed. Reginald C. McGrane (Boston, 1919), 142; Benton, *Thirty Years' View*, 1:233–35; *Register of Debates*, 22d Cong., 1st sess., 53–55, 58, 113–14.

14. Benton, *Thirty Years' View*, 1:214–19 (quotation); Cole, *Martin Van Buren*, 226–27; *Globe*, 27, 28, 30 Jan., 1, 2, 9 Feb., 22 Mar. 1832.

ther he nor Kendall planned to support the Little Magician for vice president. Yet it was a curious affair. McLane had presidential ambitions of his own and had already let it be known that he did not want Van Buren as vice president. And the conspirators' choice for a new editor—Amos Kendall—made no sense at all. Kendall had fought the BUS as much as Blair had and had joined Blair in opposing Van Buren. The only possible explanation is that the group planned to dump him later and replace him with an editor from New York. Kendall did not react to the plot especially well. He took no part in it but stood by and did nothing to defend Blair. He was probably waiting for McLane to hang himself and for the president to take charge.[15]

Jackson did. He was ready to fight because doctors had removed the bullet from his arm and his health had returned. When he learned about McLane's plot, he came to Blair's rescue and insisted that he remain as editor. He also vowed to make Van Buren vice president and presiding officer of the Senate so that, like Isaac Hill, he could return to the body that had rejected him. Then he joined the Kitchen Cabinet in a fight against the BUS. It would be an uphill battle because the BUS had the majority support not only of Congress but also, apparently, of the American people. During the struggle over recharter Biddle was able to secure 188 memorials to Congress supporting the BUS, while the administration could dredge up only 8 in opposition.[16]

Concluding that the recharter bill could not be defeated, Jackson and his advisers devised an elaborate strategy to slow the bill's progress and set the stage for a veto. In Benton's words the Jackson men would "assail [the BUS] at all points, display the evil of the institution, [and] rouse the people." Jackson confided in Kendall, Blair, Taney, Benton, Hill, and other insiders, told his official cabinet nothing, and said nothing about who would write the veto. In the House the Jacksonians delayed the recharter bill by forcing a long investigation of the BUS. Then on May 5 the *Globe* accused the BUS of bribery, and

15. Webb to Van Buren, 31 Dec. 1831–7 Jan. 1832, Cambreleng to Van Buren, 4 Feb. 1832, Van Buren Papers; Montgomery Blair, "Sketches of F. P. Blair, Sr.," 13 May 1858?, Benjamin Gratz to Blair, 24 Jan., 21 Feb. 1833, Blair-Lee Papers; Van Buren, "Autobiography," 589. The best treatment of this plot is Latner, *Presidency*, 115–16, 242 n. 100. Terry Shoptaugh suggests that McLane wanted Kendall out of the Treasury Department. Shoptaugh, "Amos Kendall," 267–68.

16. *Globe*, 14 Jan. 1832; Blair to Van Buren, 28 Jan. 1832, Van Buren Papers; Jackson to Blair, 17 Jan. 1843, Blair Family Papers; Jean Alexander Wilburn, *Biddle's Bank: The Crucial Years* (New York, 1967), 116.

five days later Kendall started editing a campaign weekly, the *Extra Globe*, with an article attacking the BUS.[17]

The coming of the Bank War invited more criticism of the Kitchen Cabinet. In March nullifier senator George Poindexter of Mississippi accused Kendall and other Jackson politicians of employing a "*trained band* of letter writers, who lounge about the public offices." He was reminding his readers that Kendall had instructed his clerks never to bring "loungers or idlers" into the office. In his attacks Poindexter became the first to use the term Kitchen Cabinet in print. "The President's press," he wrote, "edited . . . by the 'Kitchen Cabinet,' is made the common reservoir of all the petty slanders which find a place in the most degraded prints in the Union."[18]

The Bank War was briefly interrupted by the Jackson party nominating convention, which opened in Baltimore on May 21. With Jackson unopposed, the only question was the nomination for vice president, which Jackson was determined should go to Van Buren. Kendall and Blair preferred westerner Richard M. Johnson or southerner Philip P. Barbour but gave in to the president's wishes. Lewis, who represented Jackson on this matter, succeeded in squelching several attempts to defeat the Little Magician. Even though Johnson and Barbour received a few votes for vice president, Van Buren won the nomination handily.[19]

The day after the convention the Senate took up the recharter bill. In the two strongest speeches against the BUS Benton warned that it had forced the West to run up a "frightful debt" of $30 million, and Hill portrayed it as an undemocratic institution in which wealthy British aristocrats owned a large share of the stock. Did the United States, he asked sarcastically, owe anything to the Baring brothers, the marquis of Hertford, "who has his hundred thousand dollars," or Sir William Keppell, Knight of the Grand Cross of the Order of Bath, to justify granting them such "exclusive privileges"? Blair continued the attacks with editorials based on the report of the House investigating committee. Although the bill passed on June 11, the margin of twenty-eight to

17. Benton, *Thirty Years' View*, 1:235–42; Taney, "Bank War Manuscript," 224; *Globe*, 5 May 1832; *Extra Globe*, 10 May 1832.

18. *Telegraph*, 17, 27 Mar. 1832; *Globe*, 24, 29 Mar. 1832; Latner, "Kitchen Cabinet," 376. For Kendall's instructions see *Autobiography*, 318.

19. One of the plots against Van Buren involved McLane, Barry, and John H. Eaton. Harlan, "Public Career of William Berkeley Lewis," 131–35; Parton, *Life of Andrew Jackson*, 3:421; *Globe*, 22, 26 Mar., 14 Apr., 23–25 May 1832; Van Buren, "Autobiography," 581–91.

twenty was four votes short of the two-thirds needed to override a veto. Preoccupied with the tariff, the House did not plan to take up the bill until the end of the month.[20]

Before the Senate debate was over, Kendall left for Charlestown, Massachusetts, to take part in the navy court of inquiry concerning Robert B. Randolph. The court was planning to hear from purser's steward Thomas Norman, who was expected to come to Randolph's defense. While waiting for Norman to arrive, Kendall tried to discredit him by introducing evidence that he held a grudge against Eaton and had boasted about writing two of the threatening letters. As it turned out, Norman failed to appear, and the court was adjourned until December.[21]

On June 30, soon after Kendall returned from Charlestown, the House debate on the recharter bill got under way, and three days later the bill passed by a vote of 107 to 85. The next day congressmen crowded about Nicholas Biddle as he made a triumphant appearance on the floor. They were confident that the passage of the bill was "a certain harbinger of Genl. Jackson's overthrow." Such gloating could only have heightened Jackson's hatred for the BUS. On July 8 when Van Buren returned from England, he caught a glimpse of these feelings. Hurrying to the President's House in the evening, he greeted Jackson, who lay "stretched on a sick-bed." The Old Hero grasped him by the hand and said grimly, "The Bank, Mr. Van Buren, is trying to kill me, *but I will kill it!*"[22]

After receiving the bill on July 4, the president had to act promptly, for unless he vetoed it by the sixteenth, it would become law. To prevent a pocket veto, Henry Clay had arranged to extend the time for the adjournment of Congress, originally planned for the ninth, to the sixteenth. When Jackson told the cabinet that he intended to veto the bill and asked for assistance, the members agreed to help but only if he wrote a noncommittal message that would leave the door open for a future bill. Jackson, however, wanted none of this temporizing and said he would look elsewhere for help.[23]

20. Benton gave two speeches, 26 May, 2 June; Hill's speech was 8 June. *Register of Debates*, 22d Cong., 1st sess., 965–77, 1008–10, 1056–68; *Globe*, 8–21 June 1832.

21. *ASP:NA*, 4:301–20, 336–37.

22. *Register of Debates*, 22d Cong., 1st sess., 2651–3335; Roger B. Taney, "Bank War Manuscript," 223; Van Buren, "Autobiography," 625.

23. John Bach McMaster, *A History of the People of the United States from the Revolution to the Civil War*, 7 vols. (New York, 1907), 6:139–41; Taney, "Bank War Manuscript," 226; Barry to Susan Taylor, 4 July 1832, Barry, "Letters," 13:233; Jackson to Van Buren, 14 June 1832, Jackson, *Correspondence*, 4:448.

The authorship of the Bank veto was a matter of importance in 1832, but for a long while thereafter historians and biographers showed little interest. In 1860 James Parton assumed Kendall to be the author but touched only briefly on the message. William Graham Sumner said nothing about the author. Finally, fifty years later John Spencer Bassett concluded that Taney had written the heart of the veto but that "some such purveyor of balderdash as Isaac Hill or Amos Kendall" had tacked on an introduction and a conclusion.[24]

The discovery of Taney's recollections of the Bank War in 1929 seemed to confirm him as the author. Taney recalled that the president called him in on July 7, showed him a draft of the veto written by Kendall, and asked him to rewrite it. Taney said that he then spent three days with Andrew J. Donelson and Levi Woodbury, rewriting the message, and gave no indication that Kendall was involved. On the basis of this story Marquis James and Arthur M. Schlesinger Jr. credited Taney with writing the message.[25]

But when Lynn L. Marshall went to the Jackson papers at the Library of Congress, he found only one complete draft of the message—a long, much-deleted, much-corrected manuscript, almost entirely, original text and corrections, in Kendall's hand. Marshall concluded that Kendall, not Taney, wrote not only the first draft but also most of the revision. Furthermore, he gave Kendall credit for many of the ideas and suggested that he was probably working on the veto before the bill reached the president.[26]

Marshall's analysis was correct on all points, but more can be said about the drafting of the veto. Kendall was the obvious choice to be the author. Blair's writing was too unsophisticated, Hill's too harsh, Benton's too pompous, Taney's too dull. Kendall alone had the imaginative, passionate, democratic style demanded for this emotional, political subject. He had seen the BUS at work before and during the Panic of 1819, he had attacked it on many occasions, and he and Jackson agreed completely on the subject. The veto was so important that it is impossible to believe that the president waited until the last minute to call on Kendall. Jackson must have given him the assignment some time in the spring.

24. Parton, *Life of Andrew Jackson*, 3:406–10; William Graham Sumner, *Andrew Jackson*, 2d ed. (Boston, 1899), 319; John Spencer Bassett, *The Life of Andrew Jackson*, 2 vols. in one (1911; reprint, Hamden, Conn., 1967), 617–20.

25. Taney, "Bank War Manuscript," 224–27; Marquis James, *Andrew Jackson: Portrait of a President* (New York, 1937), 302–3; Schlesinger, *Age of Jackson*, 89–92.

26. Two other drafts—both in Donelson's hand—were unimportant copies of Kendall's work. Marshall, "The Authorship of Jackson's Bank Veto Message," *Mississippi Valley Historical Review* 50 (1963): 466–77.

Kendall's article on the BUS in the *Extra Globe* on May 10 gives further evidence that he was already working on the veto. In it he complained that the recharter bill would give BUS stockholders "a gratuity of *seventeen millions of dollars*," a claim that was repeated almost exactly in his draft of the veto message. Additional proof lies in the timing of the veto. Jackson did not receive the recharter bill until July 4, and Kendall presented a complete draft seventy-two hours later. The draft was too long (twelve thousand words), too coherent, and too carefully documented to have been written in such a short time. He must have started it no later than May, for he was out of town much of June. Jackson asked his cabinet for help with the veto but did so only as a formality. Kendall had been at work for some time.[27]

In writing his draft Kendall had a roomful of sources: files of the *Globe*, editorials from the *Argus*, the House and Senate reports on the BUS, and a memorandum written by Jackson. He quite likely also had copies of Spencer Roane's "Hampden" essays in 1819 attacking John Marshall's opinion in *McCulloch v. Maryland* and David Henshaw's pamphlet *Remarks on the Bank of the United States*, published in 1831. Toward the end of his work he had the congressional debates over the BUS, a memorandum from Taney, and a second from Jackson. He certainly had other materials, for the methodical Yankee loved to collect pamphlets and documents.[28]

Kendall started his draft with the republican theme taken from his days in Kentucky that the powers granted the BUS were a danger to the republic. These "powers and privileges," he wrote, "are subversive of the rights of the states, dangerous to the liberties of the people, and of doubtful constitutionality." Later when the draft was revised he made his indictment even stronger by rearranging the three charges in ascending order of importance, placing the danger to liberties at the end. He maintained the republican argument by

27. *Extra Globe*, 10 May 1832. My estimate of the length is based on the number of pages. He used sixteen sheets of paper folded once to provide four sides each, sixty-four sides (pages) in all. There were also several insertions. "Drafts of Bank Veto Message," Jackson Papers; Marshall, "Authorship of Jackson's Bank Veto Message," 469 n. 10, 474.

28. Jackson, "Opinion on the Bank," Jan. 1832, "Memorandum on the Bank of the United States," c. June–July 1832, Jackson, *Correspondence*, 4:389–90, 458–59; Spencer Roane, "Hampden Essays," 11–22 June 1819, in *John Marshall's Defense of "McCulloch v. Maryland,"* ed. Gerald Gunther (Stanford, 1969), 106–54; David Henshaw, *Remarks on the Bank of the United States* (Boston, 1831); Taney to Jackson, 27 June 1832, Jackson Papers; *Globe*, 8 Sept. 1832.

devoting the first half of the draft and a large part of the conclusion to the threat posed to these liberties.[29]

To document his theme Kendall first turned to the undemocratic privileges granted the BUS. These "favors," he said, had "increased the value of [its] stock far above its par value," taking property away from "the whole community" to make "the rich richer." The charter had set up a "monopoly," based on "the erroneous idea, that the present stockholders [had] a prescriptive right, not only to the *favor* but to the *bounty* of the government." If there had to be a BUS, "why should not the government sell out the whole stock and thus secure to the people the full market value of the privileges granted?" These capitalistic arguments echoed ideas from Benton, Hill, Henshaw, Taney, and Jackson.[30]

In addition, he appealed to sectional and nationalistic resentments by pointing out that almost all of the stock was held by easterners, Englishmen, and other foreigners. Drawing from Benton, he maintained that the debts of westerners to the BUS were "a drain on their currency which no country can bear without . . . distress." Stealing from Hill, he said that the bill would make lavish gifts to the "British Aristocracy," including the Baring brothers and Sir William Keppell. If a large proportion of the stock of the BUS fell into British hands and war broke out with Great Britain, "all the operations" of the BUS would be "in the aid of the British army and navies." If there had to be a bank with private stockholders, "every impulse of American feeling admonishe[d] that it should be *purely American*."[31]

Kendall was making good use of his articles for the Relief party. In 1824 he had warned that an exclusive, powerful combination of the BUS, the "rich and well born" Anti-Relief men, and the Holy Alliance was trying to crush the people of Kentucky. In the veto the rich Baring brothers and William Keppell played the part of the wealthy Robert Wickliffe, and Great Britain that of the Holy Alliance. He raised the same "suspicions" of conspiracy. In-

29. The discussion that follows is of Kendall's draft, not the published message; the quotations are also from the draft. In locating passages, however, I have used Marshall's method of citing the paragraph in the published version in which the material appeared or would have appeared if it had not been altered or cut. Kendall, "Draft of Jackson's Bank Veto Message," par. 2, Jackson Papers; Jackson, "Bank Veto Message," 10 July 1832, *Compilation,* 2:576; Marshall, "Authorship of Jackson's Bank Veto Message," 468 n. 8.

30. Kendall, "Draft of Jackson's Bank Veto Message," par. 3–7.

31. Ibid., par. 4, 14, 15, 18, 19; *Register of Debates,* 22d Cong., 1st sess., 970, 1056–66.

stead of drawing back "the curtain [from] the Holy Alliance of America," he now "unveiled . . . the practices" of the BUS.[32]

Kendall loaded the first half of his draft with scores of negative, antiprivilege, emotionally charged words. Most survived in the veto message: "privilege" eighteen times, "monopoly" and "power" sixteen each, "foreigner" fourteen, "exclusive" eleven, "rich" nine, and "favor" eight. The words and the arguments were often extravagant, sometimes foolish and deceptive. Few believed that the BUS threatened the people's liberties. There was little likelihood that the British would get control of the BUS or dictate its policies in wartime. Kendall knew full well that the West needed the capital provided by the BUS and that the United States needed foreign investors. But he was crafting a political manifesto, not an economic treatise.[33]

Halfway through the draft Kendall shifted to a more moderate, subdued tone as he took up the constitutional and states' rights parts of his charge. Bassett and others have argued that he was now drawing on the unadorned prose of Taney's memorandum. To a degree he was. Kendall, for example, wrote that he would "examine the details" of the recharter bill without "calling in question the general principle." This marked a shift from his usual reliance on high-flown general principles to Taney's preference for factual precedents.[34]

But Taney was not the only one to influence this section. When Kendall wrote that Congress could set up monopolies only for patents and copyrights, he was using an argument made earlier by Henshaw as well as Taney. In another instance he borrowed from Benton as well as Taney when he argued that if Congress could establish one bank, it could obviously establish others. Thus the recharter bill was unconstitutional because it denied a later Congress the right to set up a second bank.[35]

Kendall also continued to fall back on his own work. In discussing *McCulloch v. Maryland* in 1819 he too had made the point that Congress was being denied the right to charter a second bank. His crucial assertion that the

32. For the Kentucky quotations see Kendall, *Wictorian Dinner*, iii; *Argus*, 11 Feb. 1824. For the "practices" quotation see Kendall, "Draft of Jackson's Bank Veto Message," par. 42. Kendall first expressed his concern about the "wealth and power" of the BUS in his editorial on the BUS in the *Georgetown Patriot*, 11 May 1816. He may also have drawn from Henshaw's *Remarks on the Bank*. See also Marshall, "Authorship of Jackson's Bank Veto Message," 472.

33. For the largest concentration of these words see Jackson, "Bank Veto Message," par. 3–5.

34. Kendall, "Draft of Jackson's Bank Veto Message," par. 24.

35. Henshaw, *Remarks on the Bank;* Taney to Jackson, 27 June 1832, Jackson Papers; Benton speech, 2 June 1832, *Register of Debates*, 22d Cong., 1st sess., 1008–9.

president shared the power of interpreting the Constitution with Congress and the Supreme Court went back to 1822 when he had challenged the exclusive power of the court of appeals to overturn the Replevin Act. A third example was his argument that Congress had the right to set up a "fiscal agent" but not a bank with all the "surplus powers" of the BUS. In 1819 he had said that the government could "act through agents" but could not "clothe its agents" with excessive powers. In all three instances Taney had made similar arguments in his memorandum, but they were hardly new to Kendall.[36]

At the end of his draft Kendall returned to the theme of the threat to the people. "It is to be regretted," he wrote,

> that the rich and powerful too often bend the acts of government to their selfish purposes. Distinctions in society will always exist under every just government. Perfect equality of talents, of education, or of wealth, cannot be produced by human institutions. In the full enjoyment of the gifts of Heaven and the fruits of superior industry, economy, and virtue, every man is equally entitled to protection by law; but when the laws undertake to add to these natural and just advantages artificial distinctions, to grant titles, gratuities, and exclusive privileges, to make the rich richer and the potent more powerful, the humble members of society—the farmers, mechanics, and laborers . . . have a right to complain of the injustice of their Government. There are no necessary evils in government. Its evils exist only in its abuses. If it would confine itself to equal protection, and, as heaven does its rains, shower its favors alike on the high and the low, the rich and the poor, it would be an unqualified blessing. In the act before me there seems to be a wide and unnecessary departure from these just principles.[37]

In this much-quoted paragraph, which was retained almost verbatim in the final version of the veto, Kendall turned to positive words—"just," "equality," "protection," "industry," "virtue"—to unite the American people behind the president. The paragraph contains the essence of Jacksonian democracy. The acceptance of "distinctions in society" makes it clear that the veto is an attack on government privilege, not, as some have suggested, on capitalism. The metaphor of the rain taken from the Sermon on the Mount sets a limited purpose for government—to provide equal protection for rich and poor. This moderate, democratic position expressed in republican words aptly reflected

---

36. Kendall, "Draft of Jackson's Bank Veto Message," par. 21, 26, 34; *Argus,* 12 Sept. 1822; *Autobiography,* 215, 217; Taney to Jackson, 27 June 1832, Jackson Papers.

37. Kendall, "Draft of Jackson's Bank Veto Message," par. 44.

the views of most Americans, who hated privilege but accepted economic in-equality.[38]

The editing began on July 7 and went on for three days. Just as Taney recalled, he, Donelson, and Woodbury took part, but, contrary to Taney's rec-ollections, Kendall was there and did much of the work. They met in painter Ralph Earl's room across from Jackson's office on the second floor of the Pres-ident's House. Old Hickory looked in frequently and made sure that the veto was what he wanted. Van Buren, who was in Washington for the last two days, approved of the message, but had little, if any, "direct agency" in preparing it.[39]

Why did Taney say nothing about Kendall? According to Marshall, the blame rested on Blair, who feuded with Kendall in the early 1840s. By 1849, when Taney started writing his recollections, Jackson had died and his advisers were jockeying to write the history of his administration. Blair was afraid that Kendall, who had already published several chapters of a biography of Jackson, would "make himself the hero" when he got to the administration. So he urged Taney and Van Buren to write their memoirs in order to offset Kendall. It is reasonable to suspect that Blair may have convinced Taney to minimize Kendall's role in the Bank veto.[40]

In three days the group trimmed a wordy, repetitious, twelve-thousand-word manuscript into an eight-thousand-word presidential paper. Gone were the statistics showing how much individual stockholders had profited. Ken-dall's assault on the British became a much briefer attack on foreign stock-holders in general, with no mention of the Baring brothers or William Keppell. Two of three claims that the BUS made "the rich richer" were de-leted. Three references to the shedding of blood were expunged, including the charge that the "vampire Aristocracy" of Britain had "drain[ed] the life blood from the British nation" and now was "cast[ing] its eyes on the fresh features of young America."[41]

38. For the view that the Jackson movement and the Bank veto were an attack on capitalism see Sellers, *Market Revolution*, especially 325–26; for the opposite and more convincing view see William E. Gienapp, "The Myth of Class in Jacksonian America," *Journal of Policy History* 6 (1994): 232–59.

39. Jackson to Van Buren, 7 July 1832, Van Buren Papers; Van Buren, *Inquiry into the Origin and Course of Political Parties in the United States*, 314–15.

40. Blair to Van Buren, 11 Nov. 1849, Van Buren Papers; Marshall, "Authorship of Jackson's Bank Veto Message," 474–75.

41. Kendall, "Draft of Jackson's Bank Veto Message," passim, especially par. 1, 2, 4, 9, 15, 46; Jackson, "Bank Veto Message."

But no matter how many words were changed and paragraphs stripped away, the tone, the argument, and the structure remained the same. It was still Kendall's and Jackson's message, or more accurately, the message Kendall had written synthesizing the ideas of many Jacksonians. He wove together the states' rights concerns of Roane with the hatred that Jackson, Hill, Blair, and Benton felt for the BUS and the aspirations of bankers like Henshaw who hoped to profit from its fall. Aware of McLane's belief that the BUS had done an efficient job of monitoring the economy, Kendall avoided attacking the way it operated and said surprisingly little about its alleged corruption. Conscious also of the Relief men who had prized cheap money, he omitted his own hard-money belief that the paper money system of the BUS had caused financial crises.

When the veto was made public, the Jacksonians gave all the credit for the message to the president. Blair was so thrilled by "the moral spectacle" of Andrew Jackson fighting back "the insidious enemy" that he compared the veto to the Declaration of Independence. From Virginia Thomas Ritchie lauded the president for his "manly and fearless" message. It was, said Van Buren, the most popular act of Jackson's life. When it was suggested that Kendall or someone else had done the writing, the *Globe* denied it, insisting that the message was "a transcript of the President's own mind." Any slight alterations came from Jackson's "constitutional advisers" in the cabinet. Blair and probably Kendall himself felt that it was safer to say that the president wrote the document with perhaps a little help from the respectable cabinet than to admit that it came from the pen of a disreputable member of the Kitchen Cabinet. Kendall never challenged this view. Late in life he said that "the old hero wrote the most of his own messages."[42]

The National Republican press, however, had no difficulty identifying Kendall, "the oracle of the scrub-cabinet," as the author of the veto. One newspaper asked, "Are the People of the United States willing to have Amos Kendall to rule over them in the name of Andrew Jackson?" The editor of the *New York Commercial Advertiser* knew that Kendall had written the veto because no one in "the cabinet proper" was ever called on when "an appeal [was] made to the populace." It is ironic that Kendall's contributions to American politics, such as creating the Kitchen Cabinet and writing the Bank veto, were proclaimed by the opposition, not by his own party.[43]

42. *Globe*, 12 July, 8 Sept. 1832; *Richmond Enquirer*, 13 July 1832; Van Buren to Hamilton, 15 July, 5 Aug. 1832, Hamilton, *Reminiscences*, 246, 247; *Autobiography*, 686.

43. *Philadelphia National Gazette*, 12 July 1832, quoted in Daniels, "Amos Kendall," 175; *Intelligencer*, 4 Sept. 1832; *New York Commercial Advertiser*, 24 July 1832, reprinted in *Boston Courier*, 6 Aug. 1832.

In the eyes of this opposition Jackson had become an antirepublican king. Biddle described him as a mad monarch "biting the bars of his cage" and called his veto "a manifesto of anarchy." The *National Intelligencer* said he had acted like a despot usurping legislative powers. When the veto was sent to the Senate, Clay compared the president to the king of France for claiming the right to initiate legislation, while Webster said that the veto "extends the grasp of executive pretension over every power of the government." Webster also skillfully laid bare the economic fallacies in the document. But the criticism could not change the outcome. The bill was repassed in the Senate but again fell short of a two-thirds majority.[44]

One of the harshest assaults on the veto was unwittingly also one of the most perceptive. In identifying Kendall as the author, the editor of the *Commercial Advertiser* said that whenever the president "address[ed] the prejudices of the vulgar," he used "vulgar instruments." The editor also made fun of the veto by referring to it sarcastically as the "vindication of the rights of THE PEOPLE against our overbearing and wealthy aristocracy." That of course was exactly what Kendall had in mind. Like his editorials in Kentucky elections, the veto was aimed directly at the great "vulgar" mass of the "populace," not at the "wealthy aristocracy." It appealed to the worst in Americans—their fear, envy, sectionalism, and chauvinism—but also the best: their democratic egalitarianism. Never before in the history of the new country had such evocative, direct words been used to attract such a wide audience. With its broad appeal, its attacks on aristocracy and privilege, and its populist, bold style of writing, the Bank veto was an important step forward for democracy.[45]

It also had an immediate impact on American politics. *Niles' Register*, for example, paid more attention to the bank question than to any other issue except the tariff, which was a favorite of the publisher, Hezekiah Niles. The images and emotions aroused by the veto, together with the election campaign that followed and the changes in the party, turned a squabbling Jackson coalition into a more tightly knit political party. The name Democratic was not adopted officially until 1836, but Jackson, Kendall, and Blair all used it in the 1832 election. The veto became the centerpiece of the campaign. Biddle was

44. Biddle to Henry Clay, 1 Aug. 1832, Biddle Papers; *Intelligencer,* 14 July 1832; *Register of Debates,* 22d Cong., 1st sess., 1221–40, 1265–74, 1296.

45. *Commercial Advertiser,* n.d. and 24 July 1832, in *Courier,* 13 July, 6 Aug. 1832. Mary Ryan says that "the frank exaltation of democracy had become the presumption of national politics with Jackson's bank message in 1832." Ryan, *Civic Wars: Democracy and Public Life in the American City during the Nineteenth Century* (Berkeley, 1997), 9.

so certain that the American public would consider it a radical, dangerous document that he sent out thirty thousand copies. When he discovered that many Americans liked it, he started distributing copies of Webster's Senate speech instead. The Jacksonians also circulated copies of the veto message, and Blair printed extracts from sixty-eight different newspapers supporting it. Both party organs, the *Globe* and the *National Intelligencer*, published a series of editorials discussing the veto and the BUS.[46]

In their series, which ran all summer and fall, Blair and Kendall changed the direction of the Bank War by reviving the charge of corruption and by asking for the removal of the deposits. Calling the BUS a *"Gambler's Bank,"* they described the ways in which it had corrupted newspaper editors and politicians. On September 17 they brought up a plan that Kendall had hinted at in 1829. The only way to deter the BUS from its "tyrannical and oppressive course," they said, was "to withdraw the national deposits from the control of the Bank" and put them in "well managed State institutions."[47]

As in most summers, official Washington cleared out after the adjournment of Congress. The exodus was greater than usual because of a terrible epidemic of cholera spreading down the East Coast. Kendall, Blair, and Lewis, however, remained in the city to run the election. Although Jackson was at the Hermitage all summer, he did his best to keep up with the campaign. When he heard that Joseph Gales of the *National Intelligencer* had censured the administration's patronage policy, the president asked Kendall to prepare "a good reply." He was sure that Kendall would give "Joe such a dressing as will quiet him."[48]

46. Between Sept. 1831 and Sept. 1832 there were 248 references to the tariff, 113 to banking, 94 to railroads, and 46 to nullification. *Niles' Register,* index. See also *Globe,* 29 Oct., 30 Nov. 1831, 25 Jan., 1 May, 12 July–20 Oct. 1832; *Intelligencer,* 14 July, 4 Sept., 4–24 Oct. 1832; Jackson to Van Buren, 18 Nov. 1832, Jackson, *Correspondence,* 4:490; Kendall to Van Buren, 2 Nov. 1832, Van Buren Papers; Biddle to Webster, 27 Aug. 1832, Biddle, *Correspondence,* 191–92; William E. Ames, *A History of the National Intelligencer* (Chapel Hill, 1972), 52. Ronald P. Formisano does not believe that the Bank veto played such an important role. In his view only an elite minority cared about the BUS issue. If so, as Richard B. Latner and Peter Levine once asked, why was it given so much attention? Formisano, *The Birth of Mass Political Parties: Michigan, 1827–1861* (Princeton, 1971), 11–12; Latner and Levine, "Perspectives on Antebellum Pietistic Politics," *Reviews in American History* 4 (1976): 15–24.

47. *Globe,* 12 July–19 Oct. 1832.

48. For the cholera see *Niles' Register* 42 (1832): 354, 371, 389, 404, 408, 419, 450–51. Both Barry and Kendall lost a kitchen slave to the plague. Barry to Susan Taylor, 4, 17 July, 9, 16 Aug. 1832, Barry Papers; *Intelligencer,* 24 July 1832; Jackson to Kendall, 23 July 1832, Jackson to Lewis, 18 Aug. 1832, Jackson, *Correspondence,* 4:465–67.

In the election the Democrats depended heavily on the *Globe* and the *Extra Globe*. The two newspapers were running more efficiently than in the past because Blair had hired John C. Rives to serve as business manager. The shrewd, shaggy, "matter-of-fact" Rives, who stood six feet five inches tall and weighed 245 pounds, complemented the scrawny, often mercurial Blair and brought order to the office. The *Globe* was at last making money. Its circulation had climbed to six thousand, and the State Department had awarded Blair a lucrative contract to publish the *Diplomatic History of the American Revolution*.[49]

In running the campaign Kendall took advantage of his party contacts in the Northeast. He had written Gideon Welles the previous fall requesting a list of Jackson men to whom he could send information. He also wrote Hartford postmaster John M. Niles, saying that they must prepare for a "war to the knife" and asking for the names of Jackson postmasters and newspaper editors. In northern New England he relied on Isaac Hill, who hoped to carry Vermont and Maine as well as New Hampshire. One Clay newspaper in Maine complained that bundles of the *Extra Globe* were being sent into almost every town. When the Clay men lashed out at Hill, Blair denounced the "coalition prints" for their *"farrago of abuse."*[50]

Copies of the *Globe* and the *Extra* were also being mailed to New York and the western states by the thousands. With Clay running for president, the Kentucky election in August was again the opening round of the national campaign. Kendall made sure that copies of the veto and Benton's BUS speech went to his friends in the state. "You must try," he wrote, "by an efficient organization and rousing the patriotic enthusiasm of the people, to counteract the power of money." The veto proved to be a double-edged weapon, helpful in Jackson strongholds but harmful in Clay counties such as Fayette.[51]

49. Frederic Hudson, *Journalism in the United States from 1690 to 1872* (New York, 1873), 238–40, 244–45 (quotation). In addition the *Extra Globe* had eight thousand subscribers. *Globe*, 10 Apr., 19 May, 8, 11 June 1832; *Extra Globe*, 10 May 1832; Smith, *Press, Politics, and Patronage*, 250–51; Jackson to Edward Livingston, 21 July, 8 Sept. 1832, Jackson, *Correspondence*, 4: 464–65, 473.

50. Kendall to Welles, 12 Sept. 1831, Kendall to Niles, 26 Jan. 1832, Welles Papers, LC; *Globe*, 18, 21 Aug. 1832; Robert V. Remini, "Election of 1832," *History of American Presidential Elections 1789–1968*, ed. Arthur M. Schlesinger Jr., 4 vols., vol. 1 (New York, 1971), 510.

51. William H. Seward to Weed, 19 Aug. 1832, Thurlow Weed Papers, University of Rochester, Thomas C. Clarke to Nicholas Biddle, 12 Sept. 1832, Nicholas Biddle Papers, LC, both quoted in Gerald J. Baldasty, "The Washington Political Press in the Age of Jackson," *Journalism History* 10 (1983): 68; *Globe*, 2 Oct. 1832; W. O. Butler to Kendall, 20 May 1832, Blair and Rives Papers, LC;

Kendall sought to bolster the state parties by promoting a network of Hickory Clubs. Hoping to offset the influence of the BUS, which had its main office in Philadelphia, he set up two clubs in Pennsylvania. To tie them all together and give them "tone and character" he founded the Central Hickory Club in Washington. Duff Green called it a "mongrel group," which did not "intend to sleep" until it had achieved its goal of "wresting power from the people."[52]

The club also gave Kendall the opportunity to publish an address that served as a national Jackson platform. It started with a declaration of principles blending republican ideals with the more partisan democratic ideas of the Jacksonians. Amid republican echoes from the past, such as the propositions that state governments were "limitations of power" and that all governments should be "simple and cheap," were familiar democratic phrases—that congressmen must "obey the instructions . . . of their constituents" and that "the humble members of society" had the "right to complain" when the laws "grant . . . exclusive privileges." The address defended the Jacksonians against the charge of proscription by saying that the administration had a republican "duty" to "fill all offices" with men *devoted to popular rights.*[53]

Jackson won reelection with 219 electoral votes to 49 for Clay and 18 for two other candidates. Now presiding over a somewhat more balanced party than in 1828, he carried two additional northern states—New Hampshire and Maine—and two fewer in the South. Although the BUS was the major issue, its impact is difficult to assess. It drew voters to the polls, but the voter turnout percentage remained the same as in 1828. It did not determine the outcome of the election. Jackson lost Philadelphia and western New York because of the veto, but carried both states. The BUS issue helped him in Massachusetts but not enough to win. It has even been argued that the veto message hurt Jackson, for his percentage of the popular vote dropped slightly from 56 percent in 1828 to 55 percent in 1832, mostly because of a decline in Pennsylvania. It is the

Kendall to ——, 25 July 1832, Miscellaneous Manuscripts, Kendall, Amos, New-York Historical Society; Jackson to Lewis, 18 Aug. 1832, John Breathitt to Jackson, 23 Aug. 1832, Jackson *Correspondence,* 4:466–67, 469; Clay to Webster, 27 Aug. 1832, Webster, *Papers,* 3:188.

52. *Globe,* 6 Aug., 13 Oct., 1 Nov. 1832; *Telegraph,* 2, 7, 8 Nov. 1832; Duff Green to Calhoun, 23 Oct. 1832, *The Papers of John C. Calhoun,* ed. Robert L. Merriwether, W. Edwin Hemphill, Clyde Wilson, and Shirley Bright Cook, 28 vols. (Columbia: University of South Carolina Press, 1959–2003), 11:667–68.

53. *Globe,* 13 Oct. 1832.

only time that a president lost ground and yet was reelected. Perhaps, it is said, Jackson would have done better without Kendall's aggressive Bank veto.[54]

That argument misses the main point. Biddle and Clay had challenged Jackson by pressing for recharter in an election year and had every prospect of winning. But Jackson vetoed the recharter bill and won the election by a decisive margin. He won because of his own popularity, his party's network of state committees, clubs, and newspapers, and the political power of Kendall's message. The circulation of the Bank veto, the *Extra Globe,* and other campaign materials showed how mass communications could enhance American democracy. Like the "Wictorian Dinner" in 1824 and the bargain charge in 1828, the Bank veto made the difference in 1832.

Two of the party's chief victims, Thurlow Weed in New York and Duff Green in Washington, had no doubts about why Jackson had won. Weed complained that "it was easy" for the Jacksonians "to enlist the laboring classes against a 'monster bank' or 'moneyed aristocracy.'" He told his anti-Jackson friends that "as a popular question, two sentences in the veto message"—the one on foreign ownership of stock and the claim that it made "the rich richer and the poor poorer"—would "carry ten electors against the bank for every one that Mr. Webster's arguments and eloquence secured in favor of it." The veto was a winning issue for the Jackson men.[55]

According to Green, the Jackson officials "take their cue from the party, and few, very few, read any but the party paper, and he who controls the leading papers control[s] the party. What press is the organ of the Jackson party? *The Globe!* Who is the master spirit of the Central Hickory Club? Amos Kendall!! Who controls the Globe? *Amos Kendall!!!* Thus is all political power resolved into the hands of Amos Kendall!" Once again the opposition was determining Kendall's place in history.[56]

---

54. Ibid., 17 Sept., 1 Oct. 1832; Petersen, *Statistical History of the American Presidential Elections,* 20–21, 172–78.

55. Thurlow Weed, *Autobiography of Thurlow Weed,* ed. Harriet A. Weed (1883; reprint, New York, 1970), 371–73; Benson, *Concept of Jacksonian Democracy,* 53. For the relationship between the Bank veto and the bargain charge see Marshall, "Genesis of Grass-Roots Democracy," 285–87.

56. *Telegraph,* 8 Nov. 1832.

# 13

## REMOVING THE DEPOSITS

In the months following the election Jackson was forced to shift much of his attention to nullification in South Carolina. A national crisis began on November 24 when a South Carolina state convention nullified the tariff acts of 1828 and 1832. In his annual message on December 10 the president issued a sober warning to the nullifiers, and his proclamation to South Carolina a week later left no doubt that he would enforce the collection of customs duties. Later, when he asked Congress for the necessary military authority, Congress responded with the Force Act.[1]

Kendall's attention was also diverted. Early in November he wrote Martin Van Buren two surprising letters recommending that the Democrats fight nullification by forming a Union party that would admit National Republicans and deal "moderately" with Bank men. He followed in late November and early December with editorials in the *Globe* calling for a Union party and proposing lower tariffs that would appeal to the Unionist minority in South Carolina.[2]

But the Bank War was still on. Over the same span of time almost a dozen editorials against the BUS poured out of the *Globe*, and Blair repeated his call for the removal of the deposits. In his annual message Jackson denounced the BUS for failing to provide the funds needed to redeem a large government bond issue. In retaliation he called on Congress to pay the debt by selling the government's shares of BUS stock. He also hinted at removal of the deposits by urging Congress to determine whether they were "entirely safe" in the BUS. Six days after the proclamation he asked Tennessee con-

1. Jackson, "Fourth Annual Message," "Special Message," 16 Jan. 1833, "Proclamation," 10 Dec. 1832, *Compilation,* 2:591–606, 610–32, 640–56.
2. Kendall to Van Buren, 2, 10 Nov. 1832, Van Buren Papers; *Globe,* 26, 29 Nov., 4, 7 Dec. 1832.

gressman James K. Polk to start another investigation of the BUS. That "Hydra of corruption," he warned, was "only scotched not dead."[3]

During the nullification winter Polk got the congressional investigation under way and brought in a bill to sell the government's shares of the BUS. Hoping to find corruption, he enlisted the help of three of the government directors on the board of the BUS and members of the Kitchen Cabinet, including Kendall and Reuben M. Whitney. The latter was a former associate of Biddle, who had left the BUS to work for the administration. He was so active in the Bank War that Bank men mentioned him in the same breath with Blair and Kendall. Evidence of corruption was inconclusive—loans, for example, had been given to enemies as well as friends of the BUS—but the *Globe* continued to call the BUS an unsafe depository for government funds. Polk's efforts proved unsuccessful. His bill to sell the BUS stock was rejected, and on March 2 the House endorsed a committee report declaring the deposits safe.[4]

The resolution of the nullification crisis and the adjournment of Congress in early March 1833 ended any necessity for a Union party and left Jackson free to continue the Bank War. It would not be easy, for Congress was opposed to removing the deposits, and aside from Taney and the Kitchen Cabinet, hardly any of the president's subordinates liked the idea. Blair could not convince William B. Lewis, and Kendall had the same difficulty with McLane and Van Buren. His conversation with the Little Magician was unusually heated for two men who normally held themselves in check. According to Kendall, Van Buren "warmly remonstrated" with him for continuing to "agitate" the subject. After more "excited" talk Kendall flew into a rage and stormed out of the room. Unless the BUS was "stripped of the power" to receive the deposits, he shouted, it would use the power to carry the next election for the opposition.[5]

Jackson's task was made even more difficult by a clause in the BUS charter

3. *Globe*, 1 Nov.–11 Dec. 1832; Jackson, "Fourth Annual Message," *Compilation*, 2:599–600; Jackson to Polk, 16 Dec. 1832, Jackson, *Correspondence*, 4:501.

4. Whitney to Polk, 27 Jan. 1833, *Correspondence of James K. Polk*, ed. Herbert Weaver, Paul H. Bergeron, and Wayne Cutler, 9 vols. to date (Nashville, 1969–), 2:54–55; Kendall to ——, 31 Jan. 1833, Amos Kendall Papers, Chicago Historical Society; John Sergeant to Biddle, 6 Mar. 1833, Nicholas Biddle Papers, LC, quoted in John M. McFaul and Frank Otto Gatell, "The Outcast Insider: Reuben M. Whitney and the Bank War," *Pennsylvania Magazine of History and Biography* 41 (1967): 121; *Globe*, Dec. 1832–Jan. 1833; *Register of Debates*, 22d Congress, 2d sess., 1707–22, 1898–1902, 1922–36.

5. Parton, *Life of Andrew Jackson*, 3:503–5; *Autobiography*, 374–76.

giving the secretary of the Treasury—not the president—the sole power of removal. It has been suggested that Jackson had this requirement in mind when he made plans to replace Secretary of the Treasury McLane with William J. Duane of Philadelphia. The arrangements, which were made in the fall of 1832 but not announced until the following spring, called for McLane to move to the State Department while Edward Livingston became minister to France.

Some have assumed that Jackson was trying to replace McLane with someone who would remove the deposits, but that seems unlikely. First of all, the original impetus for the cabinet shifts came not from Jackson but from Livingston. Second, there was no indication that McLane would refuse to make the removals; even though opposed to the idea, he told Kendall in March that he would cooperate if Jackson insisted. Third, the idea of appointing Duane started with McLane, not Jackson. The president accepted the idea because Duane was from Pennsylvania, was the son of the famous Republican editor William Duane, and had a record of opposing the BUS. But Jackson never thought to ask him about removal. The selection of Duane was more slipshod than calculating.[6]

In spite of the uncertainties Jackson plunged ahead. On March 19 he distributed a memorandum to his cabinet and other advisers asking whether the BUS was a safe depository, whether its charter should be renewed, and if not whether it should be replaced by a new national bank or by state banks. He left no doubt about his own views. The administration, he said, must "maintain . . . the ground gained by the veto" and never allow the BUS to be rechartered. He was willing to consider a new national bank in the District of Columbia but first wanted to try "a full and fair experiment" with state banks. He obviously planned to remove the deposits.[7]

In preparing his reply Kendall had to balance the overall situation, the president's position, and his own goals. Removing the deposits and setting up a system of state banks to handle them would be difficult and would invite attacks. The BUS was still popular in the Congress and in most parts of the

6. Thomas P. Govan and Bray Hammond both assume that Jackson shifted McLane in order to appoint someone who would remove the deposits. Govan, *Nicholas Biddle: Nationalist and Public Banker, 1786–1844* (Chicago, 1959), 227; Hammond, *Banks and Politics in America from the Revolution to the Civil War* (Princeton, 1957), 413. There is some possibility that McLane knew that Duane would oppose removal. Kendall to Jackson, 11 Aug. 1833, Jackson, *Correspondence,* 5:150–53; Munroe, *Louis McLane,* 356–61, 384; Van Buren, "Autobiography," 593–99; *Autobiography,* 377.

7. Jackson to Taney, 12 Mar. 1833, *Maryland Historical Magazine* 4 (1909): 297–98; Jackson to members of the cabinet, 19 Mar. 1833, Jackson, *Correspondence,* 5:32–33.

country. To many Americans removal would seem tyrannical and vindictive. With its many branches and vast reserves the BUS had the power to retaliate against the deposit banks by collecting their notes and demanding specie.

Knowing that most of the cabinet responses were likely to be negative, Kendall wanted to encourage Jackson, defend the use of state banks, and offer arguments that would appeal to the president and that he could use to win over Congress and the public. As for himself, he sought to destroy the BUS because he considered it a threat to democracy, but his primary reason was to stimulate and strengthen the Democratic party. Removing the deposits would accomplish this by fatally weakening the party's most dangerous enemy and by enabling the administration to set up a system of loyal, Democratic deposit banks, comparable to the chain of Democratic newspapers.

So Kendall replied with the republican imagery and attacks on the BUS that he had used in Kentucky and in the Bank veto. The "power" and the "abuses and corruptions" of the BUS, he began, were too great to allow it to keep the deposits or be rechartered. Any sort of national bank, even with reforms, "impairs the morals of our people, corrupts our statesmen and is dangerous to liberty." A "decisive act" was needed to "reunite and enspirit" the Democratic party. Jackson must act at once to crush the "great enemy of republicanism." He reassured the president that a system of state banks would outperform the BUS and would not be shaken by any BUS retaliation. If Jackson let this "critical moment" pass, he warned, the BUS would succeed in electing a weak man as the next president, would soon have a new charter, and would "forever thereafter" rule the nation. The Old Hero's endorsement showed that he was in full agreement. Kendall's arguments, he wrote, "confirm all my opinions . . . on this great question. . . . The Bank must be put down, or it puts down our liberty, and rules by its corruption."[8]

The only other letter of support came from Taney, who used similar rhetoric, accusing the BUS of "abuses of power" and calling for "prompt, firm, and decisive action" to defend the "purity of our institutions." Among the other officials, Barry and Woodbury suggested waiting until Congress met in December. Livingston and Lewis Cass sent no answer but were opposed to re-

---

8. With his letter to Jackson Kendall enclosed a copy of a letter on removal that he had sent to McLane. The statements about the Democratic party and the state bank system were in the latter. Kendall to McLane, 16 Mar. 1833, Kendall to Jackson, 20 Mar. 1833, with endorsement, Jackson Papers. Major L. Wilson has discussed these and other examples of the use of republican language in the Bank War in "The 'Country' Versus the 'Court,'" 619–47.

moval. McLane offered a host of reasons why removal would be unwise. Van Buren, now less opposed to removal than he had been during his blowup with Kendall, agreed to support the president but also felt that it would be wise to wait for Congress.[9]

By the time Jackson received his replies, he was in the midst of an angry controversy rising out of the Randolph affair. When the court of inquiry reconvened in Washington in December 1832, purser's steward Norman finally made an appearance but had little to add to the case. A month later the court cleared Randolph of fraud but found him $4,303 in default and censured him for sloppy bookkeeping. The case was then turned over to the president, who as commander in chief had the authority to decide on punishment. Jackson ignored the court and dismissed Randolph from the navy because of fraud.[10]

This postscript to the Eaton affair had a violent and highly politicized ending. On May 6 Randolph tried to salvage lost honor by pulling the president's nose while he was on board a steamboat on the Potomac. After making his escape, he issued a statement saying that he had been dismissed "without just cause" because of the "malignity and conspiracy of John H. Eaton and Amos Kendall, worthy associates of their malicious and imbecile master." In Virginia dinners were held in his honor. The *United States Telegraph* and the *National Intelligencer* defended him, while the *Globe* denounced him for fraud and assault. Jackson, who believed that he had been publicly insulted, wrote an article for the *Globe*, calling the "dastardly and cowardly" assault part of a political conspiracy to assassinate him. Randolph, however, was not arrested for the attack until Jackson left office and then was not convicted.[11]

The exaggerated republican language used by Kendall and Taney to describe the BUS and the resort to a traditional code of honor in the Randolph affair reflect the unevenness of change in the early republic. Political language and codes of behavior had not changed as rapidly as politics and the economy. Although a new language of democracy had appeared, language for the liberal

9. Van Buren to Jackson, Mar. 1833, Taney to Jackson, Mar. 1833, McLane to Jackson, 20 May 1833, Jackson, *Correspondence*, 5:24–25, 33–41, 75–101; Barry to Jackson, Mar. 1833, Woodbury to Jackson, 2 Apr. 1833, Jackson Papers; *Autobiography*, 376.

10. "Proceedings of a Court of Inquiry in the Case of Lieutenant Robert B. Randolph, of the Navy," *ASP:NA*, 4:301–48; *Globe*, 23 Jan. 1833; Jackson, "Order," 18 April 1833, Jackson Supplement.

11. *Globe*, 7–11, 13–18, 21–25 May, 1, 3–5 June 1833; John M. Belohlavek, "Assault on the President: The Jackson-Randolph Affair of 1833," *Presidential Studies Quarterly* 12 (1982): 361–68; Jackson, "Draft of editorial," c. 13 May 1833, Jackson Papers; Jackson to Van Buren, 12 May 1833, Jackson, *Correspondence*, 5:74; *Niles' Register* 44 (1833): 177, 45 (1833): 292.

economy had not kept up. Politicians like Kendall had to fall back on the ingrained republican phraseology to express the real sense of economic crisis that they felt. Jackson and Kendall depended on these expressions to paint the BUS as a corrupt institution endangering the republic. Clay and Biddle used them to portray the president as a corrupt dictator endangering liberty.[12]

Kendall learned about the affair while he was in the Hudson Valley in New York. According to the *Globe* he was on his way to visit his family in Dunstable because of the recent death of his mother, but instead he stopped to visit his brother George in Catskill and then went on to Albany to see Edwin Croswell, the editor of Van Buren's political organ, the *Albany Argus.* While there he had dinner with a number of "warm-hearted friends," one probably Van Buren. Kendall may well have been there to discuss the selection of banks to receive the federal deposits.[13]

When he returned to Washington, he found the president preparing for a tour of the Northeast. McLane, Cass, and Andrew J. Donelson were to leave with the president in early June; and they would be joined by Van Buren and Levi Woodbury in New York. It may seem odd that Kendall was not invited. He had many political friends in New England, and the tour was scheduled to go through Lowell, Massachusetts, not far from Dunstable. But party politicians with reputations like those of Kendall, Blair, and Lewis were not the sort that presidents took on triumphal tours.

Besides, there was much for him to do in Washington. On May 29 William J. Duane arrived to take over the Treasury Department. Barely forty-eight hours later Whitney came to his lodgings and informed him that Jackson would soon direct him to remove the deposits. The next evening Whitney called again, accompanied this time by Kendall, whom Duane had never met. Kendall intended to explain the president's position, but, noticing how angry Duane had become, he held his tongue. When Duane finally had a chance to talk with Jackson, he protested this bold attempt to "reduce me to a mere cipher." Instead of removing the deposits on his own, he suggested waiting for the approval of Congress or the judiciary. Jackson, however, insisted that he

12. Wilson, "The 'Country' Versus the 'Court,'" 645–47; Kenneth S. Greenberg, "The Nose, the Lie, and the Duel in the Antebellum South," *American Historical Review* 95 (1990): 57–74; Bertram Wyatt-Brown, "Andrew Jackson's Honor," *JER* 17 (1997): 1–36.

13. Kendall to Jackson, 9 May 1833, Jackson Papers; *Globe,* 8 May 1833; Kendall to Jane Kendall, 7, 17 May 1833, in *Autobiography,* 325–27. Van Buren was apparently in Albany because a letter addressed to him in New York was forwarded to that city. Samuel C. Allen to Van Buren, 13 May 1833, Van Buren Papers.

had to act promptly to prove that a system of deposit banks could work. If not, Congress would be encouraged to recharter the BUS. He said he would send Duane a full statement of his views from one of the stops on his tour.[14]

Duane's opposition had caught everyone by surprise and left the question of removal of the deposits up in the air. When Jackson left on June 6, he had with him a paper that Kendall had recently prepared defending removal, but the administration had no plan for organizing the deposit banks. The president said he would discuss the entire matter with Van Buren in New York. This worried Kendall because he knew that Van Buren would side with Duane and that no one would be there to counter his arguments.[15]

He had to work fast. On June 9 he wrote Van Buren, asking him to support prompt removal and outlining a plan. The government would select "primary" banks in the major coastal cities, which in turn would choose banks in the interior, subject to the approval of the secretary of the Treasury. The banks would be regulated by the secretary and would be required to carry on the duties currently being performed by the BUS. For a man who believed that "the world is governed too much," Kendall was calling for a good deal of regulation. To avoid any "charge of harshness," the government would not remove the deposits all at once but would withdraw them gradually as the need for funds arose. The administration would have to move promptly in order to "take the last dollar" out before Congress convened in December.[16]

Kendall's paper and letter carried the day. After conferring with Van Buren and reading both of Kendall's documents, the president made up his mind to go ahead. He sent Duane two letters. The first, a statement of Jackson's views on removal, was almost identical with Kendall's paper. The second, which contained detailed instructions for setting up the deposit banks, was copied directly from Kendall's letter to Van Buren. Duane was to remove the deposits by September 15.[17]

Jackson returned to Washington on July 4 but was too exhausted to see Duane for a week. When they finally got together, he quickly rejected the secretary's arguments for waiting until Congress convened in December. On

14. William J. Duane, *Narrative and Correspondence concerning the Removal of the Deposits* (1838; reprint, New York, 1965), 5–9.

15. Ibid., 7–9.

16. Kendall to Van Buren, 9 June 1833, Van Buren Papers.

17. Jackson to Andrew Jackson Jr., 17 June 1833, Jackson to Duane, 26 June 1833, Jackson, *Correspondence*, 5:110–28; Kendall, "Statement on Removal of the Deposits," June 1833, Jackson Papers; *Autobiography*, 377–78.

July 20 he appointed Kendall special agent to negotiate with the state banks. He gave him great freedom of action, even allowing him to rewrite any of Duane's instructions that he considered inhibiting. Jackson then left for a vacation at the Rip Raps, a tiny government-owned island in Chesapeake Bay, leaving behind an administration deeply divided by the Bank War. Even Taney, it was said, had "flin[ch]ed and doubted." Because of the great uncertainty the president took Blair along to give him advice and help him prepare a statement on removal. Blair's wife and family accompanied them.[18]

Kendall's official assignment was to find half a dozen large banks sound enough and willing enough to handle the federal deposits, but his real goals were political. When asked later about the criteria for selecting the banks, he said that he preferred those "which are in hands politically friendly," but "if there are none such then we must take those which are in control of opposition men whose feelings are liberal." Jackson was unnecessarily concerned about finding such banks. Long before Kendall started out, a number of state bankers, almost all "friendly," had sent in feelers. They included Taney's banking associate Thomas Ellicott in Baltimore, Whitney's brother-in-law William D. Lewis in Philadelphia, Van Buren's friend George Newbold in New York, and other bankers from as far away as New Orleans and Natchez, Mississippi.[19]

Kendall's overriding political task was to convey an air of inevitability, to convince bankers and politicians that Jackson was certain to remove the deposits and that the state banks were eager to receive them. Wherever he went he sent word ahead to let political friends know he was coming. Once there he visited banks, met Democratic leaders, wrote letters to politicians and newspapermen, and kept Jackson and Blair informed of his progress. Newspapermen followed him closely, Democrats supporting him, opposition writers snapping at his heels. The *National Intelligencer* called his appointment "one of the worst . . . that could have been made."[20]

18. *Autobiography*, 378; Duane, *Narrative*, 38–93; Levi Woodbury, "Levi Woodbury's 'Intimate Memoranda' of the Jackson Administration," ed. Ari Hoogenboom and Herbert Ershkowitz, *Pennsylvania Magazine of History and Biography* 92 (1968): 510 (quotation).

19. Kendall to Niles, 2 Oct. 1833, John M. Niles Papers, Connecticut Historical Society, quoted in Frank Otto Gatell, "Spoils of the Bank War: Political Bias in the Selection of Pet Banks," *American Historical Review* 70 (1964): 36; see also 37 n. 8; George Newbold et al. to Van Buren, 20 Feb. 1833, The Papers of Martin Van Buren, Microfilm, 1987; Martin Gordon to Louis McLane, 21 Dec. 1832, Whitney to Jackson, 18 Mar. 1833, Powhatan Ellis to Jackson, 2 July 1833, Jackson Papers.

20. *Globe*, 25, 31 July, 2, 12 Aug. 1833; *Intelligencer*, 31 July 1833.

The first stop, on July 28 at Baltimore, went as planned. After holding conversations and exchanging letters with eight banks, he was able to report that three, including Ellicott's Union Bank of Maryland, were willing and qualified to receive the deposits. Not surprisingly he leaned toward Ellicott's bank, saying that it offered "security in good stocks." During his week in the city Kendall met with former Democratic congressman Isaac McKim and re-assured him that the BUS would not be able to "make mischief." He wrote to Blair, asking him to tell the Virginia newspapers to "dismiss their timidity" and support removal. He sent Jackson the cheering news that plenty of strong banks were waiting to take the deposits and included the unsupported rumor that Duane was ready to resign.[21]

Kendall's week in Philadelphia, the home of the BUS, went less smoothly. Many of the banks refused to deal with him, leading him to suspect that Biddle had been applying pressure. He also had to cope with newspaperman James G. Bennett, who had become part owner of the *Philadelphia Pennsylvanian*. Although a Democrat, he was in cahoots with McLane and was spreading the rumor that Jackson had given up the idea of removal.[22]

Whitney and William D. Lewis, however, were there to ease the way at the Girard Bank, where Lewis was cashier. Kendall and Whitney held court with local politicians, defending "the propriety" of removing the deposits without waiting for Congress. Whitney boasted that Congress would not dare "oppose the old hero" and claimed that the government had the power "to break a branch" of the BUS. Kendall passed the word that Duane and McLane would have to leave the cabinet if they continued to oppose removal. When the week was over, Kendall had the names of several sound banks that were "not only willing but desirous to undertake the service."[23]

Kendall continued to do well in New York, but less so in Boston. In New York, where he needed several large banks, seven, including the important Bank of America, were ready to take deposits. Boston was far less cordial. Only two of twelve banks—the Commonwealth and the Merchants—were

---

21. Kendall to Ellicott, 26 July 1833, Roger B. Taney Papers, LC; "Report of Amos Kendall," 1833, RG 56, National Archives; Gatell, "Spoils of the Bank War," 37; Kendall to Jackson, 2 Aug. 1833, Jackson, *Correspondence*, 5:145–46 (first two quotations); Kendall to Blair, 3 Aug. 1833, Blair-Lee Papers (last quotation).

22. Gatell, "Spoils of the Bank War," 39–41; *National Gazette*, 7 Aug. 1833, cited in Daniels, "Amos Kendall," 201; Pray, *Memoirs of James Gordon Bennett*, 160; Kendall to Bennett, 31 July 1833, in Hudson, *Journalism*, 447–48; *Autobiography*, 382–83.

23. Govan, *Nicholas Biddle*, 239; Kendall to Duane, 10 Aug. 1833, "Report of Amos Kendall."

interested, and his only contact was his old adversary David Henshaw. Fortunately he had not cut his ties with Henshaw and was able to convince both banks to join the system.[24]

The news that Jackson and Blair were receiving at the Rip Raps was not as good. Hundreds of letters were arriving "entreating" them to give up plans for removal, and two ordinarily reliable members of the administration were showing feet of clay. First Van Buren wrote to say that he wanted to check with the Albany Regency before committing himself. Soon afterward Taney advised the president "not to proceed further" unless he had completely made up his mind. Jackson was now facing an administrative breakdown almost as bad as the one during the Eaton affair.[25]

To keep the president from losing heart, Kendall sent two rather pointed letters from New York. On August 11 he insinuated that McLane had known that Duane was opposed to removal when he suggested his appointment. Three days later he described a surprising breakfast encounter with McLane and Van Buren. McLane had offered a compromise in which the administration would issue an order for removal but not make it effective until after Congress met in December. Kendall told Jackson that he opposed the idea and would go along only if McLane and Duane pledged to lobby for the plan in Congress. He knew that Duane would never agree.[26]

Jackson reacted just as Kendall had hoped. As soon as he received the first letter, he wrote a stern letter to Van Buren, repeating the "mortifying" story about the choice of Duane and mentioning rumors that Van Buren was "a friend to the Bank" and opposed to removal. He warned the vice president that such stories would do them both "*much harm.*"[27]

After only two days in Boston, Kendall went up to Dunstable to spend the weekend of August 17–18 with his failing father. It was a sad visit, made even worse by the mysterious disappearance of his youngest brother, Timothy, who was married and had four children. Hoping that the "painful occurrence" would be cleared up, Kendall stayed on for two extra days, but it was still unex-

24. Kendall to Duane, 10, 27 Aug. 1833, "Report of Amos Kendall"; Kendall to Jackson, 11 Aug. 1833, Jackson, *Correspondence*, 5:150–53; Gatell, "Spoils of the Bank War," 43–45, 50–51.

25. Blair to Van Buren, 13 Nov. 1859, in Van Buren, "Autobiography," 607–8; Van Buren to Jackson, 29 July 1833, Van Buren Papers; Taney to Jackson, 5 Aug. 1833, Jackson, *Correspondence*, 5:147–49.

26. Kendall to Jackson, 11, 14 Aug. 1833, Jackson, *Correspondence*, 5:150–53, 156.

27. Jackson to Van Buren, 16 Aug. 1833, ibid., 5:158–59.

plained when he left. Timothy eventually returned, but there is no record of what happened.[28]

Kendall started back to Washington just as Jackson and Blair were ending their vacation at the Rip Raps. When he stopped in New York on August 25, he was alarmed to find that many of the merchants and bankers were unable to get advances from the New York branch of the BUS. Biddle had started a policy of reducing loans, either to protect the BUS in case of removal (as he explained it) or to frighten Jackson into calling it off (as Jackson interpreted it).[29]

Now afraid that Jackson might give up the fight, Kendall wrote again, arguing that the best way to solve the problem was not to call off removal but to start it immediately. Once the state banks received the deposits, they would have "the means . . . to accommodate the merchants." The question was "*immediate removal* or *no removal*." Kendall overlooked one important possibility. If Jackson removed the deposits, Biddle was likely to reduce BUS loans even further, leaving some merchants still without loans.[30]

After a monthlong trip, Kendall arrived back in Washington on August 29. He submitted a list of forty-seven banks, a majority of which offered good security and were willing to receive deposits. Of these he recommended seven: the Union Bank of Maryland in Baltimore; the Girard Bank in Philadelphia; the Bank of America, the Manhattan Bank, and the Mechanics Bank in New York; and the Commonwealth and Merchants Banks in Boston. The selections were a triumph for party patronage. Five of the banks were "friendly" Democratic banks, the other two (the Bank of America and the Manhattan Bank) "liberal" opposition banks. All seven had important party connections: Taney and Whitney for the Baltimore and Philadelphia banks; Van Buren and New York congressman Campbell White for the New York banks; and David Henshaw for the banks in Boston.

The large number of available banks was another example of the tremendous growth of the economy since the turn of the century. In 1800 the four cities had only two banks each—not counting the BUS—or a total of eight,

28. Kendall to Jane Kendall, 13 Aug. 1833, in *Autobiography*, 329–31; Kendall to Jackson, 25 Aug. 1833, Jackson, *Correspondence*, 5:169 (quotation).

29. Kendall to Jackson, 25 Aug. 1833, Jackson, *Correspondence*, 5:169; Hamilton to Jackson, 13 Sept. 1833, Hamilton, *Reminiscences*, 261–65; Biddle to Walter Lenox, 30 July 1833, Biddle to Webster, 13 Aug. 1833, Biddle, *Correspondence*, 212–15. For Biddle's side of the story see Govan, *Nicholas Biddle*, 240–41.

30. Kendall to Jackson, 25 Aug. 1833, Jackson, *Correspondence*, 5:169–70.

one-sixth of the number on Kendall's list. This expansion of capitalism made it possible to remove the deposits, but when Kendall came to justify his report, he relied upon an old-fashioned republican argument. He was sure that state deposit banks would provide all the services performed by the BUS without "the concentrated power" that made it so "dangerous to the purity of our government & the liberties of our people."[31]

Kendall, then, had accomplished his financial goal, but the political goal was another matter: Jackson still had precious little support for removal. Taney was back on board, but McLane, Duane, and Cass were opposed. Van Buren had written an evasive letter and showed no inclination to return to Washington to join in the fight. Removal could lead to another cabinet breakup, something Jackson would do anything to avoid. After seeing Kendall and Whitney in Philadelphia, James G. Bennett knew that there was a serious rift in the administration. Early in September he wrote Jackson accusing Kendall of "treacherously attempting" to seize power from the cabinet. Bennett hoped that removal would be aborted and Kendall, Blair, and Whitney forced out. Then he could move in to edit the *Globe*.[32]

But Jackson felt that the country was behind him and was much heartened by Kendall's report. On September 15 he informed Taney that he would remove the deposits. Three days later he sent a message to the cabinet explaining his decision. He and Blair had worked on the statement at the Rip Raps, using Kendall's paper and letters and adding material of their own about the dangerous powers of Nicholas Biddle. When they returned to Washington, they gave it to Kendall for editing and then to Taney. The theme remained republican. Jackson told the cabinet that the conspiracy and despotism of the BUS threatened the character of the government, the "morals of the people," and the "purity of the elective franchise."[33]

When Duane refused to remove the deposits, the president dismissed him and gave his position to Taney. It is interesting that he did not offer it to

31. Kendall to Duane, 27, 28 Aug., 4 Sept. (quotation) 1833, "Report of Amos Kendall"; Kendall, "Epitome of Actions of State Banks," c. 4 Sept. 1833, Duane Family Papers, American Philosophical Society Library; Hammond, *Banks and Politics*, 144–45.

32. Van Buren to Jackson, 4 Sept. 1833, Jackson, *Correspondence*, 5:179–82; *Autobiography*, 386–87; Bennett to Jackson, 10 Sept. 1833, Jackson Supplement.

33. Duane, *Narrative*, 96–100; Jackson to Taney, 15 Sept. 1833, Jackson, *Correspondence*, 5:188. Jackson and Blair, "Draft of Paper Read to Cabinet," Jackson, *Correspondence*, 5:192–203; Jackson, "Paper Read to the Cabinet on Removal of the Deposits," *Compilation*, 3:5–19 (quotation); *Globe*, 20 Sept. 1833.

Kendall or Blair, perhaps for the same reason that he had not taken them on his tour. Thanks to Jackson's graciousness and his statement that no one was required to endorse his decision, harmony prevailed and no one except Duane left the cabinet. The reluctant Van Buren was mollified by the appointment of his New York friend Benjamin F. Butler as the new attorney general.[34]

The new banking system went into operation on October 1 with Kendall acting as Taney's unofficial assistant. Taney followed Kendall's plan of removing the deposits gradually, with one crucial exception. Anticipating that Biddle would try to destroy the deposit banks by collecting their notes and demanding specie in return, he devised a way to keep the banks liquid. Taney issued drafts on the BUS of $500,000 each to the four New York and Philadelphia banks and one for $300,000 to Thomas Ellicott's Union Bank of Maryland. If Biddle attacked any one of the five banks, it could use its draft to satisfy his demands, but not to make investments. On October 4 the plan backfired when Taney's friend Ellicott used two-thirds of his draft to pay his own personal debts. Faced with a scandal potentially far worse than the Tobias Watkins case, Taney called Ellicott in and chastised him in Kendall's presence but took no steps to punish him. Ellicott remained at the bank and continued to embarrass the administration. Taney and Kendall had only themselves to blame.[35]

During the rest of the fall Biddle continued to reduce his loans, and Taney pulled money out of the BUS faster than planned. The Girard and the Manhattan Banks presented their drafts on branches of the BUS, and $350,000 was suddenly withdrawn from the Savannah branch. The administration tried to force Biddle to lower interest rates by lending these funds out cheaply, but the plan failed when Biddle cut back his loans even further. By the end of the year the government had reduced its deposits from $10 million to $5 million, and Biddle had ordered loan reductions of $9 million.

The abrupt contraction drove interest rates up to 18 percent and brought on a severe panic. Unable to get credit, employers started laying off workers. New York merchant Philip Hone noted glumly that "panic prevail[ed]" on the stock exchange. Jackson blamed the situation on Biddle for drastically reduc-

34. *Globe*, 20, 27 Sept. 1833; Duane, *Narrative*, 100–114; *Autobiography*, 386.

35. Taney to Jackson, 17 Sept. 1833, Jackson, *Correspondence*, 5:192; *Autobiography*, 388–90; Taney, "Roger Brooke Taney's Account of His Relations with Thomas Ellicott in the Bank War," ed. Stuart Bruchey, *Maryland Historical Magazine* 3 (1958): 58–74, 131–52; Jacob P. Meerman, "The Climax of the Bank War: Biddle's Contraction," *Journal of Political Economy* 71 (1963): 380; Gatell, "Spoils of the Bank War," 38–39.

ing his loans, but the government's removal policy was equally to blame. If the federal deposits had been phased out slowly between 1833 and 1836, the panic might have been avoided.[36]

With no turning back, the administration expanded the system, adding fifteen banks during the fall. John C. Calhoun protested that the Democrats were "bestowing" the government funds "on *favorite and partisan banks.*" The National Republicans began calling them "pet banks"—an apt name since almost all were "friendly." At the head of the banks in Washington and Richmond were John Van Ness, once chairman of the Jackson central committee, and John Brockenbrough, cousin of Thomas Ritchie. In choosing banks in Maine, New Hampshire, and Connecticut Kendall followed the advice of Isaac Hill, Levi Woodbury, John M. Niles, and Gideon Welles.[37]

Late in December Henry Clay offered resolutions in the Senate censuring the president for dismissing Duane and removing the deposits. "We behold," he said, "the usual incidents of approaching tyranny." When he came to Kendall's tour in his speech, he looked up at the gallery and said with a sneer, "An agent was sent out—*and such an agent!*" at which point, according to the *National Intelligencer,* he was "interrupted with bursts of applause." Democrats came to Kendall's defense. His classmate Senator Ether Shepley of Maine praised him "for his intellectual powers, for his singleness and purity of purpose." The *Globe* ridiculed Clay for his "theatrical" performance and his "horrible grimace."[38]

The resolutions were adopted, and the attacks continued. Duff Green published another letter from Bennett to Jackson accusing Kendall of conspiring against the cabinet. A popular lithograph showed a mob running after Jackson and shouting "Send back the deposites!" The disgusted president is saying, "By the Eternal . . . I find I've been a mere tool to that Damn'd Amos and his set." When rumors leaked out that Kendall had asked a New York brokerage to transport government funds to Europe, he decided to publish the correspondence to show that he was not working in "collusion" with "Wall

36. Meerman, "Climax of the Bank War," 380–85; Kendall to William D. Lewis, 20 Oct. 1833, Lewis-Neilson Papers, Historical Society of Pennsylvania; *Niles' Register* 45 (1833): 97, 146, 265, 389; Philip Hone, *The Diary of Philip Hone, 1828–1851,* ed. Allan Nevins (New York, 1936), 106; "Drafts of Jackson's Fifth Annual Message," Jackson Papers; Jackson, "Fifth Annual Message," *Compilation,* 3:30–31.

37. *Globe,* 30 Jan. 1834 (quotation); Gatell, "Spoils of the Bank War," passim, especially 52–58; Niven, *Gideon Welles,* 110–11; Kendall to Duane, 28 Aug. 1833, "Report of Amos Kendall"; Hill to Woodbury, 5 Oct. 1833, Hill Papers; Isaac Waldron to Kendall, 24 Aug. 1833, Letters from Banks, National Archives. The only opposition bank was the Bank of Louisville, but it was soon replaced by a Jackson bank.

38. *Register of Debates,* 23d Cong., 1st sess., 58–94, especially 86, 234; *Globe,* 3 Jan. 1834.

Street brokers." The publication had just the opposite effect on Joseph Hop-kinson of Philadelphia, who told Daniel Webster that he had never heard of such a "bold assumption of power."[39]

With all the criticism the administration could ill afford to let any of the deposit banks fail. In March 1834 the situation became extremely serious. Three nondeposit banks in Maryland had failed, the deposit banks in Rich-mond and Washington were close to collapsing, and three deposit banks had voluntarily given up their government funds. When Clay started an investiga-tion of the Union Bank of Maryland, Kendall told Ellicott that the safety of his bank was of "*immense*" importance. The administration could "stand the stopping of other banks [but] if the '*Pets*' begin to go, it is impossible to ap-preciate the consequences." "For Heaven's sake," he implored, "fortify your-selves so that *you can stand amidst ruin*."[40]

The Union Bank survived, none of the deposit banks failed, and two of the three that gave up deposits rejoined the system. By springtime the panic was over. A tremendous inflow of gold and silver from England and France enabled the deposit banks and the BUS to provide loans and reduce interest rates. Wholesale prices had fallen only 13 percent, and they started up again in April. With prosperity returning, the House of Representatives passed resolu-tions opposing the recharter of the BUS and supporting the deposit bank sys-tem. The votes ended any thought of rechartering.[41]

The administration still had to deal with Clay's censure resolutions, which represented a strong challenge to the powers of the president. Late in March Jackson asked Taney, Kendall, and Attorney General Butler to help him prepare an official protest. In the protest the president fell back on the same theme of protecting the people's liberties that he had used in vetoing the BUS and removing the deposits. He went further, however, in his claims of executive authority. He not only defended the president's right to remove of-ficers at will but also asserted that he had custody over almost "every species of property belonging to the United States," a claim that he later retracted.[42]

39. Bennett to Jackson, 4 Dec. 1833, Jackson Supplement; *Globe,* 9 Dec. 1833; Bernard F. Reilly Jr., *Catalogue of American Political Prints, 1766–1876* (Boston, 1991), 66; *Niles' Register* 45 (1833–34): 299–300; Hopkinson to Webster, 27 Dec. 1833, Webster, *Papers,* 3:296.

40. Gatell, "Spoils of the Bank War," 38–39, 55–56; Gatell, "Taney and the Baltimore Pets," *Business History Review* 39 (1965): 205–27; *Globe,* 14, 18 Apr. 1834; John M. McFaul, *The Politics of Jacksonian Finance* (Ithaca, 1972), 37–42; Kendall to Ellicott, 15 Apr. 1834, Taney Papers.

41. Gatell, "Taney and the Baltimore Pets," 221; McFaul, *Politics,* 41; Meerman, "Climax of the Bank War," 381–88; *Register of Debates,* 23d Cong., 1st sess., 2869, 3475–77, 4467–69.

42. Jackson to Kendall, 1 Apr. 1834, Jackson Papers; *Globe,* 24 Apr. 1834; Jackson, "Protest," 15 Apr. 1834, *Compilation,* 3:69–93.

The opposition refused to back down. The Senate ignored the protest and frustrated the president on a number of other occasions. Earlier in the session it had rejected four of Jackson's nominations for directors of the BUS. Jackson resubmitted the same names, together with a message drafted by Taney and Kendall. Brushing aside the charge that the directors had spied on Biddle, he contended that their reports were needed to protect the people from the "machinations" of the BUS. Late in the session the Senate rejected the nominations for the second time and blocked the nomination of Taney as secretary of the Treasury. Jackson was forced to name the less controversial Levi Woodbury secretary of the Treasury and Mahlon Dickerson of New Jersey secretary of the navy. When McLane resigned as secretary of state in June, Jackson replaced him with John Forsyth of Georgia.[43]

This second chapter in the Bank War had even more influence on American politics than the Bank veto. Between September 1833 and September 1834 the index to *Niles' Register* had almost 700 references to banking compared to about 150 to the tariff, nullification, the Post Office, railroads, and slavery combined. The removal of the deposits destroyed the BUS, but it was not as much a Democratic political victory as the veto of the recharter bill was. The Bank veto had shown Jackson as a country hero fighting off a corrupt BUS; removal of the deposits left him in the minds of many a court despot, influenced by a Kitchen Cabinet, stretching his powers to destroy a legitimate, constitutional bank. While the Bank veto gave birth to the Democratic party, removal brought on the Whigs, who campaigned in defense of liberty under the republican banner of antityranny, anticabals, and antipartyism. The new party was composed of old National Republicans, Anti-Masons, Nullifiers, and business and reform groups—the union of Clay and Calhoun that Kendall had predicted. The political confrontation over the BUS accelerated the process toward the American two-party political system that began to flourish in the election of 1840.[44]

43. *Register of Debates*, 23d Cong., 1st sess., app., 310–16; "Nomination of Directors to the Bank of the United States," 11 Mar. 1834, *Compilation*, 3:41–48; "Votes on the Nominations of Taney, St. Clair, and Stevenson," *Senate Journal*, 24 June 1834.

44. *Niles' Register*, index. Although Ronald P. Formisano does not put as much emphasis on the Bank War as I do, he does say that it contributed to a high turnout of voters in Massachusetts in 1834. Formisano, *The Transformation of Political Culture: Massachusetts Parties, 1790s–1840s* (New York, 1983), 253–56. For the rise of the two-party system see William G. Shade, "Political Pluralism and Party Development: The Creation of a Modern Party System, 1815–1852," in *The Evolution of American Electoral Systems*, ed. Paul Kleppner et al. (Westport, Conn., 1981).

# 14

## POSTMASTER GENERAL

On June 9, 1834, a short time before the changes in the cabinet, the Whig majority in the Senate Post Office and Post Roads Committee brought in a report exposing corruption in the Post Office. The most flagrant example was the practice of "extra allowances," by which a favored contractor won a contract by bidding low and then was granted extra allowances for very little extra service. The report accused Postmaster General William T. Barry and Chief Clerk Obadiah B. Brown of receiving loans from contractors and of giving Democratic friends large printing contracts. Brown later resigned.[1]

The report came as no surprise to Barry, who had complained in February that his position was "an arduous one . . . increasing in its complexities." Barry was not competent enough to handle the Post Office. A miserable administrator, he knew little about the mail routes and sometimes wrote contract agreements on undated scraps of paper. He had shown great naiveté in accepting favors, once boasting that a contractor would furnish his daughter with a free trip to Washington in "a separate coach . . . as a compliment to me." Under his regime the quality of postal service had steadily declined. Letters were being delivered late, and mail thefts were on the rise. Owing to his sloppiness and the expansion of services, the Post Office had incurred deficits in four out of five years, including an enormous shortfall of $313 million in 1833.[2]

With the Bank War over, the Post Office scandal threatened to replace the BUS as the main issue in national politics. The Post Office was an inviting target because it was growing at such an astonishing rate. The volume of letters and newspapers had doubled since Barry took office. Henry Clay blamed

1. *Register of Debates,* 23d Cong., 1st sess., 1914–16, 1919–69, 2075, app., 215–42; *Globe,* 4 Dec. 1833, 8 Mar., 12, 13, 14, 18, 26 June 1834; White, *Jacksonians,* 253–63.

2. Barry to James Taylor, 27 Feb. 1830, Barry to Susan Taylor, 22 Feb. 1834, "Letters of William T. Barry," *William and Mary College Quarterly* 14 (1905–6): 21, 238; *Register of Debates,* 23d Cong., 1st sess., app., 231.

the corruption on the Democratic spoils system and proposed limiting Barry's power to appoint postmasters.[3]

The change in issues from the BUS to the Post Office meant that Kendall was no longer at odds with most of the cabinet officers. That is not to say that he was actually close to any of them. He had never been friendly with Cass, Woodbury, and Forsyth, and he hardly knew Butler and Dickerson. He was close to Barry, but there had always been tension between them over patronage, and Barry was now angry that Kendall was not defending him. His relations with Blair were also strained. Blair felt that Kendall was not writing enough to justify his $800-a-year salary and yet was often getting credit for articles that Blair had written. He also suspected that Kendall had stood by and done nothing when McLane tried to oust him in 1832. In short, Kendall remained what he had always been—a Jackson man and nothing else.[4]

For the first summer since he arrived in Washington he had time to be at home. The Kendalls had moved again, this time to the corner of 18th and I Streets NW, where they had enough land to grow potatoes and turnips, keep a cow, and raise chickens and pigs. They had five children: Mary Anne, fourteen, Adela, twelve, and William, eleven, from Kendall's first marriage; Jeannie, six, and John, two, from the second. According to one of his neighbors, Kendall at home was much different from his public image. He had read so much "invective" against him that he had expected to find a "burly man . . . with bowie knives in his belt" but found instead a man "spare of figure, with a face full of kindness and thought, and of pleasant, courteous, and gentle manners." He often saw Kendall "stretched out on the floor, with his own children and mine romping around and upon him."[5]

Kendall continued to be a good husband. His second marriage was no less loving and happy than the first, and there was less friction. Jane was so good-

3. John, *Spreading the News*, 4–6, 243–44, 248; *Statistical History*, 497; *Register of Debates*, 23d Cong., 1st sess., 836.

4. Barry to Susan Taylor, 22 Feb. 1834, Barry, "Letters," 14:238. The *Globe* had yet to win any congressional printing, but its executive printing had finally reached the $15,000 that Kendall had promised, and its circulation (6,480) was now twice that of the *Intelligencer*. *Globe*, 13 Nov. 1833, 1, 3 Jan., 28 June 1834; John C. Rives, Memorandum to Blair, 30 Nov.–12 Dec. 1842, Rives to Kendall, 21 Dec. 1842, Blair to Kendall, 24 Dec. 1842, Van Buren Papers; Kendall to Rives, 28 June 1834, Blair-Lee Papers.

5. William Greer, *A Full Directory of Washington City* (Washington, 1834); Weis, *Early Generations of the Kendall Family*, 166–67; Kendall to Jane Kendall, 3, 9 Aug. 1833, in *Autobiography*, 325–26, 328; Columbia Institution for the Deaf and Dumb, *Proceedings of the Board of Directors of the Columbia Institution, Eulogistic of the Late Amos Kendall* (Washington, 1870), 9–11.

natured that she rarely irritated him, and his fussiness did not bother her. A plump, sturdy woman, she willingly cared for the children, worked in the garden, and tended the animals. Amos, who loved her dearly, bantered with her affectionately, once comparing her ample "*flesh*" with his bare bones. He happily bore the responsibility for her family. After he found a job for Jane's father in his office, the Kyles were able to move into the city near the Kendalls. Amos was comfortable with his in-laws and was much more at ease with his "mild temper[ed]" father-in-law than he had been with his own "high temper[ed]" father.[6]

Kendall's reputation as the power behind the throne made him the subject of much public scrutiny. It was during the next few months that he attracted the attention of Francis J. Grund and Harriet Martineau. Grund found his appearance "one of the most striking" he had ever seen. Kendall's face, he wrote, was "pale, wearing the imprint of over-exertion; but his large eyes are full of animation, and his forehead the highest and broadest I ever saw." Martineau was shocked by "the extreme sallowness of his complexion" and the "perfect whiteness" of his hair, which she attributed to "disease."[7]

Both Grund and Martineau remarked on Kendall's reclusiveness, which they blamed on overwork, poor health, and a puritanical distaste for "the dissipations of society." Several of his more class-conscious countrymen, however, believed that it was a sense of inferiority that kept him out of polite society. Jackson's Tennessee confidant Alfred Balch said that Kendall had "been too long accustomed to the cat & dog politics of Kentucky & has too much zest for such politics. To me he does not look like a gentleman and therefore I could not talk with him. The truth is if a man is not raised a gentleman he never can be one." The New York diplomat Nathaniel Niles wrote patronizingly that Kendall's mind was a "peculiar one," useful only for "*certain objects*," such as destroying the BUS.[8]

None of these estimates quite hit the mark. Kendall kept out of the public eye primarily because he was a shy, busy man who generally did his work behind the scenes. He had never liked public speaking—in school, in college, or in politics. Furthermore, he was a political operator, not an office seeker, and

6. Kendall to Jane Kendall, 16 Aug. 1853, in *Autobiography,* 547–49; Greer, *Directory;* Kendall to John, 10 Oct. 1852.

7. Grund, *Aristocracy in America,* 299–300; Martineau, *Retrospect of Western Travel,* 1:238–39, 258.

8. Balch to Trist, Sept. 1831, Nicholas Trist Papers, LC; Niles to Rives, 23 July 1833, William C. Rives Papers, LC.

he had little need for public appearances. And not the least important, he could not afford to entertain.

Kendall's persistent lack of money requires some attention. Even though he received a high salary and had managed to sell his mill, he had little cash and was more in debt than ever. The reason was that like many Americans he was speculating in western lands. America was in the midst of the great land boom of the 1830s, in which the annual sales of public lands had jumped from about a million acres in 1829 to almost 5 million in 1834 and would reach 20 million in 1836. Kendall had borrowed $10,000 to buy parcels of land in Louisville and had acquired shares valued at $30,000 to $50,000 in the Boston Land Company. He also had land in Illinois. Although he denied any impropriety in these deals, it seems clear that he had taken advantage of his political connections. The $10,000 came from the Girard Bank, one of the banks he had selected to receive the federal deposits. He got the land from the Boston Company at a low price because the directors of the company wanted to use his influence with the president, who was responsible for disposing of Chickasaw land. The sums involved were not small. A sum of $50,000 in 1834 was the equivalent of more than $1 million today.[9]

Needing a better-paying job, Kendall asked Jackson in the summer of 1834 if he could act as his subagent in selling the Chickasaw land. The "fatality" of his "private affairs in the West," he wrote, made it essential that he change jobs. In August his Kentucky friend Thomas P. Moore, who was back from Colombia and had joined him in his land speculations, asked the president to send Kendall and himself as ministers to Spain and Russia. None of the requests were granted, but the president was made aware of Kendall's plight.[10]

Both Jackson and Kendall were concerned about the Post Office. In his annual message of 1834 Jackson called for changes and included a proposal from Kendall placing all postal revenues under the Treasury Department. Within two months the Senate responded with a bill that included Kendall's

9. He had apparently disposed of the land he acquired from the Bullock family in 1816. Kendall to William D. Lewis, 30 June 1834, 8 July 1836, Lewis to Kendall, July 1834, Lewis-Neilson Papers; Kendall to John, 23 June 1851, 22 Nov. 1853; Kendall to Brodhead, 7 Sept. 1835, Daniel D. Brodhead Papers, LC; *Register of Debates*, 25th Cong., 3d sess., app., 387–88; John C. Rives to Blair, 30 Nov.–12 Dec. 1842, Van Buren Papers. For Kendall's defense see Kendall to Dawson, 6 Sept. 1836, Moses Dawson Papers, LC.

10. Kendall to Jackson, 19 July, 21 Aug. 1834, Jackson to Kendall, 8 Aug. 1834, Moore to Jackson, 28 Aug. 1834, Jackson Papers.

suggestion and put restrictions on extra allowances. The House was unable to take it up before adjournment in March. By this time rumors were flying that Barry would be replaced—perhaps by Kendall. French chargé Alphonse Pageot reported that Van Buren wanted the shift because he needed Post Office reform to win the next election. Aware that something had to be done, Jackson offered Kendall the position, which paid $6,000 a year, twice the fourth auditor's salary. Kendall accepted but insisted that the president give him a recess appointment and hold back his nomination until the end of the next session of Congress. That way he could be sure of a year on the job. The president took care of Barry by appointing him minister to Spain.[11]

When Kendall took office on May 1, 1835, the reaction was not as partisan as might have been expected. Democrats, of course, applauded the choice, pointing out that he was a "thorough going republican" with "straightforward, unbending integrity," unusual "perseverance," and great "firmness of character"—"exactly the man to correct [Barry's] errors." A few Whigs feared his partisanship. Philip Hone was dismayed that Jackson had rewarded "the favorite member of the Kitchen Cabinet" with such an important post. Calhoun feared that if Van Buren and Kendall "play[ed] their game with dexterity . . . the country [would] sink insensibly under the sway of despotick power."[12]

But a number of important Whig editors praised the appointment. According to Hezekiah Niles the Post Office position "require[d] a clear head for arranging routes, and adjusting accounts, indefatigable industry [and] unflinching resolution [in all of which] Mr. Kendall is eminently distinguished." Joseph Gales and his partner William W. Seaton expected Kendall to "correct many of the abuses," and editor Horace Greeley of the new literary weekly the *New-Yorker* agreed. These favorable comments suggest that opponents may have hated Kendall's partisanship but were not blind to his ability. They also indicate that the Post Office controversy was not of the same magnitude as

11. Kendall to Jackson, 25 Nov. 1834, "Drafts for Sixth Annual Message," ibid.; Jackson, "Sixth Annual Message," *Compilation*, 3:116–17; *Register of Debates*, 23d Cong., 2d sess., 392, 1351, 1364–65, 1391. Democratic congressman Francis O. J. Smith had predicted the change. Smith to "Bro Can," 14 May 1834, Francis O. J. Smith Papers, Pageot to Henri de Rigny, 28 Mar. 1835, Francis W. Dawson Papers, both at Duke University Rare Book, Manuscript, and Special Collections Library; *Autobiography*, 331, 335–36. Barry died in Liverpool before taking over his new post.

12. *Globe*, 2, 5, 7, 11, 12, 13, 21 May 1835. Hone, *Diary*, 158; Calhoun to Francis W. Pickens, 19 May 1835, Calhoun, *Papers*, 12:534.

the Bank War. Jackson could not have gotten away with appointing Kendall secretary of the Treasury.[13]

Kendall justified his Whig support by starting out in a moderate, nonpartisan way. He sent a reassuring letter to his friend Caleb Butler, now Whig postmaster of Groton, who wondered whether he would lose his position. Kendall replied that as long as he performed his duties "with fidelity," he "need have no fear." The Post Office would not remove "good, faithful and quiet men whatever may be their political opinions." He repeated the promise in a circular to all postmasters. Whigs, of course, had grown skeptical of such statements, but for the time being Kendall lived up to his words.[14]

He followed the same policy in his Washington office. During the first eight months he removed only one clerk (and a Democrat at that) from a staff of eighty-nine. He even resisted pressure from Jackson to remove three clerks of "dissipated habits." Kendall, however, did manage to appoint a friend or two when he had openings from resignation or retirement. He promoted Preston S. Loughborough to replace Chief Clerk Obadiah B. Brown and later brought in two of his old clerks—his former newspaper partner Robert Johnston and his Dartmouth classmate Joseph Perry.[15]

Kendall moved more aggressively in other areas. To improve the moral tone of the office he made a point of publicly refusing offers of loans and free stagecoach rides. He issued a code of behavior like the one in his old office. "Punctual attendance . . . will be expected." Clerks must be "scrupulous in refraining from the use of public property for their own benefit." No one was to accept "any present of value or any pecuniary favor from any contractor."[16]

To get control over the contractors Kendall temporarily suspended all

13. *Globe,* 7 May 1835; *New-Yorker,* 24 Dec. 1836. *Niles' Register* showed far less interest in the Post Office than in banking. Between Sept. 1831 and Sept. 1834 the index contained 928 references to the BUS and banking and only 82 to the Post Office. Between Sept. 1834 and Aug. 1836 *Niles* paid more attention to the Post Office, but there were still only 151 references to the Post Office compared to 272 to the BUS and banking. For the Post Office as a political issue see John, *Spreading the News,* 248–52.

14. Kendall to Butler, 13 May 1835, Kendall Papers, LC; *Autobiography,* 433–34.

15. He also promoted Alex Kyle. Kendall, "Report of Postmaster General, with Statement of Clerks Employed," 19 Jan. 1836, 24th Cong., 1st sess., Ex. Doc. 84; Kendall, "Report . . . Relative to an Increase of Salary of the Clerks in the General Post Office," 9 May 1836, 24th Cong., 1st sess., S. Doc. 362; Jackson to Kendall, 21 May 1835, Jackson Papers; *Globe,* 10 May 1832, 5 Aug. 1835.

16. *Autobiography,* 337–38; Kendall, "Report of the Postmaster General," 1 Dec. 1835, 24th Cong., 1st sess., S. Doc. 1, p. 429.

extra allowances. The new policy brought him into conflict with two of the largest contractors, James Reeside, whose red carriages could be seen all over Pennsylvania, and the firm of Richard C. Stockton and William B. Stokes, which carried the mails along the post roads running out of Baltimore. Reeside soon quit and sued the government; Stockton and Stokes continued to carry mail but later sued in a case that plagued Kendall for many years.[17]

Postmasters received close attention. Kendall reprimanded Postmaster Lynch of Pittsburgh for carelessness and warned him that "the only safety" lay in "perpetual vigilance [and] unceasing industry." During the summer he named special agents to investigate thefts in half a dozen states. In September he sent a form letter to more than a hundred postmasters telling them to gather up unused mailbags and return them to the proper routes. To keep the postmasters on their toes he published in the *Globe* a weekly newsletter, which included lists of postmasters who had defaulted or had been fined.[18]

Before Kendall had been in office three months, he was suddenly caught up in the growing struggle over slavery. The sectional truce over the issue had come to an end early in the 1830s as northerners began to form abolition societies and southerners intensified their defense of slavery. The expansion of the post office and the invention of new steam printing presses made it possible for the American Anti-Slavery Society to distribute thousands of copies of pamphlets and newspapers such as *Human Rights* and the *Emancipator*. But abolitionism met strong resistance. In the North, where many considered it an unwarranted attack on an established institution, there were more than a dozen antiabolitionist riots. Southerners, already frightened by the Nat Turner slave insurrection in 1831, considered abolitionism a flagrant attempt to stir up larger slave rebellions.[19]

Slaveowners were outraged in 1835 when the American Anti-Slavery Society started sending its propaganda into the South. When about a thousand pamphlets arrived in Charleston, South Carolina, on July 29, Postmaster Al-

17. *Autobiography*, 337, 350–51.
18. On the duties of postmasters see Kendall to D. Lynch, 19 June 1835, Kendall to Postmaster, Buffalo, N.Y., 9 Sept. 1835, PMGLB; *Globe*, 7 July, 11 Sept., 12 Nov. 1835. On theft, see Kendall to J. Edward Pratt, 19 June 1835 (2 letters), Kendall to William B. Taylor, July 1835, Kendall to Postmaster, Maysville, Ky., 12 Dec. 1835, Kendall to U.S. Attorney, Richmond, Va., 9 Feb. 1836, Kendall to N. D. Coleman, 10 Feb. 1836, PMGLB.
19. Bertram Wyatt-Brown, "The Abolitionists' Postal Campaign of 1835," *Journal of Negro History* 50 (1965): 227–29; Carl E. Prince, "The Great 'Riot Year': Jacksonian Democracy and Patterns of Violence in 1834," *JER* 5 (1985): 1–19.

fred Huger enforced a state law prohibiting him from forwarding such publications. That evening a small group of vigilantes broke into the post office, seized the pamphlets, and later burned them before a large crowd. The alarmed Huger sent an anguished letter to Postmaster Samuel L. Gouverneur in New York City, where the pamphlets had been mailed, pleading with him not to forward any more. Huger also wrote to Kendall, asking for instructions for dealing with pamphlets that were "inflammatory and incendiary—and insurrectionary in the highest degree."[20]

Kendall faced a dilemma. As postmaster general he was required to make certain that the post office transmitted all newspapers and almost all pamphlets and magazines. As a newspaper editor and a defender of the rights of the people, he could hardly oppose the free circulation of the mails. But he had lived for fifteen years in a slave state, owned slaves himself, and believed in states' rights. Like many Democrats, he considered abolitionism dangerous to the unity of his party and to the Union. And, furthermore, he needed southern votes to be confirmed.

In his reply Kendall sided with slavery. Although admitting that he had "no legal authority to exclude newspapers from the mail," he said he was "not prepared to direct [Huger] to forward or deliver the papers." The post office had been created "to serve the people" of all the states, and not "to be used as the instrument of their destruction." He told Huger that they "owe[d] an obligation to the laws, but a higher one to the communities in which we live." Kendall concluded that he would neither "sanction" nor "condemn" Huger's action, but made it clear that he was giving him permission to intercept the publications.[21]

Kendall then sought the support of the president, who was vacationing at the Rip Raps. He explained that in order to exclude "the inflammatory matter . . . from the mails . . . with as little noise and difficulty as possible," he had "give[n] no instructions" but had allowed postmasters to follow the "intimations" that he had given Huger. Jackson gave his approval and said that he "regret[ted] that such men [could] be guilty of the attempt to stir up amongst the South the horrors of a servile war."[22]

20. John, *Spreading the News*, 257–59; Alfred Huger to Samuel L. Gouverneur, 1 Aug. 1835, in "Postmaster Huger and the Incendiary Publications," ed. Frank Otto Gatell, *South Carolina Historical Magazine* 64 (1963): 194; Huger to Kendall, 29 July 1835, in *Richmond Enquirer*, 25 Aug. 1835.

21. Kendall to Huger, 4 Aug. 1835, in *Globe*, 12 Aug. 1835.

22. Kendall to Jackson, 7 Aug. 1835, Jackson to Kendall, 9 Aug. 1835, Jackson, *Correspondence*, 5:359–61.

Secretary of State John Forsyth wanted to go even further. He wrote to Van Buren on August 5, complaining that the administration was showing too much "tolerance [toward] the wretches scattering fire-brands." He added that "a little mob discipline of the white incendiaries" was needed and "the sooner" Van Buren "put the imps to work the better." Van Buren sent the letter to Attorney General Benjamin F. Butler, who must have shown it to Kendall. Postmaster Gouverneur also sent word from New York that he would no longer forward abolitionist materials to southern states. Kendall told him that it was "justifiable to detain papers" in order "to prevent insurrections and save communities." The administration's united stand stopped the flow of pamphlets to the South and ended the immediate crisis.[23]

Kendall's suppression of the mails enraged opponents of slavery and defenders of free speech. William Leggett of the *New York Evening Post*, who had praised the Bank veto, called Kendall's letter to Huger "practical nullification." According to Philip Hone the Charleston policy let the "subservient tools of Jackson, Kendall, & Co." use the excuse of "patriotism" to stop "the circulation of all publications opposed to the reigning dynasty." Harriet Martineau, who had joined the American Anti-Slavery Society, could not understand such undemocratic behavior by a man of "Kendall's wit." She surmised that he was seeking southern votes.[24]

Kendall defended his actions with the questionable premises that the pamphlets were "calculated to . . . produce discontent, assassination, and servile war" and that the states were independent and had the right to "protect their interest in slaves." Neither individual states nor the federal government, he wrote, had the right to interfere with slavery in any state. He went so far as to say that the southern states had adopted the U.S. Constitution in order to gain "more perfect control over" slavery. Since the federal government had the constitutional duty to protect the states "against domestic violence," it had the right to stop transporting mail that would lead to insurrection.[25]

This extreme states' rights, proslavery position went well beyond the usual Democratic argument that abolitionism was an unconstitutional danger to the Union. By encouraging postmasters to violate the law, Kendall himself was

23. Forsyth to Van Buren, 5 Aug. 1835, in William Allen Butler, *A Retrospect of Forty Years, 1825–1865* (New York, 1911), 78–79; Kendall to Gouverneur, 22 Aug. 1835, in *Globe*, 1 Sept. 1835.

24. *New York Evening Post*, 12 Aug. 1835, *New York Advertiser*, n.d., in *Niles' Register* 48 (1835): 449; Hone, *Diary*, 171; Harriet Martineau, *Society in America*, 3 vols. (London, 1837), 1:60–61.

25. Kendall, "Report," 1 Dec. 1835, 397–99.

acting contrary to the Constitution. By calling for a higher law, he was using the same arguments as the abolitionists and the nullifiers, both of whom he opposed. Kendall, who had done so much to promote democratic, antimonopoly, antiprivilege sentiments in Jacksonian Democratic thought, was now adding undemocratic proslavery arguments.

There are, of course, reasons to explain his behavior. As he had told Jackson, he had no intention of causing any political "difficulty" for the party by defending abolitionists. He was afraid that the circulation of more pamphlets would only provoke more riots and lead to a Democratic defeat in the next election. And he was not alone, for his party, indeed a majority of adult white Americans, supported his position. In the next few months the Democratic party made a series of proslavery moves to keep southerners loyal and win the coming election. Jackson proposed a bill to ban abolitionist publications in the South. New York Democrats held antiabolitionist meetings in Albany and New York City, and Isaac Hill chaired one in New Hampshire. In October 1835 a Democratic mob followed Forsyth's advice by disrupting an antislavery convention in Utica, New York.[26]

Now half a year into his new administration, Kendall was making great progress toward one of his main goals, paying off the Post Office debt. He was helped by the financial boom after the panic, which increased mail revenues, and he had devised a method for making post office income more quickly available for paying debts. Rural postmasters, who customarily sent their revenues to Washington, were instructed to pay the money directly to contractors. In this way Kendall was able to speed up the payment of current obligations and save surpluses for paying off old debts. Before his first year in office had ended, he had wiped out the entire debt.[27]

Kendall also had plans for using the railroads. The first railroad had

26. *Albany Argus*, 31 Aug., 5, 7 Sept. 1835; *New-Hampshire Patriot* (Concord), 21 Sept. 1835; Howard Alexander Morrison, "A Closer Look at Utica's Anti-Abolitionist Mob," *New York History* 62 (1981): 64–79. For the role of slavery in the 1836 election see William G. Shade, "'The Most Delicate and Exciting Topics': Martin Van Buren, Slavery, and the Election of 1836," *JER* 18 (1998): 459–84. For the transformation of race relations in the 1830s see James Brewer Stewart, "The Emergence of Racial Modernity and the Rise of the White North, 1790–1840," ibid., 181–217. For a discussion of how some Jacksonians could be antiabolitionist yet also antislavery see Daniel Feller, "A Brother in Arms: Benjamin Tappan and the Antislavery Democracy," *Journal of American History* 88 (2001): 48–74.

27. *Autobiography*, 338–41; Kendall, "Report," 1 Dec. 1835, 389–90; Kendall, "Report of the Postmaster General," 5 Dec. 1836, 24th Cong., 2d sess., H. Doc. 2, p. 508.

started operation in 1828, and by 1835 almost a thousand miles of track had been laid. A traveler would soon be able to ride by train from Washington to Boston. Kendall hoped to use the railroads to speed up mail delivery but was quickly disenchanted when they took advantage of their monopoly to ask for outrageous rates. For daily one-way service between Washington and Baltimore they demanded $250 per mile per year—far more than the $100 Kendall expected to pay. The railroads also balked at running at night and refused to adjust their schedules to the needs of the post office. Kendall became so frustrated that he threatened to have Congress designate the railroad lines as post roads and let the Post Office run its own trains over the tracks.[28]

The Post Office dominated the agenda when Congress convened in December. In his annual message Jackson urged Congress to reorganize the Post Office, take up the problem of the railroads, and pass a law "prohibit[ing] . . . the circulation . . . of incendiary publications." In his own report Kendall requested an additional auditor and another assistant postmaster general so that he could divide the General Post Office into four offices—appointments, contracts, inspection, and accounting. In addition the Senate would have to deal with Kendall's nomination.[29]

Jackson's proposal to ban incendiary publications ran into a snag when southerners on the special Senate committee dealing with the question refused to support it. If the government was given the right to take this step, they reasoned, it might someday use the same power to abolish slavery. Instead the committee proposed a bill forbidding the circulation of any publication banned by state law, but even this expansion of national power was defeated. In the House the majority on the Post Office and Post Roads Committee favored some sort of federal restriction but never brought a bill to the floor. Southerners accepted these setbacks with good grace because Kendall's restrictive policy had made a special law unnecessary. Furthermore, their focus had changed as abolitionist societies started directing hundreds of antislavery petitions toward Congress. Debates over how to handle the petitions took up a

28. *Statistical History*, 427; Kendall, "Report," 1 Dec. 1835, 395–97, 403–8; Richard R. John, "Recasting the Information Infrastructure for the Industrial Age," in *A Nation Transformed by Information: How Information Has Shaped the United States from Colonial Times to the Present*, ed. Alfred D. Chandler Jr. and James W. Cortada (New York, 2000), 68–70.

29. Jackson, "Seventh Annual Message," *Compilation*, 3:174–76; Kendall, "Report," 1 Dec. 1835, 399–403; *Autobiography*, 342. The Democrats were gaining strength in the House. They elected James K. Polk Speaker and, for the first time, Blair and Rives printer. *Register of Debates*, 24th Cong., 1st sess., 1945–48.

large percentage of the time in both houses. Gag rules were finally passed in which the petitions were accepted by each body and then tabled in the House and rejected in the Senate.[30]

Efforts to reform the Post Office also faced obstacles. A bill to regulate the railroads was drawn up in the Senate but was tabled in April 1836 when John C. Calhoun protested that it gave Kendall too much power in setting rates. The House Post Office and Post Roads Committee reported a tentative reorganization bill in January but requested no action. The bill would be changed considerably before it was debated.[31]

Through the fall and winter Kendall waited anxiously for his appointment to be taken up. He was so anxious that he wrote Daniel D. Brodhead, trustee of the Boston Land Company, asking him to sell his shares in the company so that his enemies would not be able to call him a speculator. He apparently got rid of the stock, but whether in time to influence the confirmation process is not clear. As he waited, Kendall had good company, for Jackson had nominated Andrew Stevenson for minister to Great Britain and Roger B. Taney for chief justice. Stevenson had already been rejected once, and Taney had been turned down both for secretary of the Treasury and justice of the Supreme Court. The death of Chief Justice John Marshall the previous summer gave the stubborn Jackson another chance. The confirmation of the three Democrats, which was delayed until mid-March, loomed as large as those of Isaac Hill and Kendall six years earlier.[32]

As the winter of 1835–36 wore on, Kendall's chances for confirmation grew. The Democrats were only one short of a majority in the Senate, and the opposition was divided between Whigs and southern Nullifiers. On the afternoon of March 15 the administration finally brought Taney's name to the floor, and he was confirmed by a surprising twenty-nine-to-fifteen margin.

---

30. For the Senate debate over incendiary publications see *Register of Debates*, 24th Cong., 1st sess., 383–85, 1093–1171 passim, and 1721–37, over the gag rule, 72–838 passim; for the House debate over the gag rule, 1961–2537 passim. Hiland Hall, an antislavery Whig on the House Post Office and Post Roads Committee, tried to present a minority report opposing restrictions but was ruled out of order. He published it in the *Intelligencer* on April 9, 1836. Ibid., 1101–3, 1199–1209, 2944–46; Richard R. John, ed., "Hiland Hall's 'Report on Incendiary Publications': A Forgotten Nineteenth Century Defense of the Freedom of the Press," *American Journal of Legal History* 41 (1997): 94–95.

31. *Congressional Globe*, 24th Cong., 1st sess., 140.

32. Kendall to Brodhead, 7 Sept. 1835, Brodhead Papers. No Boston Company land appears on a list of Kendall's landholdings in 1851. Kendall to John, 23 June 1851.

Even though it was growing dark, the Democrats pressed for a decision on Kendall. After many Whigs walked out in disgust, he was confirmed twenty-five to seven. Since eleven of Kendall's votes were from slave states, his pro-slavery handling of the Charleston affair had paid off. But the two confirmations and Stevenson's the next day were due primarily to Democratic cohesiveness.[33]

Although the House Post Office and Post Roads Committee was split six to three Democratic, it was working harmoniously on the reorganization bill. The members agreed on the need to get control over revenues, disbursements, and contracts, and they knew each other well. Four had served on the committee the year before, and six lived close to each other in two boardinghouses near the General Post Office. They also had easy access to Kendall, who had recently moved into a nearby house. The most active members of the committee were Democrats Henry W. Connor of North Carolina, who was chairman, and Abijah Mann of New York, as well as Whigs George Briggs of Massachusetts and Hiland Hall of Vermont. Briggs and Hall represented the growing antislavery sentiment among northern Whigs.[34]

The committeemen started with the 1835 Senate bill and began adding provisions. They regulated contract practices such as extra allowances. They responded to Whig protests about patronage by requiring the consent of the Senate in appointing postmasters with commissions of $1,000 or more. The committee also voted to fine or imprison "any postmaster" who "unlawfully detain[ed] . . . any letter, package, pamphlet, or newspaper, with intent to prevent its . . . delivery." The clause was not, as it appeared, a repudiation of a ban on incendiary publications (the majority on the committee favored such a ban) but was more likely aimed at partisan postmasters who held back opposition publications.[35]

Kendall played a major role in shaping the bill. He had initiated the idea of turning revenues over to the Treasury, and the committee acceded to his request for another auditor and a third assistant postmaster general. His most subtle and overlooked contribution appeared in the requirement that the postmaster general submit "specific estimates" of the funds needed from Congress.

33. *Globe,* 16, 18, 19 Mar. 1836; *Intelligencer,* 16–19 Mar. 1836; Robert V. Remini, *Andrew Jackson and the Course of American Democracy, 1833–1845* (New York, 1984), 316.

34. Goldman and Young, *United States Congressional Directories,* 291–92, 296, 301.

35. "An Act to Change the Organization of the Post Office Department," 2 July 1836, in *Register of Debates,* 24th Cong. 1st sess., app., xxix–xxxiii; John, "Hiland Hall's 'Report,'" 105–6.

By introducing the phrase he was trying to get Congress to give up its policy of specific appropriations, which tied the hands of administrators. The proposal was the same as the one he had made when he was fourth auditor. After his confirmation Kendall made several other suggestions that got into the final bill. The most important was the power to establish an express mail, which would provide an alternative to using the railroads. Another was a simplified scale of postage rates that rose in uniform five-cent steps.[36]

When the House took up the bill on May 19, Whigs tried several times to reduce the postmaster general's power. Edward Everett moved to make the new auditor responsible solely to the secretary of the Treasury rather than to the secretary and the postmaster general. He also wanted the assistant postmasters general appointed by the president with the consent of the Senate rather than by the postmaster general alone. Henry Wise of Virginia sought to reduce the postmaster general's "arbitrary" authority over contracts, while James Harlan of Kentucky tried to require him to file a reason for every dismissal. But in spite of the evident hostility toward Kendall, each amendment failed.[37]

With abolitionist societies no longer sending pamphlets into the South and with antiabolitionist state laws in place, there was no great opposition to the section on freedom of the mails. Democratic committee member Ebenezer Shields of Tennessee moved an amendment banning incendiary publications, but Hiland Hall defeated it by reading a statement by James Madison supporting the liberty of the press. Thus the section on the freedom of the mails remained in the final bill, but it never had any effect because it was never enforced. With the amendments out of the way, the reorganization bill sailed through both houses almost untouched and was signed by the president on July 2, 1836.[38]

In his later years Kendall claimed too much credit for the act and exaggerated its importance. He did, indeed, contribute many important ideas and bore much of the responsibility, but it was not, as he claimed, "drawn under [his] supervision." A large share of the credit must go to Connor, Hall, Briggs, and

36. To make it easier to prosecute thieves, he asked for a provision punishing accessories after the fact. "Act to Change the Organization of the Post Office"; Kendall to Connor, 16 Mar. 1836, PMGLB.

37. *Register of Debates*, 24th Cong., 1st sess., 1769–75, 1849–52, 3779–3810 (quotation, 3783), 4063–67, 4105–33, 4390, 4535–37.

38. Ibid., 3806–9; "Act to Change the Organization of the Post Office"; John, "Hiland Hall's 'Report,'" 105.

Mann in the House and Thomas Ewing and Felix Grundy in the Senate, who put the bill together and saw it through Congress. The act went a long way toward correcting problems, but it was not a major political reform. After holding the new auditor's office for many years, Peter G. Washington concluded in 1851 that the act had failed to end the political role of the postmaster general in making mail contracts. The failure was not surprising, given the high priority Kendall placed on the role of the political party.[39]

Some scholars, however, have called the act the beginning of modern American bureaucracy and Kendall "the architect of Jacksonian administrative reform." According to this argument Jacksonian Democracy had introduced a new system of bureaucratic government run by "faceless functionaries" rotated in and out of office. There is something to be said for the argument. There were numerous examples of bureaucratic beginnings during the Jackson era, and Kendall had the makings of a good bureaucrat. In his first report as fourth auditor he said that he "wanted no discretion" in performing his duties but wanted to be able "to turn to some law or lawful regulation for every allowance that [he was] called upon to make."[40]

Yet Kendall did not create a bureaucracy. The Post Office Act was a bipartisan, not solely a Democratic, effort. Precedents for many of the bureaucratic practices under Kendall can be found under pre-Jacksonian postmasters general, and there was no sudden increase in the number of Post Office administrators in Washington during his regime. Furthermore, Kendall, Hill, and Van Buren were hardly "faceless functionaries," and Kendall's motives for Post Office reform—just as for rotation in office and the destruction of the BUS—were political, not institutional. And finally, Kendall made no effort to build the esprit de corps among his employees that is so essential to a bureaucracy. Kendall was a good bureaucrat, but he was not trying to create a bureaucracy for its own sake.[41]

39. *Autobiography,* 338–47; John, *Spreading the News,* 337 n. 164.

40. The bureaucratic interpretation is part of Lynn L. Marshall's thesis that Jacksonian Democracy was a new movement of ordinary men. Marshall, "Strange Stillbirth of the Whig Party," 445–68 (quotations, 452, 457–58, 468). See also Matthew A. Crenson, *The Federal Machine: Beginnings of Bureaucracy in Jacksonian America* (Baltimore, 1975), especially 20, 104–15.

41. The number of officers and clerks under Kendall remained steady at about 90. About half were transferred to the Treasury Department in 1836, but they are included in this study. There was an increase in employees under Barry from 43 to 89; but this was a period of Post Office growth, and no one has accused him of being a bureaucrat. *Globe,* 10 May 1832; Kendall, "Report," 19 Jan. 1836; Kendall, "Report," 9 May 1836; Kendall, "Letter," 3 Jan. 1838, 25th Cong., 2d Sess., H. Doc. 58, pp. 2–3; John M. Niles, "Letter," 6 Jan. 1841, 26th Cong., 2d Sess., H. Doc. 49, pp.

The first innovation stemming from the act was the express mail, which Kendall hoped would make the post office "independent of the rail-roads." Late in July he announced a service from New York to New Orleans, using horseback and light coaches, that would average ten miles an hour (a very fast speed in 1836) and cut the time from two weeks to one. To publicize the express mail he made special arrangements to deliver copies of Jackson's final annual message from Washington to New York in record time. Kendall was so intent on proving that his express was faster than the railroads that it became his hallmark. In the background of an engraving of Kendall two years later the artist depicted an express rider finishing ahead of a train.[42]

The high rates of the express mail brought it into the ongoing political debate over postage and the railroads. Kendall and the majority of Democrats supported both the express mail and the high rates because they benefited southern and western, often Democratic, newspapers at the expense of the large, often Whig, newspapers on the East Coast. The express mail made it possible for news to reach the interior much faster than the eastern newspapers, and high rates kept up the cost of mailing the newspapers. Kendall had counted on this advantage when he was editor of the *Georgetown Patriot* and the *Argus of Western America*. He and Democrats like him also backed the express mail because it gave them a way to punish the monopolistic railroads, which they detested as much as they did the BUS.[43]

The spoils system was an even more important political issue. Kendall may have eased Whig fears with his circular and the retention of his staff, but as time passed there was reason to believe that he was not living up to his promises. By March 1837 he had removed about 180 postmasters and by the end of that year perhaps a dozen clerks from the General Post Office. Removing 180 postmasters in almost two years was hardly proscription, but added to the 874 Barry had already removed, it demonstrated a strong commitment to party patronage.[44]

---

2–4; *Statistical History*, 497. Richard R. John denies the existence of a Jacksonian bureaucracy. John, *Spreading the News*, vii–ix, 105, 126–28, 247–48.

42. *Globe*, 25 July 1836; Kendall, "Report," 5 Dec. 1836, 512–13 (quotation); Kendall to various postmasters, 25, 28, 30 Nov., 1 Dec. 1836, PMGLB. The engraving was in *United States Magazine and Democratic Review* (Washington) 1 (1838): 402. A copy is on the cover of this book.

43. Kendall, "Report," 5 Dec. 1836, 512–13; *Expositor*, 13 June 1843; Blair to Van Buren, 14 July 1836, Van Buren Papers; Richard B. Kielbowicz, *News in the Mail: The Press, Post Office, and Public Information, 1700–1860s* (New York, 1989), 58–64.

44. "A dozen" is simply an estimate. After the transfer of clerks to the Treasury Department in 1836, there were 45 left in the General Post Office. Of those, 30 were gone by the end of 1837. Some may have died or retired, but there still must have been more than a few removals. The

A sampling of Kendall's patronage cases shows how he operated. He convinced Jackson to appoint party insider Gideon Welles postmaster of Hartford even though a coterie of Democratic bankers and the entire House delegation (all Democrats) went to the president on behalf of banker James Dodd. On the other hand he ignored the ultimate insider Isaac Hill when Hill wanted to remove the postmaster of Sutton, New Hampshire. Kendall followed the advice of the local congressman and public opinion by removing the postmaster of Clearspring, Maryland, for "unpleasant" behavior toward his opponent. When Kendall arrogantly refused to explain the removal, he was castigated in the House by Henry Wise.[45]

The most visible case involved Postmaster Samuel L. Gouverneur of New York City. Gouverneur, a Democrat, had cooperated in the Charleston affair, but he was unpopular with the Van Buren machine. When Kendall informed him that his accounts were more than $100,000 in arrears, Gouverneur sent three long but unconvincing explanations. In one withering sentence Kendall lectured him about keeping accounts: It "is truly unfortunate," he wrote, "in a case where figures are the principal guide to truth," that an official "expects to make it more plain by a volume of verbiage than by a simple account current." Jackson replaced Gouverneur with a Van Buren man.[46]

His appointment of Albert Hocker as postmaster of Stanford, Kentucky, met with criticism because Hocker had campaigned for Kendall's close friend Thomas P. Moore. The House passed a resolution demanding information, but Kendall scornfully refused. There was no such problem in Virginia, where Democrat David Campbell, soon to be governor, pressed hard to remove a local postmaster. Kendall and Jackson welcomed the opportunity to please an influential Virginia family, and they remembered that Campbell's candidate

number 180 for postmasters removed was determined by multiplying the number removed in Jackson's second term (392) by the percentage of the time Kendall held the office (46 percent). John, *Spreading the News*, 223–24, 239; *Globe*, 23 Apr. 1839; Kendall, "Report," 19 Jan. 1836; Kendall, "A List of the Officers and Clerks," 22 April 1836, 24th Cong., 1st sess., H. Doc. 235; Kendall, "A Statement of the . . . Compensation of the Clerks Employed in the Post Office Department," 3 Jan. 1838, 25th Cong., 2d sess., H. Doc. 58.

45. Kendall to Jackson, with endorsement, 7 Jan. 1836, Jackson Supplement; Niven, *Gideon Welles*, 134–37; William Moore et al. to Kendall, 15 Feb. 1836, Kendall Papers, Dartmouth College Library; Augusta Worthen, *The History of Sutton, New Hampshire* (1890; reprint, Concord, 1975), 186, 707; *Register of Debates*, 24th Cong. 1st sess., 4121–31 (quotation, 4122).

46. Gouverneur was the only major city postmaster removed in 1836. Kendall to Gouverneur, 4, 12 Feb., 15, 17 (quotation), 23 Mar., 9, 20 Apr., 11 May 1836, PMGLB; *Niles' Register* 50 (1836): 313; Jackson to the Senate, 2 July 1836, Jackson Supplement.

had supported the removal of the deposits. Quite understandably, he was appointed.[47]

The episodes show a postmaster general who did not hesitate to act on his own, sometimes arrogantly, but who more often worked collegially with others in the party. Jackson had become increasingly comfortable with party patronage and often took part in important cases. Except in the Maryland case, the will of the party carried more weight than the will of the voters. Ideological considerations played a part in the cases of Welles, Gouverneur, and the Virginia candidate, but in general loyalty, friendship, personality, partisanship, and political clout were more important.

During these first two years under Kendall the post office was enjoying a remarkable period of expansion and financial recovery. Congress established 747 new mail routes, revenues increased 37 percent, and the number of miles the mails were carried increased 26 percent. Thanks to the nationwide boom the post office had annual surpluses of $567,000 and $813,000, the two largest until the end of the Civil War.[48]

Fully occupied in the Post Office, Kendall had little time for advising and writing for the president. Despite his passion for hard money, he was not part of the administration's unsuccessful effort to block the Deposit-Distribution Act of 1836, which expanded the number of deposit banks and distributed the government surplus to the states. And Woodbury, not Kendall, was responsible for Jackson's specie circular, which required gold or silver for the purchase of public land.

He still, however, had influence with Jackson. When American general Edmund P. Gaines marched into Texas in 1836 soon after independence had been declared, the Whig press accused him of invading Mexico, which still laid claim to the region. Kendall wrote Jackson in late July, saying that most Americans and "the people of other nations [would] pronounce [Gaines's move] wrong." The United States was "already considered responsible" for the independence movement because its "enterprising and restless young men fill the ranks" of the Texas army. "What," he asked, "would have been our sensations towards Mexico if we had seen her young men pouring into South Caro-

47. *Register of Debates*, 25th Cong., 3d sess., 387; John Campbell to David Campbell, 16 Nov. 1835, Arthur Campbell to David Campbell, 13 June 1836, George W. Hopkins to David Campbell, 22 June 1836, Campbell Family Papers.

48. Kendall, "Report," 1 Dec. 1835, 387; Kendall, "Report," 5 Dec. 1836, 518–19; Kendall, "Report of the Postmaster General," 4 Dec. 1837, 25th Cong., 2d sess., S. Doc. 1, p. 794; *Globe*, 25 July 1836; *Statistical History*, 497.

lina" during nullification. Jackson, who had already taken steps to restrain Gaines, agreed and soon ordered the general to "religiously observe and maintain" the American policy of neutrality.[49]

Early in August Kendall wrote again while he was visiting the Philadelphia navy yard. The commander of the yard was having difficulty hiring workers because private employers had given in to the workers' demand for a twelve-hour day, while the navy required a longer day. Philadelphia Democrats, who had won this "concession of the richer classes," were annoyed that the only exception was the federal government. Kendall, who hated to upset a local party, thought that the "point ought to be conceded." Jackson agreed at once and ordered the secretary of the navy to adopt the twelve-hour day in Philadelphia.[50]

It is tempting to use these two letters to portray Kendall as the moral conscience of the administration, fighting for the rights of Mexicans and workingmen, but he was doing neither. Despite his strong words against the invasion, he was not an anti-imperialist. Toward the end of his letter on Texas he predicted, "The time will come when Mexico will be overrun by our Anglo-Saxon race, nor do I look upon it as a result at all to be deplored. I believe it would lead to the . . . improvement of Mexico." In the navy yard affair he was more interested in party harmony than in helping workers.[51]

In the long view Kendall played a major part in electing Van Buren president in 1836. His work in building the party made it possible for the Democrats to elect a party man in place of a hero. His two years in the Post Office deprived the Whigs of a campaign issue. He and Blair helped secure the nomination of Richard M. Johnson for vice president. And his defense of slavery in the Charleston affair smoothed the way for southern Democrats to back a northern candidate. Van Buren's firm antiabolitionist stance enabled him to hold most of the South.

Yet in the actual campaigning Kendall played a relatively minor part, and if anything was a Whig target. He was forced to rebut—not very successfully—the charge that he was urging postmasters to campaign. In one cartoon

49. Kendall to Jackson, 30 July 1836, Jackson Papers. Jackson to Kendall, 12 Aug. 1836, Jackson to Edmund P. Gaines, 4 Sept. 1836, Jackson, *Correspondence,* 5:420–21, 423–24.

50. Kendall to Jackson, 7 Aug. 1836, Jackson Supplement (quotation); Remini, *Andrew Jackson and the Course of American Democracy,* 340–41.

51. Robert V. Remini, for example, cites the Navy Yard letter to prove that "Jacksonianism was not a movement of small businessmen [but] was more concerned with workingmen." Remini, *Andrew Jackson and the Course of American Democracy,* 340–41.

he was ridiculed as a prude uninterested in the lovely French dancer Celeste when she was introduced to the cabinet. In another, demons from Hell lamented that "dear Amos" was so busy in the Post Office that he had no time to "write for us" in the campaign. "Who [else]," said one, "can lie like him." In the end Kendall's long-term contributions were evident. Van Buren carried four New England states (Jackson had won none in 1828), and in the South he lost only two states that Jackson had won in 1832.[52]

On November 19 Jackson suffered a severe hemorrhage and was bedridden for some time. As he fretted in his room, his mind ran back over the last eight years and he wondered whether he had done everything possible to return the country to hard money and reform the banking system. Calling in Kendall one evening, he spent several hours reviewing their record. After Kendall left, Jackson's mind was still unsettled, and he dashed off a note asking whether they should urge Congress to charter a national bank in the District of Columbia to serve as "a model for the States" and to "check the paper system and gambling mania that pervades our land."[53]

The president had a final chance in his last annual message but chose to look back rather than forward. In the section on banking, which Kendall wrote, he contented himself with attacking the BUS and criticizing the Deposit-Distribution Act for "produc[ing] a spirit of wild speculation." The president and Kendall also had a chance to take a strong stand on the Texas question, but they failed to offer any policy on recognizing or annexing the new nation.[54]

A week later, on December 14, Kendall was feeling "quite indisposed" and went to bed early. Between three and four in the morning he was awakened by a fire in the building that housed the General Post Office and the city post office. He and several of his clerks raced inside the building and saved many of the records by carrying books and papers across the street to Kendall's house. The fire destroyed the building but brought one benefit. Kendall could now move his offices to new quarters near the Treasury Department, to which the Post Office was now closely tied.[55]

52. Blair to Jackson, 19 May 1835, Jackson, *Correspondence,* 5:348–49; *Niles' Register* 51 (1836): 137–38; Reilly, Catalogue of *American Political Prints,* 79–80, 94–96; Shade, "'The Most Delicate and Exciting Topics.'"

53. Jackson to Kendall, 24 Nov. 1836, Jackson, *Correspondence,* 5:438–39.

54. "Drafts of Eighth Annual Message," Jackson Papers; Jackson, "Eighth Annual Message," *Compilation,* 3:236–59.

55. Kendall to John M. Robinson, 3 Jan. 1837, PMGLB; Benjamin Brown French, *Witness to the Young Republic: A Yankee's Journal, 1828–1870,* ed. Donald B. Cole and John J. McDonough (Hanover, N.H., 1989), 70.

Although Jackson still had two months left to serve, his administration was essentially over. It was now eight years since Kendall had come to Washington and met the men with whom he would work under Old Hickory. One by one they had drifted away, Green and Calhoun during the flare-up with the president, and Eaton, Ingham, Branch, and Berrien in the great purge. Poor Barry had died. Hill had left, returned, and now had left again to become governor of New Hampshire. Donelson had resigned after the death of his wife. Many of their replacements—Livingston, McLane, Taney, and Cass (now minister to France)—had failed to last through to the end. Kendall, Lewis, and Van Buren were the only original Jackson men left, and Lewis had very little power.[56]

John Quincy Adams had watched these comings and goings with intense interest. Jackson's presidency, he wrote,

> has been the reign of subaltern knaves . . . who have made him believe that it was a heroic conception of his own to destroy the Bank of the United States. . . . Two political swindlers, Amos Kendall and Reuben M. Whitney . . . have got into their own hands the overflowing revenue of the country. . . . Van Buren has had the address to persuade [Jackson] that he is the only man who can preserve and perpetuate the principles of his administration.[57]

Adams was too tied up by his contempt for these Jacksonians to realize what had taken place. The men around Jackson were not "knaves." They were politicians who had created a new type of political party held together by patronage and run by ordinary men (Adams called them a "mediocrity"). These Democrats were democratic in many ways: they believed in political egalitarianism, they appealed directly to the voters, they rejected deference, opposed privilege and aristocracy, and brought out the voters. But as they had shown in the Eaton affair, the Charleston affair, and the removal of the southern tribes, their democracy had no place for women, blacks, or Indians. They were unusually attentive to slavery and showed little interest in social or economic reform. Adams now faced four more years of the Democracy.

---

56. Woodbury and Blair also remained, but they were not part of the administration until 1830–31.

57. Adams, *Memoirs*, 9:311–12.

# 15

## VAN BUREN

On his way to the Capitol on inauguration day, Kendall could see that the "soft-spring snow" was melting away in the warm sun. It would be a splendid day for Martin Van Buren to take office. At noon Kendall and the other cabinet officers marched onto the east portico of the Capitol to watch the new president take his oath. In his inaugural Van Buren promised to follow the republican principles of his predecessors and gave no indication that he would make any changes. After the ceremony the cabinet members retired to the President's House, where they received guests and dined for the last time with Old Hickory. Three days later he left for home.[1]

Down Pennsylvania Avenue at Masonic Hall the Washington Democrats were holding their own dinner. Had Kendall been there, he would have been pleased, perhaps surprised, by the attention he was receiving. The dinner began with an ode entitled "Farewell to the Chief," which he had written especially for the occasion. The ode, said the toastmaster, "disclose[d]" in Kendall "a *heart* worthy of its pre-eminently talented *head.*" More significant were two other toasts praising him for his "uncompromising" opposition to "monopolies" and his "devotion to the cause of democracy." These rank-and-file local Democrats knew Kendall well and recognized his role in shaping these basic party beliefs. Before the dinner was over there had been six toasts in his honor, more than for anyone else except Jackson and Van Buren.[2]

Two days later Van Buren held his first cabinet meeting. The only new member was Jackson's old friend and loyal Unionist planter Joel R. Poinsett of South Carolina, who was replacing Lewis Cass as secretary of war. Van Buren told Jackson that his cabinet "worked together harmoniously," but he must not have been thinking of Kendall. All winter long there had been per-

---

1. *Globe,* 6, 8 Mar. 1837.
2. Ibid., 16 Mar. 1837.

sistent rumors that Secretary of State John Forsyth was threatening to resign if Kendall was retained. The most damaging issue, the national currency, was dividing the cabinet and the party into hard-money advocates such as Kendall and Francis P. Blair; moderates, including Van Buren and treasury secretary Levi Woodbury; and the soft-money Conservative Democrats, led by Senator William C. Rives of Virginia. The *National Intelligencer* tried to paint Kendall as the "most influential" member of the cabinet, but whether he would have as much influence with Van Buren as he had had with Jackson was far from certain.[3]

Van Buren's hopes for continuity were dashed in mid-March by the Panic of 1837, in which many banks failed or suspended specie payments. Already under pressure to change Jackson's hard-money policies, he promptly called a cabinet meeting for March 22 to discuss the specie circular. Everyone but Kendall favored rescinding it, but Van Buren decided to wait and keep the decision in his own hands. Advice from the outside was mixed: merchants, who wanted more money in circulation, asked for repeal, while hard-money Democrats, particularly Jackson, advised him to remain firm. Van Buren was also listening to another hard-money man, treasury clerk William M. Gouge, who had devised an independent treasury plan, in which the government would keep its money in subtreasuries instead of banks. On May 3 an angry delegation of New York merchants urged the president to call a special session of Congress, and a week later a run on the New York banks forced all but three to suspend payments. Meeting daily with his cabinet, Van Buren finally called a special session to convene in September.[4]

Kendall responded to the crisis by using the Post Office to show that the subtreasury system would work and that the government could get along without banks. He stopped depositing funds in banks that had suspended the use of specie, and he extended the policy of having postmasters turn their revenues directly over to contractors. Postmasters were to pay or receive nothing but specie or notes payable in specie. The regulations won the backing of Jackson

3. Van Buren to Jackson, 24 Apr. 1837, Van Buren Papers; *Globe,* 23 Mar. 1837; George R. Pavel to Polk, 23 Dec. 1836, Polk, *Correspondence,* 3:800–801; *Intelligencer,* 19 July 1837, in Daniels, "Amos Kendall," 249–50.

4. *Globe,* 20 Mar. 1837; Mahlon Dickerson, "Diary" (typescripts), 22 Mar.–30 May 1837, Mahlon and Philemon Dickerson Papers, Manuscript Group 13, New Jersey Historical Society; James C. Curtis, *The Fox at Bay: Martin Van Buren and the Presidency, 1837–1844* (Lexington, Ky., 1970), 68–76; Van Buren, endorsement on third copy of "Questions to his Cabinet," 24 Mar. 1837, Van Buren Papers.

and Blair but were unpopular with bankers, Conservative Democrats, and editors such as Horace Greeley, who considered the policies cumbersome and unworkable. When Boston postmaster Nathaniel Greene tried to enforce them, an "overflowing" protest meeting forced him to adopt a compromise credit system. John Quincy Adams's son Charles Francis decided that Kendall's "infatuation" with hard money would "soon destroy him." The critics were right. So many banks had suspended specie payments that Kendall's orders were impossible to enforce.[5]

Kendall also met resistance when he blamed the British for the panic. In a letter turning down a dinner invitation he urged Democrats in Philadelphia to declare their "independence" of the "powers at home" who were "degrad[ing] and oppress[ing] their own country [by following] foreign alliances." His message made sense because the panic was clearly international, but his wild chauvinism laid him open to extravagant criticism. Mordecai Noah charged that Kendall was trying to lure the American people into a foolish war with Great Britain.[6]

An ugly lawsuit added to Kendall's difficulties. In 1835 he had refused to pay the contracting firm of Stockton and Stokes extra allowances of $122,000. A congressional relief bill ordered a review of the case, and a year later the firm was awarded the entire amount with an additional $40,000 tacked on. When Kendall agreed to pay the original sum but not the extra $40,000, Stockton and Stokes won a writ of mandamus from the chief justice of the U.S. circuit court of the District of Columbia ordering him to pay the full amount. During the summer of 1837 Kendall appealed the decision before the full circuit court in a case that was significant because it involved the question of executive-legislative supremacy. Stockton and Stokes argued that the congressional review had turned the payment into a nondiscretionary, ministerial act. Kendall contended that it was discretionary, at the will of the executive.

    5. Kendall, "Report of the Postmaster General," 4 Sept. 1837, in *Niles' Register* 53 (1837): 25; Kendall to O. H. Dibble, 9 May 1837, Kendall to Alfred Huger, 27 May 1837, Kendall to Edward J. Mallett, 29 May 1837, Kendall to S. H. Connor, 25 July 1837, PMGLB; Curtis, *Fox at Bay*, 75; *Globe*, 15, 22, 23, 31 May, 19 July 1837; Jackson to Kendall, 22, 26 May, 23 June 1837, Kendall to Jackson, 6 June 1837, Jackson Papers; *New-Yorker*, 1 Apr., 27 May 1837; Charles Francis Adams, *Diary of Charles Francis Adams*, ed. Aida DiPace Donald, David Donald, Marc Friedlander, and L. H. Butterfield, 8 vols. (Cambridge, Mass., 1964–86), 7:244–45 (quotations), 279–80, 287–89.

    6. Kendall to John Thompson et al., 1 July 1837, Kendall Papers, Dartmouth College Library; *Globe*, 13 July 1837.

The court ordered Kendall to pay, but he dug in and appealed to the Supreme Court.[7]

By the end of the summer Kendall was beginning to realize that despite his prominence and his popularity with the local party he had little influence with the new president. It was not surprising. He and Van Buren had never been close, he had taken little part in the election campaign, and the president was getting advice from New Yorkers and Virginians, many of whom distrusted Kendall. One Virginian, Congressman William Campbell, believed that Van Buren's only hope for success was "to get clear" of Kendall. An angry New York Democrat blamed party losses on Kendall and urged the president to send him "to the moon." In Washington Van Buren's closest advisers were Gouge, a Pennsylvanian, and three key New Yorkers, Attorney General Benjamin F. Butler, Congressman Churchill C. Cambreleng, and Senator Silas Wright.[8]

Blair had also lost ground. Gideon Welles and Levi Woodbury were so alienated by the *Globe* that they were talking about starting a new party newspaper. Woodbury went so far as to assist John L. O'Sullivan in setting up a radical Democratic journal, the *United States Magazine and Democratic Review*. Unhappy with Blair's harsh attacks on banks, Conservative Democrats established another newspaper, the *Madisonian*, and succeeded in taking the House printing away from the *Globe*. Blair managed to win the Senate printing and the *Globe* remained the party organ, but Blair's role in the administration was no longer what it had been under Jackson.[9]

Neither Kendall nor Blair, therefore, had any real influence on Van Buren's message to the special session of Congress. Kendall's only contribution was a memorandum showing how his Post Office regulations could be extended to the entire government. Otherwise the principal sources were Gouge and Van Buren himself. The president blamed the panic on a "spirit of reckless speculation" in Britain and the United States. He called for Gouge's indepen-

7. Carl B. Swisher, *History of the Supreme Court of the United States: The Taney Period, 1836–64* (New York, 1974), 158–61; Kendall to Stockton and Stokes, 3 July 1835, Kendall to Virgil Maxcy, 24 Sept. 1836, PMGLB; Kendall to Jackson, 27 Dec. 1836, Jackson Supplement; Kendall to Jackson, 6 June, 11 Aug. 1837, Jackson Papers; *Globe,* 22, 26, 28, 29 June, 1 July 1837.

8. William B. Campbell to David Campbell, 16 Oct. 1837, 3 Jan. 1838, Campbell Family Papers; Kearney to Van Buren, 12 Nov. 1837, Van Buren Papers.

9. Curtis, *Fox at Bay,* 81–83, 114; Welles to Van Buren, 9 June, 24 July 1837, O'Sullivan to Van Buren, 8 Feb. 1840, Van Buren Papers; *The Madisonian* (Washington), 16 Aug. 1837; *Globe,* 7 Sept. 1837; Smith, *Press, Politics, and Patronage,* 250.

dent treasury plan, but in order to keep paper money supporters in line, he also suggested a new issue of treasury notes. During the session the independent treasury made its way through the Senate only to be tabled in the House.[10]

Even though he was outside the inner circle, Kendall remained on good terms with the president. After Congress adjourned, he and one of his daughters—probably Mary Anne, who was seventeen—joined Van Buren, navy secretary Mahlon Dickerson, and the Poinsetts on a short excursion to Berkeley Springs in the northern panhandle of what is now West Virginia. On October 23 they started out in a coach and four on the Rockville Road and by evening had reached Hyattsville, Maryland. Here they spent a restless night "suffer[-ing] with [the] heat" and listening to "the Catydids singing." Up early the next morning, they drove through Frederick and continued on to Hagerstown. After passing workers digging the Chesapeake and Ohio Canal, they forded the Potomac River and arrived at the springs. Unfortunately, a heavy rain set in, and they stayed only a day before starting back. On the morning of the twenty-eighth they dismissed the coach and four, boarded the canal packet, and by evening were back in the city.[11]

Kendall's six-day vacation with such wealthy sophisticates as Van Buren, Dickerson, and Poinsett was one of several indications that he was no longer quite the recluse who had intrigued Harriet Martineau. He and Jane were now dining out occasionally and attending the theater, usually with members of the cabinet. They would soon rent an expensive, ten-room mansion off Connecticut Avenue, two and a half miles northwest of the city. It was a handsome house on high ground with sweeping views, and they called it Jackson Hill. There they began to entertain, but still only a little. Over a twelve-month stretch, for example, Dickerson received well over sixty dinner invitations, but none from the Kendalls.[12]

One reason for the limited social life was Kendall's health. Soon after his outing, he fell into an illness that confined him for most of the winter and

10. Van Buren, "Special Session Message," 4 Sept. 1837, *Compilation*, 3:324–46; Kendall, "Remarks on the Management of the Public Revenue," Sept. 1837? Van Buren Papers; Cole, *Martin Van Buren*, 306–12.

11. Dickerson, "Diary," 23–28 Oct. 1837.

12. Ibid., 1 Sept. 1836–1 Sept. 1837, 24 Nov. 1837, 12 Mar., 13, 14, 19 May 1838. For a description of Jackson Hill see Jefferson Morley, "The Ghosts of Jackson Hill," *Washington Post Magazine*, 13 Sept. 1998, 12–16, 28–29.

brought on a sense of "alarming change." The pain in his right arm, probably arthritis, was so severe that he could hardly write. When it spread to his right foot, the doctor thought for a while that it was gout. His struggle with Stockton and Stokes deepened his malaise. On March 17 the Supreme Court ruled that he had had no discretion in the Stockton and Stokes case and that the Post Office must pay the extra allowance. The decision opened the possibility that the contractors might sue Kendall personally for having delayed the payment.[13]

In Congress the Democrats failed again to pass the independent treasury bill, and Van Buren was forced to give up the specie circular, which was repealed in the spring. These setbacks and the hard times that had gripped the country threatened the administration and prompted Van Buren to make party changes. Before the year was over he had replaced two cabinet members—Dickerson and Butler—and two major customs collectors—Samuel Swartwout in New York and David Henshaw in Boston. Depressed by his difficult winter and his declining role in the administration, Kendall thought of joining the exodus. On July 30, 1838, he sent a feeler to Van Buren describing his poor health and wondering if he could be appointed minister to Spain. Van Buren replied immediately that he would be glad to accommodate him but made no specific offer. The president's willingness to let him go reinforced Kendall's misgivings.[14]

But Kendall still had a role to play in the party. Toward the end of the summer the skies were finally brightening for the Democrats; prices were rising, and banks were beginning to resume specie payments. The party had just won elections in Illinois and Maine and hoped to take back Ohio in the fall. Kendall made plans to visit the state, after which he would examine his land holdings in Illinois and then visit Old Hickory in Tennessee. Traveling night and day along the National Road, he arrived in Columbus, Ohio, about the first of October. He stayed only a few days, hardly enough time to have much impact on the election, but when the Democrats won a week later, Henry Clay blamed the "extraordinary" Whig defeat on Kendall's visit. Noting "how easy

13. Kendall to Jackson, 6 Feb. 1838, Jackson Papers; Van Buren to Jackson, 17 Mar. 1838, Kendall to Van Buren, 30 July 1838 (quotation), Van Buren Papers; Swisher, History of the *Supreme Court*, 161–64.

14. Niven, *Martin Van Buren*, 429–35; Kendall to Van Buren, 30 July, 13 Aug. 1838, Van Buren to Kendall, 6 Aug. 1838, Van Buren Papers.

it was" for the postmaster general "to issue orders to his deputies," he charged that "a profuse and corrupt use [had] been made of the public money." Kendall said only that the Democrats had won because they were better organized.[15]

Kendall still gloried in the way that civilization was penetrating the "dark region" of the West. As he continued on to Indianapolis, he found the National Road "full of wagons, cattle, men, women, girls and boys wending their way to golden fields beneath the setting sun." They were paying a heavy price because a plague of bilious fever was "caus[ing] an awful mortality." He feared that "the conquest of these forests probably cost as much human life as the conquest of nations." Yet despite it all, people were "hurrying on," hoping to "extend the dominion of civilized man."[16]

On leaving Indianapolis he headed northwest across the Wabash River to Danville, Illinois, where he owned a 200-acre farm, 1,280 acres of prairie land, and three lots of timber, all together worth about $5,000. While there he took Democratic congressman Zadoc Casey aside and chastised him for voting against the *Globe* for printer after having received favors from the administration. Passing up a chance to see land that he owned in Springfield, Illinois, he turned south to Louisville and Nashville.[17]

On October 20 a weary Kendall stepped off the stagecoach at the gate of the long driveway leading up to the Hermitage. There, waiting for his mail, stood "the good old chief," coatless despite the "raw, cold" fall weather. He looked well, Kendall wrote, but no longer moved with his old "elasticity." It was a proud moment for Kendall, for he was one of the few Jackson men, aside from the Tennesseans, to visit the Hermitage. Van Buren did, but not until 1842; Blair, Woodbury, Taney, Cass, Hill, among others, never had the honor. He wrote to Jane enthusiastically: "The General's house is a palace. . . . I have a [large] chamber . . . most tastefully furnished." Jackson, who had been saddened by the recent death of his artist friend Ralph Earl at the Hermitage, was delighted to see another old companion.[18]

The main reason for Kendall's visit was to look through Jackson's papers.

15. McCormick, *Second American Party System*, 267–68; Kendall to Van Buren, 20 Oct. 1838, Van Buren Papers; Clay to Nathaniel P. Tallmadge, 31 Oct. 1838, Clay to Francis T. Brooke, 3 Nov. 1838, Clay, *Papers*, 9:242–43, 245–46.

16. Kendall to Van Buren, 20 Oct. 1838, Van Buren Papers.

17. Ibid.; Kendall to John, 23 June 1851; Samuel McRoberts to Polk, 16 Nov. 1838, Polk, *Correspondence*, 4:608–11.

18. Kendall to Jane Kendall, 20 Oct. 1838, in *Autobiography*, 267–69; Kendall to Van Buren, 20 Oct. 1838, Van Buren Papers.

A lively rivalry had broken out among the Old Hero's friends to see who would write his biography. Blair, Roger B. Taney, and George Bancroft, who had completed two volumes of his *History of the United States,* were interested. Jackson, however, had already promised Kendall that he could take on the task. During the next three weeks he worked steadily on the papers, but found time for a little politicking, such as helping Jackson line up a candidate to run for Congress. Before leaving he wrote Van Buren to warn him about John C. Calhoun, who had just returned to the party. He blamed the failure of the independent treasury bill on Calhoun's insistence on a rigid specie clause and reminded Van Buren of the danger from a southern sectional party.[19]

When he arrived home in late November, Kendall found the administration shaken by news from New York. The Whigs had won the state election, and Samuel Swartwout had escaped to Europe owing the government $1.5 million. Henry Wise took advantage of the opportunity to deliver another attack on Kendall and the Democrats. They "came into power," he said, to "*reform*" the government but found only Tobias Watkins, who had defaulted with a paltry $3,000. He accused Kendall of corrupt land speculation and blamed him for the rise of a spoils system. He called him Jackson's "*thinking* machine, and his *writing* machine—ay, and his *lying* machine." Kendall was "chief overseer, chief reporter, amanuensis, scribe, accountant general, man of all work—nothing was well done without the aid of his diabolical genius." It was an unintended tribute.[20]

Whigs kept up the pressure with a Senate resolution on February 12, 1839, asking Kendall to report the names of all postmasters removed since Van Buren took office. Trying to show that removals were nothing new, Kendall sent in a report that went back to President James Madison. He also scrambled to uncover other shortages and removed defaulting postmasters in New Orleans, Mobile, and Portland, Maine. The most prominent person under scrutiny was Samuel L. Gouverneur, whose default case had not yet been settled. Kendall had sued Gouverneur for $100,000, but by the time the case was settled in May 1839 the amount of the default had been reduced to $20,000.[21]

19. Taney to Jackson, 3 July 1837, Van Buren to Jackson, 17 Oct. 1837, Jackson to Van Buren, 29 Oct. 1837, Jackson, *Correspondence,* 5:495, 516, 518; McDonough, *Index to the Andrew Jackson Papers,* xii; John Catron to Polk, 27 Oct. 1838, Polk, *Correspondence,* 4:589; Kendall to Van Buren, 6 Nov. 1838, Van Buren Papers.

20. *Congressional Globe,* 25th Cong., 3d sess., 5, 19, app., 384–404.

21. Ibid., 178, 212, 220; *Globe,* 23 Apr., 29 May 1839. Van Buren to Jackson, 30 July 1839, Van Buren Papers; Selah R. Hobbie to Van Buren, 28 Aug. 1839, PMGLB.

The defaults were only part of Kendall's troubles in the Post Office. His hard-money policy had failed, and because of the depression the department suffered huge deficits in 1838 and 1839. Even with congressional help he was unable to take advantage of the railroads to speed up the mails. In 1838 Congress carried out the first half (but not the second) of his threat to turn the railroads into post roads and run postal trains over them. The railroad act of that year designated the lines as "post routes" and authorized him to pay the companies up to 25 percent more than he was paying for "similar transportation." Kendall offered the railroads substantially more than the $250 a mile they had demanded in 1835, but it was still not enough. In the summer of 1839 only 10 percent of the mails were being carried by railroads and steamboats.[22]

Late that summer Kendall received word that his father, now eighty-four, was dying. He reached Dunstable on August 10 and found the old man still living and able to "talk a little in a whisper." Thirty-six hours later he was dead. His father, he told Jackson proudly, had "met death with the same calmness that he went about" his daily affairs. He was "a good man and a good Christian" who had never "incurred a single breath of censure on account of his moral and religious deportment." After reading the letter "again & again," Jackson wrote back, "How noble the spectacle to witness, the death of a real Christian! . . . He lived to be prepared for death, and in his life learned how to die." Zebedee's death quite likely brought Kendall a measure of relief. The image of his father had weighed heavily on him; now that he was gone, perhaps he could live more on his own terms.[23]

He was no sooner back from Dunstable than he learned that Stockton and Stokes were suing him for $100,000 (over $2 million in today's money). Already burdened by increasing expenses and heavy debts, no longer the savior of the Post Office or the power behind the president, Kendall now faced a suit that could wipe him out. He needed a new job and more money. The presidential election offered a way out. In the spring of 1840 Blair and Rives asked him to become editor of the *Extra Globe*, a position that would pay far more over the next half year than the $3,000 he would earn in the Post Office. He

22. *Statistical History*, 497; Kendall, "Report of the Postmaster General," 3 Dec. 1838, 25th Cong., 3d sess., S. Doc. 1, pp. 666–67; *Globe*, 26 Sept. 1838; Hobbie to Conway Robinson, 3 Nov. 1838, Kendall to C. Robinson, H. Rhodes, and C. Osborne, 29 Nov. 1838, Kendall to George Plitt, 24 Dec. 1838, Kendall to D. Wager, 29 June 1839, PMGLB; Kendall, "Report of the Postmaster General," 30 Nov. 1839, 26th Cong., 1st sess., S. Doc. 1, p. 613.

23. *Globe*, 7 Aug. 1839; Kendall to Jackson, 29 Aug. 1839, Jackson to Kendall, 10 Oct. 1839, Jackson Papers.

resigned abruptly on May 9, citing ill health, and was replaced by Senator John M. Niles.[24]

Any evaluation of Kendall as postmaster general must first consider the economy. During the boom years under Jackson he brought order to the department, wiped out its debt, helped pass the Post Office Act, and deprived the Whigs of a political issue. The depression years under Van Buren were marked by deficits and failures in dealing with the money question and the railroads. Of much greater long-range consequence, however, were two other policies—blocking abolitionist pamphlets at Charleston and using the Post Office for political purposes. The first was a misguided decision that helped turn the Democratic party in a proslavery direction. It benefited the party in 1836 but severely restricted American democracy. The second deserves another look.

Kendall was frequently attacked for his use of patronage. Even fellow Democrat John Campbell complained when he learned that Kendall had "given a certain [Virginia] gentleman a *hint* that if he and his family were not *active in the cause* he could not hold the Office of Postmaster." There is no doubt that he was responsible for a large number of removals. As has been shown, he removed perhaps a dozen members of his staff and about 180 postmasters while Jackson was president. Under Van Buren he removed about 670 postmasters, making a total of 850 in five years. If the Barry and Niles years are added, Kendall had influence over about 1,900 removals (1.8 percent of all postmasters per year). This was certainly a change in policy; the number and percentage of removals were considerably greater than the 223 postmasters (1.0 percent per year) removed by John McLean during the Adams administration.[25]

But the consequences of the change are less clear. If McLean had remained postmaster general under Jackson and Van Buren and had continued his 1.0 percent rate of removals, he would have removed 1,111 postmasters dur-

24. Swisher, *History of the Supreme Court*, 164–65; *Kendall v. Stokes et al.*, 44 U.S. 506–14; Kendall to Jackson, 4 Mar. 1840, Jackson Papers; Kendall to Van Buren, 9, 16 May 1840, John C. Rives to Blair, 30 Nov.–12 Dec. 1842, Van Buren Papers; Van Buren to Kendall, 15 May 1840, Amos Kendall Papers, MHS.

25. John Campbell to David Campbell, 2 Mar. 1840, Campbell Family Papers; Kendall, "Post Office Report," 22 Feb. 1839, in *Globe*, 23 Apr. 1839; John, *Spreading the News*, 223–35, 238–39. I have estimated the number of removals for Kendall and Barry in Jackson's second term and for Kendall and Niles in Van Buren's term by prorating source data according to each postmaster general's time in office.

REMOVAL OF POSTMASTERS, 1825–1841

| Postmaster general | No. of postmasters at start of presidential administration | No. of removals[a] | Percent per year[b] |
| --- | --- | --- | --- |
| McLean, 1825–29 | 5,677 | 223 | 1.0 |
| Barry, 1829–30 | 8,004 | 423 | 5.3 |
| Barry, 1830–35 | 8,004 | 451 | 1.1 |
| Kendall, 1835–37 | 8,004 | 180 | 1.2 |
| Kendall, 1837–40 | 11,767 | 670 | 1.8 |
| Niles, 1840–41 | 11,767 | 168 | 1.7 |
| Combined Jacksonian PMGs | | 1,892 | 1.7 |
| Granger (Whig) Mar.–July 1841 | 13,409 | 1,085 | 8.1[c] |

SOURCES: Kendall, "Post Office Report," 22 Feb. 1839, in *Globe*, 23 Apr. 1839; John, *Spreading the News*, 223–35, 238–39.

[a] Number of removals for Kendall and Barry in Jackson's second term and for Kendall and Niles in Van Buren's term prorated based on each postmaster general's time in office.

[b] Percentage removed per year of the total at the start of the presidential administration.

[c] In only 4.5 months.

ing those Jacksonian years—about 790 removals fewer than the actual number dismissed. Whether this relatively small difference (65 per year out of an average of about 11,000 postmasters) was enough to damage the work of the post office can be questioned.

Perhaps it was, for the percentages were much greater in certain categories. As has been discussed earlier, the removals were likely to be in the most important, high-paying positions and in the more hotly contested sections of the country, the North and the West. Furthermore, the change posed a threat to post office morale and the power of the central government. Under McLean postal employees were the respected agents of the national government; they held their jobs as a public trust and were not likely to be removed. Under the states' rights Jackson men they were loyal to their party, not the nation. They were, as Kendall wrote in an office circular, "hirelings," who could be "promoted, or discharged at the discretion" of their superiors. And the change had a lasting effect. When the Whigs took over, they removed almost 1,100 postmasters in less than five months.[26]

26. John, *Spreading the News*, 127–28, 206–56; *Niles' Register* 50 (1836): 330 (quotation).

But such damaging consequences must be weighed against the advantages or even the inevitability of party patronage. The rise of political parties and the resultant party patronage were closely tied to the growing self-interested and democratic spirit of the early republic. By getting out the vote and publicizing issues, parties played an important part in the rise of democracy. When Kendall used the word "hirelings," he placed it in the context of democracy. The "offices," he insisted, were "the property of the people, and the officeholders" were their "hirelings." Democrats, Whigs, and eventually Republicans enthusiastically accepted the party system. For good and for bad, patronage became a fixture in democratic politics.[27]

Kendall's five years in the Post Office revealed the complexity, the strengths and flaws in his character. He showed his integrity and perseverance in resisting pressure from contractors. His firmness enabled him to turn down requests for favors, even from Andrew Jackson. His letterbooks give a good idea of his orderliness and industry. These traits made him a strong, tough administrator. When contractors in Vermont wanted him to extend a questionable postal route, they enlisted the help of Congressman Isaac Fletcher, who had grown up with Kendall in Dunstable. After several unsuccessful efforts, Fletcher told them in disgust that Kendall had "an iron fist" and that "scolding & quarrelling [would] avail them but little."[28]

This toughness would have meant little if he had not also known what he was talking about. He was a master of detail. When contractor Breedlove of New Orleans wanted his compensation increased because he was losing money, Kendall refused on the grounds that the losses were the result of mismanagement. In examining the contractor's books, he had found that Breedlove was losing up to $50,000 a year because of "unsuitable boats" that were constantly breaking down. Kendall was not, however, bound by details and could see the larger picture. He based East Coast mail schedules on the laissez-faire premise that since the United States was "peculiarly a business community," preference must be given to "its great commercial centre," New York, over its "political centre," Washington.[29]

27. *Niles' Register* 50 (1836): 330.

28. Kendall to Calhoun et al., 3 Oct. 1837, Kendall to Calhoun, 31 Mar. 1838 (summaries), Calhoun, *Papers*, 13:591–92, 14:250; Kendall to Buchanan, 10 June 1836, James Buchanan Papers, Historical Society of Pennsylvania; Kendall to William C. Rives, 21 May 1835, Rives Papers; Kendall to Jackson, 29 June 1839, 4 Mar. 1840, Jackson Papers; Fletcher to E. B. Chase, 28 Jan., 5 June 1838, Kendall Papers, Dartmouth College Library (typescripts).

29. Kendall to Breedlove, 3 Dec. 1839, Kendall to J. I. Cohen, Northern Pennsylvania Railroad, 29 June 1838, PMGLB.

Kendall's Yankee thrift and strict morality added an edge to his perform-ance. As Isaac Fletcher ruefully remarked, Kendall was "sharp &. . . . close for a bargain" and always acted "as though he were giving from his own purse." He would not give Willis H. Blaney a reward for arresting and convicting a thief because he was not sufficiently involved in the conviction. In dismissing Cranston Laurie for intemperance Kendall lectured the man for letting his "appetites" and behavior "destroy" him.[30]

These strong qualities had a dark side. What some saw as firmness David Campbell considered obstinance and Alfred Balch labeled "vanity and self consequence." New York cartoonist Napoleon Sarony depicted Kendall stand-ing with his arms folded, rejecting a claim from a contractor, and saying, "I obey no laws . . . I make my own." Kendall's mastery of detail was often ap-plied in an overbearing way, his thrift could be sly miserliness, and more often than not his morality was self-righteous and condescending. Kendall swung from one extreme to another.[31]

Two contemporary vignettes brought out the complexity and the extremes in his character. The *United States Magazine and Democratic Review* portrayed him as the ideal democrat. He had grown up "among the hardy and true-hearted yeomanry" of Dunstable, had fought the banks in Kentucky, and had rooted out "corruptions" in Washington. The sketch was accompanied by a picture showing him seated with his legs crossed, dressed immaculately, read-ing the *Richmond Enquirer.* His eyes were piercing, his jaw firm, his hair gray not white, his body thin but not emaciated.[32]

Whig writer John Pendleton Kennedy published a much less flattering picture in his political satire *Quodlibet.* Kennedy drew a hilarious picture of the Democratic party in the mythical town of Quodlibet, which boasted a party newspaper entitled "The Quodlibet Whole Hog." It was edited by a caricature of Kendall named Eliphalet Fox, "a thin, faded little fellow, whose . . . physi-ognomy [was] melancholy, his cheek sunken." Fox's "temper" was "sour and peevish," and he fought like a cat, "showing . . . spring nails." In his previous

30. Fletcher to E. B. Chase, 10 Mar. 1838, Kendall Papers, Dartmouth College Library (type-script); Kendall to Laurie, 15 Dec. 1838, Kendall to G. W. Toland, 27 Dec. 1839, Kendall to Blaney, 16 May 1840, PMGLB.

31. Balch to Polk, 2 Dec. 1844, Polk, *Correspondence,* 6:387; Reilly, *Catalogue of American Politi-cal Prints,* 142.

32. *United States Magazine and Democratic Review* (Washington) 1 (1838): 402–12. For a copy of the picture see the cover of this book.

position he had borrowed money and had grown "bilious, atrabilious, patriotic and indignant [and gone] for REFORM." There was a lot of Kendall in both sketches.[33]

In May 1840 Kendall's character and partisanship were political issues. The opposition reacted cynically to his resignation. The *Alexandria Gazette* found it "astonishing" that Kendall was suddenly so "poor" that he had to be given a high-paying position when everyone could remember his land speculations. In *Quodlibet* one of the characters reports that Kendall's health was "so much shattered by the diseases of the Post-office, that he is compelled to retire; and as his physician prescribes 'the excitement of composition' as his only cure, he is about to devote himself to the Extra Globe."[34]

The election campaign had opened in December 1839 when the Whigs nominated General William Henry Harrison, the victor at Tippecanoe. They mounted a vigorous campaign, portraying "Old Tippecanoe" as a frontier hero and using the log cabin as their symbol. Since the nomination of Van Buren was unopposed, the major question for the Democrats was whether to keep Vice President Richard M. Johnson on the ticket. Many southerners had turned against him for living with a mulatto woman. As Kendall well knew, the colonel had been living this way most of his adult life, but with the intensification of the race question, such an arrangement had now become a serious political liability.

Kendall's relationship with Johnson was affected by the change. In 1836 he had successfully supported his old friend for vice president, but now he altered his position. In August 1839 he received a letter denouncing the colonel for living "openly and shamelessly . . . with a buxom young *Negro wench.*" Kendall forwarded the letter to Van Buren with the comment that he was "shocked" and "washed [his] hands of any future responsibility for [Johnson's] support." Although asked a number of times about his choice for vice president, he refused to take a stand.[35]

He had no such reluctance in promoting the *Extra Globe.* To build up its circulation he asked each of the thirteen thousand postmasters to find sub-

33. Kennedy, *Quodlibet* (Philadelphia, 1840), 83–92.

34. *Globe,* 11 May 1840; Kennedy, *Quodlibet,* 239.

35. —— to Kendall, 12 Aug. 1839, Kendall to Van Buren, 22 Aug. 1839, Van Buren Papers; Meyer, *Life and Times of Colonel Richard M. Johnson,* 34–42; John Catron to Polk, 5 Nov. 1839, Cave Johnson to Polk, 28 Nov. 1839, Polk, *Correspondence,* 5:286–87, 316; Jackson to Kendall, 6 Apr. 1840, Jackson Supplement; Kendall to Cave Johnson et al., 9 June 1840, James K. Polk Papers, LC.

scribers, provided the task was "compatible" with their political "inclination and sense of duty." The request must have angered many of the Whig postmasters, but the *Globe* blithely maintained that only "a few . . . returned rude and insulting replies." Similar letters to Democratic officeholders and newspaper editors set a democratic tone. Every "Farmer, Mechanic and Workingman" should have a subscription, and those who could not afford it should band together to get one. Hinting at patronage, he promised that "the true-hearted men who may aid me . . . shall have no cause to repent their exertions."[36]

To distribute papers and get out the vote, the Democrats organized a special network of Minute Men. Kendall asked George Bancroft to put the "ball in motion" in Massachusetts on the Fourth of July. Added help came from hundreds of Democratic census takers, who combined politicking with their official duties. An old reliable tool was the network of Democratic newspapers, augmented by special campaign editions, the *Rough-Hewer* in Albany, the *Crisis* in Richmond, and *Old Hickory* in Illinois.[37]

But the Democrats faced hard going. When the depression worsened in late 1839 and 1840, they alienated many by saying that people should not look to the government for help. Van Buren's program of hard money, low tariffs, and the independent treasury, which Kendall promoted, had little appeal for an electorate that wanted more money and higher prices. Kendall and his party responded no better to the Panic of 1837 than Kendall had to the Panic of 1819.

Kendall's party address, which he distributed with the prospectus for the *Extra Globe*, was particularly disappointing. It was far more negative than his Hickory Club address in 1832 and relied more on rhetoric. Whigs were trying to "drown the voice of reason in . . . Huzzas for the newly-found hero." Their "log-cabins, cider-barrels . . . and drunkenness" showed "CONTEMPT FOR THE PEOPLE." They were "buying up Senators by the dozen" with money from "the *monster bank*." Van Buren's name appeared only once in the address, and the independent treasury bill, which finally passed on July 4, was ignored.

36. *Globe*, 26 May, 7 ("compatible"), 10 July 1840; Kendall to postmaster of Iberia, Mo., 20 May 1840, George Champlain Sibley Papers, Missouri Historical Society ("true-hearted"); Kendall to Polk, 20 May 1840, Polk Papers ("Farmer"); Kendall to Bancroft, 20 May 1840, George Bancroft Papers, MHS.

37. Kendall to Bancroft, 30 June 1840, Bancroft Papers; Robert Gray Gunderson, *The Log-Cabin Campaign* (Lexington, 1957), 84–87.

In the 1832 address he had mentioned Jackson twenty-one times and defended his policies on the BUS, nullification, and rotation in office.[38]

As in 1836 slavery and race played an important role in the campaign. Between mid-July and mid-August 1840 the *Globe* brought up the subject in eight issues. The case of Navy lieutenant George Mason Hooe, who was convicted of having several sailors cruelly whipped, put the Democrats on the defensive. When Van Buren upheld the decision even though the testimony of black witnesses had been used against Hooe, Congressman John Minor Botts of Virginia and other Whigs accused him of sympathizing with blacks and siding with abolitionists. The Democrats tried to turn the tables. Kendall published a pamphlet accusing Botts of serving on a congressional committee in which a third of the members were abolitionists. Botts, he said, was associating with *"the LEADERS of this crusade against* [his] *own constituents."* Blair joined in by labeling Harrison as an abolitionist. None of the charges had any substance.[39]

With the campaign going against them, the Democrats fell to squabbling. Gideon Welles wrote to John M. Niles, accusing Blair of being too complacent and devoting too much attention to abolitionism at the expense of an economic issue, the special favors being granted corporations. Both Niles and Kendall responded defensively. It was easier "to *grumble,*" said Kendall, "than to *thunder.*" If Welles would "send more *good thunder* . . . we will give [his] bolts full play." He defended the *Globe*'s emphasis on Harrison's Federalism and denied that the corporation issue was "the great battle of 'Gog and Magog.'" Kendall no longer seemed willing to take on monopoly and privilege.[40]

He was prepared for defeat. The Democrats, he told Welles in August, had been content with "talking and working themselves into a self-deceiving confidence." Three months later his fears were realized. Van Buren lost by

38. *Mr. Kendall's Address to the People of the United States* (Washington, 1840), American Antiquarian Society; *Globe,* 13 Oct. 1832.

39. *Globe,* 14, 15, 17, 21, 29 July, 6, 11, 13 Aug., 5, 11 Nov. 1840; Kendall, *The Case of Lieutenant Hooe—A Notable Instance of Whig Honesty* (Washington, 1840); Kendall, *Abolition!! Infatuation of Federal Whig Leaders of the South* (Washington, 1840). David Waldstreicher uses the election to show the "racialization of American politics." "Nationalization and Racialization," 52–56.

40. Niven, *Gideon Welles,* 186–91; Niles to Welles, May 1840, Kendall to Niles, 9 Aug. 1840, Niles to Welles, 12 Aug. 1840, Welles Papers, LC. For the election of 1840 see Michael F. Holt, *The Rise and Fall of the American Whig Party: Jacksonian Politics and the Onset of the Civil War* (New York, 1999), 89–121.

150,000 votes, carrying only seven states. More opposed to the antislavery movement than ever, the *Globe* called the election a day of "Abolition jubilee." Thanks to the new two-party political system, the new means of communication, and the discontent of the depression, over 80 percent of the eligible voters came out to the polls, a far higher percentage than in any previous presidential election and the third highest in American history. It is ironic that in this election, often considered a high point in the rise of American democracy, Kendall, who had contributed much to the rise, was on the losing side.[41]

41. Kendall to Welles, 13 Aug. 1840, Welles Papers, LC; Niven, *Gideon Welles*, 190; *Globe*, 5 Nov. 1840. The only elections with a higher percentage of voting were those of 1860 and 1876. William N. Chambers, "Election of 1840," in Schlesinger, *History of American Presidential Elections*, 1:680.

PART FOUR

*Kendall Green*

# 16

## PRIVATE LIFE

Not waiting for the election returns, Kendall left on a trip west, but no matter how far he went he could not escape the unpleasant news. At Wheeling on November 10, he wrote Jane, "[Whigs] saluted me by firing a cannon under the windows of the room where I slept." On board the steamboat the next day, he could not avoid a conversation with the colorful Whig campaigner John W. Baer, known as the Buckeye Blacksmith. In Cincinnati "a band of 'Tip's' musicians" gathered at the house where he was staying and "sang several of their songs, winding up with diverse groans." Having carried Pennsylvania, Ohio, Indiana, and Kentucky, the Whigs ruled the Ohio.[1]

Kendall was on his way to see his second daughter, Adela, now eighteen, who had married Dr. Frederick B. Culver and moved to Westport, Kentucky, close to Louisville. Visiting them was Kendall's seventeen-year-old son, William Zebedee. As soon as Kendall arrived, he dispatched Dr. Culver and William to Arkansas to start developing 8,500 acres of cotton land that he had acquired on the Mississippi River. The two men traveled to the site, where Culver gave William the task of putting up fences and returned to Kentucky. Left on his own, a thousand miles from home, with very little money and no friends, William was as unhappy as his father had been when he arrived in Lexington. During the next year he suffered through several serious bouts of bilious fever. Not until 1842 was he back in Washington.[2]

Kendall's land in Arkansas was the most recent of the speculations that had used up much of his income. Since coming to Washington he had earned a great deal of money: $48,000 from the government, $22,000 from the *Globe* and the *Extra Globe,* and smaller amounts from the sale of his mill, his share

---

1. Kendall to Jane Kendall, 13 Nov. 1840, in *Autobiography,* 429.

2. William Z. Kendall to Amos Kendall, 29 Aug. 1841, William Z. Kendall to Jane Kendall, Dec. 1841, Kendall Papers, Dartmouth College Library; *Globe,* 2 Sept. 1843.

in the *Argus,* and his stock in the Boston Land Company, a total of at least $90,000. Most of it—even much of his income from the *Extra Globe*—was gone. Part of it went to pay down payments and installments for his western lands. Some went for lawsuits and travel. And more than a little was lost in 1840 when the Chase Land Company, one of his latest investments, failed.[3]

Another drain on Kendall's resources was his standard of living. Ever since he had been appointed postmaster general, he and his family had been living well. He and Jane dressed fashionably, drove about in a carriage and a cariole, sent their children to private schools, and paid a high rent for Jackson Hill. His personal estate was sixth highest in his ward. He had been able to put on rather splashy weddings for Adela in 1839 and for Mary Anne and her fiancé Daniel Gold less than a year later. He and Jane were no longer Washington outsiders.[4]

Now suddenly he was trapped. The election was lost, the *Extra Globe* was shut down, and he had very little income. Almost all of his assets were lands currently depressed in value, his debts had not gone away, and he was being sued. In search of a solution he thought of moving to New York to publish a newspaper, but that became impossible when he lost his personal damages case with Stockton and Stokes. The award was reduced from $100,000 to $12,000, and a second trial was ordered, but since Kendall lacked the money to pay, he was not allowed to leave the District of Columbia. So in February 1841 he started a small biweekly newspaper—really a magazine—which he called *Kendall's Expositor.* There seemed to be room for the paper since the *Democratic Review* had moved to New York, but income came in slowly. During the summer of 1841 he had to postpone payment on two sizable notes.[5]

Complicating the situation was the question of where to live. With two

3. In 1842 Blair estimated that Kendall's income since 1829 had been $110,000, but he was including $9,000 in loans and land worth $30,000 from the Boston Land Co. The loans came after 1840, and I believe that Kendall sold the land at a large discount. John C. Rives to Blair, 30 Nov.–12 Dec. 1842, Blair to Kendall, 12 Dec. 1842, Van Buren Papers; Blair to Jackson, 16 Dec. 1843, Jackson, *Correspondence,* 6:250; Samuel Lawrence to Amos Adams Lawrence, 26 May 1840, Amos Adams Lawrence Papers, MHS; Kendall to Richard Smith, 12 Jan., 12 July, 1841, Kendall Papers, Filson Historical Society.

4. Corporation of Washington, Wards 4 and 5, "General Assessment," 1839–1843, National Archives; *Intelligencer,* 25 Nov. 1839, 14 Aug. 1840; Kendall to Jackson, 12 Nov. 1839, Jackson Papers; Kendall to John, 26 May 1851.

5. *Autobiography,* 355; Kendall to Blair, 16 Dec. 1842, Van Buren Papers; Swisher, *History of the Supreme Court,* 165; *Expositor,* 3 Feb., 15 Sept. 1841; Kendall to Corcoran, 17 May, 23 Sept. 1841, William W. Corcoran Papers, LC.

daughters married, Kendall no longer needed a ten-room house. Prudence dictated renting a smaller place, but he had never given up his dream of having a farm of his own. In the fall of 1841 he agreed to pay $9,000 for 102 acres of wooded land in northeast Washington, about two miles from the Capitol, and started putting up a house. He called the property Kendall Green. "There," he told Van Buren, "in the alternate use of the *plough* and the *pen,* I expect to spend the balance of my life." This was an unrealistic expectation because Kendall had not farmed seriously since he was a boy and had disliked it then. It was also unrealistic financially. Unable to make any down payment, he had to sign an agreement to pay the owners, John and Anna Farley, $1,800 plus interest each of the next five years.[6]

Kendall's problems continued to mount. The second jury confirmed the judgment of the first and gave Kendall a year to pay, during which time he had to stay in the District of Columbia. If he failed to pay, he would be sent to debtor's prison. Kendall appealed to the Supreme Court. Meanwhile the Metropolis Bank was suing him for $2,000. With the *Expositor* still not doing well, his situation was becoming desperate.[7]

Finally realizing that he and his family must reduce their lifestyle, Kendall took drastic steps. He first tried to return the property and rent it, but the Farleys turned him down. Then, despite the cold and wet of winter, he moved his family out of Jackson Hill and into the small, flimsy, unfinished, one-floor house at Kendall Green. Any thought of a large permanent home was abandoned. In addition, he told Jackson, he "stopped buying on a credit, took [his] children from school, set them at work, and went to work" himself cutting down trees to sell for firewood. It was a great comedown for Jane, but she responded with her usual "cheerful disposition" and made "the best of everything."[8]

Still needing money, Kendall had to turn to Francis P. Blair. He must have hesitated because their friendship, which had weakened during the Bank War, was fast disappearing. Kendall had promised Blair never to start a rival

6. Kendall's new house was twenty-six feet square. *Autobiography,* 440; Kendall to Van Buren, 23 Oct. 1841, Van Buren Papers; "Agreement between Amos Kendall and John and Anna Maria Farley," 2 Oct. 1841, Amos and Jane Kendall, "Answer to Bill of Complaint of John and Anna Maria Farley," 2 June 1843, United States District Court for the District of Columbia, RG 21, National Archives, copy at Gallaudet University Archives.

7. Swisher, *History of the Supreme Court,* 165.

8. *Autobiography,* 440–41 ("cheerful"); Kendall to Jackson, 5 June 1842, Jackson Papers ("stopped").

newspaper but had proceeded to publish the *Expositor.* Blair had retaliated by adding a weekly edition of the *Globe.* He began to think of Kendall as a rival for the congressional printing, now in the hands of the opposition, and suspected him of conspiring with the *Madisonian.* But Blair and Rives were about to receive $140,000 from the government for publishing the 1840 census and had money to lend. So in March 1842 they advanced Kendall $7,000.[9]

The loan kept Kendall from losing his house and his newspaper. The *Expositor* had become a first-rate journal, combining Kendall's provocative editorials with social and economic data and excerpts from the debates in Congress. Kendall's views had not changed much. He retained his old contempt for a national bank and his skepticism of paper money. He still carried a grudge against the railroads and defended high postal rates. His suspicions of the central government can be seen in his articles opposing high tariffs. Still hating Federalists and southern extremists, he considered the Democrats the reincarnation of the patriots of 1776 and the Jeffersonian Republicans.[10]

Several historians have used material from the *Expositor* to portray Kendall as a radical Locofoco Democrat, an advocate of social change and an enemy of capitalism. Some of his articles do sound radical. He still held to his view that every American had the right to the fruits of his labor. He opposed monopolies, land speculation, the spread of paper money, and special privileges for large businesses. He praised New Hampshire Democrats for taking the right of eminent domain away from the railroads.[11]

But these opinions did not make him a radical. On starting the *Expositor,* he explicitly renounced the terms "radical" and "loco foco." In an article defining democracy he said that the purpose of government was moral reform, not economic, and that efforts to put bread in the mouths of one group would only take it away from another. As the Bank veto made clear, he was seeking equal opportunity, not "equality . . . of wealth." Kendall, furthermore, had re-

---

9. After the loan, Kendall had debts of $20,000 to $30,000. Kendall to Blair, 30 Nov. 1842, John C. Rives to Blair, 30 Nov.–12 Dec. 1842, Blair to Kendall, 12 Dec. 1842, Van Buren Papers; Smith, *Press, Politics, and Patronage,* 250; Jackson to Blair, 24 Feb. 1842, Jackson Papers; Kendall to John, 23 June 1851.

10. *Expositor,* passim. A good sample of his editorials can be found in his *Autobiography,* 436–526.

11. John Ashworth argues that Kendall was an agrarian. *"Agrarians" and "Aristocrats,"* 23–24, 31. Arthur M. Schlesinger Jr. cites Kendall's determination to protect "freemen" from dependence on the rich. *Age of Jackson,* 393. See also *Expositor,* 3 Feb. 1841, 17 Feb. 1842, 24 Jan. 1843; *Autobiography,* 442.

jected Ricardo's labor theory of value during the Relief War and now made no mention of it in his article "What Is Wealth?" for the *Expositor*.[12]

Unlike radicals such as George H. Evans, Orestes Brownson, and Thomas Skidmore, he had no interest in redistributing wealth through inheritance taxes or grants of free land. Nor did he fight for other programs of broad reform. Rarely doctrinaire in his economic views, he had avoided the corporation issue in the 1840 election. Even in the Philadelphia navy yard case, he had not supported labor unions or the abstract theory of shorter hours, and he never showed much concern for the poor.

To keep the *Expositor* going Kendall needed a government printing contract. The sudden death of President William Henry Harrison and the elevation of former Jacksonian John Tyler to the presidency seemed to increase his chances. Tyler had split with Henry Clay and the main body of Whigs and had taken two former Jackson men into his new cabinet. Forgetting that he had once been at odds with the new president, Kendall began making overtures toward his administration. His gestures produced no immediate results and served only to antagonize Blair, who remained firmly opposed to Tyler.[13]

A further source of friction was the disposition of Jackson's papers. Kendall had started writing the biography and had been given some of the papers, but had not been made Old Hickory's literary executor. In July Blair tried to gain an advantage by telling Jackson that Kendall's "pecuniary embarrassments" and "impaired" health made it unlikely that he would ever finish the biography. He asked the Old Hero to change his will, so that when Kendall died, any of the papers in his possession would go to Blair. Jackson agreed in principle but put off doing anything.[14]

The conflict broke into the open in the fall of 1842 when Kendall offered to merge the *Expositor* with the *Globe* if Blair would give him another substantial loan. Blair agreed to the merger but offered only a $1,500 loan and a $1,200 job as a reporter. An angry Kendall turned down the "degrading" offer. He became angrier still when he heard that Blair was spreading rumors about his financial troubles and when he saw an announcement in the *Globe* apologizing for something he had written for the newspaper. Now thoroughly frustrated

12. *Expositor*, 3 Feb. 1841, 24 Jan. 1843; *Autobiography*, 437–44, 454. For Kendall's opposition to the labor theory of value see *Argus*, 27 Apr., 4, 11, 18 May 1820.

13. *Expositor*, 21 Apr. 1841; Kendall to Tyler, 21 Aug. 1841, John Tyler Papers, LC; *Globe*, 29 Nov., 31 Dec. 1842.

14. Kendall to Jackson, 5 June 1842, Blair to Jackson, 25 July 1842, Jackson Papers; Jackson to Blair, 7 Aug. 1842, Blair to Jackson, 6 Oct. 1842, Jackson, *Correspondence*, 6:162, 173.

and not yet recovered from a three-week sick spell, he wrote Blair on November 30, saying that he was "wounded" by his "unkind" words.[15]

The letter started a brief exchange that laid bare jealousies and hard feelings that had been festering for years. Kendall took all the credit for making Blair a success. "I introduced you" to the president, he wrote, "I created the Globe and put you at its head." He said he had protected Blair from the "hostility" of cabinet members and "cherished and nurtured" him until he became "one of the richest men in the District." Blair retorted angrily that if Kendall had been so "omnipoten[t]," why did he not set up the *Globe* on his own? The reason, he sneered, was that Kendall did not dare give up the security of his government job. Blair also pointed out that he had raised the money to keep the *Globe* afloat and denied having enemies other than Louis McLane in the cabinet. Then, reopening another wound, he accused Kendall of having taken part in McLane's plot against him.[16]

Both men appealed to Van Buren and Jackson. Blair insisted that Kendall had started the quarrel in order to smear him and get the public printing, while Kendall blamed it on Blair's jealousy. Poor Kendall had it backward. He was the jealous one—jealous of Blair's affluence and his fine home on Lafayette Square. The circumspect Van Buren stayed out of the fight, but Jackson, who feared unnecessarily that it would split the party, jumped right in. Over the next four months he and the two adversaries exchanged at least forty-six letters. Always quick to see conspiracies, he told Blair that "busybodies" such as Duff Green were responsible for the quarrel. Jackson arranged to have the two shake hands, but the ill will continued.[17]

Looking for other sources of income, Kendall set himself up as a claims agent and invited his nephew, John E. Kendall, down from Massachusetts to be his assistant. They opened an office on Pennsylvania Avenue and offered to help those seeking contracts and pensions or trying to settle accounts and claims. They would also deal in local and western real estate. Late in the summer they got their first important client: a large group of Cherokees, who had

15. Kendall to Blair, 11, 30 Nov. 1842, Blair to Van Buren, 26 Mar. 1843, Van Buren Papers; Kendall to Jackson, 12 Oct. 1842, Jackson Papers; *Globe*, 24 Oct., 12 Nov. 1842; Blair to Calhoun, 11 Nov. 1842, Calhoun, *Papers*, 16: 541–43.

16. Kendall to Blair, 16 Dec. 1842, Blair to Kendall, 24 Dec. 1842, Van Buren Papers.

17. Blair to Van Buren, 16 Dec. 1842, 17 Jan., 26 Mar. 1843, Kendall to Van Buren, 7 Dec. 1842, 3 Jan. 1843, ibid.; Blair to Jackson, 1, 23 Jan. 1843, Kendall to Jackson, 27 Jan. 1843, Jackson to Blair, 11, 17 Jan., 7 Feb. 1843, Jackson to Kendall, 8 Feb. 1843, Jackson to Silas Wright, 8 Feb. 1843, Jackson Papers.

moved west in 1817 on their own and had not shared in the $5 million granted to the main body of Cherokees when they moved twenty years later.[18]

Kendall also dabbled in slaves. In 1841 he purchased a teenage male slave named Daniel and rented him out to a planter in Mississippi with the understanding that he would be allowed to work out his emancipation. Daniel was worth about $800. Early in 1843 a letter arrived from the abolitionist Lewis Tappan, saying that he and his friends had rescued Daniel and asking Kendall to free him. Tappan offered to pay $50 for a deed of emancipation. Kendall was furious. "You steal and hide my property," he wrote, and then "propose to buy it at a sixteenth of its value." Tappan and his accomplices were little better than "the monsters who steal negroes from Africa." Protesting that his "boy" could not long survive in "a very cold region," he demanded that Tappan give him the chance to decide whether he wanted to be freed at once or be allowed to work out his emancipation.[19]

Kendall's final letter to Tappan suggests that his antiabolitionism was more than just politics. Attacking the abolitionists for their unwillingness to give free blacks social equality, he said that the "social degradation" in the North was "more wretched than ordinary slavery." He challenged the abolitionists to "practice what you preach" and allow their daughters to marry black men. He would readily let Daniel go if Tappan would arrange to marry him "into one of your most respectable families." After all, he pointed out, Daniel was "well formed, [had] fine eyes, beautiful teeth, thick lips, a nose moderately flat, a mild temper, a skin as black as jet, and [did] not smell more than other negroes." He asked Tappan to make his daughter "proud of *kissing his black lips, nestling in his black arms,* and *raising up a family of woolly headed mulattoes.*" Kendall concluded, "My Democracy has not been able to *reconcile black and white:* If yours can do it, show me the example." There is no evidence that he got Daniel back.[20]

Soon afterward Kendall bought a female slave and her infant child from one John L. Prewitt of Hancock County, Kentucky. After Prewitt's son-in-law won possession on a technicality, Kendall appealed, and a new trial was ordered. Again there is no record of the outcome, but it is clear that Kendall was not finding slave ownership easy or profitable.[21]

18. *Expositor,* 17 Mar. 1843; *Globe,* 28 Aug., 2 Sept. 1843; Kendall to J. Rogers, Western Cherokees, 26 July 1843, Kendall Papers, LC.

19. Kendall to Tappan, 18, 31 Jan. 1843, Lewis Tappan Papers, LC.

20. Kendall to Tappan, 4 Mar. 1843, ibid.

21. *Kendall v. Hughes,* in Ben. Monroe, *Reports of the Court of Appeals of Kentucky* 7 (1846–1847): 368–74.

A more immediate way to make money was to publish Jackson's biography. Kendall had been working on it spasmodically since 1840 and planned to start issuing the book in installments in the spring of 1843. He and Jackson had great hopes. The work would be modeled on Jared Sparks's *Life and Writings of George Washington* and would have a German translation. Thousands would be sold in the South and West alone. Since Kendall could not leave Washington, he sent Jane's young nephew, James McLaughlin, to the Hermitage to go over the papers and interview the Old Hero.[22]

McLaughlin found himself caught between a demanding uncle who wanted intimate details and an old man who hated to reveal much. Kendall told Jackson that they needed a "narrative . . . interspersed with anecdote" to "interest the general reader." McLaughlin pointed out that the duc de Sully and Benjamin Franklin had not hesitated to write autobiographies. But Jackson, who feared that his enemies would pounce upon mistakes, replied sadly, "Man was more charitable then." The work was slow and "painful." Every time McLaughlin "elicit[ed] some incident worthy of note," the old man would relate it in such "a lengthy and episodic" way that McLaughlin had "difficulty . . . preserv[ing] the connection." They did their best. Jackson managed to pull elusive facts from his tired mind and proofread at least half of the text. McLaughlin kept after the old man and sent thick packages of documents on to his uncle. Together they collected valuable firsthand information, mostly about Jackson's early life.[23]

Even so, the book was disappointing. It stopped short of the Battle of New Orleans, failed to make money, and was not very good history. Instead of taking advantage of his primary sources, Kendall relied on a few volumes of military orders and previous accounts. A dozen stories, including Jackson's conflict with John Sevier and his duel with Charles Dickinson, were drawn almost verbatim from a biography of Old Hickory written by his associate Henry Lee. The result was the anecdotal narrative that Kendall had sought, but the writing lacked his usual sparkle.[24]

22. Kendall to Jackson, 19 Sept., 29 Nov. 1842, Jackson to Kendall, 20 Dec. 1842, 13 Nov. 1843, George Walker to Kendall, 18 Oct. 1842, Jackson Papers; Kendall to Van Buren, 7 Dec. 1842, Van Buren Papers.

23. Kendall to Jackson, 29 Nov. 1842 (quotation), 7 Feb. 1843, James McLaughlin to Kendall, 12 Feb. 1843 (quotations), Jackson to Kendall, 9 Jan., 11 Apr., 29 Sept. 1843, 9 June 1844, Jackson Papers. Kendall to Jackson, 17 Sept. 1843, Blair-Lee Papers.

24. Kendall, *Life of Gen. Andrew Jackson* (New York, 1843–44), American Culture Series, Microfilm, No. 592.5, pp. 24, 67–68, and passim; McDonough, *Index to the Andrew Jackson Papers,*

At the same time Kendall was also preparing an article for the *Democratic Review* defending Old Hickory against the charge of ignoring a writ of habeas corpus after the Battle of New Orleans. In March 1815 a federal district judge had held Jackson in contempt and fined him $1,000. The article was part of a Democratic effort to have Congress pass a bill to return the fine. In the article Kendall pointed out that the women of New Orleans were so grateful for Jackson's efforts to protect them that they raised the money to pay the fine. The general "accepted" the money and gave it to charity. The article backfired because Whigs pounced on the word "accepted" to argue that Jackson had already been repaid. Jackson was unhappy, and Blair publicly criticized Kendall for the blunder, but interest died once the bill passed.[25]

The ill will between Kendall and Blair carried over into the battle for the Democratic presidential nomination. Blair was committed to Van Buren and suspected that Kendall and other New Englanders were intriguing with Tyler and Conservative Democrats against him. He warned Jackson that "Van Buren's Yankee friends Woodbury and Kendall [were] very apt to give him the slip." Kendall, Isaac Hill, and David Henshaw, he said, were backing Tyler in order to secure federal patronage. Hill already had post office contracts, Henshaw was secretary of the navy, and Kendall was angling for executive and congressional printing.[26]

Blair was right. Kendall was playing a careful game, backing Van Buren while sidling up to Tyler. In May 1843 he endorsed Van Buren but promised to defer to "the will of the party" and support "any other leader, whether it be Buchanan or Calhoun, Cass or Johnson," or even, he added, Tyler. When Blair accused him of backing "apostates," Kendall replied that the *Globe* spent more time attacking Democrats than Whigs.[27]

On October 17 Kendall announced that he was a candidate to be printer

---

xv. On Kendall's plagiarism see Mark Mastromarino, "Henry Lee, Jacksonian Biographer," unpublished paper, 1991, 24–28, and Henry Lee, *A Biography of Andrew Jackson, Late Major-General of the Army of the United States*, ed. Mark Mastromarino (Knoxville, 1992), i–v.

25. Kendall to Jackson 23 Nov. 1842, Jackson Papers; Kendall, "General Jackson's Fine," *United States Magazine and Democratic Review* (New York), Jan. 1843, 58–77; Remini, *Andrew Jackson and the Course of American Democracy*, 478–79, 490; Jackson to Kendall, 6 Feb. 1843, Jackson to Blair, 7 Feb. 1843, Blair to Jackson, 9 Feb. 1843, Jackson Supplement.

26. *Globe*, 15, 20, 28, 30 Mar., 4, 11 Apr., 21, 24 July 1843; Blair to Van Buren, 26 Mar. 1843, Van Buren Papers; Blair to Jackson, 29 Jan. 1843, Jackson, *Correspondence,* 6:185–86 (quotation).

27. *Expositor*, 16 May 1843; *Globe*, 14 Aug. 1843; Kendall to Marcy, 4 July 1843, 22 Aug. 1843, William L. Marcy Papers, LC.

for the House of Representatives—a job that over the previous two years had paid Gales and Seaton $260,000. It was a long shot, for he would have to defeat Blair and Rives in the Democratic caucus and Gales and Seaton in the House election. Kendall thought he had a chance if he could win the backing of fringe candidates Isaac Hill, William Cullen Bryant of the *New York Evening Post,* and Shadrach Penn of Kentucky and use them to unite supporters of Calhoun, Buchanan, and Richard M. Johnson. To attract the printers he dropped hints that he would share the printing, and to get caucus votes he argued that he would win the House because he would get votes from Whigs and Tyler men. A concerned Blair told Jackson that there was "a strong combination" against him.[28]

At the caucus the Blair men made Kendall's task unusually difficult by forcing through a rule requiring a two-thirds vote for all nominations. Then Cave Johnson of Tennessee followed with an excited speech pointing out the dangers of defeating the *Globe* and rebuking Kendall for his article about sharing the printing. After listening to the article read aloud, the caucus nominated Blair over Kendall by a vote of about 80 to 30. The size of the margin suggests that Kendall's combination was much weaker than expected and that he never really had a chance. Blair later defeated Gales and Seaton in the House election. He was "amaze[d]," he told Jackson rather smugly, that Kendall had challenged the *Globe* after all that he and Jackson had "done for him."[29]

Now persona non grata, Kendall had to get back in the good graces of the party. Only a day or two after the caucus he sent Cave Johnson a "conciliatory" letter asking him to "say something to remove the suspicion cast on his 'political integrity.'" When Johnson refused, Kendall publicly denied the "ungenerous misrepresentations" that had been made against him. He also tried to ingratiate himself with Van Buren, who seemed likely to secure the nomination. He warned him of a plot to dump him at the convention and offered to reveal the names of the conspirators. After Van Buren came out against the annexation of Texas, Kendall urged him to amend the statement by promising

28. *Expositor,* 17, 28 Oct. 1843; Smith, *Press, Politics, and Patronage,* 250–51; Montgomery Blair to Jackson, 20 Nov. 1843, Blair to Jackson, 6 Dec. 1843, Jackson Supplement; Blair to Jackson, 26 Nov. 1843, Jackson, *Correspondence,* 6:244–45.

29. Johnson to Polk, 9 Dec. 1843, Polk, *Correspondence,* 6:372–76; *Globe,* 5, 7 Dec. 1843; Blair to Van Buren, 10 Dec. 1843, Kendall to Van Buren, 19–20 Apr. 1844, Van Buren Papers; Blair to Jackson, 6, 16 Dec. 1843, Jackson, *Correspondence,* 6:248–50.

to support annexation if the convention voted for it. But he received no encouragement from the Little Magician.[30]

Once James K. Polk won the nomination, Kendall fell in line. During the campaign he published letters to Whig candidate Henry Clay reminiscent of his letters to Clay in the 1828 election. As moralistic as ever, he told Clay that his swearing, card playing, and dueling made him "unfit" to be president. Still speaking to the common people, he wrote that "there are always two parties . . . the *Democracy* and the *Aristocracy*." Clay and the Whigs represented the latter. Polk liked the letters and used them in his home state of Tennessee, which had gone Whig in 1836 and 1840. The Democrats ran a good race in Tennessee, losing it by only 113 votes, and Polk won the national election by a narrow margin.[31]

Kendall wasted no time demanding a share of the spoils. As president of the Democratic Association in Washington he asked Polk to consult with him before making appointments. He enlisted Jackson's support for assignment as minister to Spain. By early December, however, he had changed his mind and wanted to stay in the city as postmaster and play a role in the administration. His hopes were raised when Polk's adviser, Congressman Aaron V. Brown of Tennessee, arranged for him to write the inaugural address. Brown accepted Kendall's draft but urged Polk to have it revised. The section on the tariff, he said, painted Polk as a protectionist, and the part on state debts to European countries was badly handled. These and a particularly flowery passage on national unity were changed in the final version.[32]

Polk still did not offer Kendall a position. Jackson kept after him to find something for "poor Kendall," but other Tennesseans thought differently. Alfred Balch, always critical of Kendall, wrote scornfully that as postmaster general he had done "Van Buren more injury than 10,000 of his bitterest enemies." Cave Johnson warned that Kendall's Democratic Association consisted of nothing but "*cliques*" intent on "*serv[ing] themselves*" through an all-out "*pro-*

---

30. Johnson to Polk, 9 Dec. 1843, Polk, *Correspondence,* 6:373; *Expositor,* 19 Dec. 1843; Kendall to Van Buren, 19–20, 29 Apr., 13, 16 May 1844, Van Buren Papers.

31. The letters were published in the *Expositor,* 14, 27 Aug., 10 Sept. 1844, reprinted in the *Nashville Union* and the *Nashville Star Spangled Banner,* and are excerpted in Clay, *Papers* 10:94–97 (quotations).

32. Kendall to Polk, 16 Nov. 1844, Polk Papers; Kendall to Jackson, 18 Nov. 1844, 5 Jan. 1845, Jackson to Kendall, 23, 28 Nov. 1844, Jackson Papers; Brown to Polk, 5, 14, 23, 30 Dec. 1844, Polk, *Correspondence,* 6:398–400, 427–28, 456–59, 476–80; Charles Sellers, *James K. Polk Continentalist, 1843–1846* (Princeton, 1966), 209–10.

*scription.*" Even Brown advised Polk not to appoint Kendall to any spoils-sensitive position.[33]

Polk decided not to select Kendall or any other holdover from the Jackson–Van Buren years. Instead major appointments went to his friend Cave Johnson, northerners William L. Marcy and George Bancroft, and southerners Robert J. Walker and John Y. Mason. In April 1845 Jackson asked Blair plaintively: "What is the President doing for Mr. Kendall? He was to have had the city post office." Blair was the wrong person to ask. He still disliked Kendall, and as a Van Buren man and a less than committed expansionist, he had no influence with Polk. Soon after his inauguration Polk forced Blair out and set up Thomas Ritchie, a strong expansionist, as editor of a new party organ, the *Washington Union*. Ritchie had been one of the original Jacksonians, but as a sharp critic of patronage, he had often been at odds with the administration.[34]

So the old Jackson men—Kendall, Blair, and Van Buren—were left on the outside. And the Old Hero himself was dying. Kendall knew that the end was near. When he wrote Jackson on May 31, he said he "feared" that his letter might not find him "in the land of the living." He told his old friend, "The glories of earth have been yours; the glories of Heaven await you." The letter reached the Hermitage several days after the Old Hero had died.[35]

Jackson's death left the handling of his papers and biography unresolved. Blair took control of the papers, but many documents remained with Kendall and others. Kendall talked frequently of going back to his writing, but money, not the biography, was uppermost in his mind. There had been several hopeful signs. The abolition of debtor's prison in the District had freed him to travel, and the Supreme Court had set aside the damages award. But on the other side of the ledger the *Expositor* had gone out of business. After four years of maneuvering he had lost any hope of returning to political office and had found no reliable source of income. Kendall would have to look outside of government and journalism to support his family.[36]

33. Balch to Polk, 2 Dec. 1844, Brown to Polk, 5 Dec. 1844, Jackson to Polk, 13, 16 Dec. 1844, Johnson to Polk, 20 Dec. 1844, Polk, *Correspondence*, 6:387, 398–400, 425–26, 437–39, 443.

34. Blair to Jackson, 30 Mar., 17 Apr. 1845, Jackson to Blair, 9 Apr. 1845, Jackson, *Correspondence*, 6:393–94, 397, 400–401; Smith, *Francis Preston Blair*, 162–68.

35. Kendall to Jackson, 31 May 1845, Jackson Papers.

36. Kendall delivered some of the papers to Blair in 1849 but retained a good many others. Some of these were lost in a fire and others found their way to the Library of Congress. McDonough, *Index to the Andrew Jackson Papers*, xv–xxi; *Autobiography*, 360, 525–26; Kendall, "Memorial . . . for Certain Losses Sustained by Him," 15 Dec. 1845, 29th Cong., 1st sess., H. Doc. 37.

# 17

## THE TELEGRAPH

Kendall had been living with astounding increases in the speed of communication all of his life. When he was a boy, news of the death of George Washington took fifteen days to reach Dunstable; when he was forty, copies of Andrew Jackson's annual message arrived there in only a day and a half. He had seen the changes firsthand in 1827 when he traveled from New York to Washington in half the time it had taken in 1814. His express mail had cut the time for mail delivery between New York and New Orleans from two weeks to one. The climax came on May 29, 1844, when news of James K. Polk's nomination traveled from Baltimore to Washington almost instantaneously over Samuel F. B. Morse's telegraph.[1]

The telegraph was a product of the great popularization of science in the years following the War of 1812. Morse was only one of over fifty inventors who built some sort of an electromagnetic telegraphic device before 1840. Not a scientist himself, he could not have built the telegraph without the help of Alfred Vail and Leonard Gale and the research of the renowned scientist Joseph Henry. Morse's telegraph prevailed because it was better built, less complicated, and less expensive than the others and because he was able to fight off the claims of his rivals. To develop the telegraph Morse formed a partnership in which he owned nine-sixteenths of the patent, Vail one-eighth, Gale one-sixteenth, and former congressman Francis O. J. Smith of Maine one-fourth. After securing a patent in 1840 and winning an appropriation from Congress in 1843, the partners (or patentees as they were called) built the telegraph line that brought the news from Baltimore to Washington.[2]

1. Pred, *Urban Growth and the Circulation of Information*, 14–15; Carleton Mabee, *The American Leonardo: A Life of Samuel F. B. Morse* (New York, 1943), 276–79.

2. David Hochfelder, "Taming the Lightning: American Telegraphy as a Revolutionary Technology, 1832–1860" (Ph.D. diss., Case Western Reserve University, 1999), 7–8, 31–36, 172–73; Robert L. Thompson, *Wiring a Continent: The History of the Telegraph Industry in the United States 1832–1866* (Princeton, 1947), 8–33.

Morse planned to sell the patent rights to the government and, perhaps, also to private interests, but he dreaded the prospect of dealing with the legal and business problems that would be involved. He had brought Smith into the partnership to handle such matters but had soon lost trust in him. Smith had concealed the fact that he was Morse's partner while he remained a congressman and worked to pass the appropriation bill. He continued to hide his connection with Morse while his company was building the Baltimore line. After it was completed, Morse confided in Alfred Vail that he was "sick at heart" about Smith. Too moral to tolerate such behavior but too weak to stop it, he needed help.[3]

In the winter of 1845 Morse came to Washington to sell the rights to the government. While he was there, he ran into Kendall and talked with him at length about the telegraph. The subject was not a new one for Kendall. Ever since he was a boy he had been interested in machinery and concepts such as perpetual motion. In the Post Office he had set a high priority on speed. Frustrated by the railroads, he had started the express mail and had thought seriously of building an optical telegraph system. He was present on February 20, 1838, when Morse gave the cabinet a demonstration of his electromagnetic telegraph, and from then on was "strongly of the opinion that the project ought to be adopted and fostered by the government." The more he and Morse talked, the more interested Kendall became.[4]

On February 25, 1845, he sent Morse a glowing letter describing his vision of the future of the telegraph. Like his express mail, it would bring news to all parts of the Union long before the large East Coast newspapers could get there. Newspapers would become purely local. And since financial correspondence would be sent by telegraph, the mails would have much less need for speed and would rely less on the railroads. Once the new administration understood how much money the telegraph could save the Post Office, it would surely buy the rights. With his usual energy and optimism he promised to draw up a "Journal of Improvement" for the telegraph and put it in the hands of every member of Congress.[5]

Morse was so impressed with the letter and so desperate for help that

3. Thomas L. Gaffney, "Maine's Mr. Smith: A Study of Francis O. J. Smith, Politician and Entrepreneur" (Ph.D. diss., University of Maine, 1979), 218–20, 282–83; Morse to Alfred Vail, 11 June 1844, Morse Papers, LC.

4. Kendall to John M. Robinson, 8 Feb. 1837, in *Globe*, 15 Feb. 1837; Dickerson, "Diary," 20 Feb. 1837; *United States Magazine and Democratic Review* (Washington) 1 (1838): 410–11 (quotation).

5. Kendall to Morse, 25 Feb. 1845, Morse Papers.

he asked Kendall to become business agent for the three-fourths share of the partnership owned by himself, Vail, and Gale. Kendall would receive 10 percent of proceeds up to $100,000 from the sale of the patent and 50 percent of any excess. When Kendall accepted on March 10, a delighted Morse told Gale that they had hired "perhaps the most competent man in the country" to manage their affairs.[6]

And also one of the most ambitious. A few days later Kendall came back to Morse with an offer to buy him out for $100,000—an amazing sum ($2.4 million in today's money) for someone as strapped for cash as Kendall. The offer shows his overwhelming desire to make money and his willingness to think big and take risks. It was another example of the opportunities in antebellum America. Within a few months Kendall had closed down a newspaper, tried unsuccessfully for a patronage job, been named agent for the most exciting new technology of the day, and now wanted to buy into it. But like so many of his dreams, this one was unrealistic. Morse was interested because he needed money for a trip to Europe, but the deal fell apart when he insisted on a down payment greater than the $10,000 Kendall offered.[7]

Now resigned to being agent, Kendall started making plans for the industry. Since Congress had adjourned in March without buying the telegraph, the question of government or private ownership was unsettled. Morse, Vail, and Gale wanted the government to control the telegraph by regulating private companies. Smith insisted on selling only to private companies. Even if they all agreed and the government proved willing, the matter would not be entirely settled, for other inventors with new devices were waiting in the wings. Kendall liked the idea of selling to the government, but whether the patentees did or not, he wanted a unified system centered on New York. Having seen the importance of New York for commercial, postal, and railroad business, he envisioned it as a great hub with telegraph lines running off in all directions.[8]

---

6. Kendall signed two separate contracts, one with Morse and Gale, the other with Vail. "Agreement between Samuel F. B. Morse and Amos Kendall," 10 Mar. 1845, Western Union Telegraph Company Collection, National Museum of American History Archives Center; Kendall to Morse, 4 Mar. 1845, Morse to Gale, 11 Mar. 1845, Morse Papers; Thompson, *Wiring*, 14, 38.

7. Kendall to Morse, 14, 21 Mar. 1845, Morse Papers.

8. Smith to Kendall, 6 Aug. 1845, Smith Papers, Maine Historical Society, coll. 38; Hochfelder, "Taming the Lightning," 61–62; Mabee, *American Leonardo*, 283; Thompson, *Wiring*, 28–31, 39–40.

In May 1845 Kendall organized a corporation, the Magnetic Telegraph Company, to build a trunk line from New York through Philadelphia to Baltimore, where it would tie in with the existing line to Washington. A clause in the charter left open the possibility of future sale to the government. Since few Americans were enthusiastic about the telegraph, he had a hard time finding investors, and half of the money had to come from Smith's relatives and his own. Kendall, who was elected president, invested $500. After $15,000 had been raised, the company issued shares of stock valued at $60,000, half to the subscribers and half to the Morse patentees, for the rights to use the patent. Kendall's troubles with the railroads continued as they refused his requests for rights-of-way, forcing him to string wires along old New Jersey wagon roads.[9]

Morse and Kendall felt strongly that the telegraph should be run in a democratic and moral way. To prevent speculators and other powerful interests from getting control, they put a clause in the charter stating that the company's telegraph lines must be "opened alike to all men" on a "first to come . . . first served" basis. Kendall's touch can be seen in regulations such as the one requiring operators to be well-mannered and another forbidding them to send "angry or impertinent messages" to other operators.[10]

Meanwhile, three other companies were being formed to connect the trunk line with the North and the West. A group of stagecoach and express company men started building the New York, Albany & Buffalo Telegraph Company along the Erie Canal. In New England Smith and others set up the New York & Boston Magnetic Telegraph Association. And in June Kendall contracted with Irish immigrant Henry O'Rielly to build west through Pennsylvania. O'Rielly was obligated to connect his line with the trunk line (presumably at Philadelphia) by December. To carry out the contract he organized the Atlantic, Lake & Mississippi Company. In order to control the companies the patentees demanded half of the stock, but in the case of the O'Rielly line, they settled for a quarter of the stock and wrote controls into the contract.[11]

The formation of the companies brought Kendall into regular contact with two New Englanders with whom he had much in common. Samuel F. B. Morse, who was two years younger than Kendall, had been born in Charleston, Massachusetts, only thirty-five miles from Dunstable. His father was the

9. Thompson, *Wiring*, 41–44.

10. Ibid., 43–44; "Articles of Agreement and Association, Constituting the Magnetic Telegraph Company . . . May 15, 1845," ibid., 446–51.

11. Ibid., 57–63, 70–73, 452.

Reverend Jedidiah Morse, who had written the popular geography book that had once so enthralled Kendall. Both Morse and Kendall were brought up as Congregationalists, were educated at private academies and colleges, and eventually became Jackson men.

But there the similarities ceased. Morse came from more comfortable circumstances than Kendall. Much weaker and gentler than Kendall, he was born to say yes and be sorry, Kendall to say no and be glad. Morse hated the contentious world of business, the world in which Kendall yearned to succeed. Morse was also far more cultivated. Famous as an artist as well as an inventor, he traveled in the company of refined men such as James Fenimore Cooper and painters Asher Durand and Henry Inman. Never as dedicated to the Jackson party as Kendall, Morse once made an unsuccessful foray into politics as nativist candidate for mayor of New York.[12]

Kendall had more in common with Francis O. J. Smith. They both came from towns near the Massachusetts–New Hampshire border, went to nearby academies, studied law, edited Jackson newspapers, built state Jacksonian organizations, and were involved in land speculation. But they differed in character, for Kendall was moral, honest, and unpretentious, while Smith was often immoral, dishonest, and showy. He had built a mansion outside of Portland, Maine, where he held balls and rode in a carriage with a pair of blood grays and a black coachman. Often called "Fog" because of his initials, Smith was soon the dominant telegraph man in New England.[13]

The first dispute with Smith arose over selling the telegraph to the government. Kendall preferred to sell because he had seen the advantages of a national system when he was postmaster general. Smith, however, believed that they could get four or five times as much privately. "Whoever can lessen the power . . . of government," he told Kendall, "confers a blessing upon the people." He had "no patriotism" for the government and "no . . . love for . . . the 'dear people.'"[14]

Kendall's reply showed that he was no democratic zealot and certainly no enemy of capitalism. He told Smith soothingly that he had no "special love for the people" either and sought only "to make the most money in the shortest time that we can honestly." He added, however, that it might be better to take less from the government immediately than to wait for private buyers.

---

12. Mabee, *American Leonardo;* Paul J. Staiti, *Samuel F. B. Morse* (Cambridge, Eng., 1989).

13. Gaffney, "Maine's Mr. Smith"; Thompson, *Wiring,* 57–58.

14. Smith to Kendall, 6 Aug. 1845, Smith Papers, Maine Historical Society.

There was always the risk, he pointed out, that someone else might invent a better telegraph or that popular sentiment might turn against the Morse device. The *"certainty"* of getting "wealth" was better than years of "difficulties and perplexities." Tell me what you want for your quarter share, he told Smith expansively, "$100,000, $200,000, $250,000," and we will try to get a proportionate price from the government. Thus two prominent Jacksonians spoke for a generation of capitalists.[15]

The concept of a federal telegraph had considerable support. The *Philadelphia Enquirer* reported public opinion "decidedly" in favor of the idea as the only way to guarantee "regularity" and low rates. Others went further. The *National Intelligencer* wanted the telegraph "in the hands of the Government, and independent of any private interests." A "merchant" writing in the *New York Courier and Enquirer* was aghast at the thought that a Wall Street firm might gain control of the telegraph. The *New York Journal of Commerce*, however, considered the telegraph too expensive and too unreliable to justify government ownership.[16]

The decision rested with a traditional laissez-faire Democratic administration. Kendall approached Polk but got no encouragement. Postmaster General Cave Johnson was more ambivalent. In his 1845 annual report he recommended government ownership as a way to prevent speculation and to avoid paying "exorbitant prices" to the monopolistic railroads, but he also warned that the cost of the telegraph might be too high. Assuming that Johnson was dickering to get the telegraph cheaply, Kendall considered reducing the price in return for 50 percent of the net income. That would "give us millions of dollars," he told Smith. He tried out the plan with the chairmen of both of the Post Office committees with no success. The Mexican War offered one last chance, but a Senate bill for a telegraph from Washington to New Orleans ran afoul of John C. Calhoun and other extreme states' righters. All hope ended in December 1846 when the government leased the Baltimore line to private interests. It was eventually sold to the Magnetic Company.[17]

Fortunately for Kendall the private lines were flourishing. By the summer of 1846 his dream of a telegraph hub in New York had been realized, as the

15. Kendall to Smith, 12 Aug. 1845, ibid.

16. *Intelligencer,* 25 Oct. 1845 (quotations), 18 June 1846; *New York Journal of Commerce,* cited in Hochfelder, "Taming the Lightning," 275.

17. "Report of the Postmaster General," 1 Dec. 1845, *Congressional Globe,* 29th Cong., 1st sess., app., 19–22; Kendall to Smith, 31 Aug., 25 Nov., 12 Dec. 1845, 12 Feb., 8 May 1846, Smith Papers, Maine Historical Society; Thompson, *Wiring,* 34.

metropolis was linked with Boston, Buffalo, and Washington. In addition Smith was now building his own line from Buffalo along the Great Lakes, and O'Rielly had worked west from Lancaster, Pennsylvania, well beyond Harrisburg. He did not, however, connect Lancaster with the trunk line at Philadelphia until September, nine months after the December deadline. O'Rielly was not entirely at fault, but Smith, sensing an opportunity to get rid of a competitor, jumped on the omission as a reason for taking the patent away from the Irishman.[18]

Kendall had his own reasons for checking O'Rielly, for the two had entirely different visions for the telegraph. O'Rielly dreamed of many independent lines run by "capitalists" of the West. There, he said, "*Yankee* enterprise [would be] quickened by the energies of a *newer* country." To accomplish this he started dividing the Atlantic, Lake & Mississippi Company into subcompanies. Kendall held to his vision of a monopolistic system running out of New York under the control of the Magnetic Company. There was only "one *sine qua non*," he told Morse, and that was "*the unity of the lines*." He believed that O'Rielly's subdivisions violated the contract, which restricted him to setting up "a line," not "lines," under the "terms and conditions" of the Magnetic Company. After fighting banking and railroad monopolies, Kendall was now struggling to create one in the telegraph business.[19]

He was willing to negotiate with O'Rielly, but Smith kept insisting that they enforce the December deadline. Even Kendall lost patience when O'Rielly started issuing stock without asking permission from the Morse patentees. On November 4 Kendall and Smith canceled O'Rielly's contract, but O'Rielly was so popular that he felt strong enough to go ahead anyway. Westerners liked his headlong enthusiasm and believed his charges that Kendall and Smith were unscrupulous eastern promoters. Henry R. Selden, president of O'Rielly's original company, said that Kendall "must be taught that

18. For a short time O'Rielly thought that he had satisfied the contract, because he had been told that the trunk line might run through Lancaster rather than Philadelphia. Thompson, *Wiring*, 43, 50, 61, 66, 75–76, 81–83.

19. Kendall to O'Rielly, 11, 15 Nov. 1845, O'Rielly to Smith, 29 Dec. 1845 ("capitalists"), Alfred Vail Papers, Smithsonian Institution Archives; O'Rielly to Kendall, 17 Aug. 1845 ("Yankee"), Kendall to O'Rielly, 12 July 1845, Henry O'Rielly Papers, Historical Society of Pennsylvania; Kendall to Morse, 19 Feb. 1847, Western Union Collection ("one sine"); Thompson, *Wiring*, 73–75; "The O'Rielly Contract," 13 June 1845, ibid., 452–53 ("a line"); Hochfelder, "Taming the Lightning," 177.

we are not to be made use of, like cattle, to launch his ship." A telegraph war seemed likely.[20]

Kendall was doing better in the South. His experience with the express mail had convinced him that a telegraph line to New Orleans could be extremely profitable. Having failed to get the government to build the line, he decided to build it himself. By November 1846 he had organized the Washington & New Orleans Telegraph Company and was seeking rights-of-way along the railroad tracks in Virginia. The work moved ahead rapidly but at some cost to Kendall, who was often sick and felt that he was bearing "the whole weight" of the project. When the Virginia legislature passed a bill to incorporate the company in March 1847, Morse gave him full credit for the "glorious triumph."[21]

Kendall then tried to get the Virginia Board of Public Works to invest in the project. Painting a bright future for the telegraph, he boasted that the Magnetic Telegraph Company was "realizing over 30 per cent on [its] investment." When the board refused, Kendall warned that "the business men of Richmond better *give* the $2,000 than be without the telegraph another year." The money was soon raised, and the railroads were more generous with rights-of-way than in the North. With this kind of support all along the way, the Washington & New Orleans was expected to reach its destination in another year.[22]

By the spring of 1847 Kendall was feeling "overwhelmed" by his responsibilities. He was president of the Magnetic Company, treasurer of the Washington & New Orleans, and Morse's agent in dealing with a growing number of other lines. The Magnetic presidency was the most troublesome. He was responsible for everything from raising money to buying posts and coping with

20. Thompson, *Wiring,* 83–89; Kendall to O'Rielly, 2 Sept. 1846, Francis O. J. Smith Papers, New York Public Library; Kendall to O'Rielly, 29 Sept. 1846, Henry O'Rielly Papers, New-York Historical Society; Kendall to O'Rielly, 12 Oct. 1846, O'Rielly to Kendall, 13 Oct. 1846, Kendall and Smith to O'Rielly, 4 Nov. 1846, Vail Papers; H. R. Selden to S. L. Selden, O'Rielly Papers, New-York Historical Society, quoted in Thompson, *Wiring,* 88n.

21. Thompson, *Wiring,* 139–42. Kendall to Alfred Vail, 26 Nov. 1846, 11 Jan. 1847, Morse to Alfred Vail, 20 Jan., 27 Mar. 1847, Vail Papers.

22. Kendall to Morse, 1, 26 Apr. 1847, Western Union Collection; Kendall, Agent, to J. Brown Jr., 2d Auditor, Washington, 25 Mar., 27 Apr. 1847, Board of Public Works (RG 57) Internal Improvements Companies, BWP-198, Accession #30030, Washington and New Orleans Telegraph Company, Box 249, ALS, State Records Collection, Archives Research Services, Library of Virginia, Richmond; Thompson, *Wiring,* 142–43.

vandalism, and a small group including Alfred Vail was finding fault with his work, especially his failure to spend time in New York. There was some justification for the criticism, but the company lacked the funds to subsidize much traveling or even pay Kendall's salary. After ten months he had received only $900 of his $2,250 annual stipend.[23]

Smith posed another problem. With his growing telegraph empire, he often put his own interests ahead of those of the other patentees. Since he owned one-fourth of the patent, he could make it difficult for Morse to sell the rights. To clear the air Kendall offered to divide control of the patent by drawing a line running east and west along the southern boundary of New York, through the middle of Ohio and the southern part of Indiana and Illinois. Smith would control the sale of patent rights north of the line and Morse and Vail south of it. (By this time Morse had bought out Gale and now owned five-eighths of the patent, Vail one-eighth.) Morse and Vail would waive all future rights to stock in companies north of the line, while Smith would give up rights in those to the south. To accomplish this and maintain the one-to-three ratio between Smith's holdings and those of Morse and Vail, the two sides would have to exchange shares of stock. On June 22, 1847, the patentees accepted the proposal and signed an agreement. If properly carried out, it offered the best way to maintain the Morse monopoly with the least amount of bickering.[24]

A few days later Kendall stepped down as president of the Magnetic Company. He was giving up a $2,250 salary, but Morse and Vail had made his resignation possible by rewriting his contract. The original agreement, giving Kendall 10 percent of the proceeds from the sale of the patent, had been based on the assumption that there would be a large cash payment from the government. When that fell through and it became clear that the rights would be sold entirely for shares of stock in private companies, Kendall had to accept his 10 percent in stock that paid uncertain dividends. To make up for the uncertainty, Morse and Vail agreed to pay him 10 percent of cash income and 50 percent of all stock received. Since Morse and Vail had already received stock

23. Kendall to John, 7 Feb. 1847 (quotation); George Vail to Alfred Vail, 27 Oct. 1845, 13 Aug. 1846, Kendall to George Vail, 9 Oct. 1846, Vail Papers; Kendall to Smith, 12 Feb., 8 June, 26 July 1846, Smith Papers, Maine Historical Society.

24. Kendall to Morse, 9 Mar. 1847, Western Union Collection; Kendall to Smith, 10 May 1847, Smith Papers, Maine Historical Society; Morse to Alfred Vail, 22 June 1847, Vail Papers; Thompson, *Wiring*, 101–3.

with a par value of $200,000, the new arrangement was said to have given Kendall "the largest interest in the Morse patent."[25]

Hoping that they had solved the problems in their own ranks, Morse and Kendall now addressed the challenges from rival entrepreneurs armed with other telegraphic devices. They adopted a four-pronged strategy. They would strengthen their patent, win privileges in state legislatures, sue their rivals, and appeal democratically to an American public that was now becoming interested in the telegraph. Between 1846 and 1848 they twice rewrote the original patent and won a second patent to cover the receiving magnet. They had had success in the Virginia legislature, but they had failed to win an injunction against O'Rielly in the federal district court of Pennsylvania. To win public backing, Kendall published a series of articles in the *Washington Union* designed to rebut the claims of other systems and dispel false ideas such as the notion that lightning bolts might run along the wires and "explode through the body of the operator."[26]

In the fall of 1847 the telegraph war in the West began in earnest when O'Rielly completed lines to the Great Lakes and down the Ohio River. Smith was worried about the future of his own western lines, and Kendall was afraid that O'Rielly's People's Company, already in Louisville, would move on to New Orleans and get there before the Washington & New Orleans. Ignoring the territorial agreement, Kendall and Smith joined forces to form a rival company, the New Orleans & Ohio, which would connect Pittsburgh with New Orleans by way of Cincinnati and Louisville. Early in December the two men started down the Ohio River for Louisville and soon encountered the worst flood in eighteen years. The trip was a wild one as the steamboat was swept along on the crest of the floodwaters. On reaching Louisville, the captain spent an hour just mooring the boat. Not until midnight were Kendall and Smith safely settled in "a comfortable [hotel] room with a blazing fire."[27]

Louisville was in enemy hands. South of the city the People's Company

25. There was one exception. Kendall got only 10 percent of the stock from the profitable New York, Albany & Buffalo. Kendall to Thomas M. Clark, 14 June 1847, Kendall Papers, LC; Kendall to Morse, 5 Aug. 1845, "Agreement between S. F. B. Morse and Amos Kendall" (including 1846 agreement), 21 June 1848, Western Union Collection; James D. Reid, *The Telegraph in America and Morse Memorial* (New York, 1879), 320 (quotation); Thompson, *Wiring*, 44.

26. Hochfelder, "Taming the Lightning," 168, 180–84; *Washington Union*, 2, 5, 17, 22, 25, 31 Aug. 1847; Swisher, *History of the Supreme Court*, 488–89.

27. Thompson, *Wiring*, 145–49; Kendall to Alfred Vail, 29 Nov. 1847, Vail Papers; Kendall to John, 28 Dec. 1847.

was outstripping the New Orleans & Ohio in a race to see which would be first to reach Nashville. Inside the city handbills and newspaper articles were praising O'Rielly and charging the Morse interest with "calumny and fraud." When Kendall and Smith set up a meeting to explain their case, hardly anyone came. O'Rielly was claiming the right to use the Morse patent on all his lines except the one to New Orleans, and for that one he had a new device, called the Columbian, which supposedly did not infringe on the Morse patent.[28]

To counteract these claims Kendall published an article in the *Louisville Daily Journal* just before Christmas. As in his many writings on the BUS, he aimed his remarks at common people and accused his opponent of corrupt practices. O'Rielly, he said, was plotting "to *accomplish a stupendous speculation* . . . [to] establish a . . . monopoly over the entire Western country." Turning to his main concern, he argued that O'Rielly had violated his contract by forming more than one company and operating independent of the Magnetic Company. "It was the obvious intention" of the Morse patentees and the entire country, he wrote, that the telegraph, like the post office, should be "under one management." There could be but "*one line* . . . one board of trustees," for "UNITY [was] stamped upon [the] contract." He warned that if O'Rielly had his way, there would be five companies between St. Louis and Boston, thus increasing the number of officers and operators, raising rates, and making it impossible to fix blame for garbled or lost messages. With this nice balance of contract law, capitalistic efficiency, and moral responsibility Kendall was denouncing O'Rielly's monopoly and making the case for his own.[29]

Unable to count on western public opinion, Kendall turned to state legislatures and federal courts. During their four weeks in Louisville he and Smith laid the groundwork for the incorporation of their company in Kentucky and for a court injunction against O'Rielly's use of the new device. After Smith returned home, Kendall moved on to Nashville, Tennessee. His company was already chartered in the state, but he wanted some way to keep O'Rielly's company out. On January 14, 1848, he was satisfied when a bill was passed prohibiting the incorporation of any telegraph company that encroached on a federal patent. In Frankfort later in the month, he found the Kentucky legislature poised to incorporate his company. The act was passed soon after he left. Looking ahead to the pending patent case, he made a point of dining with

28. Thompson, *Wiring*, 128n, 149–50; Kendall, *Morse's Telegraph and the O'Rielly Contract* (Louisville, 1848).

29. Kendall to Morse, 9 Dec. 1847, Western Union Collection; Kendall, *Morse's Telegraph*.

federal district judge Thomas B. Monroe, who was likely to be the presiding judge.[30]

Late in the summer Kendall, Morse, and O'Rielly arrived in Frankfort for the trial, which as expected had been assigned to Monroe. Morse was accompanied by his young new wife, Sarah, who was both speech and hearing impaired. The plucky young bride, who was working hard to improve her speech, made a deep impression on Kendall and revived his interest in the deaf. As an old Kentucky hand Kendall was in his element. At the Weisiger Hotel, where they were all staying, the proprietor was none other than Thomas Theobald, who had once rented him a room in Georgetown. When another old acquaintance, governor-elect John J. Crittenden, came by, Kendall was the one to make the introductions. But not everyone was favorably impressed. Henry Clay's friend Thomas B. Stevenson reported that "the expression of [Kendall's] countenance excites the idea of a famished wolf. It makes one hungry just to look at his lean, lank jaws, his restless, eager eyes, and his voracious hooked nose."[31]

Kendall was also in his element in court, for it was obvious that he knew the judge. On one occasion O'Rielly wondered out loud "how far [Monroe had] made up his mind under the benevolent efforts of Kendall." The trial, which was held in the judge's chambers between ten in the morning and three in the afternoon, attracted great public attention. It was, said the *Philadelphia American,* "one of the most important lawsuits contended for in the United States." Morse's lawyers made a strong argument against O'Rielly's Columbian telegraph and would probably have won the case even without Kendall's connection with the judge. In early September Monroe gave a sweeping ruling that O'Rielly was not to use his new telegraph device in Kentucky.[32]

Within a few months, however, O'Rielly had installed another new telegraph, named for its inventor, Alexander Bain. Kendall won a temporary injunction against its use in Tennessee in July 1849, but a similar suit in Kentucky was postponed until October. During the summer Kendall looked for ways to counter the strategy of O'Rielly's new lawyer, Salmon P. Chase of Ohio. Chase was undermining Morse's credibility by describing the ways in which

30. Kendall to Alfred Vail, 13, 14 Jan. 1848, Vail Papers; Kendall to Jane Kendall, 4 Feb. 1848, in *Autobiography,* 534–35; Thompson, *Wiring,* 153–54.

31. Mabee, *American Leonardo,* 304–7; Stevenson to Clay, 29 Aug. 1848, Henry Clay Papers, LC, quoted in Remini, *Henry Clay,* 278.

32. Swisher, *History of the Supreme Court,* 489–90 ("how"); Mabee, *American Leonardo,* 307–8 ("one").

he had benefited from the work of Joseph Henry, secretary of the Smithsonian Institution, and Dr. Charles T. Jackson of Boston. Morse should have admitted his debt, especially the role of Henry in long-distance telegraphy, but he played into Chase's hands by refusing to make any concessions.[33]

On the first day of the trial Kendall made a speech in which he made up for Morse's unfortunate remarks, and from then on the trial went Morse's way. Judge Monroe, who was again presiding, upheld the Morse patent against all devices. There were certain qualifications that would send the case on to the Supreme Court, but even so it was a bad setback for O'Rielly, who would now find it almost impossible to raise money. Kendall, who often overreacted to success and failure, was so enthused by the verdict that he apologized to Morse for going easy on Jackson and promised to "crucify" him before the public. After almost five years in the telegraph business Kendall seemed to hold the upper hand.[34]

The same five years had brought great changes in Kendall's private affairs. Early in 1845, before he threw in his lot with Morse, he and Jane had given up any thought of a country home and had returned to a rented place in the city. Kendall's sole source of income was the claims agency, and it was not doing very well. The main family concern was for the three older children. Mary Anne and Daniel Gold were living in the unfinished farmhouse while Daniel held a minor government position. Kendall was trying to find twenty-two-year-old William a job in the Treasury Department. Adela and Frederick Culver were still in Kentucky. The younger children—teenagers Jeannie and John and two little girls, Fannie and Marion—were in the background.

The claims agency continued to struggle. Early in 1845 two important clients, Alfred and Arthur Benson of New York, lost their government contract to transport naval supplies and emigrants to the Pacific coast. When Kendall met them in New York to discuss the matter, they were joined by Mormon leader Samuel Brannan, who needed help in taking a shipload of members to California. Kendall brokered a deal in which he would keep the Polk administration from interfering with the migration, and the Mormons would give him

33. Thompson, *Wiring*, 156–57, 191; Swisher, *History of the Supreme Court*, 491–94; Kendall to Morse, 6 Dec. 1849, Morse Papers; Hochfelder, "Taming the Lightning," 191–99.

34. Kendall to Morse, 20, 22 Oct., 12 Nov. 1849, Morse Papers; Kendall to John, 25 Oct. 1849; Swisher, *History of the Supreme Court*, 494–95. Two years later Kendall published a pamphlet ridiculing Jackson. Kendall, *Morse's Patent. Full Exposure of Dr. Charles T. Jackson's Pretensions to the Invention of the American Electro Magnetic Telegraph* (Washington, 1852), American Antiquarian Society.

and the Bensons half of any land they might acquire in California. On February 4, 1846, the ship left for California without incident.[35]

Kendall did other favors for the Mormons. In June 1846 he and a Mormon agent called on President Polk to get permission for a battalion of five hundred Mormon soldiers to march to California. Polk gave permission but with the understanding that the men would march with U.S. forces, not on their own. The president wanted to avoid antagonizing the Californians, who feared a Mormon invasion and would not take kindly to an independent army. But despite these services, Kendall and the Bensons received no land. The agency had its only real success when the government agreed to give the major client, the western Cherokees, a share of the $5 million granted to the whole tribe. Even then Kendall received no immediate payment, because there was no specific provision for an agent's fee.[36]

Other family events had been more traumatic. In August 1845 Kendall was in New York on telegraph business when the news came that William had been killed in Washington. Just before dusk on August 18 he had been present when his friend Josiah Bailey got into a fistfight with William Rufus Elliott. A short time later he and Bailey ran into Elliott on Pennsylvania Avenue, where he was waiting for them armed with an iron cane and a revolver. Young Kendall, who was unarmed, tried to wrestle the cane away from Elliott but was shot to death in the scuffle. The aftermath was distasteful and long drawn out. Elliott was the brother-in-law of Kendall's adversary, Blair's partner John C. Rives, and there were rumors, later disproved, that William and Bailey had been carousing with questionable women. The case went to a grand jury and dragged on for five months until Elliott was discharged on grounds of self-defense.

The family horrors were not over. In December 1845 Amos and Jane received word from Missouri, where the Kyles had moved, that Jane's mother and brother had been burned to death as they tried to save stacks of grain from a wind-blown prairie fire. Three years later, in January 1849, Daniel Gold died,

35. Will Bagley, ed., *Scoundrel's Tale: The Samuel Brannan Papers* (Spokane, 1999), 76–83, 105–8, 119–25; Kendall to Polk, 8 June 1845, Polk Papers; Kendall to Bancroft, 10, 25 Nov. 1845, Bancroft Papers; Bernard De Voto, *The Year of Decision 1846* (Boston, 1942), 235–37, 494–95.

36. James K. Polk, *The Diary of James K. Polk during His Presidency, 1845 to 1849*, ed. Milo M. Quaife (Chicago, 1910), 1:445–46, 449–50; De Voto, *Year of Decision*, 237–42; S. C. Stambaugh, Amos Kendall, George W. Paschall, and M. St. Clair Clarke, *A Faithful History of the Cherokee Tribe of Indians* (Washington, 1846), Kendall Papers, LC. The Western Cherokees finally paid Kendall's estate $25,000 in 1880. J. M. Bryan, agreement with Kendall estate, June 1, 1880, ibid.

leaving Mary Anne a widow with two children. Kendall was accustomed to untimely death. His mother and father had lost five children, and he and his two wives had now lost seven. His wife Mary had died in 1823, and only recently his youngest child, Marion, had come close to dying. But these latest deaths were unusually painful, especially the first three, which were so sudden and violent. Though Kendall had learned to be resigned to the will of God, he believed that his "calamities" were as great as those of Job.[37]

Amidst it all the younger children had been establishing their identities. The change began in the fall of 1846 when Jeannie, seventeen, and John, thirteen, were sent off to Dickinson College in Carlisle, Pennsylvania. It proved to be an ideal place for the tall, intelligent, strong-willed Jeannie, but since John was so young, his father had to arrange for him to board with one of the professors. The plan worked well. Fat, red-faced William "Bully" Allen kept a close eye on John, bought him a pair of green spectacles, provided him with spending money, and sent his father encouraging reports.[38]

After the death of William it seems strange that Kendall would part with his only remaining son at such a young age. He did it because he remembered his own education and because he wanted to prepare John to carry on when he was gone. He tried to maintain some control over the boy by sending him regular letters that John was told to bind in a book. "*Knowledge,*" he wrote in the first, "can not fail to make you more respected, more powerful." With it John could become an "orator, statesman, philosopher or divine," callings that Kendall had found beyond his own reach. In his second letter he sent the sober message that John must not be "elated by riches or discouraged by privation." There was "nothing more ridiculous than for men to assume a superiority over their fellow men because they have *money.*" It was the mind that made the difference. Kendall had every right to warn against discouragement, for he had overcome many privations, but the advice about riches was hypocritical.[39]

The letters continued for many years. He corrected his son's spelling, laid

37. French, *Witness*, 178–79; *Washington Daily Union*, 18 Aug. 1845; Kendall to ———, 21 Aug. 1845, Throop and Martin Family Papers, Manuscript Division, Department of Rare Books and Special Collections, Princeton University Library; Kendall to Smith, 19, 25 Aug., 15 Dec. 1845 (quotation), Smith Papers, Maine Historical Society; Kendall to Van Buren, 13 Oct. 1844, Van Buren Papers; ——— to James Kyle, 28 Nov. 1845, Kendall to Alex Kyle, 12 Dec. 1845, in *Autobiography*, 531.

38. Kendall to John, 6 Nov. 1846, 18 Apr. 1847; Robert Emery, President of Dickinson College, "Report on J. Kendall," 27 Nov. 1846, Kendall Papers, Dartmouth College Library.

39. Kendall to John, 25 Oct., 6 Nov. 1846.

down rules of capitalization, warned him not to repeat words, and told him to keep his sentences short, a rule he himself did not always follow. He used the Ohio River flood to draw a moral lesson. It is said, he wrote, that half of the world does not know how the other half lives, but this time "misery was driven from her house and the world saw itself as it is." He concluded on a more typically materialistic note that "the loss of property compared to the wealth of the West, [was] but as the humblest rill which contributed to the raging flood."[40]

Both Jeannie and John were on hand in July 1849 when Kendall found time between court trials to return to Dartmouth for a class reunion. Jeannie came up from Washington with her father. John came over from Keene, New Hampshire, where he was studying with Joseph Perry, no longer at the Post Office. John would enter Dartmouth in the fall. After staying up most of the night waiting for a train, Kendall arrived late, tired, and harried, but his cares vanished when he saw so many of his old friends among the fourteen returning classmates. Of the eight surviving members of the Gymnasion Adelphon, six were at the reunion, including the two that he most admired, Daniel Poor and Perry. Poor was something of a celebrity; he had just returned from thirty-two years in Ceylon and India and was touring the country, raising funds for his missions.[41]

Kendall, who cared about his position in the class, was treated with the respect that he craved. He was asked to preside over part of the meeting and at commencement was awarded the honorary degree of doctor of laws. The biography that he submitted for a class publication was revealing: a third of the text concerned his family; another third his life in Kentucky; and most of the rest his work as journalist and telegraph agent. Curiously, he said almost nothing about his twelve years in the government and mentioned Andrew Jackson only once. Perhaps he felt a need to preserve party secrets, perhaps he feared reviving old stories in which he had been ridiculed, perhaps he hated to remind his friends that he was now excluded from party councils. The same reticence about party politics can be seen in his often autobiographical letters to John. The reluctance to write about Jacksonian politics may also have contributed to his continuing failure to complete his life of the Old Hero.[42]

40. Kendall to John, 20 Nov. 1846, 28 Dec. 1847 (quotation). There are 127 letters from Kendall to John.

41. Kendall to Alfred Vail, 11 July 1849, Vail Papers; Kendall to Morse, 25 July 1849, Morse Papers; Kendall to John, 22 Apr., 15 July 1849; Class of 1811, *Minutes of Their Meeting in 1849*.

42. Class of 1811, *Minutes of Their Meeting in 1849*.

After the reunion, Kendall left Jeannie and John in Dunstable with their cousins, aunts, and uncles and returned home. He and Jane spent the rest of the summer preparing for a long-awaited change—the move back to Kendall Green. For several years they had been working on the farmhouse, enlarging the first floor and adding a second. When they moved in during the fall, the roof was still not finished, and they suffered some inconvenience during several heavy rainstorms. The renovation was also costing more than Kendall had planned, and he felt continually "pressed" for funds. He was very much annoyed when John bought a rocking chair, a stove, and a carpet for his college room. These items, he wrote sternly, were entirely "unnecessary." They may have made John "comfortable," but they made his father "uncomfortable."[43]

The five years since 1845 had been bittersweet. Kendall had lost a son, a son-in-law, a mother-in-law, and a nephew, all long before their time. Yet he had prospered. He had returned in triumph to Kentucky and Dartmouth and had a son following in his footsteps. He had moved into the farmhouse that he had been talking about ever since the Court War. He had established himself successfully as Morse's agent. After toying with the idea of government ownership, he had defended his vision of a Morse telegraph monopoly against the freewheeling independent capitalism of Henry O'Rielly. It is not too much to say that the first five years of the telegraph industry had been Kendall years.

43. Kendall to John, 16 Aug., 5 Sept. (quotation), 10 Nov. 1849.

# 18

## TELEGRAPH CONSOLIDATION

Kendall may have won the first round of the telegraph wars, but the industry was evolving too rapidly to allow any time for complacency. During the Kendall phase the length of wire in operation rose from 40 miles to 12,000 miles; the number would double in the next two years and would reach 84,000 miles by the end of the Civil War. The amount of money available for rival lines was also about to explode. Capital accounts in banks, which had hovered around $200 million since 1845, would double in the 1850s. Even more threatening was the emergence of new telegraph instruments. In January 1850, 2,000 of the 12,000 miles of wire belonged to companies using rival devices; two years later the number was 5,000 out of 23,000. It would be hard to turn Kendall's dream of Morse "UNITY" into reality.[1]

The greatest immediate challenge, however, was not growth but the lack of harmony in the Morse ranks. In the North, Kendall and F. O. J. Smith were constantly at each other's throats. As Kendall saw it, Smith was violating the territorial agreement by setting up rival lines, conveying patent rights unilaterally, and refusing to give Morse and Vail stock to which they were entitled. By the fall of 1849 Kendall and Smith were exchanging harsh, sometimes childish letters even worse than the Kendall-Blair correspondence in 1842. In one instance Kendall said that he had long "ceased to expect . . . justice or fair dealing" from Smith, to which the latter replied sanctimoniously that someday Kendall would "regret" such a statement.[2]

The fighting became public in April 1850 when Kendall criticized the way Smith was running the Boston & Portland, Maine, line, in which Morse and Vail had a small interest. Because of its location the line controlled the flow of

---

1. Thompson, *Wiring*, 241, 408; *Statistical History*, 625.
2. Kendall to Morse and Alfred Vail, 8 Sept. 1849, Morse Papers; Kendall to Smith, 10, 22, 30 (quotation) Nov., Smith to Kendall, 10 Dec. 1849, Smith Papers, Maine Historical Society.

news from Europe, which arrived by ship at Halifax, Nova Scotia. Once telegraph lines were completed between Halifax and Portland in the fall of 1849,
the news could go smoothly from Halifax to New York, but only if Smith let
it pass along his line. Smith's monopoly became an issue when competition
grew between a Boston newsagent who worked for Smith and Daniel H.
Craig of the New York Associated Press. To help his agent, Smith refused to
transmit Craig's messages.[3]

Kendall protested that Smith had no right to stop messages over "legitimate Morse lines" just to punish Craig. The telegraph should be "the servant
of the public and not its master." He warned Smith that his behavior could
backfire and help "the pirates" who were trying to steal Morse's patent. Furious at being lectured to, Smith attacked Kendall for his "dictation" and threatened to go after him in a "war to the knife and the knife to the hilt." The
controversy was ended by a strange combination of events. The telegraph lines
north of Portland—all Morse lines—sided with Kendall and Craig by giving
Craig priority in sending news from Halifax to Portland. There it was put on
a waiting express train for Boston. On June 22 the train became unnecessary
when O'Rielly completed construction of a telegraph line from Portland to
Boston.[4]

After another year of jousting, Morse and Kendall decided to take Smith
to court in New York. In the winter of 1851–52 Morse's lawyers drew up a six-
hundred-page bill in chancery to enjoin Smith from doing any further harm
to the interests of Morse and Vail. One of the more interesting charges was
that Smith had arbitrarily given O'Rielly the right to use the Morse patent in
the upper part of the Old Northwest. Smith challenged all allegations and
prepared his own countersuit. Fully expecting to win the case, Kendall sent
Smith a nasty letter, saying that the court would "judge" him for the "mischief"
he had done. At the start of the trial in the late fall of 1852 he told the court
that Smith's "perverse, grasping and fraudulent conduct" had cost Morse
thousands of dollars. But in spite of the rhetoric and the mass of detail, Kendall lost the case. He and Smith would have to coexist.[5]

3. Thompson, *Wiring*, 226–39.

4. Kendall to Smith, 1 Apr. 1850 ("legitimate"), Smith to Kendall, 10 Apr. 1850 ("dictation"),
Kendall to *New York Globe*, 18 Apr. 1850, Smith Papers, Maine Historical Society; Kendall to
Morse, 22 Apr. ("war"), 28 July 1850, Morse Papers; Thompson, *Wiring*, 236–37.

5. Kendall to Smith, 30 Jan. 1852, Smith Papers, Maine Historical Society; Kendall to Alfred
Vail, 9 Dec. 1851, Vail Papers; *Samuel F. B. Morse and Alfred Vail against Francis O. J. Smith.
Affidavit of Amos Kendall on part of Plaintiff* (New York, 1852); Thompson, *Wiring*, 190–91.

Kendall's hopes for unity were also being disappointed in the South. The Washington & New Orleans Company reached New Orleans in July 1848 but the line was so badly built that the company immediately began losing money. As treasurer, Kendall was blamed for the losses and was attacked by the same sort of cabal that had plagued him in the Magnetic Company. At the annual meeting in July 1849 southern dissidents took advantage of his absence to cut his salary and elect Elam Alexander of Georgia president.[6]

The problems of the Washington & New Orleans were tied in with those of the other two lines to the South, Morse's New Orleans & Ohio, and O'Rielly's People's Telegraph, both of which had finally reached the Crescent City. The rivalry among the three lines became so intense that the only solution seemed to be consolidation. In 1851 and 1852 Kendall took two trips to Louisville to try to get the two Morse lines to divide up the business. When this failed, the New Orleans & Ohio merged with its enemy, the People's Company. After the second meeting, Kendall had to rush back to Washington and defend his actions at a critical meeting of the Washington & New Orleans.[7]

For a man who was frail and in his sixties, these trips to Kentucky—this was the tenth in five years—were wearing, but he put up with them with surprising grace. In a letter to Jane in November 1851, he described good-naturedly an all-night stagecoach ride from Cumberland, Maryland, to Wheeling, Virginia. It was, he said, "the most uncomfortable night I ever spent." As the coach traveled along the plank road, it "seemed to have no more spring than a wagon; the seat was a bad one; it was very cold; and any relief by changing position out of the question." All of a sudden one of the doors flew open and Kendall's hat blew out. Only by shouting "lustily" could he get the driver to stop. As the driver sat sullenly, "muttering curses," Kendall leaped out in the rain and "recovered [his] hat by a run of some two hundred yards."[8]

Alfred Vail did not attend the crucial Washington & New Orleans meeting, but if he had, he would have voted against Kendall. After being Morse's right-hand man in the early years, Vail had to stand by and watch Kendall usurp his position. Jealous of Kendall's rapid rise, he had joined the anti-Kendall group in the Magnetic Company and later in the Washington & New

6. George Wood to Alfred Vail, 9 July 1949, Kendall to Alfred Vail, 11 July 1849, 7 July 1851, Vail Papers.

7. Kendall to Morse, 1 Dec. 1851, Morse Papers; Kendall to Alfred Vail, 13 Oct. 1851, 22 June, 1 July 1852, Kendall to Alfred and George Vail, 7 June 1852, Vail Papers; Thompson, *Wiring*, 197; Kendall to Morse, 5 Nov. 1852, Western Union Collection.

8. Kendall to Jane Kendall, 15 Nov. 1851, in *Autobiography*, 544–45.

Orleans. He called Kendall "a deep revengeful man [who would] harbour a grudge until he [could] make you feel it," and accused him of "kick[ing] up a row" with Alexander because he would not "submit to [Kendall's] dictation." Vail thought Kendall was overrated and took great delight in exposing his mistakes.[9]

The conflicts continued for the next two years and widened to include Benjamin B. French, who in 1847 had replaced Kendall as president of the Magnetic Company. French had lost the office in 1850 when Kendall failed to support him but managed to be elected treasurer in 1853. That same year Alexander finally outmaneuvered Kendall and pushed him out as treasurer of the Washington & New Orleans. But a year later Kendall collected enough proxies to oust both Alexander and French and have himself and his nephew John E. Kendall elected president and treasurer of both companies. French wrote angrily that he had "never witnessed a meaner transaction in [his] life."[10]

Amidst the infighting Kendall and Morse were hoping for a final, unambiguous Supreme Court decision upholding their patent. The high court took up O'Rielly's appeal of the 1849 case in December 1852, a few days after the unfavorable New York decision. Morse's lawyers made the aggressive claim that the patent applied not only to the telegraph device but also to his new uses of old concepts. Salmon P. Chase, now U.S senator, countered that the claim was too broad—that Morse was trying to patent a scientific principle rather than a specific invention. On January 30, 1854, the court unanimously upheld the Kentucky decision and endorsed Morse's patent. A four-to-three majority, however, rejected his broad claim. The decision worried Morse and Kendall because it seemed likely to encourage other inventors to test the patent.[11]

In spite of the new problems, Kendall's income continued to grow. The estimated value of the Morse patent was now something over half a million dollars, four times its value when Kendall became agent. In the spring of 1851 Kendall's annual income had reached $8,000, and a year later it exceeded $10,000, considerably more than he had earned as postmaster general. By 1851 he owned $320,000 in telegraph stock, $50,000 in contracts for future stock,

9. Alfred Vail to George Vail, 22 June 1848, 16 June, 8 July (quotations) 1854, Alfred Vail to Kendall, 13 July 1851, 29 June 1852, Vail Papers.

10. Kendall to John, 11 July 1853; French, *Witness*, 214–15, 251–52; Kendall to Morse, 1 Aug. 1854, Morse Papers.

11. *Henry O'Rielly et al. Appellants v. S. F. B. Morse et al.* 56 U.S. 62–63, 601, 617; Kendall to Morse, 1, 5 Feb. 1853, 11, 31 Jan. 1854, Morse Papers; Swisher, *History of the Supreme Court*, 496–504.

$28,000 in land, and $70,000 in potential income from the claims agency. With debts of $30,000 his net worth was $438,000. In only six years he had risen from an unemployed politician to a businessman of considerable means.[12]

The sudden affluence came at the right time, for the Kendalls were now dealing with the demands of a growing extended family. After the death of Daniel Gold in 1849, Amos and Jane had become responsible for Mary Anne Gold and her two children. Then two years later they received a telegram from the Culvers, in Kentucky, saying that Adela had given birth to a daughter (their third child) and had contracted bilious pneumonia. On her deathbed she and Dr. Culver decided that it would be best if Mary Anne raised the three children along with her own at Kendall Green. After being responsible for only four unmarried children in 1849, Amos and Jane were now burdened with five children and five grandchildren.

The two deaths, coupled with Kendall's concern about his own mortality, prompted him to start planning his estate. To deal with the immediate situation he arranged to give Mary Anne $10,000 in Washington & New Orleans stock and Adela's children a similar amount in shares of the New Orleans & Ohio. In addition Dr. Culver put a large share of his own property in trust for his children and promised to give Mary Anne $90 a month and the use of a servant for their care. Looking further ahead, Kendall put the farm and some of his "best stocks" in trust for Jane and their two young daughters, Fannie and Marion. Two years later he gave each of his other two children, Jeannie and John, $10,000 in stocks. As paternalistic with his other children as he was with John, he attached strings to the gifts. His children were not to sell the stock without consulting him. They were never to get carried away by their good fortune and must always show Christian "moderation" in their enjoyment of their "blessings."[13]

The Kendall clan had another member. Amos and Jane spent the Christmas holidays in 1851 making arrangements for the January wedding of Jeannie and lawyer William Stickney. It was the first time Kendall Green had been the scene of such a festive event. Kendall was especially pleased that Morse's niece, Elizabeth, attended. After the ceremony the newlyweds had no time for a honeymoon, because Kendall took them to New York, where Stickney joined

12. Kendall, however, doubted whether he could raise more than $200,000 from his assets at any given time. Kendall to John, 26 May, 23 June 1851, 25 Apr. 1853, 28 Aug. 1854; Kendall to Morse, 9 Dec. 1852, Western Union Collection.

13. Kendall to John, 26 May (quotation), 23 June 1851, 18 (quotation), 25 Apr., 6 June 1853.

the lawyers working on the Smith case. Kendall was still thrifty. Even though he could easily have afforded to stay at the Astor or the Irving House, they all roomed at a cheap boardinghouse to save money. A little defensive about hiring his son-in-law, he told Morse that they needed another lawyer because of all the lawsuits and pointed out that Stickney would cost less than anyone else.[14]

As Kendall's estate grew, there was money to send Marion and Fannie to Mr. Cushman's school in Washington, to enable Mary Anne to take her son Willie to Baltimore to see a dentist, and to give Jeannie and Fannie a vacation in Bridgeport, Connecticut. With the help of a gardener and a tenant farmer, Amos and Jane maintained a large garden, decorated the yard with roses, and built an elegant fence around Kendall Green. They also gave money to the E Street Baptist Church, which they had been attending since 1847, even though Amos refused to become a member.[15]

In 1853 Kendall made another trip to the West, this time to visit his landholdings in Illinois. Early in August he set out for the rising city of Chicago, where he met his land agent, Alvah Gilbert. On the train ride to Bloomington the next day the scenery was so striking that he described it to Jane in great detail. The prairie was an "interminable meadow of grass," with no animals, no people, no houses. He felt as though "the managers of the steam monster . . . had lost their way and were plunging onward recklessly, without purpose or destination." At Bloomington they shifted to a stagecoach for an uncomfortable all-night ride to Springfield. When Gilbert, who was rather portly, came down hard and broke the coach seat, Kendall casually propped it up with a suitcase. Their discomfort was rewarded the next day when they sold one of their farms and were offered more than $11,000 for another.[16]

That same spring John was twenty-one and in his final year at Dartmouth. By a wonderful coincidence he had fallen in love with Lizzie Green of Groton, the daughter of Eliza Lawrence Green, the woman with whom his father had once been so infatuated. In those early days the Lawrences, especially those in Boston, had never quite accepted Kendall, and the feeling lingered. In 1840 Samuel Lawrence told his brother condescendingly that

14. Kendall to Morse, 17 Jan. 1852, Western Union Collection; Kendall to John, 25 Jan. 1852; Kendall to Morse, 5 Jan. 1852, Morse Papers.

15. Kendall to John, 17 July, 13, 27 Oct. 1851, 22 Nov. 1853; Kendall to Jane Kendall, 15 Nov. 1851, in *Autobiography*, 544–45; George W. Samson, *In Memoriam* (Washington, 1869), 16–17.

16. Kendall to Jane Kendall, 15 Aug. 1853, in *Autobiography*, 547–49; Kendall to John, 22 Nov. 1853.

Kendall had been a capable auditor but lacked the "talents" to succeed as a cabinet officer. But by 1853 the Kendalls had risen socially, and John was able to move easily into the elite world of the Lawrences. Recognizing the change, Kendall commented wistfully that John must be finding Boston society "agreeable" and "instructive."[17]

Once Kendall realized that John was in love, he sent him a flurry of letters encouraging the match. He liked "Miss Lizzie," saw her "attractions," and wanted to see John married as soon as he could support a family. In the next few weeks he sent money to pay off John's college debts and informed him of his $10,000 inheritance. To say that Kendall was making sure that his only son married well would be too cynical. The letters are so caring and transparent that they simply show a father reliving the past and trying to do right by his son.[18]

Soon after John graduated in August 1853, he became Kendall's general assistant. He manned the office, carried messages, inspected lines, and worked with the superintendent of the Washington & New Orleans. Kendall was grooming John and William Stickney to take over his responsibilities and planned to pay each of them an eighth of his annual income and a quarter of the excess over $8,000. With the prospect of this sort of income John could support a wife; late in 1854 he and Lizzie were married.[19]

John was the seventh member of the family brought into the telegraph business. Daniel Gold had been a stockholder and trustee, Dr. Culver and Jeannie Stickney held minor jobs, brother George was running a telegraph office, William Stickney served as an attorney, and John E. Kendall left the claims agency to become a contractor. Kendall's nepotism was no secret. He had been criticized for it when he was fourth auditor and postmaster general, and only recently Alfred Vail had accused him of "trying to get his family provided for in all the telegraph offices that are good for any thing." None of this of course bothered Kendall, who held the old view that it was his paternal duty to take care of his family.[20]

Though looking ahead to his retirement, Kendall was not yet ready to take the step, because he still had the goal of a Morse telegraph monopoly. In

17. Samuel Lawrence to Amos Lawrence, 26 May 1840, Lawrence Papers; Kendall to John, 20 Mar. 1853.

18. Kendall to John, 20 Mar. (quotation), 4, 18, 25 Apr., 6 June 1853.

19. Morse to Kendall, 30 Sept. 1854, Morse Papers; Kendall to John, 7 May, 4, 6 Sept. 1854, 23 Apr. 1855; Kendall to John Kendall and William Stickney, 28 Aug. 1854, Kendall Papers, MHS.

20. Alfred Vail to George Vail, 8 July 1854, Vail Papers.

1852 the three Morse lines in the East had absorbed O'Rielly's competing Bain lines, while in the West, as noted, the New Orleans & Ohio had taken over the People's Company. To consolidate further, Kendall invited the Morse companies to send delegates to a convention in Washington, which opened on March 5, 1853. Representatives came from the three eastern lines and the two to New Orleans as well as the three remaining O'Rielly companies that were using the Morse telegraph. Smith signaled his willingness to cooperate by attending. The delegates formed the American Telegraph Confederation, with Kendall on the executive board and an office in Washington. They adopted common signals and abbreviations and uniform procedures for dismissing officials but refused to give up any of their companies' independence.[21]

The emergence of new entrepreneurs paved the way for more serious consolidation. In Rochester, New York, Hiram Sibley had purchased rights to a telegraph invented by Royal E. House of Vermont and had organized the New York & Mississippi Valley Printing Telegraph Company. By 1853 he had a line from Buffalo to Louisville. A year later Cyrus W. Field and Peter Cooper of New York formed the New York, Newfoundland & London Electric Telegraph Company to connect Halifax, Nova Scotia, with St. John's, Newfoundland, and lay an ocean cable from there to the British Isles.[22]

The rise of the new company in New York strained relations between Kendall and Morse. Eager to get the use of Morse's name, Field and Cooper asked him to be their honorary electrician. The impulsive Morse not only accepted but also invested $10,000 in the venture. He was so excited about it that he allowed the company to use his patent without charge on a new line from Canada to New York and promised to do all he could to get his own companies to transmit messages for the Newfoundland Company at half price. An astonished Kendall told Morse that he had been taken in. If he gave away his patent rights, stockholders who had paid for them would feel cheated, and no company would want to give a 50 percent discount. Kendall also bluntly pointed out that the concessions would reduce his income as Morse's agent.[23]

Morse, however, was in no mood to listen. He felt himself in a strong position because he had just received a seven-year extension to his original patent. At the same time he was unhappy about his income from the telegraph, which had fallen short of the $12,000 a year that he had expected. He

21. Thompson, *Wiring,* 194–96, 259–61; Kendall to Morse, 4 Apr. 1853, Morse Papers.
22. Thompson, *Wiring,* 264–69, 299–300.
23. Kendall to Morse, 16 May, 5 June 1854, Morse Papers.

was of course a rich man—his investments were worth at least $300,000—but he felt poor. He was having a hard time supporting his two mansions in Poughkeepsie, New York, and he found it "mortifying . . . to be esteemed a millionaire" by friends raising money for charities and be forced to admit that he was not. If things got no better he might have to give up one of his houses and move in with one of his sons.[24]

Annoyed by Kendall's scolding, Morse dashed off several pointed letters in the summer of 1854, criticizing his performance and contending that their contract had expired with the granting of the extension. If he wanted to be rehired, Kendall would have to improve his system of accounting and set up an office in New York City, where Morse spent much of his time. Most ominous, Morse doubted whether Kendall was well enough to carry on as his agent and also serve as president of the Magnetic and the Washington & New Orleans Companies.[25]

Shaken by the letter, Kendall responded at once. Yes, they should have an office in New York City. No, their contract had not expired. He admitted that the accounts had not been kept "as they should have" but shifted the blame to one of his clerks, who, he pointed out, had been recommended by Morse himself. He chided Morse for being "too gloomy" and promised that dividends would be much better in another few months. Realizing how dependent he was on Kendall, Morse capitulated. He reassured Kendall that he had confidence in him, and he never repeated his demands or tried again to abrogate the contract. But his doubts about his income and Kendall's health kept resurfacing.[26]

By the summer of 1855 Field and his friends were ready to expand down the East Coast. Morse told Kendall excitedly that Field was ready to buy them out and free them from their "anxieties, and cares." His hopes seemed fulfilled in August when Field offered to lease the Magnetic Company, the New York, Albany & Buffalo, and the Washington & New Orleans, but a month later the offers were withdrawn. On November 1 the New York, Newfoundland & London Company was reorganized as the American Telegraph Company and announced that it owned a new telegraph instrument invented by David E.

24. Hochfelder, "Taming the Lightning," 184; Mabee, *American Leonardo*, 301, 356; Morse to Kendall, 29 June, 27, 29 July, 25 Sept. (quotation) 1854, Morse Papers.

25. Morse to Kendall, 22, 29 June, 17, 27 July 1854, Morse Papers; Morse to Kendall, 26 June 1854, Western Union Collection.

26. Kendall to Morse, 7 July 1854, Western Union Collection; Kendall to Morse, 1 Aug. 1854 (quotation), Morse to Kendall 29, 30 June, 3 Aug. 1854, Morse Papers.

Hughes of Kentucky. Ignoring Morse and Kendall, the new company started negotiations to buy several new lines along the East Coast, which were using the Bain and House devices. Field convinced the trusting Morse that he would not use the Hughes telegraph against him, but Kendall knew better. He warned Morse that Field would "hold it *in terrorem* over our heads . . . to induce us to let them have our lines at a reduced rent."[27]

The expansion of the American Company brought it into competition with Sibley's New York & Mississippi Valley Printing Company, which had reached out to Chicago and Pittsburgh. The two new empires met face-to-face when both Sibley and Field tried to gain control of the strategically located New York, Albany & Buffalo. In February 1856 Sibley pulled off a coup. Unable to purchase the contested line, he turned around and helped it lease another, smaller New York company and thus established a monopoly over the route from Buffalo to New York City. As part of the arrangement, Sibley's Printing Company received the right to send messages through Buffalo to New York. Sibley completed his rise to power a month later by reorganizing his company as the much larger Western Union Telegraph Company and threatened to move into the East.[28]

To meet the challenge, the American Company continued acquiring telegraph lines and strengthened its ties with the New York Associated Press. On March 1, 1856, F. O. J. Smith's old enemy, Daniel H. Craig, published an open letter, announcing a new line from New York to Washington that would use the "best chestnut posts and galvanized wire" and be far superior to Kendall's "rickety" lines. He advised Kendall to give up and lease Morse's entire system to the American Company. As Kendall had expected, he soon received offers for the Magnetic and the Washington & New Orleans lines much less generous than before. Shrugging off Craig's articles as "all false and mere wind," he rejected the proposals and started consolidating the Morse companies. On July 7, 1856, the Magnetic Company leased the Washington & New Orleans. Kendall was not unwilling to sell Morse's lines, but by contesting Field's expansion he hoped to force a higher price.[29]

In the winter and spring of 1857 the major players in the telegraph wars—

27. Morse to Kendall, 20 (quotation), 30 June 1855, Kendall to Morse, 22 June, 24 Nov., 7 Dec. (quotation) 1855, Morse Papers; Thompson, *Wiring*, 302–5.

28. Thompson, *Wiring*, 278–89; Kendall to Morse, 8, 11, 17 Dec. 1855, Morse Papers.

29. Kendall to Morse, 20 Feb., 3, 5, 8 Mar., 20 (quotation), 22 May, 18 July, 16 Sept. 1856, D. H. Craig to Amos Kendall, 1 Mar. 1856, Morse Papers; Thompson, *Wiring*, 299–309.

the American Company, the Western Union, and the Morse interest—were eying each other suspiciously. When Sibley came to New York in June, the sparring continued. After exploring a possible alliance with Field and Cooper of the American Company, he sat down with Kendall and Charles A. Mann of the New York, Albany & Buffalo. The three agreed to meet again in New York on July 1. Then Sibley went back to Field and Cooper and warned that Kendall was organizing against them. He also wrote to one of his western allies, Dr. Norvin Green, the driving force of a group that had leased Kendall's old New Orleans & Ohio and renamed it the New Orleans & Ohio Lessees. Someone also alerted John D. Caton of the Illinois & Mississippi Company.[30]

Morse and Kendall were unaware of what was going on. Morse had sailed on the U.S.S. *Niagara* with some of the American Company people to take part in the laying of the Atlantic cable. Kendall had been suffering from a serious ailment affecting his lungs and the muscles around his heart—quite likely pleurisy. Feeling better toward the end of June, he decided to bring Jane to the meeting in New York so that they could have a holiday. Arriving on June 26, he sent a smug letter to Morse, saying that he expected to hear that Field and Cooper had given up their plans for a telegraph to Washington.[31]

Kendall suddenly realized that something was afoot when he discovered that Green, Caton, and other westerners were in the city. Assuming that he was in charge, he invited everyone to what was now a summit meeting. During the first two sessions harmony prevailed, and a committee, including Kendall, was set up to carry out the goal of consolidation. The harmony vanished when Field and Cooper, who had not previously attended, joined the final meeting and announced that the American Company would not take part unless the companies agreed to pay for the Hughes patent. When Kendall asked why Hughes should be paid and not Morse, an exasperated Cooper accused Kendall of protecting his own companies, and Field blustered that the Atlantic cable would make the American Company invincible. Kendall was "shocked" when Green, whom he considered a friend, sided with Cooper and Field. With the meeting at an impasse, it was agreed to adjourn, and Kendall left in a rage.[32]

30. Morse to Kendall, 24 Feb. 1857, Kendall to Morse, 22 Feb., 27 Aug. 1857, 31 Mar. 1858, Green to Morse, 27 Jan. 1858, Morse Papers; Kendall to Smith, 26 Dec. 1857, Smith Papers, New York Public Library; Thompson, *Wiring*, 310–11, 317–18.

31. Kendall to George Vail, 18 June 1857, Vail Papers; Kendall to Morse, 26 June 1857, Morse Papers.

32. Kendall to Morse, 6 July, 27 Aug. (quotation) 1857, Morse Papers; Thompson, *Wiring*, 311–13.

The next day, July 2, the delegates met without Kendall and pledged to unite. At another meeting, on August 6, to which Kendall was not invited, they agreed to pay for the Hughes patent and formed an "exclusive connection" called the Six Nations. It was made up of the American Company, the Western Union, the New York, Albany & Buffalo, Green's New Orleans company, Caton's Illinois company, and O'Rielly's original Pennsylvania company, the Atlantic & Ohio. Kendall recognized the alliance as a declaration of war against the Morse interest. "No one would know from the [treaty]," he said, "that such a man as Samuel F. B. Morse ever existed."[33]

Kendall concluded—as he often did when things went awry—that he was the victim of "an act of perfidy." In this case he felt that Hiram Sibley was the villain. Sibley certainly bore much of the responsibility, but Kendall was just trying to shift the blame. Consolidation had been under way for some time, and all the telegraph leaders were maneuvering for position. The question he should have asked was why Sibley and Field had been able to beat him at his own game. Perhaps, as one historian has suggested, it was simply a case of the younger generation taking over. Maybe so, but Peter Cooper was about the same age as Kendall, and Sibley the same as F. O. J. Smith. The telegraph men did not differ very much. Almost all came from middling, farming, New England or New York backgrounds, with very few ideological difference. All except O'Rielly, who was no longer important, understood the necessity of consolidation.[34]

A significant reason for the outcome was the advantage that Field and Sibley gained from having their base of operations in New York State. This was ironic because Kendall had recognized the importance of New York ever since he took the canal boat from Buffalo to Albany. He had premised his Post Office policies on the central role of New York City, and he had wanted to move there to start a newspaper. He made the city the hub of the Morse companies, but he was never comfortable there himself, and he turned the region over to Smith in the territorial division. Field and Sibley, on the other hand, were able to raise large amounts of money in New York City and the towns along the Erie Canal.[35]

33. Thompson, *Wiring*, 313–17; "Articles of Agreement for the Union, Protection and Improvement of Certain Telegraph Lines in North America, August 10, 1857," in ibid., 504–15; Kendall to Morse, 27 Aug. (first quotation), 3 Oct. (second quotation) 1857, Morse Papers.

34. Kendall to Morse, 27 Aug. 1857, Morse Papers. For the generational thesis see Thompson, *Wiring*, 303.

35. In contrast with the Magnetic Company, which was capitalized at $60,000, Field's Newfoundland Company had a capitalization of $1,500,000, and Sibley's Western Union $500,000, which was quickly doubled. Thompson, *Wiring*, 42, 289 n. 300.

Besides, Kendall and Morse were worried about their health and looking for a way to retire. In 1857 Kendall twice brought up the subject. Aware of this, the other telegraph operators shied away. Furthermore, they were reluctant to deal with people like Kendall and Smith who were so hard to get along with. One telegraph man who had recently been fighting with Kendall called him "inflexible and unmoveable . . . suspicious as the very devil." Kendall must have confirmed this opinion when he got into the shouting match on the last day of the summit meeting.[36]

But like so many contemporaries from Henry Clay on, the telegraph men underestimated Kendall. Shortly after the signing of the Six Nations treaty he called a meeting of the Magnetic board and got a resolution to "carry the war into Africa." Putting his antipathy for Smith aside, he arranged a treaty with the New York & Boston line (now the New York & New England Union) and announced plans to tap the source of foreign news by building a Morse line to Halifax. He went to Wilmington, Delaware, to block the efforts of the American Company to secure rights-of-way for its line to Washington. To punish Green he issued patent rights for a line from Mobile to Cairo, Illinois.[37]

At the same time Cooper and Field had been weakened by the Panic of 1857 and their efforts to lay the Atlantic cable. After the first cable snapped in mid-ocean and the second proved unworkable, the idea was given up until after the Civil War. Kendall smugly observed that the New Yorkers had been so "humbled by the ill success of the Atlantic cable" that it would be much easier to deal with them.[38]

And so it was. Kendall's maneuvers, Morse's reputation, and the high quality of the Morse telegraph made the Morse lines increasingly attractive takeover targets. Since Morse's patent would expire in 1861, it was important to acquire it quickly before wildcat operators could use it free of charge. Cooper was the first to make an offer. Late in 1857 he talked with Kendall about uniting the American with the Magnetic and the New York & New England Union with Morse as president. Nothing happened for another year, but finally on October 20, 1858, representatives of the Six Nations (now reorganized

36. Kendall to Morse, 26 June, 26 Dec. 1857, Morse Papers; Thomas Rivers to Montgomery, 7, 12 July 1856, Henry A. Montgomery Collection, Memphis/Shelby County Public Library and Information Center.

37. Kendall to Morse, 27 Aug. (quotation), 14 Nov. 1857, 15 Mar., 19, 27 Apr., 5, 9 June 1858, Morse Papers; Thompson, *Wiring,* 319–23.

38. Kendall to Morse, 11 Oct. 1858, Morse Papers; Thompson, *Wiring,* 318–19, 323; Mabee, *American Leonardo,* 329–37.

as the North American Telegraph Association) voted in favor of buying out the Morse companies.[39]

Officially the offers to buy came from the new association, but the actual negotiating was done by the American Company, which planned to absorb the Morse companies. The talks went slowly at first because Smith was demanding what Kendall called the "exorbitant sum" of $300,000. In April and May 1859 Kendall and other concerned parties met in Philadelphia with no agreement. They tried twice more in the summer but failed again. By this time the meetings had become an ordeal for Kendall, who suffered from bouts of diarrhea and once went home in disgust after a blowup with Robert W. Russell of the House telegraph.[40]

Another obstacle appeared on August 13 when Craig and the Associated Press abruptly cut off foreign news service to the *Philadelphia Public Ledger*. Craig was retaliating for unfriendly remarks by the editor, who was also a director of the Magnetic Company. Assuming that Craig had the backing of the American Company board, Kendall delivered an ultimatum. Unless the board disavowed Craig's action and adopted the policy of "first come first served" before the twentieth, he would stop negotiating. When the day came, he carried out his threat. His "blood boil[ed]," he said, "to witness the prostitution of [Morse's] noble invention to purposes of fraud and oppression." His stubbornness was rewarded when the American Company announced that it would not exclude any reporter or news organization from free access to the news.[41]

Kendall then went back to the bargaining table and on October 12, 1859, reached a final agreement. Magnetic Company capital stock was exchanged at a premium of 35 percent for American Company stock. Morse and the heirs of the recently deceased Alfred Vail sold their patent rights to the company for $107,000. Smith was paid the $300,000 he was seeking for his stocks, patent rights, and claims. There are no transaction records for Kendall, but if the 35 percent premium is added to the $370,000 in telegraph stock that he owned in 1851, he now owned at least $500,000 in stock and cash. Add $70,000 in Washington real estate and western land and subtract $10,000 in

39. Kendall to Morse, 26, 31 Dec. 1857, 4 Jan., 11 Oct. 1858, Morse Papers; Thompson, *Wiring*, 324.

40. Kendall to Morse, 20 Feb. (quotation), 13, 17, 18, 20 June, 9, 20 July 1859, Morse Papers; French, *Witness*, 310–13.

41. Kendall to Morse, 24 Aug. 1859, Morse Papers; Thompson, *Wiring*, 327–29.

debts, and his net worth was $560,000. In today's currency that would be $12 million. He had become the wealthy man he had always aspired to be.[42]

The Kendalls had also gained status. In the reorganized American Company, Kendall was named to the board of directors, along with Morse, Russell, Field, and others, and his son John was made general superintendent. In recognition of the increased size of the American Company, the North American Telegraph Association revised its agreement for dividing up the telegraph business. Kendall was now at the top of a powerful company within a monopolistic association.[43]

Although the American Company had repudiated Craig, the question of how to treat news organizations was far from settled. During the winter the company continued to grant the Associated Press favorable rates and priority in the use of its lines. But on February 18, 1860, its executive committee, made up of Russell and two others, caused a tremendous stir by canceling many of the privileges. Several members of the American board, especially Field, thought the committee had gone too far. They were alarmed by the uncompromising position taken by Russell, who talked of setting up his own newspaper association. The question was disturbing to the North American Telegraph Association, none of whose members wanted a war with the Associated Press.[44]

After Craig published two outspoken pamphlets against the new company policies, Kendall replied. Listing the favors that the American Company had done for the Associated Press, he called Craig an ungrateful "blackguard" but indicated that he would not oppose the Associated Press as strongly as Russell. The American Company, he said, should "stand still" and "*make no war upon the New York Press.*" He was "ready to advance and meet [the Press] half way."[45]

For a short time in the summer of 1860 the choice seemed to be a newspaper monopoly headed by Craig or a telegraph monopoly led by Russell, but Kendall's pamphlet and changes in the American Company board brought the

42. Thompson, *Wiring,* 329–32. A year later Kendall was assessed for $257,200 in personal assets (the highest in wards 4 and 5) and $45,000 in Washington real estate (14th). These numbers are much lower than my estimates, but property assessments were often less than real values. United States Census Schedules, 1860, Washington County, District of Columbia, RG 29, reel 104, p. 97. Kendall had been paying off his debts. Kendall to John, 13 Oct. 1851, 20 Mar. 1853.

43. Thompson, *Wiring,* 332.

44. Ibid., 335–41.

45. Kendall, *Circular to the Stockholders of the American Telegraph Company* (New York, 1860).

two sides together. By October Kendall was confident that the Associated Press wanted peace and that there was hope of "mollifying even Russell." In November a committee of the American Company, including Kendall but not Russell, met at Delmonico's in New York with a group representing the Associated Press. After three sessions they found a compromise that ended the fight.[46]

Kendall's telegraph career revealed many of the same qualities that he had shown in the Post Office. His integrity was invaluable in winning public support for the new industry. His perseverance carried him back and forth from Washington to the West time after time. His orderliness and mastery of detail allowed him to juggle the affairs of dozens of telegraph lines and keep almost everything straight. And he never lost track of the big picture—unity (monopoly), government or private—and the centrality of New York and New Orleans. For the first five years he was almost indispensable.

But as time wore on, his lack of business and legal skills and his less attractive qualities—his self-pity, peevishness, and paranoia—coupled with his deteriorating health reduced his effectiveness. Just as in politics, he could not maintain harmony among his friends, and he invited hostility from his enemies. Perhaps the decline of the Morse interest was inevitable; the rising capitalists in New York City and along the Erie Canal had more money and larger goals than Morse and Kendall. Sibley was the driving force behind the transcontinental telegraph; Field kept the dream of the transatlantic cable alive. Kendall had to give way. He was smart enough (or lucky enough) to sell out at the right moment—before the outbreak of the Civil War.

---

46. Kendall to William Stickney, 2 Oct. 1860, Kendall Papers, Filson Historical Society; Hudson, *Journalism*, 614–15.

# 19

## PHILANTHROPIST AND WAR DEMOCRAT

Toward the end of the telegraph wars Kendall was making conscious efforts to improve his family's social standing. When Morse invited sixteen-year-old Fannie Kendall to visit his family at the Gramercy Park House in New York in 1855, Kendall gratefully accepted. He hoped that his daughter could remain under Morse's "guidance" for several months and learn "what society you have" in New York. Not long after her return Fannie married rising young attorney Robert Fox of Washington. The Kendalls put on another elegant wedding and were disappointed that the Morses were unable to attend. In the fall of 1860 they ventured into New York society themselves, taking their youngest daughter, Marion, to the Princess Ball. Jane was resplendent, wearing an expensive reengagement ring that she had designed herself from a selection of diamonds brought down from Tiffany.[1]

Much of the Kendalls' social standing depended on their country estate. Although a far cry from the Hermitage or Ashland, Kendall Green was something like Martin Van Buren's Lindenwald and Francis P. Blair's Silver Spring. After many improvements and additions, their farmhouse, set high on a ridge, had become a handsome mansion. Visitors drove up a broad driveway to a recessed front door set off by columns and flanked by tall windows. A balcony and two large wings gave the house an air of grandeur. The mansion was surrounded by an array of outbuildings, including cisterns, carriage houses, stables, woodsheds, and a bowling green.[2]

But the absence of the usual fields of grain and tobacco gave the estate what one observer described as a "skeleton look." In spite of his many remarks

1. Kendall to Morse, 7 Dec. 1855, 14 Dec. 1856, Morse to Kendall, 29 Dec. 1856, Morse Papers; Ted Gold, *History of Cornwall, Conn.*, in Hopson, notes for unfinished Ph.D. diss..

2. William Stickney to Edward M. Gallaudet, 16 Mar. 1870, pictures and descriptions of Kendall Green, Gallaudet University Archives.

about the agrarian life and his stout defense of slavery, Kendall showed no interest in running a plantation. He preferred, instead, to use the land for some form of business. In 1854 he started a real estate development, called "Kendallville," laying out lots, building houses, and offering horse-drawn omnibus service from Pennsylvania Avenue. When that failed, he and John decided to make money by planting grapevines and selling wine. He invested $10,000, hired several farmhands, and built a gardener's cottage, a brick and glass greenhouse, and a brick wine vault. Kendall worked occasionally in the vineyard, but John remained in New York tending to his new duties in the American Company.[3]

Amos and Jane continued to care for an extended family. They shared the mansion with their daughters Mary Anne and Marion and five grandchildren. One of the unsold houses was rented to Jeannie and William Stickney, who had a baby son, and a new house was being built for John and Lizzie. John wanted it placed up on the ridge, but his father insisted on putting it down near the vineyard, where John could *"live among the vines."* In the end it did not matter because John and Lizzie decided to stay in New York, and the house went to Fannie and Robert Fox.[4]

Kendall now had the wealth as well as the inclination to become a philanthropist. He had inherited the urge to do good from his father and had shown an interest in a variety of reforms. His concern for the deaf, which had been piqued by his acquaintance with Sarah Morse, was rekindled in 1856 when a man from New York solicited him for funds to support five deaf-mute children. After giving the man money, Kendall was shocked to discover that the man was exploiting and abusing his wards. Acting quickly, he won a court order giving him control of the children and brought them to live in another of his empty houses. Early in 1857 he secured an act of Congress establishing the Columbia Institution for the Instruction of the Deaf and Dumb and the Blind, with a grant of $150 a year for each student. Kendall was elected president and began looking for a superintendent.[5]

3. Kendall never became a successful winegrower. Hudson, *Journalism*, 246 (quotation); Wilhelmus B. Bryan, *A History of the National Capital*, 2 vols. (New York, 1914), 2:369–70; Gold, *History of Cornwall;* Kendall to John, 20 Nov., 8, 12 Dec. 1859, 18 May, 30 July, 12 Aug. 1860; Stickney to Gallaudet, 16 Mar. 1870, Gallaudet Archives.

4. Kendall to John, 12 Dec. 1859 (quotation), 4 May, 12 Aug. 1860.

5. Edward M. Gallaudet, "A History of the Columbia Institution for the Deaf and Dumb," in Columbia Historical Society, *Records* 15 (1912): 1–4; Kendall to Jacob Thompson, 22 Oct. 1857, Kendall to Peet, 11 May 1857, Amos Kendall Papers, Gallaudet Archives.

On April 21 he offered the position to Isaac L. Peet, assistant principal of the school for the deaf in New York. Peet could not accept, but he recommended Edward M. Gallaudet, whose deceased father had founded the Connecticut Asylum for deaf-mutes in Hartford, Connecticut. Gallaudet, said Peet, was a "man of liberal education, pleasing manners and brilliant talents," who had been "familiar with the sign language from infancy," because his mother, Sophia Gallaudet, was a deaf-mute. His only drawback was that he was barely twenty. Kendall immediately invited him to Washington.[6]

At their meeting it became clear that both men would be taking a risk. Kendall would have to accept a youth with no experience; Gallaudet would be leaving an established institution for a new school with little income and only a handful of students. But each recognized that he would be working with someone as moral, ambitious, and hardworking as he was. The young man may have reminded Kendall of himself at Dartmouth; the old man may have made Gallaudet think of the father that he had lost. And so they came to an agreement. Gallaudet would become superintendent with a salary of $1,000, and his mother would serve as matron for $300. They were on the job by early June.[7]

Gallaudet quickly showed his energy and imagination. As the school expanded, he took over still another of Kendall's houses and got the trustees to add $3,000 to the school budget. By 1860 he had built the enrollment up to thirty and was talking about adding a college department. He had now become a familiar figure in Washington as he rode to and from Kendall Green on a handsome old racehorse.[8]

None of this could have happened without Kendall. During the first year he made at least three appeals for funds, citing the need for furniture, bedding, groceries, and money for salaries. His wealthy banking friends William W. Corcoran and George W. Riggs each gave $500, but the bulk of the support came from Kendall himself. In addition to the two houses, he pledged $200 a year for the next five years. In 1858 when the two houses were no longer adequate, he gave $8,000 and land for a permanent, brick school building. Sound-

6. Kendall to Peet, 21 Apr. 1857, Peet to Kendall, 30 Apr. 1857, Kendall Papers, Gallaudet Archives.

7. Kendall to Peet, 21 Apr. 1857, ibid.; Gallaudet, "History of the Columbia Institution," 2.

8. Gallaudet, "History of the Columbia Institution," 3–4; Gallaudet College, *Inauguration of the College for the Deaf and Dumb* (Washington, 1864), 9.

ing like an antebellum Booker T. Washington, he said that his goal was to teach the pupils "manual labor in farming, gardening or some trade."[9]

Kendall's interest in good works did not of course extend to the abolitionist movement. He was especially contemptuous of "Christian abolitionists" such as Henry Ward Beecher who used religion to attack slavery. The church, he told a YMCA audience, should restrict itself to reforming individuals, not institutions, and should hold to the biblical rule that wives should submit to their husbands, servants to their masters, and citizens to the laws of the state. This authoritarian call for an institutional status quo echoed his long-held Jacksonian view that abolitionists threatened the stability of the Union. On a trip to New England in 1856 he was alarmed to find the people "greatly excited" over the Kansas-Nebraska Act. He feared that Democratic president Franklin Pierce, who supported the act, would be unable to travel through his homeland "without being frequently insulted."[10]

The principal danger, he believed, lay not in these "passing scenes," but in the rise of "sectional parties." He thought the security of the nation depended on having two parties, neither dominated by the North or the South. Thus he refused to follow Francis P. Blair and Gideon Welles in opposing the Kansas-Nebraska Act and joining the Republican party. Instead he backed the act, stayed with the Democracy, and insisted that the "Old Hero" would have done the same.[11]

After the Democratic candidate, James Buchanan, was elected in 1856, Kendall wrote to tell him that he now had the opportunity to save the Union. He warned that ever since the nullification crisis a small group of extreme states' rights southern Democrats had been trying to "break down" the Union and destroy the party. A similar "disunion party in the North" was frightening the South with abolitionist arguments. To save the republic, he told Buchanan, he should stick "inflexibly" with Jackson's policy of preserving the Union and resist any "further agitation of the subject of slavery." But Bu-

9. Records of Gallaudet University, Gallaudet Archives; Kendall to Jacob Thompson, 22 Oct. 1857, Kendall Papers, Gallaudet Archives.

10. Kendall, "Lecture to the Young Men's Christian Association, Washington," May 1860, in *Autobiography*, 564–70; Kendall to Morse, 18 May 1858, Morse Papers (first quotation); Kendall to John, 7 June 1856.

11. Kendall to Morse, 16 Sept. 1856, Morse Papers (quotation); Kendall to editor of the *Pennsylvanian*, 22 Oct. 1856, *Boston Public Library Monthly Bulletin* 7 (1902): 267, in Hopson, notes for unfinished Ph.D. diss.

chanan did not listen. He sided with the extreme southerners by supporting slavery in Kansas and denying that he had the power to prevent secession.[12]

Fed up with the president, Kendall started looking for moderate southern Democrats to save the Union. One such man was House Speaker James L. Orr of South Carolina, who had many northern friends and who believed that the best way for the South to protect slavery was to remain in the Union. Orr, however, disappointed Kendall by bolting the Democratic convention at Charleston, South Carolina, in April 1860 when it refused to adopt a platform guaranteeing slavery in the territories. In early August Kendall exchanged letters with Orr and was surprised to find how violent he had become. Orr believed that if Abraham Lincoln was elected president, the South should rise and resist his inauguration.[13]

Kendall sent Orr an open letter, accusing him of being part of the group trying to destroy the party and the Union. Guaranteeing slavery in the territories, he said, was a "latitudinarian and dangerous claim" of congressional power inconsistent with the republicanism of the Democratic party. If they used force to stop Lincoln, they would be met by force. He was scornful of the slaveowners of the deep South, who talked resistance even though they were losing far fewer slaves than the more conciliatory planters in the border states. If Lincoln won in November, Union men, many from the border states, would have to save the Union from "the Abolitionists of New England and the disunionists of the South."[14]

Kendall's arguments put him in the same camp with Jacksonians such as Martin Van Buren and Stephen A. Douglas and gave an early glimpse of the position later held by War Democrats. But his views were not entirely consistent. Kendall was advising Buchanan to avoid further agitation of slavery; yet he himself was defending the Kansas-Nebraska Act, which had stirred up the trouble in the first place. He was accusing Orr of being a radical, states' rights disunionist, but was also attacking him for unrepublican "latitudinarian" claims. Nonetheless the letter was well received by Unionist editors in the North and South. The Democratic *Daily Enquirer* in Memphis called it one of "the ablest Union papers of the season," while the Republican *New York*

12. Kendall to Buchanan, 7 Dec. 1856, in *Secession. Letters of Amos Kendall* (Washington, 1861), 37–40.

13. Orr to Kendall, 16 Aug. 1860, in *New York Times*, 20 Sept. 1860.

14. Kendall to Orr, 10 Sept. 1860, in *Secession*, 40–50.

*Times* crossed party lines to rally behind this spirit of "old-fashioned Jacksonian Democracy."[15]

Buchanan's party newspaper, the *Washington Constitution,* thought otherwise. According to the editor, Kendall was "a bloody monster ready to slaughter 'women and children'" by using force to stop secession. No one opposed to secession could be called a true Democrat. Kendall retorted that it was "a sad sight to see the organ of a Democratic administration" calling it "a crime . . . to defend the Constitution" by resisting secession. If Lincoln was elected, he would have to enforce the laws just as Jackson had done in the nullification crisis.[16]

Now thought of as the Jackson spokesman, Kendall published *Secession,* a series of articles based on the Nullification Proclamation. He described the government as a "perpetual Union" that could "coerce individuals [but] not states." It lacked the power to abolish slavery, but the states lacked the right to secede. He continued to believe that the main hope for saving the Union lay in the border states. When Virginians refused to secede in February, he cheered "Hoora-a-a for Virginia" and told Morse that he had great confidence in the Unionists in northern Virginia and other parts of the upper South.[17]

When war broke out in April 1861, Washington took on the appearance of a "military camp," and Kendall began to worry about the safety of his family. In May he, Jane, and Marion left to spend the summer on the seaside at Bridgeport, Connecticut, where they rented rooms from "a plain ladylike hostess," who provided "plenty of good wholesome food." On learning that John was sick with a respiratory illness at Lizzie's home in Groton, Kendall discouraged him from coming to Bridgeport, saying the damp sea air would only make him worse. Some days, he complained, it was too much for his own "feeble lungs."[18]

15. *Autobiography,* 584–86; *New York Times,* 20, 22 Sept. 1860. Joel H. Silbey does not use the terms War Democrats and Peace Democrats. He calls those supporting the war Legitimists, and those opposing it Purists. Joel H. Silbey, *A Respectable Minority: The Democratic Party in the Civil War Era, 1860–1868* (New York, 1977), 93–110.

16. Kendall to editor of the *Constitution,* 2 Oct. 1860 but not published. It appeared in the *New York Times,* 23 Oct. 1860, and later in the *Washington Evening Star.* See also *Autobiography,* 580–84; and Kendall to the editor of the *Star,* 16 Nov. 1860, Crosby N. Boyd Papers, LC.

17. Kendall, *Secession,* in *Autobiography,* 588–619; Kendall to Caton, 14 Mar. 1861, John D. Caton Papers, LC; Kendall to Morse, 13 Feb. 1861, Morse Papers; Kendall to John, 6 Feb. 1861.

18. Kendall to William Stickney, 30 Apr. 1861, in *Autobiography,* 624–25 ("military"); Kendall to John, 6 ("a plain"), 19 June, 23 ("feeble"), 28 July 1861.

On July 23 news arrived of the Union defeat at Bull Run. Robert Fox, who had watched the battle, told his father-in-law that Washington was in "great danger." A few weeks later Kendall learned that Union soldiers had set fire to the house of one of his neighbors, who was suspected of being a secessionist, and had come close to burning Kendall Green. Convinced that he could "do no good" in Washington and that the city was "no place for ladies," Kendall decided to stay away. Early in September he, Jane, and Marion rented a large house in Trenton, New Jersey, where they were joined by the Stickneys.[19]

While still at Bridgeport, the Kendalls had a visit from John, who was feeling better and was about to leave on a business trip to the West. Kendall's instructions illustrate his shrewdness and the short leash that he kept on his children. John was going to Chicago to exchange telegraph stock for real estate. Even though the stock was worth about $85,000, he could accept as little as $50,000 because of the war. Before buying any city land, he must check on its adaptability to improvements and its distance from the center of business and the lake. For farmland he was to determine the taxes, the fertility of the soil, and the proportion of prairie and timber. And if he had to deviate from these guidelines, he was to telegraph his father. John's trip was apparently successful, because on Kendall's death it was reported that he "owned a large amount of real estate in Chicago."[20]

The trip, however, was costly because John had not fully recovered from his illness. On his return he went directly to Washington and contracted typhoid fever. His father and mother reached the city just in time to be with him on December 7 when he died. Jane was so distraught that she refused to see visitors for several months. Amos accepted the loss with the same "resignation to the will of God" that he had displayed in the past, but he poured out his feelings to Morse. "Death is a familiar visitor," he lamented. "He has taken from me one wife and ten children out of fourteen [including all] four sons, not one of whom has left any children."[21]

During the winter and spring Kendall began to fear the coming of abolition. Several Union generals had freed slaves escaping through their lines, and

19. Kendall to John, 23, 28 ("great") July, 26, 31 ("no place") Aug. 1861; Kendall to George Vail, 21 Oct. 1861, Vail Papers ("do no good").

20. Kendall to John, 1 Aug. 1861; *Evening Star*, 12 Nov. 1869.

21. Kendall to John, 26, 31 Aug. 1861; *Autobiography*, 625; Kendall to George Vail, 24 Jan. 1862, Vail Papers; Kendall to Morse, 27 Dec. 1861, Morse Papers.

Congress abolished slavery in the District of Columbia and in the territories. Kendall was willing to accept emancipation as a *"result"* of the war, not as an "object," but he could sense that he was losing. In July he told Morse that he hated to see a war to save the Union turn into a war to abolish slavery. And in September he was dismayed by Lincoln's preliminary emancipation proclamation.[22]

By this time the Kendalls were back in Washington. They had been eager to return for several months because the city now seemed safe, and they wanted to join friends from the E Street Baptist Church who were forming a new church. The Kendalls were soon active in the church, which was called Calvary Baptist. Even though Kendall still refused to become a member, he soon had a great influence over the organization. As chairman of the trustees he succeeded in installing his Trenton minister, Thomas R. Howlett, in the new pulpit. He also made a number of gifts, which he arranged in such a way that he retained control. He loaned the church $35,000 without interest, but instead of giving cash, he made the dividends from $35,000 in stock available to the church. In addition he protected his own status by stipulating that anyone who attended and supported the church could share in running it— whether a member or not. These and other restrictions gave Kendall and his heirs control over the church for decades to come.[23]

For the first two years the church rented space for its meetings, while Kendall looked around for a permanent site. His first effort proved frustrating when he bought a church building for the bargain price of $6,900, only to have the sale annulled in a protracted lawsuit. Finally in 1863 he bought land at H and 8th Streets NW (keeping the title in his own name) and promised to give $15,000 to build on the site if the church would raise another $6,000. This was agreed to, and construction was scheduled to start in 1864.[24]

Kendall kept an equally firm hand on the Columbia Institution for the

22. Kendall to William H. Seward, 26 Jan. 1862, in *Autobiography*, 639–41; Kendall to Morse, 3 July 1862, Morse Papers; *Evening Star*, 12 Nov. 1869.

23. Carl W. Tiller and Olive M. Tiller, *At Calvary: A History of the First 125 Years of Calvary Baptist Church, Washington, D.C., 1862–1987* (Manassas, Va., 1994), 1–8; records of the Calvary Baptist Church, Washington, D.C.

24. Kendall to John C. Smith, 17, 20, 29 Nov. 1862, Kendall to Joseph B. Varnum, 23 Dec. 1862, fragment, 2, 23 Jan. 1863, 17 Nov. 1864, 21 Jan., 8, 10 Feb. 1865, Varnum to Kendall, 29 Dec. 1862, "Truth" to editor of the *Washington National Republican*, 31 Dec. 1862? John M. McCalla Papers, Duke University Rare Book, Manuscript, and Special Collections Library; Tiller and Tiller, *At Calvary*, 8–9.

Deaf. While he was in Trenton, he stayed in close touch by corresponding with Gallaudet and attending trustee meetings. He liked the superintendent and was pleased with his performance. Gallaudet had quickly followed up on Kendall's idea of teaching manual skills, and during the first three years of the war the enrollment had almost doubled. Still, neither Kendall nor William Stickney, who was treasurer, allowed the superintendent to overstep his bounds. When Gallaudet had the trustees change the wording on the diploma without Kendall's permission, he was sharply reprimanded. When he tried to put a privy too close to Kendall's property, he was told to move it. The "fumes," Kendall complained, "cannot fail to reach one of my houses." Poor Gallaudet had several run-ins with Stickney, who could be as fussy as Kendall. He was particularly annoyed when Stickney called his attention to a twenty-five-cent discrepancy in his accounts.[25]

In 1864 Congress fulfilled Gallaudet's goal by adding a collegiate department to the institution. It was the first college for the deaf in the country. On being notified that he had been elected president of the college, Gallaudet sent back a heartfelt letter of thanks. Kendall, he said, had become his "second father" and had given him "all the consideration, all the forbearance that my own father could have shown." At Gallaudet's inauguration Kendall showed how much he cared about the young man's work. It was "a great mistake," he said, to consider deaf-mutes "inferior," for their inadequacy was "not in the want of capacity but in the want of its development." In the growing dispute over how to teach deaf-mutes, he supported his protégé by advocating the use of hand signs, which Gallaudet's father had promoted, rather than lipreading, which was now gaining favor. His relationship with Gallaudet was the best he ever enjoyed with anyone outside the family.[26]

During the election of 1864 politics vied with philanthropy for Kendall's attention. As a War Democrat he was often at odds with his old friend Samuel F. B. Morse, who was a prominent Peace Democrat. Morse blamed

25. Kendall to Gallaudet, 24, 30 Oct. 1861, 15 Feb. 1862, 25 May 1864, 9 Sept. 1865 (quotation), Stickney to Gallaudet, 28 Jan., 3 Feb., 10 Sept. 1862, 4 May, 12 June 1863, Edward M. Gallaudet Papers, Gallaudet Archives; Gallaudet College, *Inauguration of the College for the Deaf and Dumb,* 9.

26. Gallaudet, "History of the Columbia Institution," 5–6; Powrie Vaux Doctor, "Amos Kendall, 'Nineteenth Century Humanitarian,'" *Gallaudet College Bulletin* 7 (1957): 8; Gallaudet to Kendall, 15 June 1864, Kendall Papers, Gallaudet Archives; Gallaudet College, *Inauguration of the College for the Deaf and Dumb,* 10–11; Jill Lepore, *A Is for American: Letters and Other Characters in the Newly United States* (New York, 2002).

the war on the "fanaticism" of the North and believed the slaveowners' cause "intrinsically sound." An extreme racist, Morse once compared blacks to "the Chimpanze [*sic*] or gorilla." Morse was depressed by the increasing political power of the abolitionists and felt that "madness" ruled in Washington. In February 1863 he was elected president of the Society for the Diffusion of Political Knowledge, which attacked the Lincoln administration for prolonging the war and restricting freedom of speech.[27]

Although Kendall too was critical of Lincoln, he took issue with Morse on several key points. He was less racist, and he blamed the secessionists more than the abolitionists for starting the war. He refused to censure the postmaster general for stopping the circulation of antiwar publications because he felt that some of the editors deserved "to be suppressed." He also opposed the efforts of Peace Democrats to bring about an armistice, saying that it would "lead to . . . a perpetual dissolution of the Union." War Democrats, he said, believed it their patriotic "duty . . . to support the war." With this Unionist position he maintained his Jacksonianism and avoided the accusations of treason and the taunts of being a disloyal Copperhead that were heaped upon Morse and the Peace Democrats.[28]

As the campaign evolved, Kendall became more immersed in politics than at any time since 1844. One of the first to support General George B. McClellan for president, he served on the Conservative Union National Committee, representing War Democrats and former Whigs. Between January and October he published over thirty articles, which supported the war but brought him somewhat closer to the Peace Democrats. He demanded an end to the "bad policy, military jealousy, and political ambition of the administration" and attacked Lincoln vigorously for missteps such as his interference with voting in the border states. These attacks led one military investigator to report that Kendall had "a powerful influence" in groups that were abusing the administration.[29]

---

27. Morse to Kendall, 11, 15 Feb. (first three quotations) 1861, 10 ("madness"), 23 July 1862, Morse Papers; Mabee, *American Leonardo*, 347–49.

28. Kendall to Morse, 21 Mar. 1862, 7, 12 Mar. 1863, 28–31 Mar. 1864, Morse Papers; Kendall to John D. Caton, 17, 28 Apr. 1863 ("lead," "duty"), Kendall to *Morning Chronicle*, 19 Feb. 1863 ("suppressed"), in *Autobiography*, 643–45, 648–49.

29. Kendall to Philip H. Smith, 15 Dec. 1863, Kendall Papers, Filson Historical Society; Kendall to Morse, 16 Jan. 1864, Morse to Kendall, 23 Jan. 1864, Morse Papers; Kendall, *Letters on Our Country's Crisis* (Washington, 1864), quoted in *Autobiography*, 650 ("bad"); Kendall, *Letters Exposing the Mismanagement of Public Affairs by Abraham Lincoln* (Washington, 1864), 3; J. B. De Voe,

During the summer Kendall felt obliged to answer an appeal from Lincoln's running mate, Andrew Johnson, who asked his fellow Democrats to join him in supporting the president, who was running on a Union ticket. Like Kendall, Johnson blamed secession on a "Southern conspiracy" within the Democratic party, but he went further and called the entire party proslavery. In denying the charge Kendall laid out the Jacksonian position. The party, he said, opposed the emancipation of the slaves not because of a "*love of slavery*" but because of a "*love of liberty*, of the *Constitution, and the Union.*" This was the same position that Democrats had held since the 1830s. By "love of liberty" Kendall meant liberty for white people—the doctrine of *Herrenvolk*, or master-race, democracy, in which oppression of blacks or Indians was justified as a means of providing opportunity for whites. Abolitionism and executive emancipation, so the doctrine went, violated the Constitution and endangered the Union.[30]

Kendall rejected Johnson's plea and was delighted when the Democrats nominated McClellan, a War Democrat, for president. He was less satisfied with the platform, which was written by the peace wing of the party. No longer tolerant of Lincoln's imprisonment of editors, he accepted the plank condemning the president for violating more than a dozen constitutional rights, including "arbitrary military arrest" and "the suppression of freedom of . . . the press." He could not, however, accept the call for an immediate armistice and a convention of the states to bring about peace. After the election he attacked the "peace Democrats" for their "equivocal platform."[31]

During the campaign some Democrats resorted to vulgarity and racism to brand the Republicans as believers in racial equality and racial intermarriage. In "The Lincoln Catechism" they asked, "By whom hath the Constitution been made obsolete?" and answered, "by Abraham Africanus the First." When they asked, "What are the Ten Commandments?" one reply was, "Thou

---

USN, to Col. J. P. Sanderson, 17 June 1864, U.S. War Department, *War of the Rebellion . . . Official Records of the Union and Confederate Armies*, series 2, vol. 7 (Washington, 1899), 355 ("strong").

30. Kendall to Johnson, 29 June 1864 (summary), Andrew Johnson, *The Papers of Andrew Johnson*, ed. Leroy P. Graf, Ralph W. Haskins, and Paul H. Bergeron, 16 vols. to date (Knoxville, 1967–), 7:55–56.

31. The *New York Times* went too far when it called Kendall one of the "builders" of the platform. *New York Times*, 4 Sept. 1864; Kendall to Johnson, 29 June 1864, Johnson, *Papers*, 7:55–56; "Democratic Platform," 1864, Schlesinger, *History of American Presidential Elections*, 1:1179–80; Kendall to C. L. Paschal, 21 Jan. 1865, Kendall Papers, Gallaudet Archives; R. F. Stevens to William B. Campbell, 29 July 1864, Campbell Family Papers.

shalt swear that the negro shall be the equal of the white man." There is no evidence that Kendall had anything to do with this trash; yet the racism in the Catechism was not much different from his own racist comments in his letter to Lewis Tappan or the assumptions of his *Herrenvolk* democracy. In the election the Democrats' early hopes were dashed. Bolstered by the fall of Atlanta on September 2, Lincoln was reelected by an electoral vote of 212 to 21.[32]

Kendall's efforts in the campaign were remarkable, since much of his work was done while he was suffering from the loss of his wife. Early in June Jane fell sick with typhoid fever, and it was soon evident that she would not recover. She seemed reasonably well on the evening of June 24, but before daybreak the next morning she was gone. As Kendall thought back over their thirty-eight years together, all he could say was: "We were very poor, and she was very happy. We became tolerably rich, and she was scarcely happier." The women in the church sewing circle missed her "encouraging smile." Morse remembered her as "considerate and gentle."[33]

Just as he had done when Mary died, Kendall kept at his work. Three days after Jane's death, he delivered his address at Gallaudet's inauguration, the next day he sent his letter to Johnson, a day later he signed the deed for the church property, and in the following two weeks he published two important campaign articles. He was determined not to let the loss "*ruin*" him, but it took a heavy toll. "The death of a beloved wife," he told a friend, "first awoke me to the fact that I was *an old man* [and that] almost none [were] left of the generation to which I belong." He was seventy-four.[34]

Facing life with no wife and few contemporaries, Kendall turned to the church and began to reconsider his unwillingness to join. He had never trusted the complex doctrines on which membership was based. He was too confident in his own intellect to let others explain the mysteries of God and the universe. In 1856 he sent a testy note to the Reverend George W. Samson of the E Street Church criticizing his sermon on the paradox of free will and an all-powerful God. My "mind and heart revolt," he said, "at every attempt to penetrate the counsels of God." But on March 22, 1865, amidst a revival in the church, he gave in. There was "a strong desire," he told his pastor, that he set a good "example" by joining. If he held back, he would be telling the world that "to be a good man, it [was] not necessary to be a Christian." For the first

32. Schlesinger, *History of American Presidential Elections*, 1:1214, 1220.

33. *Autobiography*, 652–54; Morse to Kendall, 30 June 1864, Morse Papers.

34. Kendall to Joseph S. Kennard, 7 July 1865, in *Autobiography*, 663–64.

time since he was a boy, he believed that he could "do more good in the church than out of it."[35]

His baptism on April 2 was headline news in the Washington press even though it had to compete with Robert E. Lee's evacuation of Richmond. Since the new church was not yet completed, the baptism took place at E Street. "Deep solemnity prevailed," said one account, as the Reverend J. S. Kennard marched down the aisle "followed by two young ladies . . . and then the venerable form of the Hon. Amos Kendall." As the choir sang "All hail the power of Jesus' name," the three "took their seats in front of the pulpit . . . enrobed for the impressive service of immersion." After the two women had been baptized, Kendall "devoutly descended the steps leading into the pool" and Kennard then baptized him.[36]

During the next year Kendall devoted himself to building the new church, which he promised would be "an ornament to the National Capital." The architect was Adolph Cluss, a German immigrant, who designed many other buildings in Washington. When the parishioners had trouble raising their quota of $6,000, Kendall paid almost the entire bill. He turned the title to the building over to the church but with certain stipulations. Determined as his father had been to have a beautiful church, he specified that the parishioners must raise enough money to pay for carpeting, seat cushions, and an organ in the sanctuary as well as a clock and a bell in one of the towers. The church was never to incur a debt greater than $1,000, and the church service must never be interrupted by the passing of collection plates. If the church violated any of these and other provisions, the building would revert to Kendall's heirs.[37]

By the spring of 1866 the work was completed. The new church was a massive, brick, Gothic structure, measuring 75 by 90 feet, with two square towers and a 180-foot wrought iron steeple. The sanctuary, which was on the second floor, seated seven hundred; its "ceiling, doors, and woodwork were gracefully arched," and light streamed in through tall stained glass windows on the sides and a round rosette window high up at either end. It was the ornament that Kendall wanted, much larger, more imposing, far more deco-

35. Kendall to George W. Samson, 15 Oct. 1856, 25 Dec. 1861, Kendall to T. R. Howlett, 22 Mar., 1 Apr. 1865, in *Autobiography*, 552–54, 655–56, 658–59; William A. Wilbur, *Chronicles of Calvary Baptist Church in the City of Washington* (Washington, 1914), 24.

36. *Washington Daily Constitutional Union*, 3 Apr. 1865; *Autobiography*, 659–60.

37. Kendall to J. B. Varnum, 17 Nov. 1864, McCalla Papers (quotation); Tiller and Tiller, *At Calvary*, 9–11, 289–92, 299; *Autobiography*, 666–67.

rated, but less graceful than the tiny meetinghouse that he remembered from his boyhood in Dunstable.[38]

At the dedication on June 3 an overflowing audience heard a sermon by George Dana Boardman, newly appointed pastor of the famous First Baptist Church in Philadelphia and later a strong voice in the social gospel movement. For Kendall it was a crowning moment, but as often happened, he was too sick to enjoy it. Suffering with a cold and a high fever, he barely managed to attend. God had sent "this disappointment," he remarked, to punish him for "anticipat[ing] too much worldly enjoyment on this occasion."[39]

Kendall had less than a month to enjoy the new church, for on June 27 he and the Stickneys left for a fifteen-month tour of the British Isles, the continent, and Jerusalem. During the journey he made great efforts to attend Baptist churches but often had to settle for other denominations. His descriptions of these services were reminiscent of his cavalier treatment of services in Boston, Washington, and Kentucky half a century before. His health was good, and nothing seemed to daunt him. He climbed Mount Vesuvius and hiked along Alpine trails, survived "fatiguing journeys on horseback," and thought nothing of "sleeping in tents within view of Bedouin robbers." He occasionally encountered poverty and was no more sympathetic than he had been on his journey to Vermont in his college days. After seeing "rude Irish hut[s]," which humans shared with "beasts and fowls," he commented scornfully that the dwellings showed "the degradation to which man [had] sunk . . . by transgressing the laws of his nature."[40]

Home at last in October 1867, he was welcomed by a gala reception at Calvary Baptist Church. Benjamin B. French reported smugly that the hall was "well filled, with well-dressed and good-looking people." While working with Kendall in the Magnetic Company and more recently in the Columbia Institution, French had changed his mind several times about his colleague. Now he had nothing but good to say. Kendall, he wrote, "has accumulated an independent fortune [and] is spending the income . . . in a manner worthy of his strong mind and excellent & generous heart."[41]

Again he had but a brief moment to bask in his accomplishments. In the midst of a heavy snowstorm early in the morning of December 15 the church

38. Tiller and Tiller, *At Calvary*, 299–300; Wilbur, *Chronicles*, 34–35.
39. Tiller and Tiller, *At Calvary*, 300; *Autobiography*, 665.
40. *Autobiography*, 668–74.
41. French, *Witness*, 546–47.

caught fire and burned so completely that the interior was gutted and only the steeple, one tower, and two walls remained standing. Kendall's life had been affected by the burning of two other buildings—the Kentucky state capitol and the Washington post office—but this fire hurt the most. Nonetheless, he appeared unshaken at the next church meeting and offered a resolution calling on the congregation to rebuild its "beautiful temple of worship. . . . without any material alteration." The motion passed without debate and Kendall was again elected to the building committee. The fire was not the financial disaster it might have been, for Kendall, now experienced in the ways of capitalism, had taken the precaution of insuring the building. The insurance paid for most of the $65,000 needed for rebuilding, and Kendall took care of the rest— perhaps $15,000. The work proceeded so rapidly that there was hope that it would be completed in a year and a half.[42]

By the spring of 1868 Kendall was convinced that his "race on earth [was] nearly run." Of course he had said this many times before, but now he was almost seventy-nine and there were more than the usual disquieting signs. His "eyesight and hearing [were] gradually failing," and his "poor walking machine [was] wearing out." He admitted being so forgetful that by the time he had finished writing a paragraph he had often forgotten "what [he] had said at the beginning."[43]

Yet energy remained, and there was still more good work to be done. At the Columbia Institution Gallaudet was hosting a conference for the heads of American schools for the deaf. During the conference, May 12–17, the delegates debated the merits of hand signs and lipreading and agreed on a compromise resolution with which Gallaudet and Kendall were comfortable. All schools for the deaf should offer "adequate" training in "articulation and lipreading" for the deaf but not for "congenital mutes." In July Congress made the future of the institution secure by increasing the number of free scholarships from ten to twenty-five and by appropriating $48,000 for additional construction.[44]

At the first graduation of the college in June 1869 Kendall called it—as he had his church—an "ornament" to the city. "What more noble invention has Christian civilization brought to man than the means . . . to enable these unfortunate children . . . of silence to receive . . . knowledge and religion?" His

42. Tiller and Tiller, *At Calvary*, 13–14; Wilbur, *Chronicles*, 33–36.
43. *Autobiography*, between 625 and 626, 675.
44. Gallaudet, "History of the Columbia Institution," 9–10.

address showed how closely his ideals for the deaf, the church, the Union, and American society in general were intertwined. He implored the graduates to live by the one "great principle" of the Bible: "obedience to law and rightful authority." He had made the same call for authority in his prewar YMCA speech attacking abolitionists.[45]

During the election of 1868 there was one last campaign letter. Speaking as "the only surviving member of Gen. Jackson's cabinet," he rejected the reconstruction policies of the Radical Republicans and supported President Johnson's policy of restoring the Confederate states without giving the freedmen the vote. He denounced Congress for adopting the unconstitutional "absurdity" that the seceding states were "conquered enemies" and for denying Virginia, Texas, and Mississippi the right to take part in the election. Congress should never have "subjected" white southerners "to the absolute control of ignorant and penniless negroes" by giving black males the right to vote.[46]

Kendall's letter expressed the indictment of Radical Republican Reconstruction that held sway in the United States until after World War II. It reflected his years in Kentucky, his career as a Jacksonian Democratic politician, his opposition to abolitionism, and his long-held belief in states' rights, black inferiority, and the Union—in short master-race democracy. It placed him shoulder to shoulder with the Democratic ticket of Horatio Seymour and Francis P. Blair's son Frank, and it reunited him politically with the elder Blair and Gideon Welles. The latter two had supported Lincoln and emancipation, but like Kendall they could not accept suffrage and civil rights for the freedmen. The letter, however, did not reconcile Kendall and Blair personally.[47]

After the election of Ulysses S. Grant, Kendall left Kendall Green and rented a place in Washington with the intention of moving in with the Stickneys, who were building a house near Calvary Baptist Church. A few days after Christmas he was one of the featured guests at a dinner in honor of Samuel F. B. Morse at Delmonico's in New York. Others who attended were future presidential candidate Samuel J. Tilden, William Cullen Bryant, the painter Daniel Huntington, and Kendall's telegraph rivals Chief Justice Salmon P. Chase, Cyrus W. Field, and Ezra Cornell. In his speech that night Morse singled out Kendall for special recognition, prompting such an ovation

45. *Autobiography,* 555–58.

46. *Letter from Amos Kendall* (Washington, 1868). American Antiquarian Society.

47. Smith, *Francis Preston Blair,* 386–89; Niven, *Gideon Welles,* 488–520.

that "the peaked little man" struggled to his feet. There he was, accepted, no longer ridiculed, but still in the shadow of a great man.[48]

The good works continued. He gave money for two mission Sunday schools and $17,000 more to establish the Kendall Mission Fund for new churches. On June 15, 1869, he signed a revised deed for Calvary Church and a month later took part in the dedication of the new building. He had already donated $6,000 to Columbian College (later George Washington University) to support a scholarship fund. When the first recipient paid a call on Kendall in July, the old man said that he might not be alive when the scholarship was completed and urged the young man to avoid temptation. Kendall's charitable gifts totaled at least $150,000, more than a quarter of his net worth.[49]

With his philanthropies arranged, he and daughter Marion left on August 2 for a vacation in the Adirondacks. No longer able to tolerate the discomforts of travel, Kendall was annoyed by a difficult railroad connection and a sixteen-mile ride in "a primitive stage" and a farm wagon. By the time he arrived at the home of his nephew Andrew Kendall, he had come down with another cold. After staying only forty-eight hours, he headed home, arriving sick and exhausted two days before his eightieth birthday.[50]

It was soon clear that he was suffering from more than a cold. He called it bilious fever, but it was probably cancer. He was confined to his bed, first at the Foxes' and then at the Stickneys' new house. The cancer spread to his liver and stomach, and he could no longer eat without suffering great pain. Now certain that he had only a short time left, he considered "hasten[ing] the end" by "abstain[ing] from food," but could not bring himself to commit "the terrible sin of suicide."[51]

Yet with all this, his mind was clear, his voice was audible, and he had much to say. "For hours continuously," Stickney recalled, "he poured forth a stream of calm, collected instruction . . . to members of his family, children and grandchildren, to officers of the institutions [and] the church he had served." He instructed his children in the gospel of wealth, saying that he had never owed them "anything more than a living and an education," and that it was "best for a man of property to make his donations to objects of charity during his lifetime . . . that he might personally superintend their appropriation." He was still in control.[52]

48. Mabee, *American Leonardo*, 367–68.

49. Tiller and Tiller, *At Calvary*, 13–14, 292–93; *New York Times*, 18 July 1869.

50. Kendall to Stickney, 6 Aug. 1869, in *Autobiography*, 684–85.

51. *Autobiography*, 685–86.

52. Ibid., 686–89.

His main regret was that he had never completed his biography of Andrew Jackson. Over the years he had brought up the subject so many times
that it was obvious that it had become "a source of self reproach." He blamed
his failure on lack of money and lack of help. When James Parton published
his critical biography of Jackson, a defensive Kendall called it "a caricature of
the noble old hero." Jackson, he told Stickney, "was as gentle as a lamb. . . .
The honest old giant opposed the Bank of the United States from principle
purely." Unwilling to take any credit away from Jackson, he made no mention
of his own role in the Bank veto. Blair's cynical assumption that Kendall
would have glorified himself if he had written a history of the administration
was wrong. Never sure of his own greatness and always a Jackson man, Kendall
could only glorify the Old Hero.[53]

Kendall's final hours were in the style of the great deathbed scenes so
prized in the nineteenth century. While his children wept at his bedside, a
choir one floor below sang "Jesus lover of my soul / Let me to thy bosom fly."
Several times he uttered words that were important to a man with his intellect
and his ability to make enemies: "I thank God he has given me my mind in
these last moments," and "I die in peace with all my fellow-men." He relied,
he said, on "that Saviour" who cares for those "who sincerely repent of their
sins." Surely Jackson would have said of Amos Kendall, as he had of Zebedee
Kendall, that "he [had] lived to be prepared for death, and in his life [had]
learned how to die." He did so at sunrise on Friday, November 12.[54]

At noon on Sunday Benjamin B. French left his home just east of the
Capitol and rode down the hill to Stickney's house at M and 6th. From there
he and the other pallbearers accompanied the coffin with Kendall's body to
the upper vestibule of Calvary Church. While the body lay in state, the pallbearers waited across the street in the home of Horatio King. The eight men
all knew Kendall and the city well, for they were an elite group, drawn from
every phase of his life in Washington. Two had served in the Post Office, two

53. For references to the biography see *Washington Union,* 5 Aug. 1847; Kendall to Jane Kendall,
16 Aug. 1845, Kendall to Stickney, 1862, in *Autobiography,* 529–30, 685–86; Kendall to Morse, 22
Feb. 1857, 5 July 1861, Morse Papers; Kendall to Van Buren, 29 Sept. 1859, Bedford Brown Papers,
Duke University Rare Book, Manuscript, and Special Collections Library; Kendall to Henry S.
Randall, 10 June 1862, Miscellaneous Collections, Historical Society of Pennsylvania; Samson, *In
Memoriam,* 25. For a sense of what Kendall would have written about Jackson's presidency see his
idealized view of Old Hickory in his Trenton YMCA speech, Feb. 1862, in *Autobiography,* 628–39.

54. *Autobiography,* 690; Jackson to Kendall, 10 Oct. 1839, Jackson Papers.

were deacons in the church, another was a telegraph official, and French represented both the telegraph and the school for the deaf.[55]

They returned at two and carried the coffin into the sanctuary. The
church was crowded. The family, close friends, and, it was reported, "many
colored servants," shared the center seats. The choir and students from the
school for the deaf filled the gallery. Following Kendall's request to avoid "os-
tentation," the service was reasonably short and simple. Four ministers, all
friends of Kendall, offered scripture, prayer, and a brief eulogy; there were no
lay speakers. At the end all sang once again "Jesus lover of my soul." Kendall
was then buried next to Jane at Glenwood Cemetery.[56]

55. King was postmaster general briefly. French, *Witness*, 606–7; "Obituary of Amos Kendall,"
*Washington Evening Star*, 12 Nov. 1869.

56. French, *Witness*, 607; Samson, *In Memoriam; Evening Star*, 12 Nov. 1869. There was a bit
of an irony in the choice of the burial plot because Glenwood Cemetery was originally the farm
of Phineas Bradley, the assistant postmaster general whose removal from the Post Office had
caused Kendall and Barry so much difficulty. Glenwood Cemetery brochure, c. 1996.

CONCLUSION

There are many reasons why Harriet Martineau found Amos Kendall so mysterious. A complex man, his life was filled with paradox, constant change, and an apparent lack of consistency. What else can be said of a class-conscious elitist who turned into an egalitarian democrat; of a young politician on the fringes of Henry Clay's party who moved to the heart of Andrew Jackson's; of a Jacksonian who condemned speculators and the "money power" but speculated himself and yearned to be rich? What else can be said of a farm boy who became a commercial capitalist; of a community-minded republican who adopted the self-centered liberalism of the new era; of a man with many talents who failed more often than he succeeded, yet retired a millionaire? Here is a generous philanthropist who showed little compassion for the downtrodden, who had an authoritarian streak, and who became the agent and friend of one of the leading nativists and racists of his time. Shortly after Kendall's death the Republican publicist John W. Forney found it "impossible to believe that this gentle, quiet, and soft-spoken man was the same whose nervous editorials aroused the resentment of the Whigs."[1]

One reason for these paradoxes and inconsistencies was Kendall's personality, which swung wildly between polar extremes, was not the same in public as it was in private, and in either case was viewed differently by friends and foes. The public Kendall was an ambitious, shrewd, intelligent man, quick to act, courageous, hardworking, determined, and always well organized. His enemies, however, saw only the self-important, self-seeking, materialistic, arrogant, stubborn, controlling, sometimes manipulative side of these public traits.

The private Kendall was far different. In his family life and in retirement Kendall was a humane, reform-minded, literary, loving, introspective, even visionary man. The negative side was less pleasant. He could be moralistic, fas-

1. John W. Forney, *Anecdotes of Public Men*, 2 vols. (New York, 1873, 1881), 2:151.

tidious, sentimental, self-pitying, and frequently insecure and depressed. This complex combination of public and private, positive and negative traits was the source of many of the paradoxes and inconsistencies.

But a more important source was the ever-changing society in which he lived. Amos Kendall started life in the restricted world of small farms, his beliefs and behavior circumscribed by family discipline, church doctrine, town tradition, and economic limits. He ended life the typical self-made man, who had mastered the individualistic, seemingly unlimited world of American capitalism. In making the transition he experienced many of the changes that made the new society possible. He went to college, shook off his allegiance to the church and his reliance on his father, borrowed money, went west, tried one job after another, and finally settled into the new profession of political editing. In the process he encountered many of the problems brought on by the new economy—the cycle of boom and bust, the conflicting demands of civic virtue and self-interest, and the widening gap between rich and poor, men and women, abolitionist and slaveowner.

This changing life encouraged inconsistency by forcing him to reassess his attitudes and assumptions. He held onto some of his early convictions— his morality and paternalism, for example—but more often he compromised or broke free. His boyhood suspicion of commercialism and monopoly carried over into the war on the BUS and his hostility toward railroads but yielded to his enthusiasm for the telegraph business. His belief in a limited central government gave way for a while to liberal nationalism but returned after the Panic of 1819. He was forever talking about returning to the farm, but it was just talk. When he first saw the smoke arising from industrial Pittsburgh, he exclaimed, "Here is my country" and committed himself to the new capitalist world.[2]

Yet the apparent inconsistency masked important themes that ran through most of his life and that he shared with many Americans. One obviously was making money. That was why he went west, why he tried so many occupations, why he chose not to live in the heart of the Bluegrass, why he started his mill, why he clung to Clay, and why he moved over to Jackson. Even while engrossed in Jacksonian party battles, he speculated in public lands, earned extra income writing for the *Globe*, accepted the position as postmaster general, and then gave it up to edit the *Extra Globe*—all for money.

Nothing seemed to work until he met Samuel F. B. Morse, and then his

2. *Autobiography*, 99.

success went far beyond his dreams. Kendall was never fully entrepreneurial, never a full-blown capitalist in the sense of being a banker or a manufacturer, but he desperately wanted to make money. He was the perfect example of Alexis de Tocqueville's famous judgment on the United States: "I know of no country, indeed, where the love of money has taken stronger hold on the affections of men."[3]

More important, however, was his belief in democracy. Kendall did not of course start out as a democrat, for Dunstable was a hierarchic, deferential community. Soon after leaving college he rejected a suggestion that he get into democratic editing. On his trip west his elitist scorn for Baptist preachers and undisciplined militiamen was far from egalitarian. Even in his early days as a Kentucky editor he still considered himself above politics and still looked down upon soldiers.

But Kentucky turned him into a democrat. The militia musters introduced him to democratic politics, and the compensation battle taught him how to appeal to the people. In the 1824 gubernatorial campaign his entertaining, populist editorials, his attacks on privilege and wealth, and his appeals to resentment and envy were examples of a new democratic style of writing. His political organization, the Relief party, publicized the issues and mobilized the voters. He used these democratic techniques on the national stage in 1828 when he exploited the bargain charge to defeat John Quincy Adams.

Yet Kendall never abandoned republicanism. In the Kentucky elections he based his message on the assumption that he represented a country party resisting a vicious court conspiracy to take liberty from the people. He often fell back on republican charges of corruption to prove the existence of a crisis. At times the republican and democratic styles were blended. In the bargain charge, for example, he attacked Clay both for republican corruption and for his refusal to obey the democratic instructions of the people of Kentucky.

When he reached Washington, Kendall continued to put his mark on American democracy. His activities and those of other often-scorned editors were steps toward broader participation in government; the patronage system accelerated the process. The chain of Jackson newspapers kindled interest in politics while spreading the party line. Kendall showed off his democratic writing style in at least ten of Jackson's formal state papers, twice as many as anyone else. The most influential was the Bank veto. With its populist style

3. Tocqueville, *Democracy in America*, 1:51.

and its concern for the liberty of the people, it became a classic combination of republican and democratic language.[4]

But there were limits to Kendall's democracy. If democracy is to work, the voters must be well informed and the government must carry out their wishes. Although Kendall's writings spread information, they often publicized positions rather than clarified issues. It is hard to prove that a majority was calling for the removal of the deposits. And the patronage system, though it increased participation in government, often produced results such as corruption, low morale, and inefficiency that the voters did not endorse.

Furthermore, participation in Kendall's democracy was limited to adult white males. In the Eaton affair he supported Jackson's efforts to end the political role of the ladies of Washington—a policy that made the government less aristocratic but also discouraged an early effort at female participation. His suppression of the mails in Charleston turned the Democratic party toward a policy of master-race democracy. The perpetuation of this policy after the Civil War kept freedmen from taking part in American democracy.

Even though Kendall supported political and social equality, he did not believe in extending it to the economic sphere. His Bank veto called for equal opportunity, not economic equality. In his essay "What Is Democracy?" he said that the duty of government was "to protect . . . personal liberty, and the exercise of equal political power," and nothing more.[5]

Kendall firmly believed that partisanship was an integral part of democracy. Other than Andrew Jackson and Martin Van Buren, no one did more to build the Democratic party. He began to think of a national party in 1827 when he wrote to Old Hickory and visited Jackson men in Washington. Once he was in the government, he did much to transform the Jackson coalition into a mass political party. He started with a system of party patronage that was designed to hold the party together. In helping Jackson prepare his first annual message he wrote statements on rotation in office, Indian removal, and opposition to the BUS that became the basis of the Jackson program. In the next two years he created a party newspaper, reshaped the party leadership with the Kitchen Cabinet, and arranged for the first national Democratic party convention. The Bank War, which he orchestrated, helped create the Democratic party and the second two-party system.

4. There were eighteen in all. Richard P. Longaker, "Was Jackson's Kitchen Cabinet a Cabinet?" *Mississippi Valley Historical Review* 44 (1957): 103–4.
5. *Autobiography*, 437–40.

Another theme running through Kendall's life was the transportation and communications revolution. No one was better acquainted with transportation than Kendall, who spent hundreds of days on horseback and in stagecoaches, on flatboats and canal boats, and aboard trains and steamboats. But his real contribution was in communications. A newspaper editor, party organizer, political propagandist, postmaster general, telegraph builder, and promoter of language for the deaf, he spent his life speeding up the flow of information. His major failure was his inability to get the cooperation of the railroads.

As a key representative of so many important themes in American life—especially democracy—Kendall justified the interest that Harriet Martineau and Francis Grund had shown in him. Even though Martineau was distressed at the way he handled the Charleston Post Office affair, she came to understand why Americans held him in such superstitious awe. And Grund knew that his friend had been correct when he credited Kendall with showing that "the various principles of democracy may be united into a system." Kendall helped build a system that made democracy work, but in the process he played a part in limiting its possibilities.[6]

6. Martineau, *Society in America*, 1:60–61; Grund, *Aristocracy in America*, 98–99.

# SELECTED BIBLIOGRAPHY

## Manuscript Collections

**American Philosophical Society Library, Philadelphia**
Duane Family Papers

**Calvary Baptist Church, Washington, D.C.**
Records of the Calvary Baptist Church

**Chicago Historical Society**
Amos Kendall Papers
George A. Simmons Papers

**Connecticut Historical Society, Hartford**
Gideon Welles Papers

**Dartmouth College Library, Hanover, N.H.**
Frederick Chase Collection
Amos Kendall Papers

**Duke University Rare Book, Manuscript, and Special Collections Library, Durham, N.C.**
Bedford Brown Papers
Campbell Family Papers
Francis W. Dawson Papers
John M. McCalla Papers
Francis O. J. Smith Papers

**Filson Historical Society, Louisville, Ky.**
William T. Barry Papers (typescripts)
Hickman Collection
Amos Kendall Miscellaneous Papers

## Gallaudet University Archives, Washington, D.C.

*John Farley and Others v. Amos Kendall and Others,* United States District Court for the
    District of Columbia, 1841–1845, RG 21, National Archives (copy)
Edward M. Gallaudet Papers
Amos Kendall Papers
Miscellaneous Papers
Records of Gallaudet University

## Historical Society of Pennsylvania, Philadelphia

James Buchanan Papers
Cadwalader Collection
Conaroe Papers
Dreer Collection
Lewis-Neilson Papers
Miscellaneous Collections
Henry O'Rielly Papers

## Houghton Library, Harvard University, Cambridge

New Hampshire Whig Papers

## Library of Congress, Washington, D.C.

Nicholas Biddle Papers
Blair and Rives Papers
Blair Family Papers
Crosby N. Boyd Papers
Daniel D. Brodhead Papers
John D. Caton Papers
William W. Corcoran Papers
John J. Crittenden Papers
Moses Dawson Papers
Joseph Desha Papers
Andrew J. Donelson Papers
Duff Green Papers
Andrew Jackson Papers
Amos Kendall Papers
William L. Marcy Papers
Samuel F. B. Morse Papers
James K. Polk Papers
William C. Rives Papers
Roger B. Taney Papers
Lewis Tappan Papers

Nicholas Trist Papers
John Tyler Papers
Martin Van Buren Papers
Gideon Welles Papers
Levi Woodbury Papers
Nathaniel Wright Papers

**Library of Virginia, Archives Research Services, Richmond**
State Records Collection

**Maine Historical Society, Portland**
Francis O. J. Smith Papers (Coll. #38)

**Massachusetts Historical Society, Boston**
George Bancroft Papers
Edward Everett Papers
C. E. French Papers
Amos Kendall Papers
Amos Adams Lawrence Papers

**Memphis/Shelby County Public Library and Information Center**
Henry A. Montgomery Papers

**Missouri Historical Society, St. Louis**
George Champlain Sibley Papers

**National Archives, Washington, D.C.**
Bureau of the Census. United States Census Schedules, 1810. Jefferson County, Kentucky (Record Group 29)
———, 1820. Franklin County, Kentucky
———, 1820. Scott County, Kentucky
———, 1830. Georgetown, District of Columbia
———, 1860. Washington County, District of Columbia
Corporation of Washington, General Assessment, Wards 4 and 5, 1839–1843
District of Columbia Administration, Probate of Amos Kendall
Post Office. Postmaster General Letterbooks (Record Group 28)
State Department. Letters of Application and Recommendation during the Administration of Andrew Jackson (Record Group 59)
———. Passport Applications, 1866 (Record Group 59)
Treasury Department. Fourth Auditor, Miscellaneous Letters (Record Group 217)
———. Letters from Banks (Record Group 56)

———. Reports of Amos Kendall, 1833 (Record Group 56)
———. William F. Sherman, comp., "Inventory of the Records of the Accounting Officers of the Department of the Treasury"

**National Museum of American History Archives Center, Washington, D.C.**
Western Union Telegraph Company Collection

**New Hampshire Historical Society, Concord**
Isaac Hill Papers

**New Jersey Historical Society, Newark**
Mahlon and Philemon Dickerson Papers (Manuscript Group 13)

**New-York Historical Society, New York**
Gustavus Vasa Fox Papers
Miscellaneous Manuscripts, Kendall, Amos
Henry O'Rielly Papers

**New York Public Library, New York**
Amos Kendall Papers
Francis O. J. Smith Papers

**Princeton University Library, Manuscripts Division, Department of Rare Books and Special Collections, Princeton**
Blair-Lee Papers
Throop and Martin Family Papers

**Smithsonian Institution Archives, Washington, D.C.**
Alfred Vail Papers

**University of Virginia Library, Charlottesville**
Albert and Shirley Small Special Collections Library

**Virginia State Library and Archives, Richmond**
Virginia Board of Public Works Papers

*Microfilm Editions of Manuscript Collections*

Supplement to the Andrew Jackson Papers. Wilmington, Del.: Scholarly Resources, Microfilm, 1986
Papers of Martin Van Buren. Alexandria, Va.: Chadwyck-Healey, Microfilm, 1987

## Newspapers and Contemporary Periodicals

*Albany Argus*, 1831
Baltimore *Niles' Weekly Register*, 1822–38
Boston *Courier*, 1832
Frankfort, Ky., *Argus of Western America*, 1816–30
Frankfort, Ky., *Commentator*, 1820
*Georgetown (Ky.) Patriot*, 1816
*New-Yorker*, 1836–40
*New York Times*, 1860–64, 1869
*Richmond Enquirer*, 1831–32, 1835
Washington *Daily Constitutional Union*, 1865
Washington *National Intelligencer*, 1828–40
Washington *Evening Star*, 1860, 1869
Washington *Extra Globe*, 1832
Washington *Globe*, 1830–43
Washington *Kendall's Expositor*, 1841–44
Washington *National Journal*, 1829–30
Washington *Union*, 1846
Washington *United States Telegraph*, 1828–37
Washington and New York *United States Magazine and Democratic Review*, 1837–39,
 1843

## Published Writings of Amos Kendall (by date)

"Amos Kendall's Ode to Freedom" [1816]. Ed. Robert P. Hay. *Register of the Kentucky State Historical Society* 68 (1970): 239–51.
*An Address on the Principles of Masonry.* Frankfort, Ky.: Amos Kendall and Co., 1823.
*Letters to John Quincy Adams, Relative to the Fisheries and the Mississippi.* Lexington, Ky.: William Tanner, 1823.
[Henry, Patrick, pseud.]. *The Wictorian Dinner.* Frankfort, Ky.: Amos Kendall and Co., 1824.
*Abolition!! Infatuation of Federal Whig Leaders of the South.* Washington, D.C., 1840.
*The Case of Lieutenant Hooe—A Notable Instance of Whig Honesty.* Washington, D.C., 1840.
*Mr. Kendall's Address to the People of the United States.* Washington, D.C., 1840.
"General Jackson's Fine." *United States Magazine and Democratic Review*, January 1843.
*Life of Gen. Andrew Jackson.* American Culture Series. New York: Harper Brothers, 1843–44. Microfilm.
*A Faithful History of the Cherokee Tribe of Indians.* Washington, D.C.: Jesse E. Dow,

1846. (Coauthor with S. C. Stambaugh, George W. Paschall, and M. St. Clair Clarke.)

*Morse's Telegraph and the O'Rielly Contract.* Louisville, Ky.: Prentice and Weissinger, 1848.

*American Electro-Magnetic Telegraph: A Brief Review of the Arguments Used against the Patents Granted to Professor S. F. B. Morse.* Washington, D.C.: John T. Towers, 1850. American Antiquarian Society.

*Morse's Patent. Full Exposure of Dr. Charles T. Jackson's Pretensions to the Invention of the American Electro Magnetic Telegraph.* Washington, D.C.: John T. Towers, 1852. American Antiquarian Society.

*Morse's Telegraph. Argument of Amos Kendall in Support of Morse's Patent for the Electro Magnetic Telegraph.* N.p., n.d. American Antiquarian Society.

Kendall to editor of the *Pennsylvanian*, 22 Oct. 1856. *Boston Public Library Monthly Bulletin* 7 (1902): 267.

*Circular to the Stockholders of the American Telegraph Company.* New York, 1860.

*Secession. Letters of Amos Kendall.* Washington, D.C.: Henry Polkinhorn, 1861.

*Letters Exposing the Mismanagement of Public Affairs by Abraham Lincoln.* Washington, D.C.: *Constitutional Union* Office, 1864.

*Letters on Our Country's Crisis.* Washington, D.C.: *Constitutional Union* Office, 1864.

*Letter from Amos Kendall.* Washington, D.C.: W. S. Wayson, 1868. American Antiquarian Society.

*Autobiography of Amos Kendall.* Ed. William Stickney. 1872. Reprint, New York: Peter Smith, 1949.

## Other Published Writings

Adams, Charles Francis. *Diary of Charles Francis Adams.* Ed. Aida DiPace Donald, David Donald, Marc Friedlander, and L. H. Butterfield. 8 vols. Cambridge: Harvard University Press, 1964–86.

Adams, John Quincy. *Memoirs of John Quincy Adams.* Ed. Charles Francis Adams. 12 vols. Philadelphia: J. B. Lippincott, 1875–77.

Bagley, Will, ed. *Scoundrel's Tale: The Samuel Brannan Papers.* Spokane, Wash.: Arthur H. Clark, 1999.

Barry, William T. "Letters of William T. Barry." *William and Mary College Quarterly* 13 (1904–5): 236–44; 14 (1905–6): 19–23, 230–41.

Benton, Thomas Hart. *Thirty Years' View.* 2 vols. New York: D. Appleton, 1854.

Biddle, Nicholas. *The Correspondence of Nicholas Biddle Dealing with National Affairs, 1807–1844.* Ed. Reginald C. McGrane. Boston: Houghton Mifflin, 1919.

Calhoun, John C. *The Papers of John C. Calhoun.* Ed. Robert L. Merriwether, W.

Edwin Hemphill, Clyde Wilson, and Shirley Bright Cook. 28 vols. Columbia: University of South Carolina Press, 1959–2003.

Clay, Henry. *The Papers of Henry Clay.* Ed. James F. Hopkins, Mary W. M. Hargreaves, Robert Seager II, and Melba Porter Hay. 11 vols. Lexington: University Press of Kentucky, 1959–92.

Derby, John Barton. *Political Reminiscences.* Boston: Horner & Palmer, 1835.

Desha, Joseph. *Governor's Message in Reply to the Resolutions Adopted in the House of Representatives on the Motion of Mr. Breckinridge* [14 Dec. 1825]. Frankfort, Ky.: Kendall, 1825.

Duane, William J. *Narrative and Correspondence concerning the Removal of the Deposits.* 1838. Reprint, New York: Burt Franklin, 1965.

Forney, John W. *Anecdotes of Public Men.* 2 vols. New York: Harper & Brothers, 1873, 1881.

French, Benjamin Brown. *Witness to the Young Republic: A Yankee's Journal, 1828–1870.* Ed. Donald B. Cole and John J. McDonough. Hanover, N.H.: University Press of New England, 1989.

Green, Duff. *Facts and Suggestions, Biographical, Historical, Financial, and Political. Addressed to the People of the United States.* New York: C. S. Wescott, 1866.

Grund, Francis J. *Aristocracy in America: From the Sketch-Book of a German Nobleman.* 1839. Reprint, New York: Harper, 1959.

Hamilton, James A. *Reminiscences of James A. Hamilton.* New York: Charles Scribner, 1869.

Hone, Philip. *The Diary of Philip Hone, 1828–1851.* Ed. Allan Nevins. New York: Dodd, Mead, 1936.

Hudson, Frederic. *Journalism in the United States from 1690 to 1872.* New York: Harper and Brothers, 1873.

Jackson, Andrew. *Correspondence of Andrew Jackson.* Ed. John Spencer Bassett and John Franklin Jameson. 7 vols. 1926–35. Reprint, New York: Kraus Reprint Co., 1969.

———. *The Papers of Andrew Jackson.* Ed. Harold D. Moser et al. 6 vols. to date. Knoxville: University of Tennessee Press, 1994–.

Johnson, Andrew. *The Papers of Andrew Johnson.* Ed. Leroy P. Graf, Ralph W. Haskins, and Paul H. Bergeron. 16 vols. to date. Knoxville: University of Tennessee Press, 1967–.

Johnson, Richard M. "The Letters of Colonel Richard M. Johnson of Kentucky." Ed. James A. Padgett. *Register of the Kentucky State Historical Society* 38 (1940): 186–201, 323–39; 39 (1941): 22–46, 172–88, 260–74, 358–67; 40 (1942): 69–91.

Leavy, William. "Memoirs of Lexington and Vicinity." *Register of the Kentucky State Historical Society* 41 (1943): 44–62, 110–35, 250–330.

Martineau, Harriet. *Retrospect of Western Travel.* 3 vols. London: Saunders and Otley, 1838.

———. *Society in America.* 3 vols. London: Saunders and Otley, 1837.

"Origin of the Democratic National Convention." *American Historical Magazine* 7 (1902): 267–73.

Padgett, James A., ed. "Correspondence between Governor Joseph Desha and Amos Kendall—1831–1835." *Register of the Kentucky State Historical Society* 38 (1940): 5–24.

Polk, James K. *Correspondence of James K. Polk.* Ed. Herbert Weaver, Paul H. Bergeron, and Wayne Cutler. 9 vols. to date. Nashville: Vanderbilt University Press, 1969–.

———. *The Diary of James K. Polk during His Presidency, 1845 to 1849.* Ed. Milo M. Quaife. Chicago: A. C. McClurg, 1910.

Smith, Margaret Bayard. *The First Forty Years of Washington Society.* Ed. Gaillard Hunt. 1906. Reprint, New York: Frederick Ungar, 1965.

Stedman, Ebenezer Hiram. *Bluegrass Craftsman, Being the Reminiscences of Ebenezer Hiram Stedman.* Ed. Frances L. S. Dugan and Jacqueline P. Bull. Lexington: University of Kentucky Press, 1959.

Swem, Earl Gregg, ed. *Letters on the Condition of Kentucky in 1825.* New York: Charles F. Heartman, 1916.

Taney, Roger B. "Roger B. Taney's 'Bank War Manuscript.'" Ed. Carl B. Swisher. *Maryland Historical Magazine* 53 (1958): 103–30, 215–37.

———. "Roger Brooke Taney's Account of His Relations with Thomas Ellicott in the Bank War." Ed. Stuart Bruchey. *Maryland Historical Magazine* 3 (1958): 58–74, 131–52.

Tocqueville, Alexis de. *Democracy in America.* Ed. Phillips Bradley. 2 vols. 1945. Reprint, New York: Alfred A. Knopf, 1980.

Van Buren, Martin. "The Autobiography of Martin Van Buren." Ed. John C. Fitzpatrick. *Annual Report of the American Historical Association for the Year 1918.* 2 vols. Washington, D.C.: Government Printing Office, 1920. Vol. 2.

———. *Inquiry into the Origin and Course of Political Parties in the United States.* 1867. Reprint, New York: Augustus M. Kelley, 1967.

Webster, Daniel. *The Papers of Daniel Webster: Correspondence.* Ed. Charles M. Wiltse and Harold T. Moser. 7 vols. Hanover, N.H.: University Press of New England, 1974–86.

Weed, Thurlow. *Autobiography of Thurlow Weed.* Ed. Harriet A. Weed. 1883. Reprint, New York: Da Capo Press, 1970.

Wise, Henry A. *Seven Decades of the Union.* Philadelphia: Lippincott, 1871.

Woodbury, Levi. "Levi Woodbury's 'Intimate Memoranda' of the Jackson Administration." Ed. Ari Hoogenboom and Herbert Ershkowitz. *Pennsylvania Magazine of History and Biography* 92 (1968): 507–15.

## Public Documents

*American State Papers: Naval Affairs.* Vols. 3, 4.
*American State Papers: Public Lands.* Vol. 6.

Clift, G. Glenn, comp. "Kentucky Marriages and Obituaries—1787–1860." *Register of the Kentucky State Historical Society* 36 (1938).

*A Compilation of the Messages and Papers of the Presidents, 1787–1897.* Comp. James D. Richardson. 10 vols. Washington, D.C.: Government Printing Office, 1897–99.

*Congressional Globe.* 1835–36, 1838–39, 1845–46.

Congressional Quarterly. *Guide to United States Elections.* 3d ed. Washington, D.C.: Congressional Quarterly, 1994.

Eliot, Jonathan, ed. *Debates in the Several State Conventions on the Adoption of the Federal Constitution.* 5 vols. Philadelphia: J. B. Lippincott, 1836.

Goldman, Perry M., and James S. Young, eds. *The United States Congressional Directories, 1789–1840.* New York: Columbia University Press, 1973.

Greer, William. *A Full Directory of Washington City.* Washington, D.C., 1834.

*Journal of the House of Representatives of the Commonwealth of Kentucky.* 1818–29.

*Journal of the Senate of the Commonwealth of Kentucky.* 1818–29.

*Kendall v. Stokes et al.* 44 U.S. 506–14.

Lanman, Charles. *Dictionary of the United States Congress.* Washington, D.C.: Government Printing Office, 1864.

Monroe, Ben. *Reports of the Court of Appeals of Kentucky.* 1846–47.

*Morse, Samuel F. B., and Alfred Vail against Francis O. J. Smith. Affidavit of Amos Kendall on part of Plaintiff.* New York: William C. Bryant, 1852.

*O'Rielly, Henry, et al., Appellants v. S. F. B. Morse et al.* 56 U.S. 601–33.

Petersen, Svend. *A Statistical History of the American Presidential Elections.* New York: Frederick Ungar, 1963.

Pruitt, Bettye Hobbs, ed. *The Massachusetts Tax Valuation List of 1771.* Boston: G. K. Hall, 1978.

*Register of Debates in Congress.* 1829–38.

U.S. Congress. Executive Documents. 1829–40.

———. House Documents. 1829–40.

———. Senate Documents. 1829–40.

———. *Senate Journal.* 1829–30, 1833–34.

*Vital Records of Dunstable, Massachusetts, to the End of the Year 1849.* Salem: Essex Institute, 1913.

"Will of William Woolfolk, 8 Aug. 1822." *Filson Club Historical Quarterly* 6 (1932): 192.

## Pamphlets and Other Primary Sources

Adams, John Quincy. *The Duplicate Letters, the Fisheries and the Mississippi: Documents Relating to Transactions at the Negotiation of Ghent.* Washington, D.C.: John Quincy Adams, 1822.

*Catalogue of Books in the United Fraternity's Library at Dartmouth College, June 1824.* Concord, N.H.: Isaac Hill, 1824.

*Catalogue of the Fraternity of Phi Beta Kappa, Alpha of New-Hampshire. Dartmouth College. 1832.* Hanover: Thomas Mann, 1832.

Columbia Institution for the Deaf and Dumb. *Proceedings of the Board of Directors of the Columbia Institution, Eulogistic of the Late Amos Kendall.* Washington, D.C.: Gibson Brothers, 1870.

Dartmouth College, Class of 1811. *Minutes of Their Meeting in 1849; Also Brief Biographical Notices of the Members.* Concord, N.H.: Asa McFarland, 1850.

Gallaudet, Edward M. "A History of the Columbia Institution for the Deaf and Dumb." Columbia Historical Society, *Records* 15 (1912): 1–22.

Gallaudet College. *Inauguration of the College for the Deaf and Dumb.* Washington, D.C., 1864.

Gouge, William M. *A Short History of Paper Money and Banking in the United States.* 1833. Reprint, New York: Augustus M. Kelley, 1968.

John, Richard R., ed. "Hiland Hall's 'Report on Incendiary Publications': A Forgotten Nineteenth-Century Defense of the Freedom of the Press." *American Journal of Legal History* 41 (1997): 94–105.

Kennedy, John Pendleton. *Quodlibet.* Philadelphia: J. B. Lippincott, 1840.

Lee, Henry. *A Biography of Andrew Jackson, Late Major-General of the Army of the United States.* Ed. Mark Mastromarino. Knoxville: Tennessee Presidents Trust, 1992.

Roane, Spencer. "Hampden Essays," 11–22 June 1819. In *John Marshall's Defense of "McCulloch v. Maryland,"* ed. Gerald Gunther. Stanford: Stanford University Press, 1969.

Samson, George W. *In Memoriam.* Washington, D.C.: Gibson Brothers, 1869.

## Secondary Sources: Books

Allgor, Catherine. *Parlor Politics: In Which the Ladies of Washington Help Build a City and a Government.* Charlottesville: University Press of Virginia, 2000.

Altschuler, Glenn C., and Stuart M. Blumin. *Rude Republic: Americans and Their Politics in the Nineteenth Century.* Princeton: Princeton University Press, 2000.

Ames, William E. *A History of the National Intelligencer.* Chapel Hill: University of North Carolina Press, 1972.

Appleby, Joyce Oldham. *Inheriting the Revolution: The First Generation of Americans.* Cambridge: Harvard University Press, 2000.

Ashworth, John. *"Agrarians" and "Aristocrats": Party Political Ideology in the United States, 1837–1846.* Cambridge: Cambridge University Press, 1983.

———. *Slavery, Capitalism, and Politics in the Antebellum Republic.* Vol. 1, *Commerce and Compromise, 1820–1850.* Cambridge: Cambridge University Press, 1995.

Barnes, Thurlow Weed. *Memoir of Thurlow Weed.* 1884. Reprint, Boston: Da Capo Press, 1970.

Belohlavek, John M. *"Let the Eagle Soar!" The Foreign Policy of Andrew Jackson.* Lincoln: University of Nebraska Press, 1985.

Benson, Lee. *The Concept of Jacksonian Democracy: New York as a Test Case.* Princeton: Princeton University Press, 1984.

Burstein, Andrew. *The Passions of Andrew Jackson.* New York: Alfred A. Knopf, 2003.

Chapman, George T. *Sketches of the Alumni of Dartmouth College.* Cambridge: Riverside Press, 1867.

Clift, G. Glenn. *Governors of Kentucky.* Cynthiana, Ky.: Hobson Press, 1942.

Cole, Donald B. *Jacksonian Democracy in New Hampshire, 1800–1851.* Cambridge: Harvard University Press, 1970.

———. *Martin Van Buren and the American Political System.* Princeton: Princeton University Press, 1984.

———. *The Presidency of Andrew Jackson.* Lawrence: University Press of Kansas, 1993.

Connelley, William E., and E. Merton Coulter, eds. *History of Kentucky.* 5 vols. Chicago: American Historical Society, 1922.

Crenson, Matthew A. *The Federal Machine: Beginnings of Bureaucracy in Jacksonian America.* Baltimore: Johns Hopkins University Press, 1975.

Curtis, James C. *The Fox at Bay: Martin Van Buren and the Presidency, 1837–1844.* Lexington: University Press of Kentucky, 1970.

Darling, Arthur B. *Political Changes in Massachusetts, 1824–1848.* New Haven: Yale University Press, 1925.

*Dartmouth Graduates and Former Students.* N.p., n.d.

Davis, Darrell H. *The Geography of the Bluegrass Region of Kentucky.* Frankfort: Kentucky Geological Survey, 1927.

De Voto, Bernard. *The Year of Decision 1846.* Boston: Little, Brown, 1942.

Formisano, Ronald P. *The Birth of Mass Political Parties: Michigan, 1827–1861.* Princeton: Princeton University Press, 1971.

———. *The Transformation of Political Culture: Massachusetts Parties, 1790s–1840s.* New York: Oxford University Press, 1983.

Freehling, William W. *The Road to Disunion: Secessionists at Bay, 1776–1854.* New York: Oxford University Press, 1990.

Govan, Thomas P. *Nicholas Biddle: Nationalist and Public Banker, 1786–1844.* Chicago: University of Chicago Press, 1959.

Green, Constance M. *Washington: Village and Capital, 1800–1878.* Princeton: Princeton University Press, 1962.

Hammond, Bray. *Banks and Politics in America from the Revolution to the Civil War.* Princeton: Princeton University Press, 1957.

Hargreaves, Mary W. M. *The Presidency of John Quincy Adams.* Lawrence: University Press of Kansas, 1985.

Heale, M. J. *The Presidential Quest: Candidates and Images in American Political Culture, 1787–1852.* London: Longman, 1982.

Hickey, Donald R. *The War of 1812.* Urbana: University of Illinois Press, 1989.

Holt, Michael F. *The Rise and Fall of the American Whig Party: Jacksonian Politics and the Onset of the Civil War.* New York: Oxford University Press, 1999.

Huston, James L. *Securing the Fruits of Labor: The American Concept of Wealth Distribution.* Baton Rouge: Louisiana State University Press, 1998.

John, Richard R. *Spreading the News: The American Postal System from Franklin to Morse.* Cambridge: Harvard University Press, 1995.

Kendall, Oliver, *Memorial of Josiah Kendall.* N.p., 1884.

Kielbowicz, Richard B. *News in the Mail: The Press, Post Office, and Public Information, 1700–1860s.* New York: Greenwood Press, 1989.

Kirwan, Albert D. *John J. Crittenden: The Struggle for the Union.* Lexington: University Press of Kentucky, 1962.

Latner, Richard B. *The Presidency of Andrew Jackson: White House Politics, 1829–1837.* Athens: University of Georgia Press, 1979.

Lawrence, Robert Means. *The Descendants of Major Samuel Lawrence of Groton, Massachusetts.* Cambridge: Riverside Press, 1904.

Lepore, Jill. *A Is for American: Letters and Other Characters in the Newly United States.* New York: Alfred A. Knopf, 2002.

Mabee, Carleton. *The American Leonardo: A Life of Samuel F. B. Morse.* New York: Alfred A. Knopf, 1943.

Marszalek, John F. *The Petticoat Affair: Manners, Mutiny, and Sex in Andrew Jackson's White House.* New York: Free Press, 1997.

Martis, Kenneth C. *The Historical Atlas of Political Parties in the United States Congress, 1789–1989.* New York: Macmillan, 1989.

Mayo, Bernard. *Henry Clay: Spokesman of the New West.* Boston: Houghton Mifflin, 1937.

McCormick, Richard P. *The Second American Party System: Party Formation in the Jacksonian Era.* Chapel Hill: University of North Carolina Press, 1966.

McCusker, John J. *How Much Is That in Real Money? A Historical Price Index for Use as a Deflator of Money Value in the Economy of the United States.* Worcester, Mass.: American Antiquarian Society, 1992.

McDonough, John J. *Index to the Andrew Jackson Papers.* Washington, D.C.: Library of Congress, 1967.

Meyer, Leland W. *The Life and Times of Colonel Richard M. Johnson of Kentucky.* New York: Columbia University Press, 1932.

Munroe, John A. *Louis McLane: Federalist and Jacksonian.* New Brunswick: Rutgers University Press, 1973.

Nason, Elias. *A History of the Town of Dunstable, Massachusetts.* Boston: Alfred Mudge & Son, 1877.

Newman, Simon P. *Parades and Politics in the Street: Festive Culture in the Early American Republic.* Philadelphia: University of Pennsylvania Press, 1997.

Niven, John. *Gideon Welles: Lincoln's Secretary of the Navy.* New York: Oxford University Press, 1973.

Parton, James. *Life of Andrew Jackson.* 3 vols. New York: Mason Brothers, 1860.

Pasley, Jeffrey L. *"The Tyranny of Printers": Newspaper Politics in the Early American Republic.* Charlottesville: University Press of Virginia, 2001.

Pessen, Edward. *Jacksonian America: Society, Personality and Politics.* Rev. ed. Homewood, Ill.: Dorsey Press, 1978.

Pred, Allan R. *Urban Growth and the Circulation of Information: The United States System of Cities, 1790–1840.* Cambridge: Harvard University Press, 1973.

Reilly, Bernard F., Jr. *Catalogue of American Political Prints, 1766–1876.* Boston: G. K. Hall, 1991.

Remini, Robert V. *Andrew Jackson and the Bank War.* New York: W. W. Norton, 1967.

———. *Andrew Jackson and the Course of American Democracy, 1833–1845.* New York: Harper & Row, 1984.

———. *Andrew Jackson and the Course of American Freedom, 1822–1832.* New York: Harper & Row, 1981.

———. *The Election of Andrew Jackson.* Philadelphia: J. B. Lippincott, 1963.

———. *Henry Clay: Statesman for the Union.* New York: W. W. Norton, 1991.

Richardson, Leon Burr. *History of Dartmouth College.* 2 vols. Hanover, N.H.: Dartmouth College Publications, 1932.

Robertson, Andrew W. *The Language of Democracy: Political Rhetoric in the United States and Britain, 1790–1900.* Ithaca: Cornell University Press, 1995.

Rothbard, Murray N. *The Panic of 1819: Reactions and Policies.* New York: Columbia University Press, 1962.

Rothenberg, Winifred Barr. *From Market-Places to a Market Economy: The Transformation of Rural Massachusetts, 1750–1850.* Chicago: University of Chicago Press, 1992.

Ryan, Mary P. *Civic Wars: Democracy and Public Life in the American City during the Nineteenth Century.* Berkeley: University of California Press, 1997.

Schlesinger, Arthur M., Jr. *The Age of Jackson.* Boston: Little, Brown, 1945.

———, ed. *History of American Presidential Elections, 1789–1968.* 4 vols. Vol. 1. New York: Chelsea House, 1971.

Sellers, Charles. *James K. Polk, Continentalist, 1843–1846.* Princeton: Princeton University Press, 1966.

———. *The Market Revolution: Jacksonian America, 1815–1846.* New York: Oxford University Press, 1991

Shade, William G. *Democratizing the Old Dominion: Virginia and the Second Party System, 1824–1861.* Charlottesville: University Press of Virginia, 1996.

Shannon, Jasper B., and Ruth McQuown. *Presidential Politics in Kentucky, 1824–1848*. Lexington: Bureau of Government Research of the University of Kentucky, 1950.

Silbey, Joel H. *Martin Van Buren and the Emergence of American Popular Politics*. Lanham, Md.: Rowman & Littlefield, 2002.

———. *A Respectable Minority: The Democratic Party in the Civil War Era, 1860–1868*. New York: W. W. Norton, 1977.

Smith, Culver H. *The Press, Politics, and Patronage: The American Government's Use of Newspapers, 1789–1875*. Athens: University of Georgia Press, 1977.

Smith, Elbert B. *Francis Preston Blair*. New York: Free Press, 1980.

Smith, Merritt Roe. *Harpers Ferry Armory and the New Technology: The Challenge of Change*. Ithaca: Cornell University Press, 1977.

*The Statistical History of the United States from the Colonial Times to the Present*. Stamford, Conn.: Fairfield, 1947.

Stickles, Arndt M. *The Critical Court Struggle in Kentucky*. Bloomington: Graduate Council, Indiana University, 1929.

Swisher, Carl B. *History of the Supreme Court of the United States: The Taney Period, 1836–64*. New York: Macmillan, 1974.

Thompson, Robert L. *Wiring a Continent: The History of the Telegraph Industry in the United States, 1832–1866*. Princeton: Princeton University Press, 1947.

Tiller, Carl W., and Olive M. Tiller. *At Calvary: A History of the First 125 Years of Calvary Baptist Church, Washington, D.C., 1862–1987*. Manassas, Va.: Trinity Rivers, 1994.

Wade, Richard C. *The Urban Frontier: The Rise of Western Cities, 1790–1820*. Cambridge: Harvard University Press, 1959.

Waldstreicher, David. *In the Midst of Perpetual Fetes: The Making of American Nationalism, 1776–1820*. Chapel Hill: University of North Carolina Press, 1997.

Watson, Harry L. *Liberty and Power: The Politics of Jacksonian America*. New York: Hill and Wang, 1990.

Weis, Frederick Lewis. *Early Generations of the Kendall Family of Massachusetts, Especially the Life of Lieutenant Samuel Kendall, Gentleman, 1682–1764, of Woburn, Lancaster, and Athol*. Lancaster, Mass., 1839.

White, Leonard D. *The Jacksonians: A Study in Administrative History, 1829–1861*. New York: Macmillan, 1954.

Wiebe, Robert H. *The Opening of American Society from the Adoption of the Constitution to the Eve of Disunion*. New York: Alfred A. Knopf, 1984.

———. *Self-Rule: A Cultural History of American Democracy*. Chicago: University of Chicago Press, 1995.

Wilbur, William A. *Chronicles of Calvary Baptist Church in the City of Washington*. Washington, D.C.: 1914.

Wood, Gordon S. *The Radicalism of the American Revolution*. New York: Alfred A. Knopf, 1992.

## Secondary Sources: Articles

Appleby, Joyce Oldham. "The Vexed Story of Capitalism Told by American Historians." *JER* 21 (2001): 1–18.

Baldasty, Gerald J. "The Washington Political Press in the Age of Jackson." *Journalism History* 10 (1983): 50–53, 68–71.

Barton, Tom K. "Henry Clay, Amos Kendall, and Gentlemen's Education: State-Supported Higher Education as a Political Issue in Kentucky, 1815–1825." *Rocky Mountain Social Science Journal* 3 (1966): 44–57.

Belohlavek, John M. "Assault on the President: The Jackson-Randolph Affair of 1833." *Presidential Studies Quarterly* 12 (1982): 361–68.

Bushman, Robert Lyman. "Markets and Composite Farms in Early America." *William and Mary Quarterly* 55 (1998): 351–74.

Cayton, Andrew R. L. "We Are All Nationalists, We Are All Localists." *JER* 18 (1998): 521–28.

Chambers, William N. "Election of 1840." In *History of American Presidential Elections 1789–1968,* ed. Arthur M. Schlesinger Jr. 4 vols. Vol. 1. New York: Chelsea House, 1971.

Cole, Donald B. "A Yankee in Kentucky: The Early Years of Amos Kendall, 1789–1828." *Proceedings of the Massachusetts Historical Society* 109 (1997): 24–36.

Cooke, J. W. "'Pride and Depravity': A Preliminary Reexamination of the Beauchamp-Sharp Affair." *Border States* 6 (1987): 1–12.

Curry, Leonard P. "Election Year—Kentucky, 1828." *Register of the Kentucky State Historical Society* 55 (1957): 196–212.

Curtis, James C. "Andrew Jackson: Symbol for What Age?" *Reviews in American History* 8 (1980): 194–99.

De Voto, Bernard. "The Easy Chair." *Harpers* 190 (1945): 500–503.

Eriksson, Erik M. "The Federal Civil Service under President Jackson." *Mississippi Valley Historical Review* 13 (1927): 519–40.

Feller, Daniel. "A Brother in Arms: Benjamin Tappan and the Antislavery Democracy." *Journal of American History* 88 (2001): 48–74.

Fish, Carl R. "Removal of Officials by the Presidents of the United States." *Annual Report of the American Historical Association for the Year 1899.* 2 vols. Washington, D.C.: Government Printing Office, 1900. 1:67–86.

Gatell, Frank Otto, ed. "Postmaster Huger and the Incendiary Publications." *South Carolina Historical Magazine* 64 (1963): 193–201.

———. "Spoils of the Bank War: Political Bias in the Selection of Pet Banks." *American Historical Review* 70 (1964): 35–58.

———. "Taney and the Baltimore Pets." *Business History Review* 39 (1965): 205–27.

Gienapp, William E. "The Myth of Class in Jacksonian America." *Journal of Policy History* 6 (1994): 231–59.

Greenberg, Kenneth S. "The Nose, the Lie, and the Duel in the Antebellum South." *American Historical Review* 95 (1990): 57–74.

Hardin, Billie J. "Amos Kendall and the 1824 Relief Controversy." *Register of the Kentucky State Historical Society* 64 (1966): 196–208.

Harlan, Louis R. "Public Career of William Berkeley Lewis." *Tennessee Historical Quarterly* 7 (1948): 3–37, 118–51.

Hofstadter, Richard. "Andrew Jackson and the Rise of Liberal Capitalism." In *The American Political Tradition and the Men Who Made It.* New York: Alfred A. Knopf, 1948.

John, Richard R. "Affairs of Office: The Executive Departments, the Election of 1828, and the Making of the Democratic Party." In *The Democratic Experiment: New Directions in American Political History,* ed. Julian Zelizer, Meg Jacobs, and William Novak. Princeton: Princeton University Press, 2003.

———. "Recasting the Information Infrastructure for the Industrial Age." In *A Nation Transformed by Information: How Information Has Shaped the United States from Colonial Times to the Present,* ed. Alfred D. Chandler Jr. and James W. Cortada. New York: Oxford University Press, 2000.

Johnson, Fred M. "New Light on Beauchamp's Confession?" *Border States* 12 (1993): 13–21.

Kulikoff, Allan. "The Transition to Capitalism in Rural America." *William and Mary Quarterly,* 3d ser., 48 (1989): 120–44.

Latner, Richard B. "The Kitchen Cabinet and Andrew Jackson's Advisory System." *Journal of American History* 65 (1978): 367–88.

———. "A New Look at Jacksonian Politics." *Journal of American History* 61 (1975): 943–69.

Latner, Richard B., and Peter Levine. "Perspectives on Antebellum Pietistic Politics." *Reviews in American History* 4 (1976): 15–24.

Marshall, Lynn L. "The Authorship of Jackson's Bank Veto Message." *Mississippi Valley Historical Review* 50 (1963): 466–77.

———. "The Genesis of Grass-Roots Democracy in Kentucky." *Mid-America* 47 (1965): 269–87.

———. "The Strange Stillbirth of the Whig Party." *American Historical Review* 72 (1967): 425–44.

Mathias, Frank F. "The Relief and Court Struggle: Half-Way House to Populism." *Register of the Kentucky State Historical Society* 71 (1973): 154–76.

Mathias, Frank F., and Jasper B. Shannon. "Gubernatorial Politics in Kentucky, 1820–1851." *Register of the Kentucky State Historical Society* 88 (1990): 245–77.

Mayo, Bernard. "Lexington: Frontier Metropolis." In *Historiography and Urbanization: Essays in Honor of Stull Holt,* ed. Eric F. Goldman. Baltimore: Johns Hopkins University Press, 1941.

McCarthy, Jeanette H. "The Strange Case of Isaac Desha." *Register of the Kentucky State Historical Society* 60 (1962): 293–303.

McFaul, John M., and Frank Otto Gatell. "The Outcast Insider: Reuben M. Whitney and the Bank War." *Pennsylvania Magazine of History and Biography* 41 (1967): 115–44.

Morley, Jefferson. "The Ghosts of Jackson Hill." *Washington Post Magazine,* 13 Sept. 1998, 12–16, 28–29.

Morrison, Howard Alexander. "A Closer Look at Utica's Anti-Abolitionist Mob." *New York History* 62 (1981): 64–79.

Pruitt, Bettye Hobbs. "Self-Sufficiency and the Agricultural Economy of Eighteenth-Century Massachusetts." *William and Mary Quarterly* 41 (1982): 333–64.

Remini, Robert V. "Election of 1832." In *History of American Presidential Elections, 1789–1968,* ed. Arthur M. Schlesinger Jr. 4 vols. Vol. 1. New York: Chelsea House, 1971.

Rothbard, Murray N. "The Frankfort Resolutions and the Panic of 1819." *Register of the Kentucky State Historical Society* 61 (1963): 214–19.

Royalty, Dale. "Banking and the Commonwealth Ideal in Kentucky, 1806–1822." *Register of the Kentucky State Historical Society* 77 (1979): 91–107.

Shade, William G. "'The Most Delicate and Exciting Topics': Martin Van Buren, Slavery, and the Election of 1836." *JER* 18 (1998): 459–84.

———. "Political Pluralism and Party Development: The Creation of a Modern Party System, 1815–1852." In *The Evolution of American Electoral Systems,* ed. Paul Kleppner et al. Westport, Conn., 1981.

Silbey, Joel H. "'To One or Another of These Parties Every Man Belongs': The American Political Experience from Andrew Jackson to the Civil War." In *Contesting Democracy: Substance and Structure in American Political History, 1775–2000,* ed. Byron E. Shafer and Anthony J. Badger. Lawrence: University Press of Kansas, 2001.

Singletary, Michael W. "The New Editorial Voice for Andrew Jackson: Happenstance or Plan?" *Journalism Quarterly* 53 (1976): 672–78.

Skeen, C. Edward. "*Vox Populi, Vox Dei:* The Compensation Act of 1816 and the Rise of Popular Politics." *JER* 16 (1986): 253–74.

Stevens, Harry R. "Henry Clay, the Bank, and the West in 1824." *American Historical Review* 60 (1955): 843–48.

Stewart, James Brewer. "The Emergence of Racial Modernity and the Rise of the White North, 1790–1840." *JER* 18 (1998): 181–217.

VanBurkleo, Sandra F. "'The Paws of Banks': The Origins and Significance of Kentucky's Decision to Tax Federal Bankers, 1818–1820." *JER* 9 (1989): 457–87.

Waldstreicher, David. "The Nationalization and Racialization of American Politics: Before, beneath, and between Parties, 1790–1840." In *Contesting Democracy: Substance and Structure in American Political History, 1775–2000,* ed. Byron E. Shafer and Anthony J. Badger. Lawrence: University Press of Kansas, 2001.

Wilson, Major L. "The 'Country' Versus the 'Court': A Republican Consensus and Party Debate in the Bank War." *JER* 15 (1995): 619–47.

Wood, Kirsten E. "'One Woman So Dangerous to Public Morals': Gender and Power in the Eaton Affair." *JER* 17 (1997): 237–75.

Wyatt-Brown, Bertram. "The Abolitionists' Postal Campaign of 1835." *Journal of Negro History* 50 (1965): 227–38

———. "Andrew Jackson's Honor." *JER* 17 (1997): 1–36.

## Unpublished Dissertations and Papers

Daniels, James D. "Amos Kendall: Cabinet-Politician." Ph.D. dissertation, University of North Carolina, 1968.

Doctor, Powrie V. "Amos Kendall, Propagandist." Ph.D. dissertation, University of Georgia, 1940.

Gaffney, Thomas L. "Maine's Mr. Smith: A Study of Francis O. J. Smith, Politician and Entrepreneur." Ph.D. dissertation, University of Maine, 1979.

Hochfelder, David. "Taming the Lightning: American Telegraphy as a Revolutionary Technology, 1832–1860." Ph.D. dissertation, Case Western Reserve University, 1999.

Hopson, Edwin N. Notes for unfinished Ph.D. dissertation on Amos Kendall. Filson Historical Society.

John, Richard R. "Managing the Mails." Ph.D. dissertation, Harvard University, 1989.

Kany, Julius Franz. "The Career of William Taylor Barry." Master's thesis, Western Kentucky State Teacher's College, 1934.

Kindig, Everett W. "Western Opposition to Jackson's 'Democracy': The Ohio Valley as a Case Study, 1827–1836." Ph.D. dissertation, Stanford University, 1974.

Marshall, Lynn L. "The Early Career of Amos Kendall: The Making of a Jacksonian." Ph.D. dissertation, University of California, Berkeley, 1962.

Mastromarino, Mark. "Henry Lee, Jacksonian Biographer." Unpublished paper, 1991.

Melton, Baxter Ford, Jr. "Amos Kendall in Kentucky, 1814–1829: The Journalistic Beginnings of the 'Master Mind' of Andrew Jackson's Kitchen Cabinet." Ph.D. dissertation, Southern Illinois University, 1978.

Shoptaugh, Terry L. "Amos Kendall: A Political Biography." Ph.D. dissertation, University of New Hampshire, 1984.

# INDEX

Randolph, John, 161

Randolph, Robert Beverley, 136–37, 139, 142, 181

Randolph affair, 136–37, 141, 142, 164, 181

Reeside, James, 199

relief meetings, 1819 (Ky.), 70–71

*Remarks on the Bank of the United States* (Henshaw), 166

Reorganization Act, 87, 91, 93, 97

republicanism, 3, 5. *See also* Dunstable, Mass.; Jackson, Andrew; Kendall, Amos—views on

*Rhode Island Republican Herald,* 149

Ricardo, David, 68–69, 74, 236–37

Richardson, William M., 27–28, 30, 34–36, 47

Richmond *Crisis,* 228

*Richmond Enquirer,* 144, 149, 226

Riggs, George W., 280

Rip Raps, Va., 184, 186, 187, 200

Ritchie, Thomas, 58, 70, 123, 171, 190, 244

Rives, John C., 174, 222, 242, 258

Rives, William C., 215

Roane, Spencer: "Hampden Essays," 166; mentioned, 70, 171

Robertson, George, 89, 91

*Rough-Hewer* (Albany), 228

Rowan, John, 103

Russell, Gervas E., 60–61, 133

Russell, J. B., 61

Russell, Jonathan, 77

Russell, Robert W., 275, 276–77

Russell, William, 81

Samson, George W., 289

Sanders, Lewis, 125, 133

Sarony, Napoleon, 226

Savannah branch of BUS, 189

Schlesinger, Arthur M., Jr., 165

Scott County, Ky., 48–50

Seaton, William W., 197, 242

*Secession* (AK), 283

Sedition Act, 96

Selden, Henry R., 251

Sevier, John, 240

Seymour, Horatio, 293

Sharp, Solomon P., 85, 90–93

Shays's Rebellion, 12

Shepley, Ether, 46, 190

Shields, Ebenezer, 206

Sibley, Hiram: builds Western Union, 269, 271; helps form Six Nations, 272–73; mentioned, 277

Silver Spring (Blair's home), 278

Six Nations, 273–75

Skidmore, Thomas, 237

Slaughter, Gabriel, 59–60, 72

Smith, Francis O. J.: opposes Morse and AK, 246, 247, 249–50, 253, 262–63; description of, 249; joins AK against O'Rielly, 251, 254–55; mentioned, 4, 245, 269, 271, 273, 274–75

Smith, Margaret Bayard, 45, 120, 134

Smith, Thomas L., 123, 145, 154, 156

Smith, William, 140, 141

Society for the Diffusion of Political Knowledge, 287

Sparks, Jared, 240

stay legislation, Kentucky: Stay Act (1820), 72; Replevin Act (1820), 74–76, 81, 169; Stay Act (1821), 75

Stevenson, Andrew, 105, 204–5

Stevenson, Thomas B., 256

Stickney, William, 4, 266–67, 268, 279, 284, 286, 291, 294, 295

Stockton, Richard C., 199

Stockton and Stokes case, 216–17, 219, 222, 234–35, 244

Stokes, William B., 199

subsistence farming, 4, 10

subtreasury plan. *See* independent treasury plan

Sully, duc de, 240

Sumner, William Graham, 165

Swartwout, Samuel, 118, 219, 221

Tammany Society, Lexington, Ky., 48

Taney, Roger B.: opposes BUS, 158, 160, 162, 165–70; and removal of deposits, 178, 180, 184, 186, 188–89; confirmed as chief justice, 204; mentioned, 21, 150, 191, 192, 213, 220, 221

Tappan, Lewis, 239

Taylor, John, 70

Tazewell, Littleton, 127–28, 136–41

Tecumseh (Indian chief), 50

telegraph

—companies: Magnetic, 248, 250–55, 264, 270, 271, 274, 275; New York, Albany & Buffalo, 248, 251, 270–71, 272, 273; New York & Bos-